RELATIONAL PSYCHOANALYSIS AT THE HEART OF TEACHING AND LEARNING

This book introduces the insights of contemporary relational psychoanalysis to educational thought and uses them as the foundation for a comprehensive model for understanding and informing teaching and learning practice. The model integrates what we know about conscious thought, motivation, and the physical body and translates these understandings in ways that are meaningful and relevant to the circumstances of practicing teachers, school leaders, and teachers of teachers. It will be of great interest to them and to those educational scholars whose attentions turn to the exigencies of the current era.

Echoing calls for inclusivity, the book stands against admonishing anyone on the right way to be a person. Instead it emphasises understanding and, in understanding, practicing well. Readers will gain a deeper appreciation of the nature of sense-making and awareness and of the practical implications of cognition as embodied, life forms as non-linear dynamic systems, and relationships as core to human development and classroom life.

It was Einstein who, in a letter to Freud, once asked for an educational solution to the menace of war. Today's urgencies – of nations divided, diminishing planetary resources, and certain ecological disasters – press for wisdom beyond our collective habit. Thankfully the once-elusive mysteries of life, mind, learning, and learning systems now yield in ways to help shape answers to Einstein's question. Relational psychoanalysts, psychotherapists, educational theorists, teachers, and those who work with them will be intrigued by the convergences and heartened at the possibilities.

Lissa D'Amour recently retired from the Faculty of Education, University of Calgary. Her 15 years working with prospective and practicing teachers followed upon and benefited from 25 years of school-teaching success in a variety of everyday contexts, from pre-kindergarten through grade 12. Today, as an independent scholar, Lissa continues to work at bringing relational psychoanalytic understanding into curriculum theory and, through curriculum theory, into the lived experiences and practical lives of teachers and their students.

"Sophisticatedly simple, this book is a 'sanctuary for the mutual meeting of minds' (quoted in this volume), one wherein apparent antinomies – progressivism v. traditionalism, theory v. practice, scientific biology v. humanist philosophy – provoke not bifurcation but stunning synthesis in Lissa D'Amour's theory of teaching and learning. Panoramic yet detailed, playful while earnest, joyful and discerning and attuned (despite past trauma, despite the dire present in which we are embedded), this book (itself a transitional object, see within) rides relational psychoanalysis to destinations solitary and shared, sublime and strategic, a sustained – and sustaining – 'a-ha' educational experience of authenticity and presence."

– **William F. Pinar**, Professor and Canada Research Chair,
University of British Columbia, Vancouver

"Lissa D'Amour has reached a brilliant and unexpected conclusion: *Relational Psychoanalysis* provides ideas and values that can be used to structure a humanistically informed way of thinking about what it means to educate people, and how to do it. D'Amour encourages people, in learning, to become ever more familiar and accepting of what they find in themselves, and between themselves and others. She argues against imposing faddish values and techniques from outside. I don't know enough about education to comment on Curriculum Theory; I am a psychoanalyst, one of the relational psychoanalysts that D'Amour cites. But with that proviso, I believe I can see that D'Amour's book is a *tour de force*, a brave and creative contribution to Curriculum Theory, and to all of education."

– **Donnel B. Stern**, PhD, William Alanson White Institute of
Psychoanalysis, New York

RELATIONAL PSYCHOANALYSIS AT THE HEART OF TEACHING AND LEARNING

How and Why It Matters

Lissa D'Amour

LONDON AND NEW YORK

First published 2020
by Routledge
2 Park Square, Milton Park, Abingdon, Oxon OX14 4RN

and by Routledge
52 Vanderbilt Avenue, New York, NY 10017

Routledge is an imprint of the Taylor & Francis Group, an informa business

© 2020 Lissa D'Amour

The right of Lissa D'Amour to be identified as author of this work has been asserted by her in accordance with sections 77 and 78 of the Copyright, Designs and Patents Act 1988.

All rights reserved. No part of this book may be reprinted or reproduced or utilised in any form or by any electronic, mechanical, or other means, now known or hereafter invented, including photocopying and recording, or in any information storage or retrieval system, without permission in writing from the publishers.

Trademark notice: Product or corporate names may be trademarks or registered trademarks, and are used only for identification and explanation without intent to infringe.

British Library Cataloguing-in-Publication Data
A catalogue record for this book is available from the British Library

Library of Congress Cataloging-in-Publication Data
A catalog record for this book has been requested

ISBN: 978-1-138-09756-8 (hbk)
ISBN: 978-1-138-09758-2 (pbk)
ISBN: 978-1-315-10481-2 (ebk)

Typeset in Bembo
by Apex CoVantage, LLC

 Printed in the United Kingdom
by Henry Ling Limited

CONTENTS

Acknowledgements	*vii*
Prologue: in which the author positions herself	1

PART I
The relational turn   5

1 Distinguishing the relational perspective	7
2 Psychoanalysis in education	15
3 Voices at education's helm	26

PART II
A dialectic theory of learning: self, other, and the transitional object   51

4 Meaning-making and the curricular object	53
5 Of minds and bodies: a few orienting tenets	73
6 Becoming self: storied in relationality, steeped in affect	88

vi Contents

7 Theorising learning: philosophies, understandings, and
perspectives over the years 113

8 Dialectics arrested: on learning's refusal 141

PART III
Into practice: for meaningful inclusion 163

9 Capacity, trust, and meaning 165

10 Rethinking twenty-first-century orthodoxy 180

11 Classrooms as holding environments 208

12 The provision of curricular objects: teaching for
discernments that matter 218

13 Selves and witnesses: teacher know your story 249

Epilogue: through angst and grace, in this together 275

References 280
Index 299

ACKNOWLEDGEMENTS

Writing this book, transgressing as it does traditional disciplinary boundaries, was always going to be a solitary venture filled with moments of self-doubt. I have many good people to thank for buoying me through that journey, but none more so than Sandy Miller, Martina Metz, and Wendy Anderson.

Sandy and Martina read, understood, and responded to selected chapters in ways that communicated belief in me and in the book's potential.

During those times when the impasses seemed insurmountable, it was always my dear friend and long-time school-teaching colleague, Wendy, who sustained me. It was for her presence, even in her absence, that I was never truly alone.

PROLOGUE

In which the author positions herself

William Pinar writes,

> Private-and-public intellectuals . . . are private in Nietzsche's sense of self-overcoming while publicly declining to employ their intellectual labor in unquestioning service to the State and in complicity with the political status quo. They work from "within." Curriculum theory, then, constitutes a public and political commitment that requires autobiographical excavation and the self-reflexive articulation of one's subjectivity in society.
>
> *(2004, p. 22)*

At heart a curriculum theorist, I begin with the personal – *my* personal – laying forth the elements of my striving in private-and-public intellectual life.

Beginning with bias

Beginnings matter. They shape unconscious habits and compose hidden biases. I had a bad start – well, quasi bad. It must have been quasi, because otherwise I would not be in a position to write here. Judge for yourself.

In 1965, at ten years old, I presented a talk to my grade 5 class on Freud's id, ego, and superego. I had learned about Freud from my father – the repeatedly rejected, high school French teacher who, almost yearly, under threat of exposure, relocated his family to yet another town in rural Ontario. My father – an early orphan and later a Hong Kong prisoner of war – used Freudian theories to rationalise, to me, his own desperate, yet calculated, wrong-doings on me. Indeed, Freud himself had believed in a daughter's "repressed wish to take her own mother's place as her father's love object" (in Pitt, 2003, p. 126). You should know that I have reason to recoil from much of what Freud judged to be true.

2 Prologue

In mid-August 1970, I walked my body, mind adrift, through the doors of the Children's Aid Society in Timmins, Ontario. Some days later, I sat alone in the upper hall of a receiving home to pen my testimony: an existence of vigilance, a story of abuse. It was two months later when a closed court hearing would settle my future. I remember the room. A man, the judge, sat behind a heavy desk. Family members – at the helm, father-abuser and mother-enabler – chose their well-being over mine, and lied. The judge was last to speak. He did not believe my story could have happened but, acknowledging the events were real enough to me to keep me running away, he ruled that I would become a ward of the state. With one man's opinion legislating my fate, I began a differently tumultuous life in foster care – a world where even after secrets are spoken they remain unspeakable. I learned early to protect the world, to protect myself, from the history of things done to me. Today, many women refuse such lessons. I join them.

Eigen writes of dramatic changes as an act of faith and a "violence intrinsic to . . . a chick breaking out of an egg" (Eigen, 1999/1981, p. 9). I seem to have determined two such essentially risky, creative destructions, each time exposing myself to the unanticipated harshness of reshaping forces beyond each shell's keeping. The second hatching occurred some 15 years ago, out of a 25-year gestation in marriage, family life, and "everyday" teaching. In the doing, particular questions have become central to me.

What broader world conditions make possible atrocities, greater and lesser, as I, and others, have experienced and continue to experience? How do we continue to be complicit, even if as yin making possible yang and vice versa? And what can I possibly do about it? The flickering image of a person in front of a tank in Tiananmen Square comes to mind. These thoughts express the crux of matters moving the work of this book. I offer it with hope and the best scholarship I can muster at the fruition of a second ten-year self-reshaping, this time in graduate studies, and then a five-year academic sojourn that ultimately disappointed. I believe we can, and must, do better. I believe that for all our precociousness as a power-wielding species, we are infants when it comes to understanding ourselves as beings in the world.

The trenches

Public educators tell of working in the trenches. As a child, these trenches were my safe haven and secure base for hiding in the open, using learning objects to tune out the deafening din of fear and shame at home. School was my earliest constant safety. A second bias, then, attends these writings. I hold near-religious hope for what education can do. That I write owes to the privilege and possibility of generous audiences there, audiences to which I played the best academic parts of me.

I entered marriage with a clear gendered self-understanding and a determination that the family we would make would be well. If not the first, then at least the second. Off-and-on-again job changes – following shifts of a husband's career, child-bearing, child-rearing, home-schooling, and finally graduate studies – meant I often found myself the new employee.

Prologue **3**

In teaching absences, I read and studied – that I might return all the wiser. Yet each new setting shaded differently what mattered and what worked. My versatility ensured me one foot in the door to any number of teaching situations. These brought humbling serendipitous lessons of circumstance as I grappled to find my footing in appointments running the breadth of preschool to high school and later graduate school – in all of Montessori, charter, private, public, urban, rural, and home-schooling contexts. A transection of society, religious beliefs, sexual orientations, ethnicities, and races has peopled my many Canadian classrooms. Students, especially in the middle grades, where I'd settled for the final decade before graduate studies, came bearing such labels as cause to segregate or integrate: gifted, cognitively impaired, dyslexic, autistic, attention deficit, oppositional defiant, affected by generalised anxiety, and the like. But nothing figured more importantly, across those myriad contexts, than what settled clearly into my awareness as a common need among students for individuation *with relatedness*, independence *with belonging*, and a place to trust in being visible, welcomed, cared for, believed in, and then prodded and intrigued, regardless of sameness or difference, hidden or visible.

In these "trenches" my students and I mucked about, playing with and working the fascinating curricular artefacts dropped there by the various programmes of study. *For the most part, it didn't seem to much matter what those curricular objects were – the point was the playing and the working.* At times my classrooms could feel like sanctuaries where shared curiosity, leaning on well-honed automaticities, would have their day. I believed that if the world was going to be a better place, it needed to begin and be buoyed by what my students and I did together with whatever worldly objects arrived for the using and perusing. I learned to recognise these curricular objects as *not* the point of learning. Instead, they were points of focus and movement for the making of precious selves in and through the world, and the making of a precious world through and in these selves. The capacity to make useful sense of what was given could not be teased from: the art of individual and collective being and becoming, the birthing of hard-won agency, and a self-trust that could accrue in grappling with cultural givens.

I choose middle

My move to scholarship was, in part, prompted by ongoing curiosity over a perplexing and pervasive problem: the popularity of what increasingly struck me as a steady supply of new techniques that seemed to offer more of the same. I began to wonder if those speaking in the name of professional development were either naïve or opportunistic.

In my K–12 teaching career, the whiff of politics began arriving in such simple ironies as mandatory professional collaboration to ease workload. Instead, I found these collaborations pulled individuals to a common mediocrity, bent to agreements (regulations really) on delivering, in the name of sameness as fairness, identical teaching regimes. These regimes would be billed as better insofar as they aligned with popular ideologies, often branded in terms of unquestioned platitudes, always in service of ameliorating the favoured inadequacies du jour.

4 Prologue

For now, I make the claim that the extensive lists of proliferating imperatives on schooling, by and large, continue to fly in the face of what is good for children and education. It will take the book to show how and why, and to suggest shifting structures of thinking. Suffice it to say that part of my move to graduate studies was to make sense of the motivations behind seemingly strange policies and politics characterising what William Pinar has described as the "nightmare that is the present" (2004, pp. 13–62). Psychoanalysis, especially with the strength of the relational turn, if moved to the heart of education could help us face our schooling nightmares. It seems to matter now more than ever.

Education faculties have camps – and my sense has been that they are not to be spoken of. Near as I can tell, trans- and interdisciplinarity seem to favour cross-campus allegiances, more so than cross-floor. My second-year doctoral class epitomises the microcosm of education. We convened weekly at three tables spanning a conference room. The humanist and "post" folks gathered on the right and the "practical" science people took the left table. A smaller contingent sat between and tried to ferret what middle might be. The year before I had been admonished to "position myself." I continue to choose a middle path unlike any I have found in the academy. Where people take sides, middle can be a lonely, misunderstood place, with few appropriate journals in which to publish. One has to be careful with words because invariably one does not know whose mouths they have been in. Moreover, it can make for messy writing when chapters traverse multiple and middling discourses. As with the non-Kleinian British object relations school, and that of its contemporary offspring, relational psychoanalysis, I expect the exigencies of middle will be disconcerting for some readers and refreshing for others.

Ultimately, this book represents an effort to bring into curriculum theory and education a re-centred psychoanalytic theory – one coherent with current neuropsychological understandings of the unconscious, as Freud might have imagined (Erreich, 2016). To that end, I have striven to conceive and communicate implications in as relevant and accessible a manner as I can muster, beginning in the first section with familiarising the reader with the difference of relational psychoanalysis, continuing in the second section to develop a theory of learning grounded in relational insights, and closing in the final section with implications for schooling. Without further ado then, we thus begin with the relational turn, its cohering inclination twice-removed from schooling: first for psychoanalysis's position in the borderlands, and second for relational psychoanalysis's radically middle orientation, barely represented among those margin-dwellers.

PART I
The relational turn

1
DISTINGUISHING THE RELATIONAL PERSPECTIVE

In the 1970s, curriculum studies in the United States realised a reconceptualisation that would transform the field globally. Fifty years later its work continues to complicate the conversation (Pinar, 2004, pp. 185–201) about socio-cultural, political, interpersonal, and intrapsychic forces at play in school curriculum. Over roughly the same period, the diverse American psychoanalytic field congealed into theoretical lines on the role of interpersonal relations in shaping psychic structure. Fifty years later a more fundamentally relational psychoanalysis has likewise transformed the contemporary field. Both transformations came into view "retrospectively" – as "self-reflectively discovered" intellectual traditions (Mitchell & Aron, 1999, p. ix). Yet the world beyond contemporary theory and practice, curricular and psychoanalytic, seems not to have noticed that the familiar melodies of these traditions now play on critically different notes (Donnel Stern, 2010) in a new key (Pinar & Irwin, 2015).

The present book seeks to address that situation and to bring the relational turn of psychoanalysis into curriculum studies reconceptualised. It begins with the relational psychoanalytic story.

In 1983, Greenberg and Mitchell's seminal book, *Object Relations in Psychoanalytic Theory*, articulated a distinctly relational sensibility that had been brewing for some time. By the turn of the twenty-first century, that sensibility had flourished enough to warrant a compendium of papers entitled *Relational Psychoanalysis: The Emergence of a Tradition* (1999). To what were these thinkers pointing and why might it be important to education today?

For one, the relational tradition names much more than any increased emphasis, in contemporary psychoanalysis, on interpersonal relations. Instead, the relational perspective radically asserts that psychic structure emanates "solely from the individual's relations with other people" (Greenberg & Mitchell, 1983, p. 20). This represents a fundamental departure from Freud's view of *inborn* libidinal and aggressive

8 The relational turn

drives at the heart of psychic structure. Contra-Freud, relational analysts understand the intrapsychic and the intersubjective as co-implicated from the start – each the context of the other.

In Part I of this book, I explore the history and premises that distinguish relational psychoanalysis from other psychoanalytic traditions and I consider the state of curriculum practice in education today. In the process, I answer two questions:

1   Isn't psychoanalysis already in education and isn't it also relational?
2   Acknowledging the marginal status of any form of psychoanalysis in educational discourses (Bainbridge & West, 2012; Britzman, 2013; Redmond & Shulman, 2008), which scholarships are most at play in defining contemporary schooling practice?

The remainder of the book focuses on a third question:

3   What difference might relational psychoanalysis make for schooling?

To that end, Part II develops a theory of learning that understands human nature as storied in relationality, steeped in affect, and radically embodied. Part III follows the theory's implications back to curricular practices in schooling.

Object relations: *from* the primacy of drives *to* the primacy of relationships

In their seminal book, Greenberg and Mitchell identified "the most significant tension in the history of psychoanalytic ideas . . . [as] the dialectic between the original Freudian [drive/structure] model . . . and an alternative comprehensive [relational/structure] model" (1983, p. 20). Michael Eigen described the fallout of the "therapy wars" as "in a way, fighting for causes . . . [and] akin to fighting for the kind of person you are or imagine you are or perhaps would like to be" (in NPAP, 2016, para. 9–13). To understand, we return to Freud.

At the turn of the twentieth century, Freud was puzzling over so many hysterics' persistent memories of childhood sexual experience – an actuality that eventually seemed too far-fetched to him. Having begun with a theory of infant seduction, he eventually opted for a theory of infantile sexuality. It seemed more plausible to him that these women's stories were actually unconscious fabrications (Haynal, 2002; Mitchell & Black, 1995/2016, pp. 207–214). To the question of why would so many women be making these things up, his answer became: childhood fantasy coupled with unconscious inborn sexual desire and its necessary suppression by civilised society. Rather than asking after the societal conditions that would make child sexual abuse possible, Freud's disbelief and consequent theoretical shift "establish[ed] individual pleasure seeking and drive discharge as the bedrock of human existence" (Mitchell, 1988, p. 404).

Distinguishing the relational perspective **9**

If Freud's first-conceived drive was a sexual one, then the first objects were libidi-nal. They were the real persons, fantasised upon from infancy as objects. That is, the theoretical objects of "object relations" were originally the targets of deep-seated libidinal drives. One could say the object was constituted as libidinal by the drive (Greenberg & Mitchell, 1983, p. 13). Later in trying to make sense of human aggres-sion, Freud conceived of the death instinct and reused the notion of the object in the context of the aggressive drive (Greenberg & Mitchell, 1983, p. 13). In both formulations, Freud's object was something real *and* a goal or target. For Freud, the "object *is* the thing which is the target of a drive" (p. 13).

Following Freud, and remaining true to his doctrines of drives and instincts, Melanie Klein developed object relations theory, which expanded psychoanalytic principles into relational realms. Working with young children, she extrapolated back to infancy and to an idea of part-objects including the breast as primary (Greenberg & Mitchell, 1983, pp. 119–150). Today, object relations theory refers to "theories, or aspects of theories, concerned with exploring the relationship between real, external people and internal images and residues of relations with them, and the significance of these residues for psychic functioning" (Greenberg & Mitchell, 1983, pp. 11–12). Notably, prior relations are what saturate internal images with present meanings. Those meanings, in turn, play into current relations. In object relations theory, we speak of external objects (actual people) and internal objects (images composed of past experiences and unconsciously brought to bear on pres-ent actual people).

Greenberg and Mitchell (1983) reordered the psychoanalytic field along a con-tinuum of approaches to object relations, beginning with Freudian drive theory and progressing to relational views. While "*drive/structure*" approaches conceived of inborn drives as the primary impetus to psychic structure, "*relational/structure*" approaches attributed intrapsychic structure as co-emerging with and through interpersonal relationships with *real* others. In other words, on the central point of object relations, Greenberg and Mitchell's gambit was to position the psychoanalytic field at the cusp of a paradigm shift.

A retrospect on psychoanalytic thought – then till now

While Berman saw relational psychoanalysis as "not a new school, but rather a broad integrative orientation focusing on Self and Other" (1997, p. 185), Mills tells of the relational turn as having been "inaugurated . . . in one stroke of the pen" – when Greenberg and Mitchell "displaced Freud's drive model" in favour of "relatedness with other human beings as the central motive behind mental life" (2005, p. 159).

Greenberg and Mitchell organise an arguably either/or continuum (from drive/structure to relational/structure) to order the two equally dogmatic storylines that had been brewing for some time in the history of psychoanalysis: the established orthodoxy and its dissenters (Berman, 2001). The orthodoxy carried on Freud's "intrapsychic libido-focus" (Berman, 2001, p. 1268) of tracking the interpersonal

10 The relational turn

"back to the vicissitudes of drive and defense, to the intrapsychic, and to . . . a one-person psychology" (Aron, 1990, p. 476). On this classical view, the human being was "a biologically closed system seeking to discharge energy in order to maintain homeostasis" (Aron, 1990, p. 476). Meanwhile, the mavericks and their followers (e.g., Jungian & Adlerian schools) gravitated to an interactional perspective and a two-person psychology (Berman, 1997, pp. 185–186). They saw the mind as an open system, always in interaction with others, and never neutral or anonymous with respect to the interpersonal field (Aron, 1990).

On the interactional side, Mitchell's second book, *Relational Concepts in Psychoanalysis* (1988), catalysed an integration of existing approaches that all saw "humans . . . [as] inherently structured in relational terms (Sullivan), develop[ing] intense attachments because they crave relatedness (Fairbairn), and develop[ing] a self in the context of relatedness (Winnicott, Kohut)" (Berman, 2001, p. 1269). In short, that "*human beings are fundamentally social, developing within, internalizing, and shaped by their relationships with important others in their lives*" (italics added) (Black, 2016, p. xxvi). As it turns out, these understandings would converge with neurobiology, infant development, childhood attachment, and organic systems theory (see Part II). Inasmuch as Mitchell's efforts fostered a coming together of splintered factions on a common ground of relationality, it was met favourably. However, given the deliberate move to supplant the classic drive/structure foundation of the established orthodoxy, it could not but provoke divisiveness.

In "Illegitimate Attacks on Classical Psychoanalysis" Mills (2005, pp. 172–176) described Mitchell's stance as a "politically driven ideology" (p. 172). He argued a false dichotomy (p. 172) and described the relational perspective as flailing in its efforts to resolve "the existence of a private inner life focusing on internal processes . . . [and] interpersonal explanations focus[ing] on transactions with others" (Mascialino, 2008, p. iv). Others warned against radically positioning the field (Frie, 2009; Mills, 2005). The controversies drew notable attention within psychoanalytic circles in the United States, but hardly beyond.

Within the United States by the turn of the twenty-first century, the relational position had become a major voice. The American field had long been priming for change: The 1960s saw the establishment of alternative psychoanalytic training programs for those "excluded . . . from the 'official' psychoanalytic institutes" (Berman, 1997, p. 196). And in 1979, the American Psychology Association founded its Psychoanalytic Division 39. Both shifts set the stage for a positive reception to Greenberg and Mitchell's book (1983), Mitchell's later elaboration (1988), and a postdoctoral relational track in psychoanalysis and psychotherapy (early 1990s) as part of New York University's alternative training program (Berman, 1997, p. 196).

By 1991, Mitchell had launched *Psychoanalytic Dialogues: A Journal of Relational Perspectives*, the future flagship journal of the International Association for Relational Psychoanalysis and Psychotherapy (IARPP, n.d.), itself inaugurated in 2001. Through the 1990s, English translations of the various works of Sándor Ferenczi[1] provided added sources of inspiration for the relational view (Berman, 1997, pp. 192–193; Haynal, 2002). Since then, the association has enjoyed continued

Distinguishing the relational perspective **11**

international growth, supported by both an educational hub in New York City's Stephen A. Mitchell Center for Relational Psychoanalysis (IARPP, n.d.) and *Psychoanalytic Dialogues*, the "top ranked psychoanalytic journal in the world, by impact factor, for 2013" (Bass, Ipp, & Seligman, December 2014).

Still, outside the bounds of the psychoanalytic world, the relational turn remains lesser known (Mitchell & Black, 1995/2016, p. 172; Redmond & Shulman, 2008). Instead, "*the version of psychoanalysis cited in most interdisciplinary efforts . . . is Freud's biologically grounded drive theory*" (italics added) (Mitchell & Black, 1995/2016, p. 172; Redmond & Shulman, 2008). Education is, of course, no exception. In 2008, Redmond and Shulman searched 150 of the topmost American colleges and universities for psychoanalytic content in undergraduate courses. They located 1,092 such courses, of which only 3 were in educational studies. Just over 75 per cent were in humanities and social sciences and only 13.6 per cent were in psychology faculties. Within those courses, most identified psychoanalytic thought "exclusively with Freud's work . . . rather than as an ongoing movement and a living, evolving process" (p. 406). They left the impression of clinical psychoanalytic practice as a historic phenomenon.

This is not to say that drive theory has become obsolete. Not by any means. Rather, it has evolved, most notably, into Kleinian, neo-Freudian, ego psychology, and Freudian revisionist forms – the latter including Lacanian theory that has powerfully influenced post-structuralist and feminist thinking (Mitchell & Black, 1995/2016, pp. 171–172, 193, & 203; Redmond & Shulman, 2008). In education, these classical versions have found their way into curriculum studies through the influence of feminists Juliet Mitchell, Julia Kristeva, and Luce Irigaray, especially and through revisionist and Kleinian perspectives applied to pedagogical practice (see, e.g., Bibby, 2011; Grumet & Stone, 2000). After Freud, and an earlier Winnicott, prior to his estrangement from Klein (see Berman, 1997, pp. 190–192; Eigen, 1981/1999, p. 10), Melanie Klein is arguably the most-cited psychoanalytic theorist in education (see, e.g., in Bainbridge & West, 2012; Bibby, 2011, pp. 97–115; Britzman, 2006, 2016; Todd, 2003, pp. 100–107). In *Education – An "Impossible Profession"? Psychoanalytic Explorations of Learning and Classrooms*, Bibby draws upon Kleinian theory to describe "relating to objects . . . [as] entirely an intra-psychic event. . . . [resting] on drives and instincts" (2011, p. 117). Significantly, it is Klein's approach alone that Mitchell and Black identify as "exceptional in retain[ing] an almost exclusive emphasis, *even more than that of classical Freudians, on inborn instinctual drives*" (italics added) (1995, n. 3, p. 263). For all these indicators, we can fairly say that psychoanalysis in education is not relational.

Convergences: post-Cartesian science and relational psychoanalysis

Science philosophers Fortun and Bernstein (1998) optimistically anticipated "wonderfully and woefully complex systems of muddy hybrid components . . . [in the] fusions, confusions, and profusions" of bridging Snow's unbridgeable cultures: the sciences and the humanities. Approaching this possibility, relational psychoanalysis, per Emmanuel Ghent (a seminal relationalist author), "is almost ideally suited to make use of insights from the dynamic systems perspective that in the last decade or two has begun to radically change the way we think in science" (2002, p. 9).

Today, psychoanalysis in education remains classically leaning (with hermeneutic and phenomenological sensibilities), narrative in form, interpretive in nature, and rich with metaphor, affect, and first-person accounts. Yet the original drive theory it invokes sits comfortably in the positivist and neopositivist science of Freud's day – steeped according to Overton (2014) in Descartes' mechanistic inheritance (p. 35) and preferring causative chains over recursive self-cause (Juarrero, 1999/2002), and having little room for biological contingencies and idiosyncrasies. This science's allure was and continues to be its promised certainty and predictive power. Seemingly at odds with any psychoanalytic tradition, such a science seeks to reduce away the unique, the enigmatic, and the individual. At the turn of the twentieth century, it could allow only one of either nature or nurture (Overton, 2014, pp. 24–25). Overton writes, "The Cartesian worldview . . . shape[s] an intrapsychic/interpersonal (nature/nurture) divide within which circular and dialectic causation are conceptually problematic" (2014, pp. 25–26). It was not a divide that Freud would bridge. Instead, his drive theory sided with nature and put instinct as unavoidable first cause.

Resolving the Cartesian split between the nobler thinking mind and the baser physical body was a challenge awaiting a maturing natural philosophy of complex life systems (see Chapter 8). Recast in that philosophy – that is, in "post-Cartesian/relational/relationist" terms (as per Overton) – humans are holistically organised selves, functioning as wholes only by virtue of the interdependence of their parts (Overton, 2014, p. 32), and of a class of "nonlinear, essentially historical phenomena . . . not already there waiting to be rolled out and therefore explained . . . [but rather formed of] uniquely individuated trajectories embodying irreversible discontinuities that emerge over time" (Juarrero, 1999/2002, p. 220). In Freud's world, any shift in philosophical perspectives from Cartesian foundations to post-Cartesian sensibilities (Stolorow, 2009, p. 144) was only a speck on a virtual horizon of conceptual possibility. Yet he managed to create a generative humanistic science to grapple in that space.

Even today, and too often in education, the Cartesian legacy is the present common sense. We find it alive and well in ever-popular computer metaphors about knowledge and learning where the ways we think are considered like software programs running on brain circuitry to receive, process, and store data (Fonagy & Target, 2007, pp. 422–423). It lives in public schooling, where there prevails a scientific method dedicated to cause-effect laws and probabilities. Even the biological sciences have no room for concepts of self-organisation and the infinite loops of recursive causation. Indeed, if we were comfortable with these ideas, it would not sound strange to speak of knowing as a kind of doing, to say that we do ourselves into our own difference, or to think of being as an ongoing state of dynamic becoming. Instead, we school students in the mathematics and sciences of additive linear causality (where, e.g., "A" and "B" cause "C," causing "D") and material causality (where, e.g., the physical topography of the brain explains observed behaviour), and, despite phenomena such as the wave-particle duality, trust-control duality (Möllering, 2005), and singular-plural-being (Nancy, 2000), we generally disavow paradox. All the while, popular educational research continues to feed a public appetite for the latest set of "things we know for sure."

Freud, a neuroscientist aspiring to an exact science of mind, faced "raw data" that instead called for the mind's storying. And so, his writing took narrative form, even as he tethered it to a science of inferred causal preconditions. Shaped in an era of C. P. Snow's *Two Cultures* (1959), with a still-naïve, heady, (neo)positivistic science, and no hope of consilience across the long-standing science-humanities fissure, psychoanalysis could not have appeared legitimate except riding upon scientific postulates that were acceptable enough to the era's assumptions about human nature. But that was over a hundred years ago.

It would take a century of evolution in philosophical thought, studies of human nature, and the sciences of life to even begin to fathom, much less live with, more humble propositions: foundations as contingent, truth as critically constructed, life forms as emergent and nested, "causation" embedded in paradoxical, recursive, explanatory forms; affect and reason intertwined and embodied, relations at the core of knowable reality, and "exchanges of recognition" (Benjamin, 1988) – even perhaps between empirical science and interpretive hermeneutics.[2] These perspectives and understandings describe a "rapprochement among the sciences" (see Overton, 2014, pp. 44–54) that together lend further support to the relational psychoanalytic orientation.

On the question of philosophical foundations, relational psychoanalytic theorists have answered roundly and clearly (Aron, 1996; Berman, 2001; Fonagy & Target, 2007; Mascialino, 2008; Mills, 2005). Its principal tenets are "the primacy of relatedness" and a "psychoanalytic hermeneutics" (Mills, 2005, pp. 158–165). Relatedness rests upon a Heideggerian intersubjective ontology where "Being-in-the-world is always already 'Being-with others'" (Stolorow, 2009, p. 155). Its hermeneutic orientation is Gadamerian (Frie, 2009, p. 16; Donnel Stern, 1997/2003), grounded in phenomenology, and linked through neurophenomenology to the sciences of mind (see, e.g., Frie & Orange, 2009; Mascialino, 2008; Donnel Stern, 1997/2003, 2010; Stolorow, 2009).

As with other contemporary traditions, the understandings and perspectives of relational psychoanalysis owe to rich shared histories with multiple lines of psychoanalytic thought. Its distinction, however, lies in its comparative orientation that intimately shades "American interpersonal tradition, Kleinian and neo-Kleinian theory, the British Independent tradition, self psychology, feminist thinking and postmodern theory" (Safran, 2016) in a pervasive post-Cartesian relational hue. It is no surprise to find, within and coterminous with relational psychoanalytic theorising, a fulsome complement of ideas from such contemporary fields as critical constructivism (e.g., see Aron, 2010, also as in Donnel Stern, 1997/2003), feminism (see especially Benjamin, 1988, 1995), non-linear dynamic systems (NLDS, e.g., Lewis & Granic, 2000; Seligman, 2005), otherwise known as relational developmental systems (Molenaar, Lerner, & Newell, 2014), infant studies (see especially Daniel

Stern, 1985/2000, 2000; Teicholz, 2009), child development (e.g., Carpendale & Lewis, 2006; Mayes, Fonagy, & Target, 2007), neuropsychology (e.g., Cozolino, 2010; Ginot, 2015), and attachment theory (e.g., De Bei & Dazzi, 2014; Fonagy & Target, 2007; Wallin, 2007). It is precisely this confluence of acumen, in meaning and insight, that I argue holds untapped potential for breathing humanistic wisdom into education. Yet within current writings in psychoanalysis in education, key relational thinkers and their critical contributions are, with the exception of Benjamin, no more than a footnote if present at all.[3]

Notes

1 Ferenczi, a former colleague of Freud, fell out with him over his view on infant sexuality (Berman, 1997; Haynal, 2002; Mitchell & Black, 1995/2016). Ferenczi wrote of a "Confusion of Tongues" (1933/1988), whereby a child's desire for approval and acceptance by a powerful adult is maligned as a desire to be sexually exploited (sexually loved) by that other; that is, where to love and be loved becomes about exploiting and being exploited (see Benjamin, 1988, Chapter 2).
2 It is worth mentioning several key works that played a critical role along the way in shifting societal openness to, if not acceptance of, these ideas. The 1960s saw Kuhn's *Nature of Scientific Revolutions* (1962) and Berger and Luckman's *Social Construction of Reality* (1966). Cartesian anxieties found address in such writings as Bernstein's *Beyond Objectivism and Relativism* (1983) and Butler's "Contingent Foundations" (1992). Post-Cartesian sensibilities gained clearer articulation through a critical trajectory from Maturana and Varela's original *Autopoiesis and Cognition: The Realization of the Living* (1972/1980) and inclusive of Lakoff and Johnson's *Philosophy in the Flesh* (1999) and Thompson's *Mind in Life* (2007).
3 In an extensive search through psychoanalytic writings in education – including theses, journal articles, and the most recent texts of Appel (1996), Bibby (2011), Bainbridge and West (2012), Britzman (2006, 2016), Pitt (2003), Salvio (2007), Taubman (2012), and Todd (2003) – for principal thinkers and/or ideas specific to the relational tradition I found but one: Patricia Ann deYoung's 2000 doctoral thesis, "Thriving on Difficult Knowledge: Poststructural Pedagogy and Relational Psychoanalysis," was influenced by doctoral committee member Alice Pitt, who worked with Deborah Britzman in theorising difficult knowledge (2003), and by her own colleagues at the Toronto Institute for Relational Psychotherapy, the only relational institute at the time in Canada.
  In regards to the textbook search, I located three uses of Benjamin's theorising: in Bibby, who is ambiguous in invoking Benjamin, registering particular objections to notions of containment and attachment; Pitt, who appropriately uses Benjamin to attend to the question of reciprocity in relations and who aptly offers questions with important implications for education; and Brown and Murphy – Brown having been my external doctoral examiner – who are the only writers to actually invoke relationality in a small section (two pages) that draws from Benjamin's theorising about infant development, with comparable attention to Ogden's notion of thirdness. Other than these references, I found two one-line mentions of Fonagy and Target (in Bibby, 2011), a reference to Eigen's seminal paper by Taubman (2012), and the mention of Ogden by Britzman (2006).

2

PSYCHOANALYSIS IN EDUCATION

Aron footnoted his book, *Mutuality in Psychoanalysis* (1996), with a telling comment: "Current classical theorists are likely to argue that their versions of classical theory are indeed relational or contain relational concepts. Granted. Nevertheless." (p. 1, n. 1).

Whereas Chapter 1 outlined the relational difference, the contexts of its emergence, and a beginning sense of its promise and absence in education, this chapter focuses on two explicit relational aims relevant to education: rendering the discourse more generally accessible and fostering an understanding of the human condition attendant to the spectrum of human experiences, from trauma and anguish to creativity and joy, especially with respect to learning. These intentions of relational psychoanalysis, together with the notable and diverse scholarships from which the tradition draws, make it radically suited to the curricular study of teaching and learning.

Accessible discourse – losses in translation

Greenberg and Mitchell (1983) described the shift from drive/structure to relational/structure in terms as stark as the Copernican revolution. Much as the Ptolemaic theories of old afforded conceptual and pragmatic power commensurate with the times, and much as they also became unwieldy in adjusting to and explaining emergent anomalies (Kuhn, 1962/1996), so too has the field of "postclassical psychoanalysis . . . fragmented into competing schools and traditions. . . . [making it] difficult for anyone who has not spent years studying the history of psychoanalytic ideas to pick up any individual psychoanalytic work and to grasp its contribution" (Mitchell & Black, 1995/2016, p. xxi). This is especially true for psychoanalytic writing in education today.

Jessica Benjamin, key relationalist and feminist author, saw a mnemonic "advantage of Freud's theory of the death instinct" (1995, p. 189): For analysts, it invoked

16 The relational turn

"clearly established" (p. 189) conceptual links. Not so for any lay public. Nonetheless, she adds, "'instinct' may best be understood not literally, biologically, but rather as a metaphor for somatic and affective states" (p. 189).

In the late twentieth century, a proliferation of alternative training institutes in the United States served to broaden and enrich an increasingly comprehensive field (Mitchell & Black, 1995/2016, pp. xx–xxiii). In opening psychoanalysis to a broader public, these changes lent a rigorous cross-infusion of disciplinary thought while promoting the "reversal of the traditional elitism and contrived obscurantism of psychoanalytic writing" (Mitchell & Black, 1995/2016, p. xxi).

Yet hard-pressed to communicate its complex, more neoclassical ideas in approachable language, psychoanalytic texts in education today, too often, exemplify what Mitchell and Black describe as an obscure, at times poetic, near-impenetrable psychoanalytic style (1995/2016, p. xxi). Consider the following example, heavy with unfamiliar language, unusual metaphors, and complex argumentation. It is fairly typical of Deborah Britzman, a notable Kleinian scholar in education (2016).

> Without a phantasy of knowledge, without that motivating fiction, and without an admission of something on the tip of one's tongue, with what one almost said, there is hardly a way to enter into mental worlds. So it is with this "witch meta-psychology." It proceeds, just as psychical life proceeds, through speculation, theorizing, accidents, and phantasying. And present conflicts will be called and addressed. The invitation is for the symptom to repeat through variations, its attempt to placate meaning by missing it. The context of the analytic setting, however, causes the symptom's confusion to create something anew, what Freud saw as "an artificial illness" (1915a). Conveyed through the transference, the displaced symptom will present itself as defamiliarization. Much earlier in the psychoanalytic archive, Freud (1905) saw aspects of these early explorations as sexual research. . . . For the little sex researcher, theory was exciting because it needed neither external proof of its own existence nor any experience to secure its grounds. Indeed, theory's only purpose was its capacity for exciting symbolization. And this intimacy between thinking and sexuality, the sexualizing of thought, may help us understand why literary styles so excite, why Freud needed Goethe, why we need our private madness.
>
> *(Britzman, 2016, p. 18)*

Rare would be the curriculum scholar or educational practitioner at ease with moving from a "phantasy of knowledge," through "witch meta-psychology" as "psychical life," and the placation of "meaning by missing it," to a notion of transference in "defamiliarisation" – and then be sufficiently compelled to concede such arguments as are made on a need for "private madness" that link the child to the "sexualizing of thought" and the thinking of literary styles in ways that "so excite." This style alone may be enough to account for psychoanalytic theory's existence on the fringes of educational discourses and peripheral to schooling practice. However exquisite and profound, the writing lends credence to a myth that psychoanalysis is "an esoteric cult requiring both conversion and years of study" (Mitchell & Black, 1995/2016, p. xx) in order to participate. The present book, in line with relational efforts, attempts to further the cause of broadened accessibility, without compromising conceptual rigour, in interdisciplinary conversations in education.

To be sure, some psychoanalytic writings in education have sought to reach general publics. Bibby's recent work designed for teachers is one such exemplar. Yet even that work, intended to communicate psychically relevant experiences in everyday language, uses descriptions so powerfully imbued with affect as to seem entirely foreign and alienating to readers – not the least of whom, in relation to the following example of a hungry crying baby, may have themselves raised rather cherub infants.

> Let us begin with the experience of hunger (for example). A growl from the stomach initiates a gnawing pain – some malevolent object has set up a chain of experiences which threaten to annihilate the baby's fragile existence: pain, loud noises in the ears tear the head, tears in the eyes blur vision, dryness in the throat scratches and generates more noise, mucus fills the nose and throat adding to the difficulties of breathing. Screaming to escape the screaming that fills its head and saturates its world with terror, the baby is "beside itself" with rage and misery. The pain is experienced as malevolent, death-dealing, terrifying. To manage the pain an object is phantasised, imagined into being, an object that has caused this pain and to which the baby can turn its fury, a malevolent object that Klein called the bad breast.
>
> *(Bibby, 2011, p. 100)*

Bibby's depiction fairly represents Kleinian perspectives, these having arisen out of pioneering work in child analysis, begun in the 1920s and controversial at the time. Today, a hundred years later and after decades of more recent revolutionary work in infant studies (see Chapters 5 and 6), it should be quite unsurprising to find Klein's descriptions thoroughly out-of-step with the present field. On the trouble of the marginal presence of psychoanalysis in education, we would do well to appreciate how compromising the foregoing two passages might be today. Unless psychoanalytic theory in education can bring itself into mindfully informed, accessible, and relevant understandings, it will continue to be dismissed out of hand.

Trauma and joy

Tracing the relational perspective back to the 1940s and its roots in the independent group of the British Psychoanalytic Society, we find a difference of perspective on the infant's inborn disposition. Marion Milner succinctly summarised the objections of the independent group when she wrote, "I think it is a pity that the expressive word 'reverie' has been so largely dropped from the language of psychopathology. . . . [A]re we going to treat all phenomena . . . as symptoms, something to be got rid of?" (1957/1987, p. 231).

18 The relational turn

The beginning years of the Society saw a feud between Anna Freud and Melanie Klein. Those most loyal to Freud followed his daughter in a direct line to today's ego psychology. Others followed Klein's revision "of an infant wired for human interaction" (Mitchell & Black, 1995/2016, pp. 113–114). Both groups took "refuge in heredity" (Winnicott, 1971/2005, p. 95) and imagined an infant primed for trauma by the precondition of inborn aggression. On this view, a third independent group differed. Later known as the British object relations school (including Fairbairn, Winnicott, Balint, Bowlby, and Guntrip of the renowned Tavistock Clinic), this group agreed with Klein on a social infant but broke with her on the premise of constitutional aggression (Mitchell & Black, 1995/2016, pp. 113–114). Describing "the concept of the death instinct . . . as a reassertion of the principle of original sin," Winnicott argued that "the history of an individual baby cannot be written in terms of the baby alone" (1971/2005, p. 95).

In short, *the infant of the British school was "wired for harmonious interaction and non-traumatic development . . . [that could nonetheless be] thwarted by inadequate parenting"* (emphasis added) (Mitchell & Black, 1995, p. 114).

On this count, it is useful to distinguish radical shifts in Donald Winnicott's works. Whereas an earlier Winnicott linked object usage "with the ruthless expression of instinctual drives" (Eigen, 1981/1999, p. 10), the later one celebrated "the infant's creativity . . . and the mother's capacity to allow it" (Berman, 1997, pp. 190–191). In educational psychoanalytic literature, Winnicott is frequently cited but without attention to this shift. Just as Ferenczi was inspired by Freud and then broke with him, Winnicott was inspired by Klein but then fell out with her. Thus, whereas the more classically oriented perspectives in education invoke an earlier Winnicott, a contemporary relational view draws from his later insights.

Schooling – classically, the subduing of instincts

We need not search far to find rather glum neoclassical leanings in educational psychoanalytic literature. Bibby, citing Frosh, writes, "Behind every action is a wish, behind every thought is an unreasonable desire. . . . [H]uman 'essence' lies in unacceptable and hence repressed impulses" (2011, p. 7), while Britzman invokes Philips, writing, "[T]here may, sometimes, be a cure for symptoms, but there is no cure for the unconscious, no solution for unconscious desire. Knowledge can't put a stop to that, only death can" (1998, p. 21).

Insofar as psychoanalysis in education has adhered to Freud's fundamental drive/structure model, it has remained entangled in Freud's era where personal memories – recovered in dreams, free associations, and verbal slippages – needed the premise of two desires, libidinal and aggressive, in order for those memories to be woven into narratively coherent, causally sensible, and culturally viable accounts. Put differently – and recalling from Chapter 1 – the first Freudian premise derived from a socio-culturally "necessary" belief that the hypersexualised memories of his female patients, women hysterics, could not have been real events. These hysterics suffered physical disabilities without obvious physical

Psychoanalysis in education **19**

impairment. Yet under hypnotic suggestion, those impairments could disappear. Wondering why and how some ideas could be elusive and inaccessible to awareness yet still wreak havoc, *Freud formulated a psychic theory of human tragedy, in a story of unconscious defence against socially undesirable and intolerable instincts* (Mitchell & Black, 1995/2016, p. 3).

Felman recapitulates and reemphasises education's first and impossible task: "The child must learn to control his instincts. . . . Accordingly, *education must inhibit, forbid and suppress.* . . . [even though this] involves the risk of neurotic illness" (Freud in Felman, 1982, p. 23). Meanwhile, repression and various psychic defences work to vigilantly seal away the "difficult knowledge" (Pitt & Britzman, 2003) of disavowed urges and prevent our coming to terms with them. Indeed, a pervasive sentiment of psychoanalytic literature in education seems to be one of commiseration with educators on their impossible role as civilising agents in an inevitably tragic human tale. Addressing teachers, Bibby gently acknowledges the dire task.

> There is no route map for an easy walk through life's vicissitudes, but I will suggest that there may be some ideas that can help us to think about the difficulties and why they might feel so hard, or downright impossible, to deal with. And that in turn can help us to develop some ideas for other ways of thinking and acting – if we can bear it.
>
> *(2011, pp. 3–4)*

Britzman observes that education "cannot tolerate psychoanalysis" (1998, p. 29). Reports have this as fairly consensual (Bainbridge & West, 2012; Britzman, 1998, 2013; Pitt, 2003; Taubman, 2011). While the psychoanalytic account of schooling tells a Freudian story of fated anguish in learning and grievous difficulty in teaching, its narrative about its own alienation in education seems too neatly explained by the general psychoanalytic premise of repression. There is much convenience in rooting resistance in "that which is repressed and fundamentally unknowable" (Bibby, 2011, pp. 6–7). If the unconscious is uncanny, and the prediscursive baby has not words to voice disagreement on interpretations made of him, then like Freud's conclusions about female hysterics, such theories form a closed loop that render them beyond adjudication. Yet all of these accounts stumble over two critical counterpoints that, as we will see, render moot the arguments, while playing our attentions in drastically altered ways as we consider learning's motivation (Chapter 7) and its refusal (Chapter 8).

Both counterpoints arise at the convergence of disciplines. Firstly, affective neuroscience locates at least seven subcortical brain systems responsible for all varieties of raw emotions, instinctual behaviours, and attendant visceral responses (Panksepp & Biven, 2012, p. 17). Two of these are rage and lust. However, it is the other five – fear, play, seeking, care, and (in abandonment and loss) care's underside, panic/grief – that relational psychoanalysis and affective neuroscience converge in naming as most critical to early attachment relations and subsequent human flourishing. Importantly, none of these systems and the affects they spawn assume interpretive

20 The relational turn

meaning except in and through interpersonal relations. The non-verbal child is quite incapable of thought, much less discerning a breast and attributing it malevolent cause (as per Bibby, 2011, p. 100, cited earlier).

Secondly, current understandings of neurophysiological processes paint a picture of highly selective formulation of unconscious and nonconscious content into conscious awareness. Most of our body's knowing and doing operates outside of conscious awareness (see Chapter 4). Psychic defences are far less likely to work by repressing what we know and far more likely to be about refusing to know in the first place; that is, we are physiologically primed to avoid spelling out those affects that bode irresolvable conflicts within the self (Donnel Stern, 1997/2003).

> In a frame of reference in which consciousness is active interpretation and not passive registration, the basic defensive process must be the *prevention of interpretation* in reflective awareness, not the *exclusion from awareness* of elements that are already fully formed. If reflective experience is created by interpretation, such experience is avoided by not interpreting.
>
> *(Stern, 1997/2003, p. 87)*

To summarise, in the classical intrapsychic model, we see a self caught in a kind of punishing Promethean coping – an inherited original sin as Winnicott suggested (1971/2005, p. 95). Refusal, resistance, and repression explain inaccessible unconsciousness. Shackled by the inherited "sins" of overzealous, unchecked life-and-death forces of libidinal and aggressive drives, the therapeutic and educational goal is to resolve our good and bad, civilising and uncivilised, self-parts. We can grow a kind of quietude of self-knowledge and self-acceptance as our defences give way and we find the courage to allow and live with the difficult knowledge of our repressed animalistic urges. Like many stories of human life, as we will see, this narrative is not without merit, but it wants for relational reinterpretation.

Schooling reconsidered – on responsibility

The Routledge Handbook of Psychoanalysis in the Social Sciences and the Humanities has described the twenty-first-century shift from psychoanalytic intersubjectivity-on-the-margins to its now-dominant relational position as nothing short of revolutionary, radically reframing "our entire view of human development and social bonds" to a contemporary way of thinking "in terms of the interpenetration of minds, conscious and unconscious" (in Benjamin, 2018, p. 1).

Significantly, a crucial difference – between, on the one hand, ready-to-roll-out aggressive and libidinal instincts at odds with socio-cultural norms and, on the other hand, a self that takes its very shape in relationality – is the difference of collective responsibility and social agency. In pointing to instinct as the source of difficulty, we are left to flounder in the inevitable. In looking to forms of relating – as sources of potential difficulty, yes, but jubilance, too – we are called instead to attend to the interplay between biophysical potentialities and interpersonal relational systems that shape meaning in life. Learning thus becomes about creative and co-creative possibility.

In so saying, my concerns about education today and my hopes in writing join those of Jessica Benjamin, who seeks

> to illuminate the larger stakes of the contemporary psychoanalytic project: its unique way of thinking about self and other, mind and affect, the psychic life of social subjects. . . . that these propositions will reach across the disciplinary barriers and enable non-psychoanalysts to access the social and philosophical implications of intersubjective psychoanalysis.
>
> *(2018, p. 1)*

If we follow the converging lenses of twenty-first-century neuroscience, dynamic systems theory, and psychoanalysis, we come to a far different story of selves than is commonly made or classically given in psychoanalysis. Each person's unfolding occurs relationally in ways to negotiate, mediate, and define a rich interweave – viscerally human and discursively societal. As species' inclinations (instincts) find expression in persons, themselves finding meaning in social systems, the challenges and possibilities of living well may fundamentally owe to slippages and fractures that inevitably occur as these forms – species, personal, and societal – each with their own timescales, temporalities, histories, and proclivities – engage each other.

Life and its vicissitudes seem to happen in a middle interpretive realm of lived experience where each self iteratively redefines and refines itself. We can think of instincts as taking their cue for expression from all that is unique and idiosyncratic in such experience. These enmeshed interactions shape the ongoing elaboration of personal and societal predilections, in the context of verbally mediated worlds of available meaning. In other words, instinctual and normative structures may be better thought of as the respective frameworks of species-specific predispositions and inherited cultural legacies that – in conversation with all that is uniquely individual and relational – work to foreclose some possibilities while opening others.

Notably, and central to relational psychoanalytic understandings, these things occur, for the most part, in ways that preclude our very capacity to render a personal account of them – that is, outside our awareness of the prior and tacit conditions that shape and shaped our being. Thus, to better address the human condition, we might consider foraging, in self and world, for memory's decaying and archival remains, that we might formulate into awareness otherwise-dissociated experiences, toward an ethical life in humble acknowledgement of degrees of opacity of selves.

We are not there yet, by any means. I submit that the reason for lack of movement entangles in societal habit, like the unconscious, generative of proclivities for discernment (see Part III) and keeping us quite oblivious to the visceral, relational, and social worlds interacting beyond our noticing. Meanwhile, in individualistic societies especially, unwavering faith in individual agency continues. I speak of the pervasive belief – reiterated in popular self-help literatures – that we are all endowed with free will and are the masters of our own conditions. If it is true that "where there is a will, there is a way" and "you can do anything you set your mind to" – as the aphorisms go – then we can rise above our circumstances. If we don't, "we have only ourselves to blame."

In the least, most people continue to take for granted what Freud, and numerous others, began to question: the conditions of our own formation, belief in our own self-transparency, and trust in our remembered self-story as the fully definitive one. In short, we are a long way from appreciating system contingencies, opacities, and complicities in the shaping of selves. Given this state of public awareness, any explanation of human difficulty that appears to privilege relationality over instinct, shared interpretive unfolding over fated drives, will be considered a narrative to visit blame on someone – especially caregivers. Thus, the story of relationality in early attachment suggested a Pandora's box that, for a near half-century, was thought best kept closed.

The tacit vigilance that permeates Bibby's chapter "Thinking in Relationships" is a prime example (2011, pp. 117–133). Writing on such hopeful relational constructs as containment, mutuality, and intersubjective thirdness (2011, pp. 118–119), she recasts them in a Kleinian logic of forsaken depressive self-acceptance (p. 120), while eliding the potential joy they speak to in teaching and learning. And she warns against the slippery slope of an orientation that could lead to blaming the mother. One can almost hear Bowlby in "his early days in the British Psychoanalytic Society. . . . when he arose defiantly to assert . . . 'But there *is* such a thing as a bad mother'" (circa 1940s, in Mitchell & Black, 1995/2016, p. 114) – a lament to which we ought now hasten to add: Enfolding that mother (that father and later that teacher) was a world conditioning her circumstances, just as, within her, lived the circumstances of her own childhood. Applying across degrees of intimacy, to all relationships – not only those between primary caregivers and their children – we can remember that there is *both* shared joy and disturbing complicity at play in our holding each other well, or not. In this realisation, with Pandora's box wide open, we can locate our greatest agency to understand, support, encourage, and inspire differently.

On joy – learning and the relational encounter

Eigen writes, "The need to be good in order to make up for being bad is a very different moment from the freedom of loving for its own sake. . . . [J]oy is not defined by a background of guilt, but is an intrinsically undefensive feeling" (1981/1999, p. 12). What, then, of those of us who find joy in parenting and in schooling, and who see that joy reflected in the children in our midst?

If it is true that "like Bion's adult clients, children hate learning from experience, and entertain magical fantasies that remove the pain of having to learn" (Bibby, 2011, p. 19), then are we – who revel in it and who seek the stretch of learning's provocation – caught in some strangely neurotic modern denial? Perhaps not. Certainly, affective neuroscience would say not (on seeking systems, see Panksepp & Biven, 2012). Could we entertain the notion that things are perhaps not the way they might classically seem? Might the narrative of inevitable trauma install, to some degree, its own repetition compulsion riding upon a melancholic want to keep joy at bay?

In any case, it may help to remember that the seeming veracity of an interpretation as matching (or not) one's lived experience has everything to do with the accepted social constructions availed to us and what we have taken and made of them. Whereas a kind of neoclassical psychoanalysis is at home speaking words and ideas that are often an affront to more sanitised and romanticised views of childhood and innocence, its tales of trauma and difficulty seem a ready fit with Foucauldian tales of human subduing and a critical theory narrative of power and control. But must we accept that we are doomed to difficulty because of counter-social inborn proclivities and their need for regulation, or is there far more at play? Must we resign ourselves to constant disillusionment, or might disillusionment instead invite movement and the creative, and iterative, re-visioning of, just as *illusive, reals*?

I am not alone in questioning the tragic tone of psychoanalytic accounts. Bibby acknowledges "an optimism and externality suggested by intersubjectivity that is missing in Klein's work" (2011, p. 117). Indeed, in the "Kleinian guilt-based account, joy would be rationalised. . . . It would have *no place in its own right, as an intrinsic part of self–other awareness*" (Eigen, 1981/1999, p. 11). For a later Winnicott too, "creativity permeates psychic life and is involved in the very birth of self and other" (Eigen, 1981/1999, p. 5). "It is creative apperception more than anything else that makes the individual feel that life is worth living" (Winnicott, 1971/2005, p. 87). Contra Freud and Klein, Winnicott's core affect is joy. And though he acknowledges that "life requires violence (hatching processes)" (Eigen, 1981/1999, p. 25) he locates hatching within a "primacy of love" (p. 25) "alive and strong enough to [be able to] use destructiveness creatively, rendering guilt superfluous" (Eigen, 1981/1999, p. 11).

Likewise, contra Lacan, for Winnicott, as for relationalists, "experiencing and object usage are *not* essentially linked with repression" (Eigen, 1981/1999, p. 16). Eigen perhaps best captures the point:

> By roughly two or three months of age (perhaps earlier), the infant may spontaneously break out into a coherent, joyous smile to a face stimulus. . . . Lacan . . . reads a seductive or controlling (adaptive mastery) element. . . . I find this smile more radically joyous, expressive of delight in recognizing personal presence. . . . To view . . . [it] merely in terms of its value for ensuring survival says little of what kind of being survives *this* way, and scarcely does justice to its surplus of expressive meaning. . . . [T]he *primary smile* . . . expresses all out, spontaneous living through faith.
>
> *(Eigen, 1981/1999, p. 19)*

Even in addressing the pervasive and persistent problems of master/slave relations, gender binaries, and domination (1988, 1995), Benjamin brings a sensitivity on the first bonds of love and, with it, the courage and promise of mutuality. The message,

24 The relational turn

like that of Winnicott's and Eigen's, is one of the "basic goodness of 'news of difference'. . . . not catastrophe. . . . [;] of dramatic unfolding rather than traumatic im- or propulsion. . . . [; and] a sense of basic harmony mak[ing] divergence revitalizing rather than essentially menacing" (Eigen, 1981/1999, p. 16).

Winnicott endorses Marion Milner's perspectives – Milner, whose background passed through Montessori educational training – when he quotes her:

> Moments when the original poet in each of us created the outside world for us, by finding the familiar in the unfamiliar, are perhaps forgotten by most people; or else they are guarded in some secret place of memory because they were too much like visitations of the gods to be mixed with everyday thinking.
>
> *(Milner, 1957, in Winnicott, 1971/2005, p. 52)*

And Milner appends, to a reprinted version of a 1945 piece, the entirety of a letter from J. D. Sutherland, medical director of the Tavistock Clinic. Citing Sutherland, Milner writes,

> I always believed, ever since Fairbairn . . . that Freud's libido theory was a handicap to the theoretical development of analysis. . . . Guntrip was to me on very solid ground when he criticized Melanie Klein. . . . Klein's work . . . is almost impossible to square with the findings on cognitive development. . . . [G]reat guilt at an early stage implies a differentiation of a self-structure. . . . This is conceivable for most researchers as the second year goes on but not in the first when Klein's oral sadistic phantasies are so powerful in their implications.
>
> *(in Milner, 1945/1987, pp. 59–60)*

As for myself, ever the pragmatist, and wanting to make sense of the joy I felt in both parenting and teaching, I am drawn to a story that can interweave the empirical and the hermeneutic in mutually reinforcing ways. It is *this* story that I *want* to follow. I seek to stay mired neither in disillusioning trauma nor in my favourite illusive real. Instead, in the face of a given world that regularly disrupts and one made of my own re-construing storying, I seek movement that I might creatively illusion myself and that world anew, and anew, again. And so, a different story is the one I *will* follow, to where it leads and from whence it came.

In denying that we are enslaved to aggressive and libidinal drives, a relational perspective serves up a fulsome dose of agency, but with commensurate responsibility that some may not want. Indeed, it calls us to know our own complicity, as self-organising systems, both unto ourselves and as elements of grander self-organising systems that we collectively comprise. In the unfolding of life relationships, the consequences of choices and of co-emerging histories do settle into connective tissue that opens and limits each subsequent possible. Thus, trauma and joy find themselves instituted into constitutional being that, in a continuity of life across space-time, dissipates outward from self to coexisting selves and forward from generation to generation. The crossings and intersections of the crests and troughs of such dissipating ripples will work to amplify, nullify, and reconfigure, for an indeterminate time, life meanings and the performances of those meanings. It seems to me that the healing called for in the world is not the taming of being but the giving of grace to these nested selves that we be – as uncertain, striving, intersecting, co-implicated, and co-implicating systems in a shared project of life.

To the tragic tale of the human condition configured by Freud, the relational turn answers with a dose of hope for a difference in education. It lives in notions that have yet to find their way into education – ideas to reframe our position *vis-à-vis* each other. These notions fall under such considerations as the following: thirdness, creative apperception, and attunement; transitional spaces where a you and a me find each other as co-subjects grappling in the taking and making of a given object-world; and affective neurobiological-interpersonal systems of striving, connecting, and belonging. As will be developed through subsequent chapters, in striving, biological seeking systems are at play in the enticement of a mercifully disillusioning "huh?" In connecting, a neurophysiology of resolutions of ambiguity rewards "a-ha" moments of new illusion-making. And in belonging, the possibility for spirit-lifting moments of subject-to-subject exchanges of recognition echoes and arises from early self-other attunement and events of co-recognition at the heart of mutuality.

3

VOICES AT EDUCATION'S HELM

The situation of education

In 2004, pre-eminent curricular theorist William Pinar described education as "a fragmented field broadly modelled after [and colonised by] the social and behavioral sciences" (p. 2).

> More than ever . . . there is the idea that if only we make the appropriate adjustment (in curriculum, in teaching technique, in how teachers are prepared, in testing, etc.), the school engine will then hum smoothly, and those test scores will soar.
>
> *(p. 176)*

The situation has not much changed. To appreciate schooling practice and whose scholarships are most influential, we will want a sense of the socio-politico-economic climate within which today's schools are embedded, how these climates and the expectations they hold for educational research influence that research and its uptake, and the severe limitations in conducting educational research in the first place.

The blind spots of evidence-based schooling practice

We can begin by considering the proliferation of privileging claims to evidence-based practice. These problematically overdraw on at least four classes of research: (a) highly contextualised *in vivo* qualitative and design-based studies in school settings, (b) laboratory-style *in vitro* studies of operationalised school-related constructs, (c) broad-scale surveys and focus-group consultations of school participants and/ or their stakeholders, and (d) meta-analyses of these studies. Both "a" (*in vivo*) and "b" (*in vitro*) studies in education are forced to play the reliable control of variables against the authenticity, relevance, and generalisability of findings to different contexts over time, not to mention the long-term effect of particular practices and their interaction. Survey and focus-group studies do not fare better. We can tap only what people and societies are conscious of and inclined to admit. "The overreliance on self-reports in personal, clinical, and attitudinal research can no longer be maintained in the face of mounting evidence that much of what we do, feel, and think is inaccessible to consciousness" (Westen, 1998, p. 361).

> [If individuals] can act on the basis of unconscious networks of association, motives, and defenses, then any approach . . . that fails to address such ubiquitous processes is likely to need substantial supplementation. The norm in human life is that people have conflicting feelings . . . and we know little about the way in which conflicting social information, and particularly information associated with contradictory affect states, is processed.
> *(Westen, pp. 356–357)*

The claim to evidence-based schooling practice goes with a kind of tunnel vision that is more ideologically driven than any consequence of scientific rigour. "Everyone . . . may reason to emotionally biased judgments when they have a vested interest in how to interpret 'the facts'" (Westen, in Carey, January 24, 2006).

Quite simply, the things that matter most in education are relational, contextual, and emergent across time. They elude scientific principles of isolation, replication, and measurement.

Politics and a confusion of knowledge and information

To be fair, the research community is generally inclined to making humble, qualified, and tentative claims. However, in more public venues the same findings are often rebranded and marketed in everyday terms to publics who want and expect certainty. In an era where information parades as knowledge, the more specifically that such claims dictate to practice and the more confidently they are expressed – usually in a language of "must" and "should" to "ensure" some desired outcome – the more compelled are teachers and administrators to put them into action and to document those actions. But "information is not knowledge . . . [W]ithout ethical and intellectual judgment – which cannot be programmed into a machine – an Age of Information is an Age of Ignorance" (Pinar, 2004, p. xiii).

Meanwhile, the growing global emphasis on "knowledge economies," with governments vying for secure enough "knowledge-based capital" (Organization for Economic Cooperation and Development), fuels a demand for reliable, valid, and monetizable scientific and technological results. In education, findings with compelling face validity and short-term predictive value stand as proxies for other forms of research validity and reliability. Regardless, compelling findings give the allure of information-as-knowledge to assuage concerned publics. As such, they become monetizable commodities, the production of which lends prestige to research and teaching institutions, installing a forward feedback loop whereby capital and credibility beget further and compounding capital and credibility.

Thus, the creation and successful mobilisation (including branding and marketing) of educational research products have become lucrative endeavours, making possible the further investment of capital from industry sponsors and favourable rewards from research-granting bodies (e.g., see Social Sciences and Humanities Research Council of Canada, 2016). At the same time, with the decline of untargeted monies to higher education,[1] liberal arts colleges have all but given way to a business model bent on the production of specialised knowledge workers.

Successful schools of education take savvy business advantage of a synergy of practices. To wit: lucrative industry partnerships and public-sector endorsements, high-level merchandising strategies that attract students and further investment, a shrinking digital world making possible online and blended courses with high volumes of students at discounted prices, the mass production and marketing of compelling facsimiles of knowledge, and a steady supply of the next quick fix for schooling – all have simply become good business in the game of staying solvent. Meanwhile, on the receiving end, the responsibility falls to teachers and school leaders to put latest techniques and technologies into proper effect – a task which presupposes all of: keeping abreast of new information and accordant techniques, trusting that these define right choices, exercising the moral imperative to do so, and believing they can. The tacit assumption, ill-suited in humanistic endeavours of most sorts, is that schools will succeed if they implement the right facts and tools and that educational research can and does provide those tools.

In contraindication, the lessons of psychoanalytic theory join those of history and of present-day neuroscience and systems theories to affirm that *individuals and societies do what they do, and want as they want, not because they lack the proper facts and tools but largely because of seemingly intangible convictions and motivations within them.* The question of personal will or won't – especially when it comes to the relationships of teaching and learning – has everything to do with our historically shaped, individual and collective capacities and desires – the sense we want, can, or should make of things. The identification of what constitutes a problem – or more deftly understood, what lies underneath and beyond a problem of our limited individual and social purview – and how it might be variously addressed goes as largely assumed and beyond the pale of the most popular of educational thought. In short, when it comes to schooling practice, we seem to be accumulating a great deal of information that, with much ado, poses as knowledge.

If, as Pinar describes it, an "Age of Information Is an Age of Ignorance" (2004, p. xiii), then it is also an age to plunder the very foundation of democracy. In a moment prescient of the 2016 American presidential election, former American Supreme Court justice David Souter said,

> I worry . . . that when problems are not addressed . . . [and] get bad enough . . . some one person will come forward and say, "Give me total power and I will solve this problem." That is how the Roman republic fell. . . . *[T]he*

day will come when somebody will come forward and we and the government will in effect say, "Take the ball and run with it. Do what you have to do." That is the way democracy dies. And if something is not done to improve the level of civic knowledge, that is what you should worry about at night.

(Souter, 2012, in Benen, 2016, para. 1)

Cicero's words "In extraordinary events ignorance of their causes produces astonishment" (from *De Divinatione*, II 22, in Hoyt & Roberts, 1922) ring ever true in a common astonishment of Trump's 2017 election to the presidency. In an age of copious supply, we humans tend to selectively draw information to fortify and justify the choices we want to make anyway.

In what seems a collectively shared dissociative moment, today's cultures seem largely to carry on as if oblivious to the very existence of any unconscious, much less recognise its import in shaping meaning and being. Meanwhile, our various societies shoulder and wield unprecedented capacities because we can, and not for knowing any better. The blinding effect of the ignorance we refuse to acknowledge, first and foremost about ourselves, couples with a bravado of unbridled confidence that puts at risk our own self-destructive demise – as much from a sabotaging hidden self within as from its outward reverberation. In conditions where ignorance couples with bombast to issue a false sense of authority and practical agency, and when publics gravitate to those leaders, then it comes as no surprise to find the depth work of psychoanalysis and curriculum theory direly needed yet readily dismissed in schooling governance and everyday educational practice.

Intellectual freedom in an audit culture

Anthropologists Shore and Wright aptly describe the audit culture of today's new managerialism.

> The substitution of trust by measurement, the replacement of academic autonomy by management control, the deliberate attempt to engineer competition and a climate of insecurity are all features of new managerialism's disciplinary grid of audit. Its aim is to inculcate new norms that supposedly "empower" audited individuals to observe and improve themselves according to new neo-liberal notions of the performing professional.
>
> *(2000, p. 78)*

On November 4, 2011, Stephen Toope, then president and vice chancellor of the University of British Columbia and chair of the Association of Universities and Colleges of Canada, presented a speech on behalf of that association (Canadian Association of University Teachers). The topic was the 2011 revision of the previous 1988 Statement on Academic Freedom (Association of Universities and Colleges of Canada, 1988, 2011). Toope highlighted five commitments from Canada's universities to Canadians, of which the following three figured prominently: *increased university*

30 The relational turn

influence on K–12 practices; rising emphasis on "evidence-based research in pedagogy, new technologies and community-focused opportunities . . . [; and the continued growth of] alliances with business and community groups" (italics added) (Berkowitz, 2011, para. 2).

There is tragic irony in a statement on academic freedom, penned by an association of universities and colleges, that makes its commitments neither to academics nor to their intellectual freedom. Rather, it is consistent with and tacitly endorses several pervasive assumptions about the production of knowledge as pivotal commodity – to wit, that (a) Educational institutions are best run as businesses dealing in the production and distribution of information-as-knowledge; (b) educational research can be usefully conducted according to the rigorous and trustworthy standards of the hard sciences while yielding findings sufficiently generalisable for widespread application in the infinitely variable contexts of schooling; (c) the preparation of teachers and school leaders should follow from research findings on the management of learning – the so-called evidence-based practices; (d) the fidelity with which teachers and school leaders adhere to such practices should be carefully monitored, judged, and regulated to ensure student achievement; (e) failures in student achievement owe to failures in the proper implementation of said findings; and (f) educational research ought to be conducted, in the first place, in solidarity with society's primary knowledge consumers (the stakeholders of business and community), who, in a democracy, should rightfully serve as final arbiters of research directions, including especially the questions that researchers pose and answer in service to these stakeholders.

In short, the most recent Canadian Statement on Academic Freedom aligns with a more globally pervasive audit culture (Strathern, 2000) and a belief that the regulated design and implementation of proper technique and technologies in schools are in the best public interest for ensuring a steady supply of human knowledge capital. An audit culture – as shall be further explored in the new management of the learning sciences ahead – does so by communicating to education faculties a distrust in its autonomous practices and of education's "knowledge workers." It presses these workers, instead, into the role of followers and servants in a stressful game of catering to the whims and desires of stakeholders – the ultimate consumers at the helm of a mercurial marketplace of information on offer as knowledge (Shore & Wright, 2000). In this way, educational researchers are hired and rewarded for their productivity in creating and marketing the very techniques and technologies that will be used in their own regulation and in the uncomplicated management of schoolteachers, school policies, and teaching practices, to the ends of readily producing student achievement. Such an "approach leads to a narrow emphasis on economy and efficiency to the neglect of effectiveness" (Shore & Wright, 2000, p. 84).

Sciences, the humanities, and big business

Governmental, economic, and societal needs converge in depending on continued growth of the more "saleable" sciences of technique and technology. On the one hand, social and psychological sciences, now with potential access to big data, inform public-relations practices that selectively appeal to and augment human desires and particular valued identities (Curtis & Kelsall, 2002). On the other hand, in many ways the technological sciences exacerbate the pace of change, fuelling by feeding an appetite for newness and a belief in the near-unlimited capacity for science to rise to the latest social, economic, and environmental challenges (Gregory & Miller, 1998). Meanwhile, the shortening shelf lives of individual and societal attentions, especially "deep" attention (Turkle, 2015), leave us jumping from one shiny idea to the next.

The misguidedness of trying to "technologise" and audit our way into educational change for a wiser and more able and just society has been soundly critiqued. Critical theorist Raewyn Connell writes,

> The . . . technicized knowledge base . . . is so impoverished that it cannot meet the social need for discourse about educational problems. So around it, there has grown up a gaudy arena of pseudo-science, fads and fakery about education, much of it promoted by the entrepreneurial consultants who have multiplied in the neoliberal world. Different consultants market brain science, boys' special learning styles, parent training, computer solutions, gifted-and-talented programmes, boot camps for troublesome kids, direct instruction, tough love, patent reading schemes, zero tolerance, charter schools and many, many more slogans, programmes and devices.
>
> *(2013, p. 109)*

Psychologist Westen has argued convincingly for "a psychodynamically informed psychological science":

> Psychoanalytic theorists have been describing, categorizing, and exploring the workings of unconscious mental processes for a century, whereas the existence of these processes has just been acknowledged in mainstream research in psychology in the last decade. . . . [I]t is no accident that psychoanalysts have been making some very sophisticated observations about unconscious processes for decades, whereas experimental psychologists have only recently acknowledged their existence.
>
> *(1998, p. 361)*

Instead they have been the cognitive-behavioural approaches that have risen to the fore in educational psychology. "They take less time . . . are cheaper. . . . [and] more conducive to measurement, however questionable . . . and reductive . . . this might be" (Bainbridge & West, 2012, p. 3).

But we must want, in education especially, to take the time needed to make lasting differences in nuanced circumstances. Doing so will benefit from the erudition of scholarships that are: at home with life's paradoxes and contingencies, reverent of the idiosyncrasies of life systems, appreciative of their co-evolving relational dynamics, and understanding of these characteristics as defying the logics of

32 The relational turn

prediction, causation, and prescriptive practice so successful in the hard sciences (Juarrero, 1999/2002).

The humanities and the arts – especially as taken up in curricular and psycho-analytic discourses – have exercised long-standing sensitivity to system contingen-cies and to the inseparability of the personal from the political, cultural, ethical, and intellectual (Pinar, 2004, p. 2). Yet given the present socio-economic-political climate (described earlier), neither curriculum studies nor relational psychoanalytic theory has enjoyed much influence in schooling practice. To date, these discourses may suffer from being ahead of their time. The previous chapter addressed the marginal presence of psychoanalytic theory in education and why the relational turn promises a difference that matters. On the side of curriculum theory – notably, *"the interdisciplinary study of educational experience"* (p. 2) and the only academic dis-cipline wholly dedicated to studying that experience (p. 2) – the reasons are differ-ent. As Pinar has argued, having "conscious[ly] abandon[ed] . . . the 'technician's mentality'" (1978, p. 210), curriculum studies continues to find much of its present scholarship and the force of independent professorial thought increasingly muzzled when it comes to action. It enjoys "no jurisdiction – and little influence – over . . . schools . . . gripped in a vise of right-wing business-minded ideologues" (Pinar, 2004, p. 62).

In short, today's insights into the natures of consciousness, the unconscious, learning, and life systems have hardly made their way into the schooling conversa-tion. If anything, borrowed buzz words, absent integrated understanding, have come to circulate in the public forum – brandished there to legitimise quick fixes that risk exacerbating the very conditions these fixes seek to ameliorate.

Of facts, gizmos, and credentials

When it comes to teacher preparation and graduate studies in education, the years have seen normal schools morph into training colleges and now professional institutions increasingly operating according to a business model with a sale-able brand and a strong marketing agenda to promote three principal education commodities.

At the risk of inviting acrimony, we might abbreviate the current predicament by parsing the commodities of schooling into three categories: *facts, gizmos, and credentials*. Whereas *facts* aggregate into information that circulates as knowledge, *gizmos* are those prized products (educational techniques and tools) advertised for their capacity to engage students en route to innovative ethical citizenry, and *credentials* promise authority and power to learning leaders and their intermediar-ies indentured to the system. As has been developed, there is a lucrative market-place for mobilising facts about learning, selling educational technologies, and advancing a credentialing industry to further justify, promulgate, and indoctrinate educators in the ongoing production of human consumptive capital. In the pro-cess, schools and faculties of education form alliances with various stakeholders and corporate sponsors that cannot but skew theory in the direction of vested interests, marketable outcomes, and a fiction of measurables as reliable proxies of things worthwhile.

Over my 40 years working across all aspects of schooling, I have witnessed first-hand this mutation of educational priorities *from*, at its best, intellectual rigour, critical thinking, and a humility that appreciates the limits of one's knowing *to*, at its worst, the advertisement of these attributes whilst engaging the opposite: that is, keeping educators preoccupied and colleges afloat, in a business of advising on and preparing teachers for a market that has the last word. To that end we see the rise in professional programmes of education of the following phenomena – granted, not all problematic, but all in service of the economics of learning: forums to showcase student productions, attract community interest, and garner stakeholder approval; competitive pricing on programmes with guaranteed scholarships to attract graduate students (we will not be undersold); online course offerings to open classes for all; part-time study, literally and figuratively; mass production of graduates (at the extreme, MOOCs: massive open online courses); stepwise credentialing; sessional instructors from the public sector filling teacher-preparation positions; notable publication records to entice granting bodies (quantity and notoriety beget quantity and notoriety); a public discourse of certainty and proof; a spirit-rousing rhetoric of everyone can (and must); exultation of that which is new, disposable, and fresh over the age-honed as age-worn; and a commitment to customer (learner) satisfaction as measured by infamous broad-scale engagement surveys, such as the National Survey of Student Engagement (http://nsse.indiana.edu), and common site-based satisfaction surveys, such as the Universal Student Ratings of Instruction (www.ucalgary.ca/usri/).

Just as these mechanisms have become part of a reshaped student body, they increasingly usurp professorial and teacher agency to responsively work the lived curricula of their classrooms (Grumet, 2010). Of such practices, Pinar speaks of "teachers . . . hav[ing] been reduced to domestic workers, instructed by politicians to clean up the 'mess' left by politics, culture, and history" (2004, p. xi) – teachers overworked yet held responsible for any failure in the clean-up (see, e.g., Gartner, 2017).

Meanwhile, cash-strapped, financially indebted undergraduate students, unsurprisingly, express their entitlement to the credentials for which they've paid. As student anxiety, depression, and suicide swell to unheard-of proportions (Goodman & Mann, 2018, June 11; Lunau, 2012, p. 64), well-meaning practitioners layer prescriptive detail into their assessment rubrics to allay fears by minimising uncertainty. With each minutia-specifying expectation, surveillance of that which can be readily observed and thus documented (in students and their teachers) increases and the possibility and the value of unexpected expressions of knowledge are erased from that which can be legitimate. In other words, only performances of understanding that can be explicitly spelled out ahead of time have value. And so, with a subtext of "Tell me what I'm supposed to do, and make it engaging," grades inflate and students find themselves frantically jumping through the very clear hoops they demanded. The clamour of these technologies of "doing" and "being done to"

34 The relational turn

(Benjamin, 2004, 2018) all but eclipses provocation and curious invitation to think, study, and engage in a quiet, self-reflexive shaping of wisdom.

What we lack seems increasingly to be trust – the area of faith in Eigen's recounting when he writes, "By faith, I do not mean belief. We literally kill each other over beliefs. Faith supports experiencing and exploration of experience. . . . by enabling unknown transformations that open reality, transformations we may sense but are unable to pin down" (2014/2018, p. 6). This kind of leap of faith that is trust cannot be renovated through efforts at control (see Part III, especially Möllering, 2005).

Who presently advises on schooling practice?

On the reconceptualisation of curriculum theory, Pinar wrote,

> The difficulties these reconceputalists identify are. . . . not "problems" that can be "solved." That concept created by technological rationality, is itself problematic. Thus, what is necessary, in part, is fundamental structural change in the culture. Such an aspiration cannot be realized by "plugging into" the extant order.
>
> *(1978, p. 210)*

New management: schools, still, as factories

The metaphor of the factory has long been applied to systems of mass public education. In tragic ways, it still fits. Whereas in the twentieth-century factory, innovation turned teachers from craftsman to assembly line workers, its twenty-first-century incarnation seems to have distanced educators from the learning interaction altogether (Grumet, 2010). Indeed, for some their removal seems the explicit intention: Consider the following futuristic vision presented by leading learning sciences theorist Keith Sawyer (2006b):

> Imagine a nation of online home-based activities . . . all connected through high-bandwidth Internet software. There would be no textbooks, few lectures, and no curriculum as we know it today. "Teachers" would operate as independent consultants . . . and occasionally meet with ad-hoc groups of students . . . on the project-based and self-directed learning that those students were engaged in. . . .
>
> Well-designed software could sense each learner's unique learning style and developmental level, and tailor the presentation of material appropriately. . . . And each student could learn each subject at different rates; for example, learning what we think of today as "fifth grade" reading and "third grade" math at the same time. . . . [Granted, i]f learning and schooling were no longer age-graded, other institutions would have to emerge to provide opportunities [to make friends, to form peer groups, and to participate in team sports].
>
> *(p. 569)*

In such a vision – its realisation already begun – teachers become, at best, designers and operators, preoccupied by their quasi-managerial roles, serving in a highly automated factory, *increasingly distanced from actual pedagogical moments.* Essig, Turkle, and Russell (2018) write of the "science fiction fantasy . . . [of] artificial intimacy" (para. 1) looming as disconcerting future reality: "There will only be widespread acceptance of artificial intimacy if we are willing to reduce what we expect from relationships to what technology can provide. And that's what we seem to be doing" (Essig, Turkle, & Russell, 2018, para. 2). As will be investigated in Part II,

> Evolution designed our neurophysiology to communicate in many ways other than verbal, an emotional activation mediated by neural processes that occur out of conscious awareness. This is how parents and babies first communicate, and this non-verbal communication continues throughout life.
>
> *(Essig, Turkle, & Russell, 2018, para. 5)*

Yet humans "lower their expectations to fit what technology provides" (Essig, Turkle, & Russell, 2018, para. 9). Unconsciously, we can and do functionally adapt to less-than-ideal circumstances, even when those circumstances and adaptations become dysfunctional over the long term (e.g., Felitti et al., 1998). When Sawyer dismisses the invaluable and incalculable criticality of intersubjective face-to-face relating in teaching and learning, even and especially with children, he unconscionably discounts the way that relationships story the affective unconscious to make meaningfully understood constructs of purportedly neutral curricular facts. Sawyer's vision joins a practice of operationalised and digitised metrics for the exercising of quality control, at a distance.

In its current incarnation quality control in education follows a tiered hierarchy from higher-level management to district consultants and administrators, to school learning leaders, to teachers who, in turn, conduct quality control on students-as-system-products. The rise of ever-new intermediary specialists endowed with "expert knowledge" joins a discourse to buttress a "normative grid. . . . for setting [institutional] targets and assessing achievements." In this way, newly minted local experts (typically, teachers with master's degrees in education) "manage the new regulatory mechanisms and systems, and judge levels of compliance or deviance" in a "therapeutic and redeeming role . . . tutor[ing] individuals in the art of self-improvement and steer[ing] them towards desired norms" (Shore & Wright, 2000, p. 62).

In the new managerialism, design serves as the latest distancing technology – according to Sawyer, aspiring to all but do away with teachers altogether. In theory, with "proper" classroom application, design-based learning tasks occupy, expand, and insert an objectively given accessible world into the conceptual space between teachers and learners. Here managerialism colludes with a limited interpretation on constructivist's principles that rightly recognise sense-making as the province of the sense-making agent (the student and not the teacher) in response to a situation that confronts, provokes, entices, and/or supports. However, popular logic has a habit of confusing (a) constructivist principles – that understand the student as the seat of sense-making – with (b) entitlement that submits the teacher to the whims of students' choices about their learning preferences. As developed in subsequent chapters, this effectively abandons the student by diminishing the teacher as a valuable witnessing subject-other. Instead, the proffered solution to student entitlement is the teacher who forgoes much explicit teaching in favour of designing compelling situations that, on their own, teach. In present conceiving, these principles play effectively into the populist culture of learning styles – however widely discredited is that discourse (see Hood et al., 2017, March 12; see Chapter 10).

At the same time, rather than develop the capacity to regulate attention, children growing up in a highly digitised, fast-paced, virtual, consumer world need only exercise the power of a mere touch of a finger (no need to even turn a dial) to make the accessible world serve their, now flickering, attentional needs. As solution to the dilemma of focused engagement, such a child has learned to command the world instead of himself and, in the doing, has shaped a mind-brain unschooled in deep attention. Increasingly the digital world entrains habits of quick judgement, likes and dislikes, and surface appearances as of greatest value. Paling by comparison, such mundane practices of having to listen to a teacher or engage oneself in quiet, independent study have fallen into notable disrepute (Cain, 2012; Turkle, 2015). This need not be the case.

> There is another way to respond to students who complain that they need more stimulation. . . . [We can teach] them that a moment of boredom can be an opportunity to go inward to your imagination, an opportunity for new thinking. . . . We can try to build their confidence that such moments – when you stay with your thoughts – have a payoff.
>
> *(Turkle, 2015, pp. 218–219)*

Returning to the factory model, today's version plays into and capitalises on the enticement value of popular trends, endorsing them and putting faith in the power of twenty-first-century technologies to manage student experiences, captivate attentions, and deliver on societal expectations. With a confluence of forces having conspired to redefine the role of teachers, that role's primary focus has become one of designing and monitoring the smooth running of the physical and now virtually expanded factory floor. In this present incarnation, the floor extends upwards to comprise, at once, several levels of concurrent tracks, synchronised to student age, and encompassing at any one moment an unwieldy spectrum of student capacities, from kindergarten entrance to high school exit. Ideally, each track should consist of eloquently conceived and eloquently sequenced choices in learning tasks, with digital information in easy reach. Moreover, the best designs foster inclusivity (see Part III for further discussion); that is, they can be completed in relative independence of the teacher and interdependently with classroom peers (see "Piaget and Vygotsky," Chapter 7), regardless of level. To accomplish such an extraordinary feat, they should be based on rich, authentic (real-world) problems, with multiple entry points and various solution paths. In theory, these principles will ensure learning tasks that are experientially relevant and academically accessible to all students. Moreover, clear, detailed assessment rubrics tell students what they should produce as demonstrations of understanding, in principle forestalling anxiety by reducing ambiguity about expectations, in practice exacerbating anxiety by conditioning a need for "no uncertain terms." Moreover, as part of the narrative, in the process of solving these engaging problems, students will learn to devise good questions and enact the highly prized design-based protocols of the STEM disciplines (science, technology, engineering, and mathematics), together, generating inquiry paths that take them into their community and the digital world, where real-life local concerns and expert knowledge can be gathered and used. As such, the featured priorities of critical thinking and innovation are purportedly developed.

In this tidy and somewhat utopian scenario, I want to point up a key discontinuity – symptomatic of a principal fault line between two simultaneous yet conflicting priorities: on the one hand for student satisfaction on the student's terms, and on the other hand for the production of capable graduates on society's terms. In other words, *the current factory model catches students between two non-negotiable identities: entitled consumer and quality-controlled product.* This issue strikes me as at the heart of several persistent personal and political afflictions, manifest in the likes of: inordinate student anxiety; parental dissatisfaction with children unschooled in the basics; and the lament of teachers who say that in preparing children for government-mandated tests, they and their students have no time for fully indulging rich tasks. *In short, these most avant-garde approaches to education seem to be placing all their bets on one radical assumption: that teachers can design and/or implement learning tasks such that students, almost inadvertently and largely on their own, develop the requisite academic skills needed for success in school and later life* – that is, including, and building up from, the fundamental "3 Rs" of reading, writing, and arithmetic, for, though the digital world provides facts at our fingertips, it seems the case that, to get to knowledge, memorising matters. Indeed, "we think with what we know" (Turkle, 2015, p. 224) and this implies the need for a strong background of facts and concepts, often, *before* knowing one needs them. Outsourced memory and flickering attention seem to be leaving everyone floundering.

In summary, despite obvious shortcomings and amid enticing student-pleasing scripts of engagement and production, the proffered solution to the educational challenges of the present era continues to be a factory model, revised according to sciences' newest outcropping of learning principles (a conglomeration of convenient "truths"), and leaning on a rhetoric of public values (many of them conflicting) around: the virtues of inclusivity and cultural diversity, the uniqueness of the individual, the soft skills of collaboration, the need for all things tangible and practical, and the democratic principles of holding institutions accountable to stakeholders and of schools as the great equalisers – all in an audit culture where responsibility devolves to the teacher as ultimate manager, designer, and quality controller. If indeed that teacher feels overworked or overwhelmed, then her solution lies in two strategies: sharing the load by foraging further in the digital world and collaborating with her fellow teachers. In this way, she can devise and implement universally effective designs to meet the unique needs of all her students.

It of course borders on mythical thinking to believe that teachers can deliver on these kinds of contradictory and conflicting one-size-fits-all expectations. Promoting myth as reality, two widely influential "knowledge industries" have taken hold: universal designs for learning (UDL), developed by the Center for Applied Special Technology (2018), and McTighe and Wiggins's (2012) Understanding by Design (UbD™), endorsed and promoted by the Association for Supervision and Curriculum Development.

Importantly, not only do effective design-based learning tasks promise to free students from the tedium of having to listen to their teachers, but also they should free teachers from actual time explicitly teaching – all the better to manage and monitor the production line. Here, research in educational psychology is at their disposal. The support is critical because, in an era of social promotion and notorious diversity, the implementation of learning tasks, if they are to succeed at all, is thought to turn, in large part, on the teacher's ability to promote and maintain a climate of inclusion that keeps all students happily working together and on track. Typically, a plethora of government-approved resources, produced in conjunction with school and applied psychologists, provides up-to-date guidance (see Chapter 10 for full discussion).

Returning again to our factory metaphor, teachers are entreated to implement these guidelines in a process of, first, scanning for students either unable to manage their own paths, unable to work well with the other students/products, or making poor differentiating choices at the "switches." If quickly identified, the good teacher can encourage them back on a track. That failing, the teacher can pull these students aside, if need be putting them on a waiting list for clinical assessment, and in the meantime setting them on remediated or further differentiated alternative paths, alongside their peers. The goal is to see struggling students, at least, stay on some inclusive track (preferably not one on a collision course or going around in circles) to reach graduation in good time and ready to serve society in manner consistent with their production.

Unsurprisingly, the more students find reasons to be engaged with each other and the learning tasks along the way – tasks that are especially captivating if digital technologies are involved and student creation can be showcased – the more likely they are to stay in school and ultimately reach the measure of achievement called graduation. This is the statistical link between student satisfaction and student success. In an assembly line that moves students forward, success literally means succession. It is simply not dropping out. As such, summative assessment should find ways to encourage and reward students as they progress. Thus, a credentialing industry working with grade inflation creates a new kind of student: the nervous test writer but confident consumer of information-as-knowledge (Molesworth, Nixon, & Scullion, 2009) and producer of projects and presentations – the twenty-first-century "title page." Here, in the new knowledge economy, the most adept graduates become those who can skilfully and swiftly gather from a world of collectables – disassembling and reassembling as needed – to produce a newest crop of marketable facts and gizmos.

The rise of the learning sciences

To the question, then, of who advises on schooling practices these days, the answer lies in a convergence of sciences rapidly consolidating under the rubric of learning sciences and successfully collaborating with business and politics. Learning sciences theorist Keith Sawyer writes,

> Leading thinkers in business, politics, and education are now in consensus that schools have to be redesigned for the new economy, and that the learning sciences are pointing the way to this new kind of school – a school that teaches the deep knowledge required in a knowledge society.
>
> *(2006b, p. 567)*

Citing the OECD Sawyer adds, "Those societies that can effectively restructure their schools on the learning sciences will be the leaders in the twenty-first century" (OECD in Sawyer, 2006b, p. 567)

Sawyer describes this new aggregate as having emerged from and being inclusive of "cognitive science, educational psychology, computer science, anthropology, sociology, information sciences, neurosciences, education, design studies, instructional design, and other fields" (2006a, p. xi). Its first journal, the *Journal of the Learning Sciences*, followed the first Learning Sciences' International Conference in 1991. The National Science Foundation's *How People Learn* (Bransford, Brown, & Cocking, 2003) is often named as the first publication in the learning sciences proper. It was an optimistic beginning. That text's conceptual sequel, *The Cambridge Handbook of the Learning Sciences* (Sawyer, 2006a), seems, however, to have taken the study of teaching and learning characterising the previous work and crystallised it into prescriptive technique favouring the new managerial sciences of distributed cognition, network theory, game theory, and design-based methodologies.

The *Journal of the Learning Sciences* describes itself today as a highly ranked (5th out of 230 in education and educational research and 7th out of 57 in educational psychology, in 2015) compendium of study on the "processes of learning, and the ways in which technologies, instructional practices, and learning environments can be designed to support learning in different contexts" (n.d., para. 1). It explicitly privileges "design in methodology and pedagogy; . . . grounding research in real-world contexts; answering questions about learning process and mechanism, alongside outcomes; [and] pursuing technological and pedagogical innovation" (n.d., para. 3). Its design-based emphases marry well with business and government interests in STEM education.

As applied to learning systems, design practices answer this question: "If learning is always unique to a specific context, then how can research ever result in sustainable products that can be disseminated and adopted in a wide range of schools?"

40 The relational turn

(Sawyer, 2006b, p. 573). In answer, the model of design experimentation involves investing a learning environment (e.g., a classroom, school, or district) with resources (typically research teams) for the purposes of effectuating systemic change and, on the fly, adapting and documenting the manner of resource investment. In theory, such change becomes the cultivating ground for the development of "curricula and software that can be transferred to many other schools with a relatively minor additional investment" (p. 573). Indeed, this was precisely the model into which I was initially hired as university researcher, charged with overseeing the research arm of a project whose conceiving predated my arrival. We were to be instrumental in the creation and study of exemplary teachers and, thus, in the "reform" of mathematics education in a select elementary school, targeted to become the hub of cascading change. Four different stakeholder groups with vested interests governed the project: a school district, a resource provider, a funder, and we the researchers. I came to know all too well just how ill-conceived such a project could be, especially in its angst-ridden effect on the heavily supervised teachers earmarked to become expert implementers of technique.

From the perspective of curriculum theory, the learning sciences could be considered a newer version of mainstream social science research – research against which, a half-century ago, Pinar warned, "While on the surface seemingly apolitical in nature and consequence, if examined more carefully [it] can be seen as contributing to the maintenance of the contemporary social-political order, or contributing to its dissolution" (1978, p. 210). Deeply worrisome is the very denial of conflicted interests as, in abject complicity, it insists on objective neutrality while tapping into a post-Cartesian story of complexity to buoy its legitimacy in the ongoing production of facts, gizmos, and credentials.

From a relational psychoanalytic perspective, it is doubly disconcerting to find that the expressed attentions of the learning sciences seem little concerned with, or accounting for, the human affective elements of learning or learning systems – especially in relation to care and belonging. Indeed, their most pervasive feature may well be the manner in which emotional relations – that shape us and from which learning takes its meaning – are systematically reduced from study even as the research serves up "curricula and software" for scaling up so-called educational reform. Though the frequent invocation of systems thinking by the learning sciences suggests an affinity to post-Cartesian understandings, its design-based preference to zooming out has the disturbing tendency to reduce learners, their teachers, and the people in schools to affectless agents, cogs really – some more co-operative than others – in a system under study. I point here to continued, and still disastrous, ethical oversights, this time in viewing human collectives. However analogous human systems may be to mathematically understood forms, we cannot pretend that sentient beings are the same as pixels on a screen. Indeed, in studies that transcend systems and their parts, a critical eye must always be maintained upon the very people whose lives and well-being are affected. This loss-of-sight joins, for me, those things I find most frightening about the direction through which the scientific study of learning seems to have emerged, in this newest iteration.

As such, for all their influence in education, the learning sciences as a group operate from a view broaching the opposite end of the spectrum of relational psychoanalysis and curriculum theory. When learning is split from considerations of emotion and human connection, or when attempts are made to put the scientific study of emotion and human connection in the service of the objectification and commodification of humans as capital, as when undertaken in collusion with business and the state, then despite and precisely because of claims to neutrality, the generalisations drawn are as questionable as they are disturbingly foreboding.

A fractured technologised field

Michel Foucault warns us that the "moment when the sciences of man became possible is the moment when a new technology of power and a new political anatomy of the body were implemented" (1975/1995, p. 193). It is a warning heeded by the reconceptualists of curriculum theory, with the challenge aptly articulated by Pinar in 1978:

> In contrast to the canon of traditional social science, which prescribes data collection, hypothesis substantiation or disconfirmation in the disinterested service of building a body of knowledge, a reconceptualist tends to see research as an inescapably political as well as intellectual act. As such, it works to suppress, or to liberate, not only those who conduct the research, and those upon whom it is conducted, but as well those outside the academic subculture.
>
> *(p. 210)*

Educational psychologist Howard Gardner included not only "a range of sciences" but also "other disciplines" for their "suggestions about how best to educate" (2016, p. 9). "None of them is definitive, but it would be foolish to ignore any of them, and we are best off if we try to draw on the range of perspectives, paying particular attention when the various indices point in the same direction" (p. 9).

Yet the field of education continues to be fractured – with some voices missing, some echoing in insular chambers, others reverberating with our very social fibre, those whose amplified sounds command everyone to listen, and others that seem more visibly alive in the political arenas of stakeholders converging on schools. Of the first and second type is psychoanalysis, with relational psychoanalysis all but missing completely. As has been seen, psychoanalytic writers in education acknowledge education's intolerance for their work. Britzman, echoing others, traces that intolerance to a "knot at the centre of relations . . . [and] the conflicted and creative process of learning" (in Pitt, 2003, p. 15). Notwithstanding some truth to this, I have earlier attributed seeming intolerance to less accessible and often off-putting language, and a disproportionate insistence on and preoccupation with the inevitability of trauma and difficulty in schooling.

If psychoanalytic theory in education could be conceived as marginalised and left-leaning in its consideration, then educational leadership and educational

42 The relational turn

psychology are pre-eminently mainstream, with a tilt to the right – that is, toward the efficient, clinically informed, certain and directed, visionary management of persons and systems. On the one hand, educational leadership with its dedication to the preparation of school administrators may well constitute the amiable face of this perspective as the face of schools. Concerned with the supervision of curriculum teaching and learning while keeping publics satisfied and coffers afloat, it develops its theories in alignment with the audit cultures of business and economics, while turning to the human sciences for insight in the strategic governance of within-house human relations and the thoughtful projection of a welcoming, responsive, and effective public image to the community at large – especially where key stakeholders are concerned. On the other hand, educational psychology enjoys the position of expert advisor, long providing governing theories of cognition, conducting research underlying certain "brain-based" schooling practices, administering clinical assessments of students, overseeing individualised treatment protocols, and generally formulating guidelines on the regulation and management of individuals and classrooms. Educational psychology serves government by advising on the supervision and direction of the people of schools. It takes a medicalised position *vis-à-vis* student needs, offering its evidence-based methods and interventions to the ends of promoting the productivity and achievement of students while seeing to their emotional well-being. In popular culture and school leadership, it contributes theories on motivation, self-regulation, mindset, and other themes of currency. Importantly, educational psychology has a long history of speaking most directly to teachers and families in a language amenable for public consumption and influence.

Of the amplified voices in education, two genres appear to have greatest currency: On the governing side of power, as we have seen, I locate the learning sciences, wherein aggregates all manner of human study, including psychology, but, importantly, adding systems theory into the mix. Taken together, the common stance of these human sciences is to tacitly accept the structures of power as conditioning an immutable reality to which we all must, practically speaking, accede. Accordingly, in the immediacy of everyday life, the learning sciences benefit from a public persona of advancing accepted-as-shared societal goals and delivering the tools to get there. On the other side and in contradistinction to the learning sciences, critical theory seeks to ameliorate present conditions by destabilising power and, with it, hegemonic constraints on the possible and permissible. It works to do so by augmenting critical consciousness about the ways in which normativity, governance, and power work in collusion to shape how anyone can and cannot be. Critical theory especially concerns itself with the empowerment of those peoples and persons confined to liminal societal spaces: the subjects of society's subjugation, objectification, and marginalisation, notably including those individuals and publics captured under such rubrics as: First Nations, Métis, and Indigenous peoples (FNMI); lesbian, gay, bisexual, transgendered, queer, two-spirited (LGBTQ2S); the (dis)abled or differently abled; and, generally speaking, all those individuals whose existences arise in circumstances of disavowal for reasons of colour, race, ethnicity, and gender, to name a few. In faculties of education, these two factions serve complementary functions, leastwise as presented to future and current school teachers especially. Critical theory is seen to bring key societal issues into public awareness and to thus contribute to the regular revision of teacher preparation programmes, professional development initiatives, and the latest educational resources – this while the structures of schooling, for all intents and purposes, go unaltered. Meanwhile, the learning sciences offer the definitive word on the particulars of how schools should be run.

In an ironic twist, both critical theorists and learning scientists profess a concern for empowerment. Whereas the critical theorist takes a radical revolutionary stance – seeking to empower the subjugated to rise up, redefine their circumstances, and revise the governing normative structures responsible for the continued propagation of such subjugation – the learning scientist promotes the status quo, arguing for a so-called practical stance of ameliorating unsuccessful persons and peoples through a combination of supportive structures and deterring ramifications meant to reorient them into right directions for achievement within the terms of meritocracy. In this latter narrative, people are independent actors in a neutral social system where power is within everyone's reach. One need only rise up within and according to the rules of the system to accede to optimal positioning within that system. Of course, this begins with understanding the rules. To this end, the learning sciences work to devise more effective and efficient techniques for coercing compliance and encouraging the kind of learning purported to engender personal recognition, stature, and agency – enough to secure the good life and a healthy stable society. However, a competitive hierarchal world, by definition, delivers the good life to society's winners. In a climate where ends do justify means, those ends are visited forward from one privileged culture and generation to the next. For there to be winners, there must be losers. In all of these problematic contexts, the learning scientist's programme is dedicated to promoting the individual attainment of power, not by revolution but, importantly, by acquiescence to power's hegemonic terms – terms that in large part deny circumstance and that instead offer programmes of correction or remediation, called reform, to promulgate a great, widely shared, fiction: *Everyone can succeed and, as long as schools and teachers co-operate with the techniques of the learning sciences, everyone will.*

Thus, in the context of everyone's concern that no child be left behind, there emerges an unexpected and perplexing alliance wherein governments work with capital stakeholders and learning scientists, all influenced by critical theorists, to fabricate guiding documents for twenty-first-century schooling, the likes of Alberta's *Competencies for Engaged Thinkers and Ethical Citizens with an Entrepreneurial Spirit* (Alberta Education, 2011). Powerfully connected with and sympathetic to business, management, and governance, the learning sciences accede to a subtle politics of democracy and decency that mandates and capitalises upon an optics of attention and concern for the subjects of critical theory's concern and lament. As we have seen, the learning sciences perform their function by the legitimacy of an alluring rubric of highly popularised but poorly understood (see, e.g., Fortun & Bernstein, 1998; Gregory & Miller, 1998) evidence-based findings arising out of design-based methodologies and practices. In short, the state of art in the learning sciences – that

44 The relational turn

new post-management technical arm of the twenty-first century's governance – is to marry technological litheness (e.g., network theory, game theory, and digital technologies as teachers of the future) to the clinical examination and social study of humans (e.g., sociology, psychology, cognitive science, and most recently complexity science).

At this point, let me share a word from Michel Foucault about the historical antecedents of these human sciences. Foucault (1975/1995) chronicles their inception in the shifting regulatory structures of late eighteenth-century, post-classical, European societies – entrance into "the age of the infinite examination and of compulsory objectification" (p. 189). It was a time of growth in the tools of examination and documentation toward a more pervasive, yet precise, institutional (jurisprudence, medical, military, workplace, and educational) disciplining and governance of peoples. These tools opened two possibilities:

> the constitution of the individual as a describable, analyzable object . . . under the gaze of a permanent corpus of knowledge . . . and . . . the constitution of a comparative system that made possible the measurement of overall phenomena, the descriptions of groups, the characterization of collective facts, the calculation of the gaps between individuals, their distribution in a given "population."
>
> *(Foucault, 1977, p. 190)*

The "small techniques of notation, of registration, of constituting files, of arranging facts in columns and tables . . . were [in Foucault's conceiving] of decisive importance in the epistemological 'thaw' of the sciences of the individual" (1975/1995, pp. 190–191). Today, these techniques arguably function on digital hyperdrive. If in the 1800s they orchestrated an insidiously effective subjugation of persons through the "play of coercion over bodies, gestures and behaviour" (p. 191), how much more effective is the experience of human surveillance today – of that sense that, at any moment, we may be being watched but not knowing when, by whom, or for what purposes? Indeed, to a telling degree, mechanisms for measurement and categorisation of persons have risen to perhaps frightening proportions. In these contexts, certain commonplace practices may not be as inconsequential or innocuous as they first seem. What is the effect on self-preoccupation and anxiety of, for example, rising self-assessing and self-regulatory practices in schools, popular self-surveillance mechanisms the likes of Fitbit (a wristband to track exercise patterns), the "How did we do?" solicitation of feedback on workers, and the publicising of reviews of products and services, including "Rate Your Teacher"? Acts of describing, judging, measuring, and normalising oneself and others – heightened in willing, public and semi-public, digital exposure (e.g., Facebook and reality television) and played upon by a market-driven economy (see Curtis and Kelsall's *Century of the Self*, 2002) – have instantiated the, now, all-too-common "procedure of human objectification and subjection" that Foucault foresaw (1975/1995, p. 192).

With Foucault, I contend that much of what ails present societies lies "in the steep rise in the use of these mechanisms of normalization and the wide-ranging powers which, through the proliferation of new disciplines [of self and other], they bring with them" (p. 306). As shall be developed, in Chapter 8 especially, the legacy of the disciplined, supervised, managed, docile subject – now schoolchild, then teacher, school leader, graduate student, and faculty member – has come to nest, as rampant anxiety, in the spirits and hearts of, now, lifelong learners: students, their teachers, and across the lion's share of Western educational systems today. In answer, the call of technological rationality rings again – in tragic irony, ever more urgent. The artful techniques for regulating delinquency and ensuring citizen compliance are those invoked to manipulate our newest populations into being free thinkers: those "engaged," "ethical," and "entrepreneurial" (Alberta Education, 2011) citizens of a global world at the ready to tackle looming, yet unfathomable, twenty-first-century challenges; citizens strong in creative problem solving, innovation, and critical thinking; and citizens adept at bringing well-honed "soft" social competencies into inclusive collaborative synergies. In short, mechanisms of tacit control and public regulation are called to render the definitive programmes for ensuring the production of, well, the exact opposite for which these tools were designed. In other words, constraint inside the box, and internalised as such, is the means by which we will produce free thinkers who can think outside of it. Is it any wonder so many are anxious?

Finally, in regards to heightened surveillance, Institutes for the Scholarship of Teaching and Learning (SoTL) are cropping up, with notable frequency, at the hub of campuses across North America. Offspring of the century-old Carnegie Foundation for the Advancement of Teaching, these institutes represent the fruition of that organisation's long-time vision "to do and perform all things necessary to encourage, uphold and dignify the profession of teacher and the cause of higher education" (from the Foundation's 1906 Congressional charter, in Shulman, 2005a, p. 24); to strengthen "American education through scientific inquiry and policy studies" (Henry Pritchett, the foundation's first president, in Shulman, p. 25); and most recently to enact a threefold vision articulated by Lee Shulman, president emeritus (1997–2008) of the Foundation – that is, to standardise teacher preparation by creating (a) centres of "teaching as 'community property' and as a scholarly practice," (b) programs of research on the pedagogies, and (c) re-examinations of the "character of the doctorate . . . since this was the degree that functioned as the 'teacher training program' for higher education and, by extension, for K–12" (Shulman, 2005a, pp. 27–28; see also Hutchings & Shulman, 1999). *It is not that I object to the dignity and improvement of teaching; it is that the dignifying of a profession in no way follows from its ongoing external regimentation.* For, although these teaching and learning workshops do highlight many valid considerations and offer worthwhile opportunities for reflection on practice, they seem also trained in the direction of a disturbing regulatory elision, from voluntary attendance at workshops to certificates of attendance, to the privileged hiring of individuals with said certification. While such programmes attract graduate students and temporary workers

46 The relational turn

seeking sessional/limited-term employment, other faculty are encouraged to join to improve their practice and document said improvement – on the principles and assumptions of these institutes. Meanwhile educational researchers are enjoined to contribute findings and garner funding toward this scholarship to ensure the production of further measurables applicable to those hired to teach, where teaching becomes the operationalisation of uniformity across course sections. To wit roughly half the undergraduate courses in most Canadian universities are at present taught by sessional instructors on limited-term contracts – these people being the cheaper labourers most eager to fall into proper step and deliver the curriculum as told (Basen, 2014).

In my own experience, good teaching is quite inconsequential to a faculty member's perceived value unless that member puts concerted effort into monetising that practice, contributing to its regulation via attendance and presentation at these SoTL workshops, promoting oneself in competitions for teaching awards, and translating personal practice into published quantitative or qualitative research aligned with current ideology – these days, for example, as the so-called signature pedagogies of best practice (Shulman, 2005b; Werklund School of Education, n.d.). In short, effective teaching, as an end in itself, is secondary to securing capital funding in the lucrative business of generating measurable markers of good practice – the problem being that these markers come to substitute for good practice itself. The problem is beautifully captured by curriculum theorist Nel Noddings.

> Educational research, like behavioral science in general, has made the error of supposing that method can be substituted for individuals. . . . Often when researchers are trying to determine whether A or B is a better method of instruction ("treatment"), they try to strip away the special qualities of teachers and students so that the various settings in which A and B are being tried can be regarded as comparable. As many variables as possible are controlled. But teachers are not interchangeable; they cannot be regarded as delivery systems or treatments. Nor are children interchangeable. One impish grin in the middle of a lesson can change what follows.
>
> *(2005, p. 8)*

In describing this fractured field, I return finally to curriculum theory/studies. In its reconceptualist movement of the late 1970s, under the direction of William Pinar, a new genre took hold. Neither traditional school technicians designing curriculum within the status quo of schooling structures nor conceptual-empiricists imported from fields outside education, this new curriculum theorist brought a "heightened awareness of the complexity and historical significance of curriculum issues" (Pinar, 1978, p. 210), consciously abandoned any role as technician, critiqued technological rationality itself, advanced comprehensive critique on what had been, and was committed to a fundamental reconceptualisation of curriculum that it might function instead in emancipatory ways (p. 211).

Today, curriculum theory's countervailing and re-centring influence draws upon the critical lenses of cultural studies, feminist theory, psychoanalytic theory, Indigenous studies, and ecocriticism, to name a few. It brings to the public forum such educational issues as revolve around new forms of citizenship, activism, public science, meaning-making, and the arts to address social injustice and assert agency in everyday life and educational settings. Its influence has and continues to move attentions to the blind spots of curriculum and to foreground curriculum as lived.

Yet over the years, problematic schooling structures have stubbornly persisted. Indeed, technological rationality seems as solidly ensconced as ever. It is in the spirit of curriculum theory reconceptualised that this book is dedicated, sitting as it does in a middle, neither promoting violent revolution nor supporting the status quo. Instead, I draw from a breadth of discourses, these read through a critical theorist's lens, in an effort to story a different possibility for schooling and an expansive collective "we." I aspire to American poet Robert Frost's "The Road Not Taken" and to the possibility of a better wisdom spawned of the past, seeded in a present, and carried to untold futures on the wings of generations who cannot but exceed our collective imagination. Yes, one can hope.

What difference might a relational psychoanalytic perspective offer?

Lewis Aron, founding relationalist, once asked, "What are the consequences of defining psychoanalysis one way or another and to whom? Under what social, economic, cultural, historical, political conditions does [doing so] lead to benefits or disadvantages" (2010, p. 1279)? His questions echo the interpretivist views of curriculum reconceptualised, per Pinar (1978).

Differences of social, economic, cultural, historical, and political convictions find their way into the words we choose and the meanings they hold for us.

The potential contribution of the relational turn to education is insightfully portrayed in the evolved meanings of two words, "subjects" and "objects," and the telling differences as we traverse three discursive fields: school systems (as reflected in common public understandings); curriculum studies (through which psychoanalysis finds its way into education); and object relations theory (within psychoanalysis proper).

In schooling systems and among the general public, objects are physical things and subjects are topics. In particular, school subjects are broad conceptual categories of study and discipline, such as mathematics, history, and language arts. School subject knowledge is accepted as drawn from either an empirically and objectively accessible world (in the sciences) or an interpersonally and subjectively accessible one (in the humanities). Here, objects and subjects have to do with both facts (truths believed about the world) and discursive traditions that govern ways of perceiving and thinking about those facts. Together facts and traditions make up information that, in assemblage, is widely taken as knowledge. Such subject knowledge officially represents and re-presents, to a society's newest inductees, the principal elements of

48 The relational turn

a particular cultural stock of tacit agreements and understandings about the world. To be offered in schools, these agreements tend to have transitioned to acceptance as neutral, unquestionable, and assumed. They comprise the "objectives" to be learned, and then measured, to determine student achievement. The interpretive elements that have gone into producing the school subjects are typically beyond the pale of the officially and consciously intended curriculum of old and new management regimes in education.

In curriculum theory, objects comprise both the given material aspects of the world (things that humans encounter physically in the world – e.g., a chair, a baby, a tree) and what we make of these aspects (qualities that humans think of as conceptually real – e.g., love, understanding, depth). Subjects, on the other hand, are thinking beings and a designation commonly reserved for individual humans. In these terms, to objectify an other is to wrongly dehumanise that other. In introducing the interpreting person-subject we come to the constraint of there being no observerless observations. That is, we can never excise our own perceiving capacities and predispositions from that which we claim to perceive and thus come to know. Accordingly, the unavoidable limits of perception compose a rider on truth, placing it within those constraints and making unanimity in perceiving, for all practical purposes, the final arbiter on any real. And there's the rub. But we are not doomed to abject relativism (see, e.g., Richard Bernstein, 1983). Contrary to current populist culture, rejecting absolute truths about any purported real and wholly accessible world need not reduce us to any number of alternative facts and truths – a discussion of which is an entirely other matter.

In psychoanalytic object relations theory, internal objects are individual-specific, enduring mental re-presentations of the entities (beings and things) of our experiential encounters in the world and that we necessarily revise each time we recall and recount a memory (Panksepp & Biven, 2012) according to ongoing unique experiences of that world. Importantly, internal objects also include self-objects: the mental self-representations that compose identity. Taken together, our mental representations define and give meaning to who and what we know ourselves and the world to be. They also shape the limits and possibilities of how we can perceive and understand ourselves and others in that world. But internal objects are not the same as the actual people (subjects) and actual things (external objects) for which the internal objects stand. Still, we need enduring representations in order to recognise anyone or anything and to organise our experience in the world. Moreover, because we cannot walk in the shoes of others, their actual being will always exceed our knowing of them. This means that, in negotiating ourselves with others in the world, we inevitably brush up against the difference between the object of them, in mind, and the subject of them, before us, in person. Our capacity to discern that difference is some function of our neurophysiological constraints on attention and awareness and the ways in which our histories have primed particular possibilities in perceiving (see Part III). Accordingly, the capacity to both recognise others and still perceive, much less accept, their difference – that is, the capacity to realise, understand, and live well with others as different centres of being – is indeed a primary developmental task and an ongoing humanistic one. It is, I contend, the crux of that which is most critical yet most neglected in education and schooling.

To the degree that we insist on understanding and treating others as the unchanging objects of our minds, we are objectifying them. That is, we treat them as the self-reinforced sum of our expectations of them. This paradox of humankind's existence makes a falsity of objectivity (as typically understood) and makes deeply problematic the objectification of persons. Thus, from an object relations perspective we return to the rudiments of a long-standing feud between the humanities and the sciences, the former acknowledging and respecting uncertainty and the latter believing that skilfully manoeuvred method can eradicate it. More specifically, it returns a tragic flaw of logic in the so-called evidence-based practices of education – that is, the folly of thinking that reductive scientific principles can deliver any directly applicable "truth" in the complex and situated matters of human relational being.

Thus, the shifting meanings of subjects and objects flag radical differences in understanding that which constitutes us in the world and the world in each of us. The starkness of difference ultimately sets the challenge and the claim for *Relational Psychoanalysis at the Heart of Education: How and Why It Matters Now*. It implies that the storying of the relational being is missing in some significant way from education and that relational psychoanalytic theory has unique value on offer in this regard.

To recapitulate Part I: I have introduced relational psychoanalysis and addressed three principal objections to its promotion for education – the first two relating to its claim as a distinct tradition.

1   To the objection that drive/structure and the relational/structure approaches are not mutually exclusive, I have attended to the difference that arises out of Mitchell and Aron's insistence that "Relational concepts do not provide understandings of different phenomena from those explored by the drive/defense model; *relational concepts provide alternative understandings of the same phenomena*" (italics added) (1999, p. xiv).

2   To the objection that psychoanalysis in education already reflects an increasingly relational contemporary psychoanalytic field, we have seen that non-relationalist drive/structure models continue to be most pervasive across, and characteristic of, an educational psychoanalytic literature that has limited influence in education proper. Insofar as it would be fair to characterise all contemporary psychoanalysis as relational, it would be a mistake to characterise that work as consistent with this newly emerged relational tradition and this speaks both to the linguistic accessibility of a relational discourse and to its sensitivity to not only trauma in learning but also joy.

And finally, to the reminder that the various learning sciences and other fields already fill the niche of informing educational practice, I point to the impossibility of successfully following through on the idealised expectations offered by these disciplining disciplines. By no means wanting to make the same mistake of presenting relational psychoanalysis as the missing regulatory form for curing everything that ails our schools, I offer it instead in the sensibility of curriculum studies, reconceptualised as discourse of consequence for helping to dislodge technological rationality from its participation in holding education hostage in an audit culture of accountability. This book draws from the transdisciplinary coherence of relational psychoanalysis to buoy the critique of current structures and to move the conversation away from technique in favour of deepened understandings about self and other in a relationally conceived and relationally mitigated sensibility, cognisant of contemporary social and political concerns in ways that might just be amenable to democratic publics.

Note

1 In Canada, government revenues to universities dropped from 92 percent in 1974 to 55 percent in 2012 (Canadian Federation of Students, 2018, p. 6).

PART II
A dialectic theory of learning
Self, other, and the transitional object

PART II

4
MEANING-MAKING AND THE CURRICULAR OBJECT

In this chapter and the four to come, I use relational psychoanalysis to realise and articulate a theory of learning. I will draw especially on Donald Winnicott's prescient understandings about transitional objects – *both given* by the world and *made* by the child. As will be developed, the point of the given and made is central to the play of co-emerging intrapsychic and intersubjective realities in any learning.

> Playing implies trust, and belongs to the potential space between (what was at first) baby and mother-figure. . . . It is in playing and only in playing that the individual child or adult is able to be creative and to use the whole personality, and it is only in being creative that the individual discovers the self.
>
> *(Winnicott, 1971/2005, pp. 69 & 73)*

Just as there is play in a wobbly stool or a supple sapling, when Winnicott invokes it, he names the latitude of movement and articulation made possible when elements of a judging reality are held in just enough abeyance for unfettered musing. In play, the thing fantasied (upon, with, and in) is reality. That is, *to play is to undertake "what if" adventures, dwelling neither wholly in prodigious fantasy nor in intransigent reality, but rather in some space between – a space Winnicott identified as transitional.* The transitional object/phenomenon – classically, the child's security blanket – broadens across a lifetime to include words (Daniel Stern, 1985/2000, pp. 170–174) and the cultural objects of school. Winnicott explains (1971/2005):

> There is a direct development from transitional phenomena to playing, and from playing to shared playing, and from this to cultural experiences. . . . I am assuming that cultural experiences are in direct continuity with play, the play of those who have not yet heard of games.
>
> *(pp. 69 & 135)*

54 A dialectic theory of learning

The play of the transitional object is the wellspring of human possibility and critical to learning as a fundamentally creative act. In play, ventures into the unknown can be safely indulged. Make-believe spaces suspend a disillusioning world while the learner grapples to make illusive sense of seemingly ambiguous circumstances. In Winnicott's transitional space, one can be oneself, but also other than oneself; and one can interact with persons and things that are themselves, but also other than themselves. For instance, in play, two chairs under a blanket are, and are not, a house; a plastic straw is, but is not, a magic wand; a girl under a crown is, and is not, royalty; and a favourite blanket, as proxy for a loving parent − or later, favoured cultural objects, such as poetry, ideas, or acquisitions − is, and is not, the thing that reassures and soothes. Importantly, questions like "Was it already there, waiting to be found as such, or did you make it up to this significance?" are not to be asked. They transgress the boundaries of subjective and objective worlds and thus go prematurely to paradox (Winnicott, 1971/2005, p. 130). Asking them amounts to calling into question the significance of make-believe excursions into what could be, eclipsing that possibility before it is ready to survive scrutiny. Just as the ephemeral apparitions of dawn's early morn become something other, in the light of day; so too do unbidden understandings, visible only out of the corner of one's eye, scatter under too-soon scrupulous attention. Where play is disavowed, learning, bereft of its chance for meaning, reduces to lifeless activity and parroted mechanical process (see especially Fonagy & Target, 2007). On these things, Winnicott (1971/2005) writes,

> Of the transitional object it can be said that it is a matter of agreement between us and the baby that we will never ask the question: "Did you conceive of this or was it presented to you from without?" The important point is that no decision on this point is expected. The question is not to be formulated.
>
> *(p. 17)*

> On the basis of playing is built the whole of man's [*sic*] experiential existence. . . . We experience life in the area of transitional phenomena, in the exciting interweave of subjectivity and objective observation, and in an area that is intermediate between the inner reality of the individual and the shared reality of the world that is external to individuals.
>
> *(p. 86)*

Following Winnicott, I forward a sensibility toward curricular objects in their most critical function as transitional phenomena whose meanings and values derive from their relational embeddedness. Learning in these terms is meaning-making between an external knowable reality, experienced as authority on objective truth, and an internal reality of subjective self-, other-, and world-making.

> Infant research teaches us that human external reality is inherently shared because it is constructed out of shared feelings, shared intentions and shared plans. As adults we may conveniently place the world "out there", but "out

Meaning-making and the curricular object **55**

there" retains its historical connections with the earlier sense of a shared interpersonal reality . . . largely built within attachment relationships.

(Fonagy & Target, 2007, p. 921)

Taking external and internal together, a final irony becomes that the world one
comes to know paradoxically includes the very self to whom it appears as a given,
and of and by whom it is also made.

Things as they seem: *either the sun rises and sets, or the earth rotates*

Let me share a brief vignette to foreshadow how relational psychoanalysis might
be implicated in a potential teaching and learning encounter. (I have flagged relational psychoanalytic terms with italics, marking them for future elaboration.) In
the example, the curricular/cultural object, and the sense to be made, is the apparent
motion of the sun traversing the sky as a function of a rotating globe. The memory
reminds me of my own shortcomings – "failing" my youngest son, 7 years old at
the time. He, however, has no recollection of the incident.

Like a dream, the story starts in the middle. I am insisting that he pay better
attention to my flashlight-and-globe model. He, likewise insistent, but also exac-
erbated and increasingly distraught, will have none of it. Gadamer reminds us
that "one does not understand by understanding the other person per se, but by
coming to a new view of what the other person is saying" (in Donnel Stern, 2015,
pp. 196–197). The change of a new view is wrought of lived experience. "Verbally
understanding, explaining, or narrating something is not sufficient to bring about
change. . . . An event must be *lived*, with feelings and actions taking place in real
time, in the real world, with real people, in a moment of presentness" (Daniel Stern,
2004, p. xiii).

The understanding I share now, the one I lacked then, is a new view of what my
son was saying. Too singularly intent on my own knowing, I could not entertain his.
Nor could I contain his affect, so preoccupied was I with mine. Instead, I pressed
him to be "rational." And isn't it odd that my need for a particular rationality arose
out of my own frustrated emotionality?

In the urgency of the moments, one following swiftly on the other, something
of a script was writing us along and it was far less about some mere fact than it was
about selves insisting on themselves. I now think us caught in what Donnel Stern
(2015) has called the *grip of the field*. Too much implicated, I did not muster the
wherewithal to pull either of us out of a *complementarity* whereby his unreasonableness made me the ineffective teacher that I could not be and my unreasonableness
confronted him with an ambiguity he could not resolve. He no doubt felt unfairly
done to (as per Benjamin, 2018, pp. 71–90 especially). Yet it was me, the adult enamoured in a fiction of absolutes, right against wrong, who was catching him in the
same fiction. It was me who did not yet "know" the reasonableness of different
perspectives on an ambiguously encountered and disconcerting real, his and mine,

56 A dialectic theory of learning

the view from the planet and the one from beyond it. Unable to change the nature of my involvement, I persisted.

> Each time one participant changes the nature of his or her involvement in the [relational] field, the possibilities for the other person's experience change as well. . . . It is meaningless, really, to claim that I *should* have been able to see beyond his rage. The field is the only relevant context.
>
> *(Donnel Stern, 1997/2003, p. 110)*

As doggedly determined mother, I would make my son in my image. Ironically, it seems I had. As teachers can often do, I pressed on, believing that if only he would co-operate and allow himself to entertain my suggestion, he would understand. Put differently, *rather than understand him, I expected him to understand me.* Rather than *surrendering* (Benjamin, 2018) to allow admission of an alternative view, his, I demanded he *submit* to me, my view, and my needs.

In Winnicottean terms, I had foreclosed a *transitional space* in which my son could have engaged the *play* of "what-if" excursions that permitted either and both to be the case. I did not know to hold safe a kind of sanctuary for the *mutual meeting of minds* (Benjamin, 2018). And I ultimately left no room for him to *resolve the ambiguity* between the given and the made – that is, the given tangible world of his lived experienced and the symbolically contrived substitute one I would have him make. In these kinds of, not uncommon, impasses we see a hint of what is at stake when learners encounter curricular objects and are called to make sense of something less theirs for the making and more ours for the giving.

In the pages that follow, I probe understandings of co-implicated mind- and world-making. I strive for an approach considerate of the views of any number of readers' lived experience – that is, from how things seem when they come to mind and to learning. I hope the traction of common ground makes accessible a proposition, rendered in the form of a model, on the nature and movement of learning. In turn, I explore a different sense of a long-standing quarrel between traditional and progressive views in education.

In the next two chapters, I deepen and elaborate the model by drawing on understandings at the intersection of psychoanalysis, neuroscience, and early childhood development. Chapter 7 follows the history of learning theories, charting these to the present moment and offering the model as next step. In Chapter 8, we return to the relational psychoanalytic lens to consider *not learning* and the defensive solution of dissociation as a function of situations that compromise capacity, trust, and meaning for the learner.

At this point, before proceeding further, we will want to address, up front, a different set of meanings and understandings from affective neuroscience and studies in consciousness that, being coextensive with relational psychoanalysis, marry well with the theory I am proposing. A second narrative addressing the interplay of the conscious, nonconscious, and unconscious mind (following Antonio Damasio, 2010, and Daniel Stern, 2004) serves this purpose. In the example, I use a ten-minute interlude from a not particularly eventful morning.

Meaning-making and the curricular object **57**

Three for morning rituals: consciousness, nonconsciousness, and the unconscious

In his preface to *The Present Moment* (2004), Daniel Stern observes that although "the experienced micro-world always enters awareness . . . [it] only sometimes enters consciousness (verbalized awareness)" (p. xiv). "Like a bird's life, [the stream of consciousness] seems to be made of an alternation of flights and perchings" (William James in Daniel Stern, 2004, p. 43). That is, instead of continuous presence, we join the dots and seamlessly fill in the spaces as though we were fully aware all of the time. Yet regardless of whether we know it, "intentional decision-making runs through the neural circuitry that underlies emotions. . . . Intentions coopt emotions to simplify things" (Juarerro, 2002, pp. 178–179).

Thus, in the micro-analysis of the present moment, we find a subtext of implicit knowing that underwrites explicit conscious awareness. Moreover, like the world in a grain of sand, "the small behaviours and mental acts making up this micro-world . . . [often express] the larger panorama of someone's past and current life" (2004, p. xiv). To illustrate what such an analysis might entail and what it could reveal, in a manner reminiscent of Stern's work, I undertook to record one such present moment – doing so in the hour after its passing. In the sequence of my recalling, here are three accounts of what I estimate as ten minutes one morning.

> *The coherent, strung together, narrative*: I lay in bed, aware of my headache, thinking of the evening before and the three-hour phone conversation that had gone past midnight my time – two hours later for the caller. I wondered what to do about him. I also resolved to limit myself to only one, not two, glasses of wine in an evening, especially so close to bedtime. Pitou, my 4.5-pound Yorkshire terrier, was anxious for me to get up. As per her usual, having seen me stir, she had gone to collect a current favourite toy – this time a tiny stuffed yellow bird with orange flappy beak and feet. She dropped it in front of me, awaiting intently, eyes trained on the bird. We played the game of toss the bird several times over – a game interrupted once by a bark from the dog next door and Pitou's need to respond.
>
> *The series of remembered present moments and accompanying thoughts*: (1) I remember noticing my head hurting and thinking it was the wine. I remember contemplating the sound of the voice on the phone from the night before, the French accent, the impression it gave me, and how I thought the man was overconfident. (I know that I was playing fetch with Pitou, but do not remember the details.) (2) At one point, I studied her eyes. I tried to tell if she was looking at me or the toy. I thought it was the toy and wondered how I knew. Then, I got my answer when I caught the white of her right eye and knew her to have taken a quick glance at me and then to have returned her gaze to the toy. (3) I also remember, at one point, noticing her wee tongue just peeking out from her closed mouth as she sat perfectly still. The exposed tongue-tip had a curious double-lobed shape, one lobe smaller, the other larger. (4) I remember a second time when that tongue showed again. It had a smoother curve this time.

58 A dialectic theory of learning

I "read this" through an awareness that this was what Yorkies did when they were content. (5) At some point, I also thought, "Oh, I get it now. The orange beak and feet of the toy ('tab-like' appendages) are what her teeth must latch onto when she so vigorously manages to shake it side to side. So that's how she gets so much movement." (6) I heard a bark outside. I was fleetingly aware of Pitou's changed focus (though I don't remember what I saw or how I knew) and this memory blurs into knowing she had left. I remember registering her barking, as background confirmation of my expectations. I remember noting that she barked a few times, but not too many.

(Importantly, throughout my interchange with the dog, the only actual moments of conscious awareness, of presentness, entailed my study of her eyes and mouth and my putting together the physical appearance of the orange tabs with a previous image of her shaking the toy. The rest of the account consists of roughly remembered mental ruminations and a blend of past and present on what was familiar and typical for us.)

The sentiments accompanying and marking the remembered moments: dismay – at myself for having had that second drink; resolve – to pour out the rest of the wine; worry – over writing time compromised by a headache and by a need to make up lost hours oversleeping; more disappointment – both in myself for not clearly voicing and enforcing my needs and, also, in the man on the phone for being yet another person who would not hear me when said I needed to go; worry – about what it meant that he was the kind to stay up till the early morning; grateful – for my dog's patience; happy – for her playful temperament; curious – about where her eyes were looking and how I would know; relieved and softened – to see her endearing wee tongue as a sign of happiness; amused – by the different shapes of the bits of tongue that showed; reassured – by her signs of contentedness that I was a good-enough puppy-mom; mildly awed – at how she was so attuned to sounds and to the distant single bark of the neighbour dog; comforted – by how predictable was her "on-guard" reaction; pleased – that she predictably came back; and relieved – that she did not continue barking and possibly disturb the other condo members.

In the foregoing recounting, one can readily observe the covert collaborations, efficient and necessarily so, between the conscious, nonconscious, and unconscious mind. The first rendition threads a coherent story by taking the moments of discrete awareness (like the bird's perchings in James's quotation) and superimposing them onto a backdrop of uneventful nonconscious happenings that went unformulated and remained thus, insofar as they were not discernibly different from past instances of similar happenings. Thanks to well-trained brain-body routines (from a lifetime of using habits, learned early), except for monitoring for anomalies, such nonconscious activities as my picking up a toy and tossing it could run underneath awareness (Damasio, 2010; Juarrero, 1999/2002). Accordingly, the connecting bits of the story are to some degree inferred. They were too familiar to be noteworthy and so they easily merged into a long history of similar experiences (Damasio, 2010, p. 285–299; Daniel Stern, 2004).

Meaning-making and the curricular object **59**

> A subjective experience must be sufficiently novel or problematic to enter consciousness and become a present moment. Present moments form around events that break through ordinariness or violate expected smooth functioning. . . . [T]he present moment carries an implicit intention to assimilate or accommodate the novelty or resolve the problem.
>
> *(Daniel Stern, 2004, p. 34)*

The second rendition represents what was novel this particular morning and therefore alerted to awareness. These are the things I thought through language – the remembered present as *formulated* into language (as per Donnel Stern, 1997/2003) and, through languaging, rendered available to my conscious mind – the parts that remained nonconscious, being still unavailable to me to write about. Importantly, noted sentiments (the third rendition) were attached to these remembered moments – affect lending the salience needed for conscious presence and later recall. Note, too, the way my social past had set me up to pay particular attentions. My world was in this grain of sand (Daniel Stern, 2004, p. 18; Donald, 2001). Writing these accounts, just inside an hour of their occurrence, the feeling states came to life with each remembrance. Juarrero (1999/2002) observes that "many if not all human emotions . . . have a cognitive component" (p. 178). I contend the converse equally the case. On the present moment, Daniel Stern writes, "even when someone is alone, that person is addressing his or her conscious mental activity for someone else" (2004, p. 22). Always, the subjective invokes the intersubjective – and with it affect. We are construed and self-construe in the social (Daniel Stern, 1985/2000).

Finally, note the richness and breadth of feeling states flickering to mind across only a ten-minute interval. It was affect – drawn of yesterday's lessons, embodied in the unconscious, and visited forward – that guided what mattered for attention and that could come to attention in a contextual field free to allow it to do so (Donnel Stern, 2015). And it was familiarity that let the rest run automatically, according to the experience-honed knowing of my nonconscious self. Indeed, my consciousness was far more preoccupied with feeling states and, as I recall, preferred to muse in the pleasurable ones while also drawn to ruminate on how to, next time, circumvent those less pleasurable.

Be reasonable: on taming emotion

As my morning example suggests and as research into consciousness and present moments solidify (Damasio, 2018; Juarrero, 1999/2002; Panksepp & Biven, 2012; Daniel Stern, 2004), in the immediacy of lived experience, conscious executive function comes into play only *after the fact* of much-quicker-to-the-scene nonconscious action-routines and an equally quick, social-affective unconscious interpreting, prompting, directing, and conditioning both attention and action, critically, according to a history of life lessons. Even as the unconscious is influencing behaviour – and, in particular, learning – it does so in a timeframe *before*, even, the reaches of awareness. That is, it is quite natural to believe oneself the conscious master of one's

60 A dialectic theory of learning

motives. But to be accessible to conscious awareness, unconscious experience must be formulated through some communicable, narratable symbol system – a condition that necessarily implicates the social. Not only does this take effort, but also it cannot proceed without language. Thus, most of what is core to our being remains inaccessible to conscious awareness. It is locked in a socially construed affective unconscious that reaches back to the interpersonal rhythms and communicative gestures of first attachment relationships (Daniel Stern, 1985/2000). Put differently, the very experiences that made thinking possible in the first place must subsequently elude us. Moreover, even those later experiences that *could* be spelled out are routinely passed over. Bodies simply can't afford the extravagance of impractical redundancy (Donnel Stern, 1997/2003). People are quite oblivious to the workings of the nonconscious, especially the unconscious, and this seems exactly the point of the efficient, behind-the-scenes, everyday functioning of these faculties.

Besides, affects have a disconcerting habit of calling up the "wild things" – of myth, fantasy, and acting out. More primordial than consciously formulated thought, and perhaps having once-too-often signalled conspicuous alarm, they express themselves through unsettling metaphorical associations that dissipate in the light of day, leaving us wondering how we could be so upset over a reality so trite. We can learn to eschew such strange feelings. That is, not wanting the feeling that some of our feelings might give us, one way of coping is by pre-emptively discounting the too-disturbing ones – and, lest there be contagion, we would prefer other people do the same. "Feelings, and more generally affect of any sort and strength, are the unrecognized presences at the cultural conference table. Everyone in the room senses their presence, but with few exceptions no one talks to them" (Damasio, 2018, p. 16).

Indeed, individuals – some more than others – can develop expertise at tuning out uncomfortable emotions and feelings. Even though such dissociative disregard may serve over the short term, it can and does wreak cumulative physiological, psychological, social, and ultimately transgenerational havoc when left to fester.

Commenting on the unpopularity of unconscious motivation as a research concept, Winnicott writes,

> The data I need are not to be culled from a form-filling questionnaire. . . .
> This where those who have spent their lives doing psychoanalysis must scream
> out for sanity against the insane belief in surface phenomena that characterises computerised investigations of human beings.
>
> *(1971/2005, pp. 192–193)*

In the name of civility, modern societies advance a reassuring illusion – that of a trustworthy, conscious, rational mind, grounded in objective reality, and confident in reasoned and bias- and affect-free thought. Yet horrifying atrocities are too often performed on the very auspices of such reason – reason bent on covering over deeply buried, untended, and dissociated affect. Quite simply, regardless of how things might seem otherwise, cognition and affect, reality and fantasy, and overt and covert wonderings are physiologically interwoven in mind as body, from birth,

Meaning-making and the curricular object **61**

according to interpersonal relational life. In that inseparability, and its appearance otherwise, I ground my theory.

Like my son's insistence on the sun circling the earth, the felt experience of a cognitive-affective divide is a reality not to be discounted. Most of us acknowledge the earth's rotation, but live as if the sun really does rise and set. How then might we likewise *surrender* to the tension of holding both perspectives in a way that refuses to *submit* to reason's enlightened acclaim (Gould, 2003; per Descartes, in Bernstein, 1983)? Surely under the banner of modernity, the turn to reason that privileged objectivity and wedded it to scientific knowledge against other ways of knowing has made us powerful – beyond our means.

A comprehensive theory of learning, accessible to teachers and schooling systems, cannot ignore a world and its experience as at once given/made, certain/elusive, conscious/unconscious, objective/subjective, and rational/emotional. We will want to contend with the contradiction of things being strangely as they seem and not as they seem. And finally, acknowledging the strange illusion of conscious control over unconscious and nonconscious processes, such an account must give due attention to the co-shaping of nonconscious, unconscious, and conscious aspects of a self, across a lifetime. With these intentions, I forward a beginning schema in Figure 4.1.

Toward a theory of learning

The affordances of visual schema come with unavoidable limitations. I begin by explicating the less obvious parts. Several nested circles, with radial arrows, encircle the self and signify two co-implicated directions of growth: inward deepening and outward opening. The circles' dashed outlines show semi-permeability between the self and world.

The elliptical swirls and arrows indicate *recursion* – a principle of self-cause that characterises non-linear dynamic systems (in education see Davis & Sumara, 2006; in psychoanalytic theory see Lewis & Granic, 2000). In recursion, each iteration of an acting agent returns a revised agent. In the model, each return to self is a return to a dialectically evolved version of that self. To quote T. S. Eliot, "We shall not cease from exploration / And the end of all our exploring / Will be to arrive where we started / And know the place for the first time" (in Benjamin, 2005, p. 198).

By dialectic I mean the Hegelian sense of one's interpretation (thesis) making possible and calling forth its contention (antithesis) and pressing the reconsideration of what we thought we knew. A great deal of thought can ensue in response to another articulation that seems not quite right, with which one disagrees – an articulation that one seeks to understand and/or to correct. In the dialectic process, however, one does not stop at the confrontation of thesis and antithesis; one continues in thought and in dialogue to arrive at a tentative mediating synthesis – a workable resolution of a heretofore unresolvable ambiguity. In this way, learning, as a process of becoming other than oneself, entails recursive dialectic revisions of the knowing we once made to accommodate newly discerned givens – assuming, of course, that learning is not rejected (see Chapter 8).

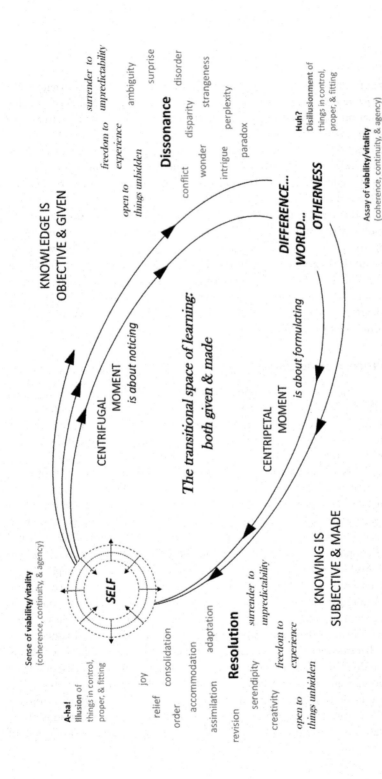

FIGURE 4.1 A tentative model of learning

Meaning-making and the curricular object **63**

The making of sense, an "a-ha" moment, is reassuring in its tentatively afforded illusion of things being in control, proper, and fitting. But in living forms, energy and matter must shift, dynamically and relationally so. "Whenever anything reaches its own perfection . . . it cannot endure to remain in itself" (Plotinus, in Benjamin, 2005, p. 199). There is unavoidable tension in the illusion of things being unsustainably "just so." Flux is the condition of possibility; stagnation the harbinger of atrophy and decay. In the model, learning, powered by such tension and life's proclivity toward assemblage (Edelman, 2006; Juarrero, 1999/2002; Maturana & Varela, 1987/1998), moves through recursive self-elaboration into and with the unknown (within and without) that it encounters and succeeds in enfolding into acceptable enough resolutions – that is, via assimilation and accommodation (as per Piaget; see Chapter 7).

In so doing, the self seeks to sustain its continuity while, ideally, deepening itself in accordance with a world that opens into a progressively expansive view. "Resolutions are a particular way of dealing with tensions" (Benjamin, 2005, p. 198). With Benjamin, I am concerned with "the kind of resolution that makes difference possible" (p. 198). For learning and difference, we will want to move through resolution and dissonance, neither resting too long at either pole. On this matter, Benjamin writes,

> Mov[ing] back and forth between poles . . . creat[es] a space that is neither simply dissonance nor simply harmony. Movement is what makes it possible to hold a tension, like that between subjective and objective awareness. . . . [I]n the flow or movement, this distinction between wave and particle, energy and matter can become moot.
>
> *(2005, p. 199)*

In the dialectics of learning, the question of whether world, other, and self are given or made remains never quite settled. There exists a kind of graceful non-urgency that accedes to and even welcomes the relentless compulsion of a life force within and out of which, sense-formulations return temporary resting places of reassuring resolution. When the impatient press of world, others, and oneself is held in mindful abeyance, a person gains, in trust, a space of flow for pondering and imagining well – as if the impasse between conscious thought and unconscious possibility were transgressed for a time.

I have followed Benjamin's (2005) usage of the idea of centrifugal and centripetal moments to parse each learning excursion. The outward centrifugal movement is about awareness, noticing differently, and realising things not previously apparent. In this gesture one risks disillusionment, and disassembling, in exchange for the opportunity in the centrifugal gesture to recover oneself anew (Winnicott on illusion–disillusionment, 1971/2005, pp. 13–18). Insofar as one feels resilient enough – that is, having sufficient self-coherence, continuity, and agency (Daniel Stern, 2000, pp. xix–xxv) to survive the assay – then risking one's illusions is worth the renewed self that might emerge, empowered, on the other side. The greater the dissonance, the more satisfying the resolution; but one can lean out too far (Benjamin, 2005,

64 A dialectic theory of learning

p. 198). The question central to learning's possibility asks, "How centrifugal can you be and still feel the elastic tension of the energy that pulls you back?" (Benjamin, 2005, p. 199).

In a self already self-aware, testing one's knowing requires trust. For a newborn, trust is an endowment undertaken naïvely, freely, and before conscious possibility. Soon, however, trust is gifted of situations that prove trustworthy – as per Winnicott's good enough mother (1971/2005), Benjamin's moral third (2018, pp. 88–90), and also as observed across mammalian species (Panksepp & Biven, 2012). Ultimately the thing trusted is that, on the other side of curiosity-indulged, one can recover oneself with revitalised self-coherence, continuity, and agency (Daniel Stern, 1985/2000) in a world renewed and enlarged with enfolded difference. In short, one trusts in one's capacity for greater individuation and belonging in learning (Benjamin, 1988, 2018; Mayes et al., 2007; Daniel Stern, 1985/2000). Given the uncertainty of ventures into new territories, I have annotated the model with a range of possible affects, including surprise, paradox, strangeness, disorder, ambiguity, disparity, perplexity, wonder, intrigue, and conflict.

On the return to self, the second phase of sense-making entails a two-part formulation of one's experience into meaningful resolution (see Chapter 5) – the visible delight of an "a-ha" that teachers look for in their students. The capacity to freely formulate also requires trust: to surrender to the unpredictability of what might be made, to the freedom to play with possible scenarios, and to an openness to the surprise of a "light coming on" as if "out of the blue" but yet somehow also arising from one's own interiority. In the model, the words flagging this experience of resonance – consolidation, relief, revision, order, creation, adaptation, assimilation, accommodation, entrainment, and serendipity – capture a different quality of quieting affirmation of tension resolved. The feeling contrasts sharply against encounters in the centrifugal unknown.

We will return to further elaborate and augment this model throughout the text. For now, I turn to its potential implication for interpreting the all-too-familiar-to-educators pendulum swings between so-called traditionalists and progressivists. Put in the contexts of the model, this ongoing debate is between learning as (traditionally) given and learning as (progressively) made. Of course, the point of a transitional phenomenon is that it can be both.

A politics of given and made: traditionalism and progressivism

Of constructivism (in all its forms) Donnel Stern writes, it "teaches us to see the inner and the outer [self] as a dialectic in continuous flux, it sensitizes us to the dialectic of time: the past is as much the creation of the present as the present is of the past" (1997/2003, p. 6). This principle is at the heart of the model. On these same constructivist principles (coextensive with interpretive philosophies – phenomenological and hermeneutic), curriculum theorists generally understand that the thing we name "knowledge," enabled and constrained within a pragmatics of power relations, is also that which humans, at some level, can and do make of what is given.

Within these contexts, the straw man of progressivism emphasises knowledge as made, while the straw man of traditionalism emphasises knowledge as given.

Schooling practice has had a long and problematic history of opposing views on whether or to what degree knowledge/knowing is best conceived as given – and therefore most efficiently guided, transmitted, and received; or whether it is made – and therefore can only be discovered, prompted, and occasioned. All accounts have these quarrels no less stormy today than in the early days of twentieth-century public education in North America.

I have no intention to point up the wrong-mindedness of either side, nor even to advocate a middle ground as many academics have done (see, e.g., Akerman, 2003, January; Ansari, 2015; Martin, 2016, June 10; Metz et al., 2016; Schoenfeld, 2004). I am no more insistent on either of these positions than I would be today insistent that the sun does or does not actually traverse the sky. Rather, I take it that things are as much as they seem (given) in lived experience as they are (made) when we put our heads together – the making of which entails formulation (eventually through the symbolic) by our rather magnificently conjuring, socially embedded, bodily construed, and relationally moved neocortices.

The quarrel of traditional versus progressive schooling practices, with its swings to either direction, has bedevilled education for over a century. In the current moment, and for several decades now, the early progressivism of John Dewey, riding on renewed constructivist principles, has enjoyed considerable resurgence – indeed with hardly a detractor from among the hallowed halls of education's elites. However, in the all-too-common version of progressivism, we find an interpretation that, to my mind, fails abysmally on a vital point, a contradiction really: *Whereas it is accepted that learners construe their own knowing, they are much less considered able to construe their own "being" as learners.* In other words, the current popular uptake of constructivism seems to neglect a tenet of life systems: that of responsive self-cause (Juarrero, 1999/2002) or, in complex systems terms, the recursion that characterises autopoietic systems (Maturana & Varela, 1972/1980; see Chapter 7) – that is, where one "does" oneself into ever-evolved being and becoming and where knowing is not separate but rather always embodied in such being. Such a tenet might best be captured in the title *The Brain that Changes Itself* (Doidge, 2007), but where self-change is radically understood to go, beyond a positive psychology of conscious affirmation and willpower, to an appreciation of the mind's unconscious motivations and nonconscious habits.

All the animals went to school: differentiation and its limits

As evidence of a troubling interpretation of constructivism, consider a common belief guiding schooling practice: Accepting that, according to personal idiosyncrasies, students make their own understanding, and that we want these students to learn particular things, then the onus falls to schools and teachers to design learning environments that spark students' natural interests and capitalise on students' intuitive learning preferences to the ends of ensuring that these same students learn

66 A dialectic theory of learning

the things we, as a societal collective, more or less agree they should learn and upon whose knowing they will ultimately be tested. In other words, in the ideal of progressive, student-centred classrooms, the circumstances of teaching and learning should be designed to fit the learners. And who could argue with that?

However, on the sacrosanct uniqueness of each learner, teachers are also beseeched not to ask those students to fit themselves to circumstances of learning, even if those circumstances would exercise student capacity in learning. A popular fable, originally written by George Reavis in the 1940s (Reavis, 1999), illustrates this point: All the animals went to school and they all had to take every subject.

> The duck was excellent in swimming. . . . but only made passing grades in flying and was very poor in running. Since he was slow in running, he had to stay after school and also drop swimming in order to practice running. This was kept up until his webbed feet were badly worn and he was only average in swimming. But average was acceptable in school so nobody worried about that, except the duck.
>
> *(pp. 6–9)*

And so it went that the rabbit, the squirrel, and the eagle, too, suffered similar fates. In the end, "an abnormal eel that could swim exceeding well and also run, climb, and fly a little had the highest average and was valedictorian" (p. 16).

Is there a point at which we do a disservice, to both teachers and students, in holding out the impossible expectation that classroom activities should be tailored to each learner's preference? In so doing, perhaps we have traded one self-fulfilling prophecy for another. That is, having once limited children by putting them into categories of achievement, do we now limit them by putting them into categories of learners? On constructivist principles, must celebrating difference and recognising uniqueness elide into a belief that student learning preferences are immutable and that students have a right to learn in their "style"? Does this mean, for example, that in a digital world of shortening attention spans, schools should indulge that trend? In short, despite a rhetoric on a brain that changes itself, we seem to believe that children cannot learn themselves into different kinds of learners. Turkle sums up the concern:

> Children who begin school with an iPad won't know that you can "force" a state of greater concentration by using media that allow you to do only one thing at a time. It's up to a more experienced generation to teach them.
>
> *(2015, p. 217)*

Trust, authority, and responsibility

For members of that "more experienced generation," to successfully teach presupposes that students trust in their teacher's authority; otherwise a great deal of classroom time will need to go to persuasion and assuagement. That is, if students do not trust their teacher to do what's best for them, then that teacher will be expected to pre-emptively justify pedagogical actions and allay the anxiety of student mistrust. All reports have trust in schooling "a commodity in short supply. . . . [among] parents, students . . . [and] educators" (Ennis & McCauley, 2002, p. 149; Dasgupta, P., 2000). Today's era of alternative truths is part of a crisis of trust that makes justifications of teaching practice into near-canonical expectations.

In such a climate, regardless of wisdom, experience, and mindful teacher inten-tion, the default position will be to question authority, especially if it goes against the grain of what students' desire and believe they should have. A short-sighted solution might be turning over teacher responsibilities to the students by way of, for example, anarchy in the classroom, taking matters to a vote, or different strokes for different folks (see Chapter 9). But there is a danger that, in delegating students with responsibility for the nature of their learning experience, we abandon them and dispossess ourselves from the responsibility that a more experienced generation must own.

Let me give an example. While teaching a course in elementary mathematics pedagogy, I came to a decision for which student input would be valuable, so I opened the matter to classroom discussion. To my surprise, after class, three students approached me concerned that I would put the matter to a vote. I reassured them that, though I valued the insights of the group, the responsibility was mine.

For another example, imagine a parent and child in a busy mall. The child is protesting that she can stay close without holding hands. The parent knows that in the jostling crowd this is unlikely. The child lacks the lived experience to properly adjudicate over the parent's reasoning. Whose reason and experience should prevail?

When learners find their pedagogue's justifications insufficiently forthcoming or compelling, those students, today, are more likely to question, feel entitled, and resist. Indeed, in the face of resistance, the point is that any teaching method is likely to fail. Thus, in an era where students have been schooled on their right to refuse, then activities that seem decidedly unprogressive – the likes of memorising a poem, listening to a talk, repeating an exercise, following a procedure, or replicating a demonstration – can hardly be satisfactorily defended, although they must be, and compellingly so, in order to be effectively used at all.

Learning to learn

I am not advocating against the rich, engaging learning tasks of progressive educa-tion, nor against student rights. I am, rather, thinking about who might productively own which responsibilities, and whose interests are served when that ownership is misappropriated. In terms of the model, I am suggesting that reinforcing the stu-dent's right to avoid that which seems uncomfortable can backfire. That is, insisting that the student be charged with the full nature of the centrifugal moment and what or how noticing should happen there can render that learner bereft of the value of a potentially disillusioning world whose encounter is adult-mediated, but always with both the learner's needs and the broader socio-cultural circumstances

68 A dialectic theory of learning

in mind.[1] These conditions foreshadow the very afflictions we see on the upswing among students today: entitlement, anxiety, and depression. Put differently, the student who needs the teacher to create an environment that will compel her to learn – even though the things to be learned (being a function of the heritage of what that society has on offer) are actually determined by neither teacher nor student – is a student poorly equipped in self-agency, agility in learning, and also self-trust to survive disillusionment or to notice, much less see, that which might be centrifugally found in a given world.

Notwithstanding the fact of constructivism, from a position of lived experience, it seems foolish to argue that knowledge cannot be given. Your telling me something might actually engender my knowing it. In everyday life, mimicry, repetition, rote learning, following procedures, and effortful practice tend to be the mainstay of learning. The repetitive practice of a toddler learning to walk or to hold a crayon and colour is not ill-conceived drudgery. Demonstrate to a child how to bob in the water and, if he trusts you and himself, he will think, "I can do like you" – striving to crudely replicate and then hone the act for the rewards of both agency and belonging. I read and follow the instructions of a recipe, including perhaps even the rationale behind this or that choice, and that knowledge becomes mine to subsequently adapt. In automating keyboard skills, it is time-constrained practice that forces an efficient, and yes mindless – that is, nonconscious – rote association between my fingers and the letters and words that appear on the screen. When children are first learning language, there is no want for attention. Videotapes taken during this period show the inordinate amounts of careful attention they direct toward the imitation of the spoken sounds they hear (Donald, 2001, p. 231).

In so saying, am I taking up a traditionalist stance? Hardly. I was myself the stubborn, curious child who insisted on formulating my own questions, following my own hunches, and stumbling in my own way. That said, this thirst for inquiry began in intercourse with a given world. Attending a lecture and engaging in quiet, focused study are invaluable modes of learning, with both centrifugal and centripetal elements – and because I needed them, I worked to learn them. Damasio (2010) writes,

> Conscious deliberation is about *reflection over knowledge*. . . . [It] has little to do with the ability to control actions in the moment and everything to do with the ability to plan ahead and decide which actions we want or do not want to carry out. . . . [M]ost important decisions are taken long before the time of execution, within the conscious mind.
>
> *(p. 287)*

Indeed, in the way suggested by Damasio, I used my conscious mind to structure my world so that my nonconscious mind could develop the habits it needed, the habits I wanted, that I might have agency in a world to which I belonged. And though not everyone can rally sufficient attention for such endeavours, one has to ask whether and to what degree current difficulties in youth today are a consequence of a self-fulfilling prophecy. Even the capacity to commit to memory has been shown to follow from practice at doing just that, but there must be committed effort – that is, trust that it might be useful (Roche et al., 2009). Contrary to what some education students studying theories of learning are want to protest, learning to learn in these ways in no way contravenes constructivist principles.

While the highly structured authoritarian classrooms of the past, in their worst caricatured scenarios, may have been all about "the given" with no room for free thought, inquiry, debate, Socratic questioning, and the like, parents today now lament a deep sense of the pendulum having swung too far the other way. In public forums parents petition governments for a re-centring movement "back to the basics" and the debates are none more heated than in mathematics – perhaps the canary in the coal mine on a disjuncture of beliefs about what is best in schooling (see, e.g., Crary & Wilson, 2013, June 16; French, 2016, June 19; McDonald, 2013, September 13). In answer, a niche market of supplementary programmes and charter and private school alternatives increasingly fills a perceived gap. All reports have long waiting lists as the norm.

The given and the made in programmes of study

This fracture between the given and the made, traditionalism and progressivism, as one or the other, has its representation in programmes of study as well. In Alberta, Canada, and many provincial and state jurisdictions, these guiding documents, to which teachers are held accountable, are parsed with several pages of front matter describing the curricular practices thought most suited to a constructivist understanding of this or that particular subject discipline. Behind this front matter one typically finds a much more extensive and detailed listing of the various learning objectives that students are intended to achieve at any particular grade level.[2] Whereas the front lays forth principles in teaching and the nature of understandings characterising the discipline, the bulk of each document is composed of the back section that details, in no uncertain terms, those curricular concepts to be known and adjudicated through fitting assessment practices. In short, assessment focuses on outcomes and could be thought to lean in the direction of knowledge as given, demonstrably so.

Thus, the learner outcomes of any curricular document seem to press teachers into a transmission approach to distributing knowledge, and this is true no matter how the front matter describes learning environments far more conducive to meaningful sense-making. This is what educators mean when they bemoan the practice of "teaching to the test" and, with it, a teaching practice explicitly intent on covering the itemised learning objectives, regardless of whether the students are "with" you.

Per the model, the traditional approach dwells in the moment of knowledge as objective and given. It is attentive to the clear sequencing of such knowledge in appropriately sized packages, procedurally followed, and religiously memorised. Here, "Read a hundred times and the meaning will appear" (Marton, Wen, & Wong, 2005) makes sense, "hooked on phonics" suits the development of skill in reading,

70 A dialectic theory of learning

and a sequenced drill and practice approach to mathematics and grammar seems most justified.

Emphasising the other moment, where knowing is subjective and made, we find the more progressive inquiry-oriented activities as appropriate strategies for occasioning that knowing. Here, good teaching is about drawing student attention to the big ideas emphasised in the front matter while encouraging them to traverse the specific content according to their own learning trajectories.

Whereas, in terms of the model, the traditional approach may have the appearance of giving short shrift to the creative side of resolution, the progressive approach might seem too thin on confronting learners with the givens of what they must know. Yet a closer consideration reveals something different at play and that difference entails the scope and breadth characterising each iteration around the circle. Do the learning activities ask the students to lean too far into difference, perhaps encountering dissonances exceeding their capacity for resolution? And does such frightful leaning compromise resolution's possibility or is there not enough intrigue in one iteration to keep learning interesting?

A constructivist model for inclusion

If we are serious about inclusive practices (Part III), then it behooves us to consider that among the most profound differences in learners is their emotional capacity to sustain engagement through dissonance and resolution. Students arrive to our classrooms with deep differences in their affective capacity to tolerate the play of movement between the given and the made – those capacities having origins in familial lessons predating formal schooling. Where one child feels overwhelmed by a task too broad, another thrives on boundaries further stretched. Problematically in my opinion, the latest educational trend describes the former tendency as fixed-minded and the second as growth-minded. This is the newest discriminating hierarchy in schools. Indeed, the widely popularised discourse of *mindset* (Boaler, 2016; Dweck, 2006/2016), complete with classroom posters on how we all can be growth-minded too, participates in a consensual cajoling of learners to comply. This is a different sort of complying. It is about being undaunted by profound dissonance and fearlessly working at resolution – all the better if effectuated collaboratively. And here, collaboration is the solution of *distributed cognition*, where knowing resides not in any one individual but rather is an emergent property of the collective. But as Nicholas Carr so astutely commented, "To remain vital, culture must be renewed in the minds of the members of every generation. Outsource memory, and culture withers" (in Turkle, 2015, p. 225).

A teacher has a choice on how far to lean out, themselves and with their students. Lived experiences are telling and matter deeply to classroom relations. There are those students and teachers for whom an open field leans too far out and creates intolerable ambiguity. On the other hand, there are those who find structure frustrating and would prefer to broaden the play of ideas. In response, the model need not shift; rather the situation wants for adjustment of the degree and direction of one's venturing into a potential area of dissonance and thus mitigating the corresponding resolution it might call for.

In other words, to accommodate breadth on the side of dissonance and across the resolutions that students might make (e.g., What is the meaning of mother to you? How many ways can you think of division? See if you can balance on one foot), we create learning situations that are safe enough to allow for many degrees of freedom and much play in the system. However, if we are going to be particular about the details of what must be made (e.g., What is the definition of mother? What is the sum of 12 and 35? Hold your balance as you walk along this tightrope), it will be better to structure less play up front. There will be students as happy one way as the other.

For another example, one can invite the class on a month-long collaborative or individual project defined by one iteration in terms of setting up the curricular structure (with many subsets of open iterations as the project unfolds under the agency of the students) and then come to specifying key properties, *or* one can take the class through structural subsets of the curriculum in ever broadening circles, each with incrementing degrees of freedom, adding intrigue for those swift in arriving at particular understandings, such that the overall effect is the same in terms of total play. Without detailing further, suffice it to say that this model has direct implications in how we might approach teaching and learning, and these want for elaboration. This remains the subject of Part III. For now, let me summarise the key points of this chapter.

Things are *and* are not as they seem: *the sun rises and sets, and the earth rotates*

For some, it seems incontrovertibly clear that objective knowledge is what matters in education and that such knowledge, existent in the material and cultural world, can and should be directly given to students. For others, it is just as clear that individual knowing is a subjective undertaking and, however intersubjectively engaged, it is ultimately at the behest of the learner. In this latter view, the teacher can only hope to design and moderate fitting enough circumstances to occasion, but not determine, learning. For over a century now, the struggle over these two contradictory positions has troubled curriculum practice. Yet in the same way that the sun rises and sets across the sky *and* it remains in (relative) place as the earth rotates, so too is the curricular object *given*, as traditionalists would have it, and *made*, as progressivists maintain. The quarrel over which interpretation accurately represents the real, and is therefore right, and which interpretation is illusion, and therefore wrong, is not resolvable. For indeed across a lifetime, as in childhood, if viable sense is to be made of any given, then reality and fantasy must have a tentative space where each can freely spar over which might better pose as the other.

How might we understand, teach, and learn well amid, these, life's impossible contradictions? A model construed upon the wisdom of relational psychoanalytic thought is one familiar with paradox. We will want to understand the tensions

72 A dialectic theory of learning

driving life's ebb and flow and sustaining the conceptual movement of learning. In refusing the collapse into either pole – that is, in keeping open transitional spaces as neither wholly given nor wholly made – dialectic movement allows those things that are given to be made meaningful and those things that are made to be in turn meaningfully given. And finally, it is in the play of curricular objects, as themselves thus transitional, that understandings can be worked out, yet never quite settled.

I turn now to Chapter 5 to parlay the model's interpretive capacity in a manner as to accord with relational psychoanalytic theory, including the various disciplines (notably, developmental psychology and affective neuroscience) with which it converses. Through investigations in the next chapter and the one after that, I intend to show how the model comes from and is consistent with leading relational psychoanalytic understandings and, at the same time, how it fits developmental and neuroscientific ones. We will begin by tracing the affective-relational lessons of infancy and early childhood that – well before any child steps through the doors of school – give rise to the meaning and pull that can be made of education's curricular objects.

Notes

1 The distinction I am making here recalls a difference between Piaget's and Vygotsky's views prioritising the role of peer interactions and student-teacher interactions, respectively, as critical in learning (see Chapter 7).
2 These days, until high school, whether students achieve grade-level objectives is typically inconsequential to their moving into the next year's grade level. However, student achievement is critically consequential to the politics of how educational institutions and schooling people will be judged.

5

OF MINDS AND BODIES

A few orienting tenets

On the one hand, neuroscientists, such as Antonio Damasio, draw upon the sciences of mind to explain the development of individual conscious being. On the other hand, relational psychoanalysts, such as Jessica Benjamin, emphasise the interpersonal and the social at the heart of individual development and unconscious and conscious being.

> The corrective responses that the brain produces on the basis of unconscious surveillance are, for the most part, not consciously deliberated. . . . Eventually . . . the surveillance job yields conscious feelings and enters the subjective mind. It is only beyond that point . . . that the responses can be influenced by conscious deliberation while still benefiting from the nonconscious process.
>
> *(Damasio, 2018, pp. 57–58)*

> Intersubjectivity . . . is now a dominant . . . view in psychoanalysis. . . . We now think in terms of the interpenetration of minds, conscious and unconscious, even mirror neuron to mirror neuron. The implications . . . have been revolutionary. They extend . . . to our entire view of human development and social bonds.
>
> *(Benjamin, 2018, p. 1)*

How do we bridge these seemingly different accounts? Who is the infant self that enters the world? How can that self be both the agent and the consequence of its ongoing becoming? From whence arise consciousness, intentionality, and agency in the first place? Can the material world and thoughts about it have meaning for themselves, or are all meanings some echo of early relational lessons in being and becoming?

74 A dialectic theory of learning

The address of the foregoing questions is large and must unfold over the course of this chapter and the next. We begin, however, in the familiar, with the feeling of an "a-ha" that strikingly marks a centripetal return to self. As the chapter proceeds we will work our way around and back to early infant perceptions and conceptions.

The centripetal moment: two phases of formulation

When we feel a new conception bubble to awareness and congeal into a coherence, this is formulation. We are literally feeling a mind-brain changing itself and settling into that change. Each change in conceiving, subtle or grand, revises the perceiver, who, thus changed, sees the world differently and so sees a different world. The centripetal return to self, depicted in the model, renders the next, centrifugal, possibility for encountering newly noticeable differences.

Notably, the formulation of the model itself is a useful instance of the thing it describes. For that illustrative value, I begin there, to consider not only the schema's very emergence and development but also how earlier happenings, reaching all the way back to infancy, provided the affective impetus to continue the effort forward.

Realisation: the "a–ha" comes to mind

A rudimentary version of the proposed learning schema first came to me a near decade ago. It was the unbidden arrival of the thing I had not sought. It emerged out of a great deal of noticing and in the midst of thought conversations with Winnicott's *Playing and Reality* (1971/2005) and two Sterns: Daniel Stern on *The Interpersonal World of the Infant* (1985/2000) and Donnel Stern on *Unformulated Experience* (1997/2003). I recognised its arrival in the surprise of a resonance, the relief of clarity, and a ring of fit. We could say that its realisation marked me in the thick of a centripetal moment – the first phase of the "a-ha" and the one to make possible an *articulation* into conscious and communicable thought (see Stern, 2010, p. xv). The felt experience of "A-ha, I-get-it-differently-now" is the unarticulated sensation of a new connection falling into place. It loses its precarious, fleeting nature when lifted from the visceral into a more tangible form, communicated (even if only to oneself) and communicable, at the ready for further articulation and elaboration.

I thus witness this process in myself even as, across 35 years of teaching, I have observed it countless times in my students. But in infancy, to the extent that the baby is *prediscursive* – that is, it experiences a world not yet organised according the conceptual groupings of words and language – then that baby, whose eyes light up with delight at some surprising resonance, knows no symbol system through which to story that experience. So where does the infant's "a-ha" land? Given I am arguing for the relevance of a model across the lifespan, it will be important to underscore, both, the profound difference in the way the centripetal return plays out before there is language and the relevance of unconscious, unthought-but-known infant experiences to later processes of symbolic representation and understanding.

Of minds and bodies **75**

The point? *If, in the prediscursive child, there can be no symbolic formulation, this does not mean that the infant does not engage in sense-making.* Neither does it mean that early life is devoid of any part of formulation. It *does* mean that, in infancy, articulation does not follow realisation, and so formulation must remain nonverbal, in the temporally shaped affective contours of the feeling of a moment and the familiarity of that feeling – that is, as the rudiments of the unconscious.

Of nonverbalised feelings (regardless of age of such incomplete formulation) three *principles of salience* seem to direct the degree of their unconscious etching in mind (a) *recurrences*, though never quite identical, that make for familiarity; (b) unexpected *disruptions* of the familiar; and (c) heightened moments of emotional *intensity* (Beebe & Lachmann, 2014, pp. 37–38; Lachmann, 2008, pp. 14–17). Studies of the recurrence, disruption, and intensity of kinds of affective encounters in caregiver-infant interactions "can shed light on similar patterns of interaction that occur . . . in life, generally" (Lachmann, p. 17). Indeed, "moments of self/other similarity tend to occur at times of high arousal and retain throughout life their ability to establish a strong feeling of connectedness, similarity, or intimacy, for good or ill" (Daniel Stern, 1985/2000, p. 107, n. 3). Lachmann describes these salient moments as transformational. Being transformational, then, on an embodied account of cognition, they are instances of learning – that is, where learning is responsive self-transformation. Thus, from the beginning, affective salience, learning, and interpersonal relations always co-implicate each other.

The difference, however, between the newborn and later life lies in the way, in infancy, these salient memories are, at once, central to the emergence of a sense of self (Daniel Stern, 1985/2000) but absent any consciously retrievable trace. Rather, they are remembered as bodily formulations – visceral, affective, relational, and procedural (Lachmann, 2008) – "the palpable experiential realities of substance, action, sensation, affect, and time" (Daniel Stern, 1985/2000, p. 71). They live as implicit memory, ensconced in habits of bodily action and reaction, and absent to awareness by the yet-to-be-developed conscious mind. In these terms, *the critical beginnings of identity take shape without any conscious consent on our part and according to forces and influences that precede our capacity to know them.*

For the infant as for the adult, a realisation, arriving unbidden as in a dream, if not verbalised while accessible, remains in a nebulous realm of bodily sensing, as a kind of latent dormancy awaiting attribution to a new moment that calls it out. In this way, it resurfaces and infuses the (strangely known but unarticulated) sense that "was" into a different present moment that "is." Otherwise, this unarticulated preverbal formulation drifts back into that collectivity of nonconscious associations comprising implicit/procedural relational knowledge (as opposed to explicit/ declarative forms). It becomes part of the intuitive sense, the powerful unversed feelings of tendency, that a person has, and reacts to, but without spelling out or being able to put a finger on what "it" is.

Of special relevance to education, the prior embodied experience is that which makes not only learning possible but also that which imbues symbolic representation with recycled meanings. That said, whereas that which is affectively embodied

76 A dialectic theory of learning

is necessarily rife with meaning, the symbolic may be taken up in a dissociated manner, vigilantly split off from meaning to serve as a way of engaging without engaging – a kind of keeping busy that can be numbing and/or soothing retreat.

Attaining a connection-of-significance between that which is embodied and the symbolic seems to be the point of the progressive call for meaningful learning discussed in Chapter 4. However, contrary to current and progressive educational dictums, owing to the complex primary formations of self-with-other, such connection need not be – indeed is unlikely to be – explicit, near, or direct (as assumed in the schooling language of, for example, authenticity and rich problem solving). The point is that, for learning to be felt as meaningful, it must connect in some way to primary affective vitalities whose meanings were rendered relationally, in primary intersubjective worlds, and recursively extensive from those worlds. Put differently, the visceral is inextricably entangled in socio-affective histories, reverberating in the present, but solidly anchored in first intersubjective lessons of embodied selfhood. It is with these thoughts in mind, that I return us to the example of my model's formulation as an instance of the thing itself.

To reiterate, as per Donnel Stern's description, the model arrived unbidden.

> Novel conscious experience is unbidden . . . the means by which we create it are not available to our inspection. . . . It is not a rare event, and it is not necessarily powerful or dramatically enlightening. . . . [It] happens routinely. In this sense, creativity is rampant in our lives.
>
> *(2015, pp. 108–109)*

It just so happened that one day, just as other thoughts regularly "come to mind," an image found me, and I was delighted by its arrival. So, I played at sketching the thing I was thinking, to see how it might look. Now, of course, the image did not come "out of the blue." By then, unbeknownst to me, it had been percolating for some time – not only through a decade of graduate studies and teaching in higher education but also, before that, through experiences that only a varied 25-year history in school teaching could give.

Articulation: closing the loop

Once initially formulated into some tangible form, I could capitalise on the power of the written – offloading memory and thought for safe keeping in visible, beyond-me form (Donald, 2001). This particular emergence went on to birth further curiosities fuelled by all manner of fascinating literatures. In a sense, I was submitting the assemblage to the scrutiny of other ways of thinking, for the intrigue of disillusionment, that it might be revised, elaborated, and honed against multiple extant realities. And so, following the initial resolution and formulation, manifold subsequent *centrifugal* swings sought out differences to be resolved in ever-revised *centripetal* returns.

Only once it was sufficiently "filled-in" did questions the likes of those opening this chapter, assume the appearance of driving the process. Indeed, such questions seemed to generate their own momentum – as if the model's churning, once begun, sustained itself forward from the tension of new queries, to new unknowns, to the affirming energy of resolution and onto new or revised questions. And if someone would have asked me what was driving my doing, if I had been asked to fill in a questionnaire about my motivation, I would have likely named these questions or similar ones.

Yet in the process, I have come to realise a deeper driver: reasons that live in my unconscious self, whose socio-affective strength I feel, even as I am not privy to their logic. I locate those reasons in early-year experiences and threads never dropped, around which my life has embroidered itself. Though I have no discursive memory of my beginning years, I have myself as the embodied sediment of those first patterned happenings. I am the construer of a narrative woven in the direction (though not the specific path) that such a body was, thus, moved to go. It is in affective vitality, drawn on earliest experiences, that I locate the ultimate wellspring propelling me to notice differently.

As for the truth of the story, leastwise the one that feels to fit today, I would say this: I work at this thing because I need to make a *good* sense of how and why I came to be me, and then to visit that understanding forward. By "good," I mean, a "force of good," forged of a past known as less that. As per Daniel Stern's recounting (1985/2000), I do it in accordance with the "agency," "coherence," and "continuity" of my sense of self, begun so long ago. That critical compulsion, *my* critical compulsion, translates now in a habit of wanting to make things better in manner that I could not do as a child. I effectuate this healing, as also a self-healing, by visiting what-good-I-might-learn forward into the lives of the students with whom I work, their students after them, and so on.

The point of this narrative is the point of all such narratives: that we indeed experience ourselves as storied in relationality and that we hold to our stories for their affective salience, wrought in the intersubjective, that imbues them with meaning and that underpins identity. For this reason, any theory of learning must reach back to and be consistent with a story of a self, making itself, in life, with others, in world, beginning in infancy – though undeniably storied from a time and into a time that socially pre-existed birth.

Beginnings: making self from givens

If we take seriously current perspectives on the embodied mind and a half century of concerted study in infant and child development, then any viable theory of learning must not only fit school-aged children and their higher-education counterparts, it will also want to accord with the early processes of the mind's psychobiological emergence. As we will see, "the emergence of organization is no more than a form of learning. . . . And learning experiences are powerful events in an infant's life. . . . [I]nfants are predesigned to seek out and engage in learning opportunities" (Daniel Stern, 1985/2000, p. 45). The child's mind and being is intersubjectively organised – in the interweave of inherited self-possibilities (as

78 A dialectic theory of learning

idiosyncratically expressed, evolutionary givens) and their unpredictable manifestations with and in the interactive matrices of psychosocial contexts (as idiosyncratically expressed, socio-cultural givens). For, as Stern also observed, though learning is not solely suited to "the exclusive purpose of forming a sense of self . . . a sense of self will be one of . . . [its] many vital byproducts" (1985/2000, p. 47).

At birth, the human brain is raw potential not yet organised by experience. We can "think of the constraining information of heredity as historical constraints now functioning as initial conditions" (Juarrero, 1999/2002, p. 176). The newborn arrives with but few, though powerful, innate species-specific propensities, a scarcity of set patterns of mind, and idiosyncratic qualities of personal vitality at the ready for fashioning selfhood in responsive interaction with a near-experience of world (Fonagy & Target, 2007; Gergely, 2007; Klin & Jones, 2007; Daniel Stern, 2000). Quite simply, newborns – having had no out-of-the-womb encounters in a shifty social place – have had nothing against which to contrast a relatively less-variant, more familiar, viscerally felt self. Accordingly, at birth, infants have no sense of distinguishable categories of being, neither of self, nor of others, objects, or world (Carpendale & Lewis, 2004, p. 87). The new mind, although flush with possibility is primarily undifferentiated. Any co-ordination between internal states and behavioural expression reflect inborn adaptations and not conscious intention (Fonagy, Gergely, & Target, 2007, p. 293). Yes, infants express basic emotions. And yes, they experience and respond to affect and sensation. But at birth, *the 'constitutional' or introspectively 'invisible self'* (Gergely, 2007, p. 58) bespeak genetically informed and environmentally occasioned differences of individual temperament. These differences come to be translated through a limited set of "primary," "universal," "prewired," "stimulus-driven" emotions, as "procedural behavioural automatisms . . . not accessible to conscious awareness and over which the baby has no voluntary control at first" (Gergely, 2007, p. 58).

And so, contrary to the model shown in Figure 4.1, there is, at the point of birth, no "a-ha" to speak of and no "illusion of things in control, proper, and fitting." Neither, however, can there be any sense of things not in control, proper, or fitting. These aspects of the model come into view only in consequence of emergent neurophysiological self-organisation. Indeed, a budding sense of self will arise in the very processes of a self feeling its own coherence, continuity, and agency – that is, insofar as there is an attuned and coherent enough witnessing other through which to know oneself. Moreover, learning, being a dialectical recursive process of self-making, means that not all components will be in view from the beginning. We begin with a self, not self-conscious of itself, yet engaging in centrifugal and centripetal encounters with an experienceable world within and without. At this point the model's aspects of openness, freedom to experience, and surrender are all inborn givens – so too, as we shall see, is trust.

Importantly then, having only fledgling, neurally networked coherence – the consequence of hazy foetal experiencing – the neonate can*not* be said to direct its own learning or attention. Instead, in a strange play of circumstances, the processes (that nonetheless, taken together, comprise the neonate) direct themselves. They do so, critically, in conversation with a sensation-eliciting world. The infant mind-brain-body is awash in all degrees of pleasant and unpleasant sensation – what Daniel Stern has termed "feelings of vitality" (1985/2000) – the felt vibrancy of a particular self's aliveness.

From sensations to internal objects

In everyday speech people use the words emotions and feelings interchangeably. I instead adopt Damasio's useful distinction, where "emotions play out in the theater of the body. Feelings play out in the theatre of the mind" (2003, p. 28). Constellations of bodily sensation are the physiological substrates of emotion; and thoughts and mental associations (both nonverbal and verbal) about emotions are the stuff of feeling. Although coming to reverberate nearly indistinguishably together as affect, developmentally at least, emotion precedes feeling (Damasio, 2003, pp. 29–31). In time, emotions triggered by feelings and feelings triggered by emotions reverberate and recycle across mind-in-body – amplified or acquiescing, as per conscious and unconscious re-emoted memories.

To begin to appreciate the way an infant comes to know and discern self from other and world, a quick overview of four sensation types will be useful (Ammaniti & Ferrari, 2013; Damasio, 2018; Edelman, 2006; Panksepp & Biven, 2012): (1) The background hum of *interoception* is the sensation of aliveness as one's body does what bodies do, mostly automatically (e.g., breathing, falling asleep, suckling, shivering, & feeling thirsty). (2) The sensation of instinctual *affective reactions* triggered by neurochemical secretions – the likes of cortisol, adrenalin, dopamine, and oxytocin – from relatively distinct subcortical regions are responsible for the primary-process emotions of fear, play, seeking, care, panic/grief, rage, and (much later in life) lust. (3) *Proprioception* communicates the feeling of one's body and its parts in spatial relation, as, for example, in vocalising, moving, relaxing, holding still, and just "being." Some movements happen in instinctual sequences like suckling. Others begin haphazardly and become crudely replicated and smoothened in a budding goal-directed capacity of, for example, a foetus sucking its thumb (Piontelli, 2006, p. 395). (4) And finally, a kaleidoscope of *exteroceptive* sensations, most notably, sight, sound, taste, smell, and touch.

These sensation capacities are, of course, non-identical across different bodies. Even subtle peculiarities at micro levels will generate striking variations of human nature that together mark each infant unique and whose physiologies Winnicott saw as the infant's "inherited potential" and the basis of the true self (in Bollas, 1993, p. 406). Bollas writes,

> The infant is born with his or her own personality. . . . a peculiar form of being, in which reality and experience will be processed in a unique and definite manner. The baby immediately begins to elaborate this intrinsic character through increasingly sophisticated mental contents.
>
> *(p. 402)*

80 A dialectic theory of learning

Affective sensations "speak" to the infant as contours of intensity over time, not as separately recognised modalities (e.g., sight or sound) (Ammaniti & Ferrari, 2013; Daniel Stern, 1985/2000). For example, what is common in father's feeding may be the *rhythm* of his breathing, the *warmth* and *scent* of his body, the *steadiness* of his arm, the *depth* of his voice, the *strength* of his heart beat, and the *gentle* way he holds the bottle. The contour of these happenings is likely to have an experienceable harmony "known" by the infant. In this example, they shape an embodied memory-become-trusted-familiar. If the baby could verbalise her thoughts, she might say, "This is that person with whom I know what to expect because this is the familiar feel of him that comes to me, in comfort, and of-a-piece." This is not to say that daddy is always as such. There will be multiple familiar daddies – for example: playful, pensive, distracted, hurried, and so forth (Daniel Stern, 1985/2000, pp. 104–112). In this way, the constellation of interactive experiences of being-with-daddy, create an internal nonverbal representation, the memory, of father as *object* within. It is to this idea of internal objects, mapped from experiences with originary external others, that a theory of object relations speaks. "An evoked companion or internal representation [internal object] or working model or fantasied union with [or way-of-being-with] mother is *no more or less than the history of specific kinds of relationships*" (italics added) (Daniel Stern, 1985/2000, p. 118).

Stern's method of real-time dynamic study of infant-parent dyads has been widely taken up and elaborated in the field (e.g., Ammaniti & Ferrari, 2013; Beebe & Lachmann, 2014; Trevarthen, 2011; Tronick, 2001) forming the basis of a compelling *intersubjective* story of *intrapsychic* emergence whereby the self-object, as fluid nonverbal sense of self, arises in concert with senses of other selves – the primary caregiver(s) being most critical. Note too, that in this conceiving, internal objects comprise, less the people themselves, and more their interactive ways-of-being-with those people.

To reiterate, internal objects, in Stern's conceiving, are the memoried interactive experiences that cluster around and characterise encounters with particular others of one's world, seminally in infancy. *They are not the same as the reality of those external others.* In this difference, we have the budding of a potential clash between the memoried other-within, as "made," and the encountered other-without, as "given." Indeed, "because of memory [as such] we are rarely alone, even (perhaps especially) during the first half-year of life. The infant engages with real external partners some of the time and with evoked companions [internal representations/objects] almost all of the time" (Stern, 1985/2000, p. 118).

Over repeated interactions, the internal object of the infant's knowing comes to assume the countenance of reliably "certain" knowledge. At the same time – insofar as the parent is multidimensional, has an interiority that remains out of view, and is necessarily evolving herself – any such certainty is illusory and vulnerable to disillusionment by the "real" external-other. Such disillusionment exercises a kind of breaching or violation of expectation; and violations of expectation, depending on the intersubjective contexts, can engender intrigue and laughter as in the game of peek-a-boo, or fear and frustration as in, for example, an infant's bewildering encounter with a sudden loss of parental responsivity in Ed Tronick's classic "still face" experiments[1] (Lachmann, 2008, Part 2). In the dynamic shaping of the internal object-other, which cannot but be different from its external object "match," we see the inauguration of a struggle – one perhaps most vociferously protested during the period of rapprochement (colloquially, the "terrible twos"). Of this struggle Winnicott wrote,

> The mother's main task (next to providing opportunity for illusion) is disillusionment. This is preliminary to the task of weaning, and it also continues as one of the tasks of parents and educators. In other words, this matter of illusion is one that belongs inherently to human beings and that no individual finally solves for himself or herself.
>
> *(1971/2005, p. 17)*

Along with the formation of internal other-objects, a sense of self takes shape. It will evolve with the infant's capacity to move, to act on things in the world, and to socially interact in ways that elicit responses from others. There will be important lessons about himself in the reflecting eyes of a potentially witnessing and attuned caregiver. The version of himself that the child sees in the mirroring face of the parental other will form the bases of self-experiences across a spectrum of attributes accepted as "me" or rejected as "not me" according to what his caregiver might make possible (Horowitz, 2014). If, for example, mother's habit is to smile in response to baby's frown, this would come to the baby as disharmonious, a striking mismatch. Should this too often be the case, it would compromise the infant's capacity to render his own coherent, self-contingent sense. He might smile for her and whimper at the same time (see Beebe & Lachman, 2014, for such examples). The issue of cause, as in, "Did I 'cause' this unpleasant disharmony or did mother?" has no answer in the baby's experience. Beebe and Lachmann (2014) describe the effect of these kinds of interactions:

> Incoherent or contradictory dialogues involve a collapse of intersubjective space in which only one person's subjective reality is recognized. The partner's initiatives are ignored, over-ridden, or not acknowledged. . . . [S]uch failures of collaborative dialogue generate contradictory internal models [objects]. Discordant information is difficult to integrate into a coherent percept, and may remain unintegrated. . . . set[ting the] origins of dissociative processes.
>
> *(p. 36)*

In such complexly interwoven tapestries of early attachment, we begin to see how primary lessons in self-realisation are intimately and inextricably entangled in lessons about ways–of–being–with others.

Critical to agency going well, is a reliable enough connection between an event happening in an infant's world and its apparent contingency on the infant's prior initiated action, that is, a correlation that implies causation. For example, a baby happily explores the question of whether something falls off the edge of the

82 A dialectic theory of learning

highchair's table each time she pushes it off the edge. The drop is fully contingent on her actions. So too have been her explorations in learning to moving her own arm. This is the reliable world of things – and notably, an "it" world less unsettling to some children for whom intersubjective contingencies may feel disconcertingly out of synch (see, e.g., Klin & Jones, 2007, discussions of autism). When all goes well, however, a far more intriguing exploration entails in watching mom's reaction with every repetition of the trick of that object falling. For there to be agency there must be predictability; the response, inanimate or social, must be experienced as sufficiently contingent on one's own initiative.

> Detection of contingency facilitates the development of a sense of agency or effectance. Neurophysiological evidence also suggests that familiarity, repetition, and expectancy constitute the most powerful organizing principles of neural functions. . . . As expectations become established, breaches or violations of expectations also exercise a powerful organizing effect on infants.
>
> *(Lachmann, 2008, p. 115)*

Whether such interactive experiences move an infant toward attachment security or insecurity turns on the ways that contingencies and their unexpected violations engender trust. That is, the infant develops a capacity to trust his own agency (to act independently) through trustworthy-enough experiences of interdependence between his actions and those of another person and the world. In this we see the interplay of two critical developmental tasks, the independence needed for individuation/separation and the interdependence at the root of relatedness/belonging. Each accrues in concert with the other.

> Once we accept the idea that infants do not begin life as part of an undifferentiated unity, the issue is not only how we separate from oneness, but also how we connect to and recognize others; the issue is not how we become free of the other, but how we actively engage and make ourselves known in relationship to the other.
>
> *(Benjamin, 1988, p. 18)*

Embodied metaphor and meaning in amodal perception

Daniel Stern introduced the expression *vitality affects* to describe the activation contours – phrasings of sensation – that an infant comes to know in a body-responsive way. Of these affective contours he writes,

> A "rush" of anger or of joy, a perceived flooding of light, an accelerating sequence of thoughts, an unmeasurable wave of feeling evoked by music, and a shot of narcotics can all feel like "rushes." They all share similar envelopes of neural firings, although in different parts of the nervous system.
>
> *(1985/2000, p. 55)*

Over time these vitality affects with their characteristic feel, become associated with affective interpretations and the particular intersubjective encounters from which they originate. Taking their qualitative value as a function of intensity over time, as per the example of daddy, earlier, these contours are *amodal*, the likes of what could be described with such words as surging, fading, explosive, intermittent, and so forth. In this way, a sound, a taste, and an emotion can all be sharp.

This amodal biophysiology grounds human experience in a metaphorical world (Lakoff & Johnson, 1999), one that goes on to speak to us in dreams, and that make poets and artists of us all. It describes the primary visceral life experience of the infant and the "solid affective/evolutionary foundation . . . [without which] higher emotional and cognitive processes . . . would collapse" (Panksepp & Biven, 2012, p. 15).

The infant is uniquely attuned to this kind of perception. Stern writes, "Infants . . . have an innate general capacity . . . to take information received in one sensory modality and somehow translate it into another sensory modality" (1985/2000, p. 51). For example, a three-week-old baby sucking on a pacifier, without having seen it, can then visually discern the one his mouth felt from the differently shaped one it did not (p. 47). Even a newborn will follow the sight of an experimenter sticking out his tongue with the action of mimicking that action (Meltzoff in Beebe & Lachman, 2014, pp. 25–26). This phenomenon of mapping one modality to another – in this case, mapping the shape of the action he sees onto the shape of the one he feels in doing it too – "appears to be well within infants' capacity by three weeks of age" (p. 49).

> The infant, from the earliest days of life, forms and acts upon abstract representations of qualities of perception. These abstract representations . . . are not sights and sounds and touches and nameable objects, but rather shapes, intensities, and temporal patterns – the more "global" qualities of experience.
>
> *(p. 51)*

> [A]t a preverbal level (outside of awareness) the experience of finding a cross-modal match . . . would feel like a correspondence or imbuing of present experience with something prior or familiar.
>
> *(pp. 52–53)*

Experiences are rarely unidimensional, making cross-modal associations the norm – that is, as long as communication is itself coherent: The contradiction of a smiling father with soothing voice who changes a diaper abruptly leaves the baby at a loss to make coherence. The persistence of contradiction, should that characterise a child's early experiences, lays a foundation of insecurity to which a child adapts, and for whom adaptations, the likes of heightened vigilance and generalised mistrust, become maladaptive in subsequent more secure settings.

> Imagine you're walking in the forest and you see a bear. Immediately, your hypothalamus sends a signal to your pituitary, which sends a signal to your

84 A dialectic theory of learning

adrenal gland that says, "Release stress hormones! Adrenaline! Cortisol!" And so your heart starts to pound. Your pupils dilate. Your airways open up, and you are ready to either fight that bear or run from the bear. And that is wonderful if you're in a forest and there's a bear.

(Burke-Harris, 2014, 7:32)

Assuming all goes well, over time and with the swiftness of infant learning, the baby comes to recognise patterns, some more familiar than others, depending on exposure, and the most familiar being the vitality affects originating in the baby's own bodyhood. "All of the stimuli (auditory, visual, tactile, proprioceptive) emanating from the self share a common temporal structure, while all of those emanating from an other share a different temporal structure" (p. 84). The baby's sense of aliveness has an invariance that marks it as different from things that are not self. Immersed in these kinds of affective experiences, the baby's senses of self and other, as distinct, from birth, obtain as differently felt, contrasting-but-quickly-familiar, qualitative coherences. And of course, with emergent familiarity comes expectation; and expectation, depending on what experience teaches a child to expect, can condition over time the anticipation of things pleasurable, things less so, or things unpredictable – all of which in turn implicate degrees of security, either compromising or sustaining trust.

On initial conditions

Stern (1985/2000, p. 8) describes months 2 to 3, 9 to 12, and 15 to 18 as "epochs of great change" with quantum leaps "in EEG recording, overt behavior, and subjective experience" (p. 8). Between these epochs are "periods of relative quiescence . . . [during which] new integrations appear to consolidate" (p. 8).

How do the quantum leaps that Stern describes come about? What initial conditions, biological processes, and worldly encounters align to trigger learning in the child? On which principles do first lessons occur? Neurobiology provides a beginning set of answers. The mind-brain-body is poised to responsive self-construing according to the following principles:

1   on a principle of neural *action potentials and long-term potentiation* – in brief, the neural equivalent of a "path laid in walking" – the intensified firing of neural pathways (assuming no other countervailing forces) results in neural learning; that is, familiar patterns of neural firing are more likely to repeat than novel patterns are likely to occur, and this owes to adaptive alterations of neural chemistry. (Panksepp & Biven, 2012, pp. 218–220);

2   on a principle of neural *re-entry* – in brief, that "neurons that fire together wire together" (Edelman, 2006) – sensations co-occurring in experience across multiple sensory channels (e.g., smelling and tasting mothers milk while suckling and feeling body-to-body touch and warmth) will obtain a heuristic wholeness that in repetition become generalised such that one sensation calls up the others

(e.g., the scent of mother's milk recalls taste, suckling, touch, warmth, and a reflex of head and body "reaching" toward the scent) and reminds the child of a *way-of-being-with* the other;

3   on a principle of *neurochemical value systems* – in brief, raw primary-process emotions, as felt pleasure and displeasure mark events with affective salience – the infant begins to associate context with accompanying self-states, and develops preferences and the capacity to anticipate situations best approached or avoided;

4   on the aforementioned principle of *vitality affects* – in brief, the felt psycho-biological contours and rhythms of bodily sensations whose affective saliences come to be associated with interpersonal happenings – the infant begins to discern between its own internally triggered vitality affects and the experience of sensations coming from without.

On this last point, it needs to be emphasised that

> Infants are not lost at sea in a wash of abstractable qualities of experience. They are gradually and systematically ordering these elements of experience to identify self-invariant and other-invariant constellations. And whenever any constellation is formed, the infant experiences the emergence of organization.
>
> *(Daniel Stern, 1985/2000, p. 67)*

Critical to the experience of emergent selfhood is a process whereby "extremely diverse events may . . . be yoked" (Stern, 1985/2000, p. 58) according to the activation contour that they share. Indeed, "infants act as though two events sharing the same temporal structure belong together" (p. 85). This is "because activation contours . . . can apply to any kind of behavior or sentience . . . [and can thus] be abstracted from one kind of behavior . . . [to] exist in some amodal form so that it can apply to another kind of overt behavior or mental process" (pp. 57–58). Importantly, what is yoked, in a present moment, is "the intentional object [whatever the mind is attentive to] and the vital bodily feelings and shifting vitality affects of experiencing" (Stern, 2000, pp. xviii–xix). It is through the input of this bodily vitality that the infant can sense itself as the felt experiencer of its intentional objects. And each moment, whereby this experiencer feels himself situated in the world, is a moment of "primary consciousness" (p. xviii). In the pulse of life, short, periodic moments of primary consciousness "offer rehearings of the continual music of living." *These experiences of primary consciousness are "not self-reflective . . . not verbalized, and . . . [endure] only during a present moment that corresponds to 'now' [italics added]"* (p. xvii). They are what mark the senses of self-coherence, self-continuity, and self-agency, as developed by Stern and depicted in the model. Stern summarises: "This is what I mean by a sense of an emergent self – experiencing being alive while encountering the world (or encountering yourself) at a given moment, an awareness of the process of living experience" (p. xviii).

86 A dialectic theory of learning

How the model of learning applies from birth

How does the proposed model accord with these understandings on new life? Donnel Stern observes that the

> unquestioning acceptance of the familiar ensures that there will be no inadvertent deployment of curiosity. . . . The capacity to see the familiar in the unfamiliar, one of the great achievements of infancy, becomes in adulthood an equally great impediment to thought's growth.
>
> *(1997/2003, pp. 62–63)*

Per his observation, the self's approach to learning changes as a function of familiarity with self and the world, and one's capacity and willingness to notice the unfamiliar. *Making the unfamiliar familiar is the work of infant construing. Undoing the familiar to find the unfamiliar within is, arguably, the work of later life.*

What one perceives, notices, in the world shifts according to one's own conceiving of it. That is, perceptive tendency is to go looking for the familiar and recognisable, doing so in accordance with what one has already conceived and so can, and is inclined to, perceive (see Chapter 12 for elaborations related to teaching). However, at birth, the newborn – absent experience out of which to have shaped any prior conceiving (neither nonverbal nor symbolic) – exhibits an initial orientation that Gopnik has described as a "vivid but distributed . . . lantern[-like]" attention (2007, p. 502).[2] At first, the baby orients to whatever in the world (internal or external) most "catches" her attention (Gopnik, 2007, pp. 503–504). In effect, she is at the whim of the engagement power of stimuli as accorded by her body's inherited tendencies to notice some things more than others – especially exteroceptive sensations. Genetic inheritance generally primes the infant to be more attentive to the external world (Gergely, 2007, pp. 58–59).

In these terms, consider first the model's centrifugal moment. Its emphasis is on *noticing*. Clearly, the infant's "thinking" mind cannot, at first, be overwhelmed by any sense of surprise, disarray, or unpredictability as per the model. The very condition of the newborn mind's non-organisation necessarily precludes expectation, much less thought, as we might understand it. The baby *can*, however, be overwhelmed in the sense of stimulation that is too much: too disharmonious, too intense, too abrupt, or too unrelenting – these constituting inborn triggers for angst (Panksepp & Biven, 2012). Neither can feelings the likes of wonder, intrigue, surprise, and trepidation apply at this point. Accordingly, in the newborn, the outward proclivity to notice its world is an instinctual given condition of sensorial receptivity (openness, freedom, and surrender, as per the model). The centrifugal moment can neither be enhanced nor impeded by preconceived expectations – at this point there are none. This state of affairs will swiftly change.

On the centripetal return of infant learning, biology, as per the foregoing principles, has ensured much in the way of resolution. Physiologically, sense-making features the neurochemically rewarded self-experiences of aliveness, given of neural self-assemblage and emergent internal neural synchronisation matched to external experiencing. Here resolution as sense-making is inherently rewarding insofar as it triggers evolutionarily selected neurochemical rewards (it feels good) accompanying biological changes that favour survival – those changes being the experience of a predictable world and, with predictability, greater degrees of agency to act on and in that world. In other words, sense-making is generally accompanied by positive vitality affects associated with (a) expanding *coherence* – as increasing interconnectivity within, that matches an increasingly predictive world without; (b) *agency* – as a corresponding ability to physically act in the world and to witness the consequences of those actions; and (c) reinforced *self-continuity* each time the sense of oneself, established in a moment, reappears in subsequent moments as familiar.

Initially bathed in unorganised concerts of sensation, the infant thusly organises itself in accordance with the world. She learns herself into being according to regularities availed and experienced. Through a biology of neural-noticing-become-experiential-being, co-triggered neurons become temporally and structurally bound into physiological-experiential associative networks primed for subsequent co-firing – and this is possible, so long as, the amodal activation contours given of the body and the world repeat themselves with enough, though not exact, virtuosity as to be recognised as familiar. In this way, nonverbal memory accrues, and the infant gains the capacity to recognise invariance against new variance across time – and so, to learn – and with such learning, to anticipate pleasure from displeasure and react accordingly.

Now, what exactly the baby learns overall – be it trust in experiences of comfort and joy or uncertainty and fear over the likelihood of discomfort and pain – pivotally turns on the nature of her experienced internal and external worlds. That is, what she learns – about herself, about her world, and about learning itself – critically depends upon the people of her near-experiencing and the ways in which they can attune to, and responsively meet, her psychobiological needs.

We leave this chapter, to pick up, in the next, the thread of relationality – the dialectics of intrapsychic and intersubjective life – into and through language, as relationality recursively builds upon itself in degrees of security and trust, ultimately conditioning the way one has learned to learn.

Notes

1 In the "still face" experiment (Tronick, Als, Adamson, Wise, & Brazelton, 1978), the parent begins by establishing a playful affective connection with the infant. After two minutes, the parent assumes a non-responsive, immobile expression for two more minutes, after which play resumes. The effect on the infant during the breach of playful expectation is profound.

2 In contrast, in maturation, the mind's consciousness primarily speaks to itself as it rallies a "spotlight" focus on the world (Gopnik, 2007, pp. 502–503). "In adults . . . [a]ttention is focused, inhibitory, and top-down . . . [I]t is reportable . . . in the service of goals, and . . . is connected to a sense of self. . . . In development, this apparently unified picture breaks apart" (2007, p. 504).

6

BECOMING SELF

Storied in relationality, steeped in affect

Insofar as we come to know and create ourselves through the eyes of significant others, most profoundly in infancy, intrapsychic well-being will intimately entangle in intersubjective relating. Studies in caregiver – infant interactions seem to have confirmed something sought in vain "in the field of psychoanalysis itself – a demonstration of how we get into each other's minds . . . long before speech . . . how recognition works in action . . . [and] new scaffolding for the idea of intersubjectivity . . . previously considered philosophically" (Benjamin, 2018, p. 2). In this chapter, we delve deeper into childhood development. We will follow the understandings of Chapter 5 – to see how they play out in observed caregiver – infant interactions, to trace the shaping of an intrapsychic world through intersubjective life, and to mark key educational implications for exploring in Part III.

First, I note a half-century of study in attachment patterns and childhood development attesting that, in caregiver – child relations, security begets security. Caregivers who possess markers of well-being at the confluence of authenticity, self-knowledge, and self-acceptance are those most inclined to the judicious outward rendering of presence with care and grace to participate in the sharing of attention and intention (Benjamin, 2018, p. 77). As research has borne out, critical in relationships with infants, children, and youth, is the adult's capacity to synchronise an acknowledging affect, without losing her centre – neither tending to the dissolution of interpersonal boundaries (psychic equivalence) nor to the vigilant maintenance of impenetrable ones (pretence, per Fonagy & Target, 2007; Target & Fonagy, 1996). In other words, if we caregivers can be well with ourselves, without "living the lie" or the fear of the unacknowledged within, then we are better able to address and deescalate the everyday ruptures of relational life and teach our children the possibility of relational repair. Neither dismissive, submissive, obsessed, nor retaliatory, we might contain the child's affective peaks and valleys, in good enough measure, including their insistences at the extremes of independence and dependence. Such security, gifted forward from one generation to the next, may be our best bet for navigating well, which is to say never perfectly, the vicissitudes of life, intimate and far-reaching.

The ability to ultimately come to a position of subject-to-subject relating in adulthood – what Benjamin calls mutuality (2018, pp. 71–90) – means perceiving others as different centres of being. Instances of mutuality are moments of co-presence, co-witnessing, and co-recognition in a tension that allows for living and learning through the intersubjective pull of difference. Attachment security supports this capacity for mutuality and relates to greater vitality, agency, and balance between dependence and independence throughout life.

As we will see – from synchronised caregiver-infant affective communions in first months, through cross-modal affective matching of internal states later in the first year, and then affective mirroring, gesture, and the pointing of language through toddlerhood – children learn to acknowledge and negotiate intrapsychic and intersubjective life; that is, life in their heads and life beyond. The alternative is an existence absent the subjective difference of others, a life alone in a world of object-others, an unstable world of: "They are and must be who I think they are. What's out there must be what I already have in mind about it." Inevitably the world will refuse to conform to one's illusions about it, even the reasonable ones. In the potential for disillusionment are precious teaching moments. But such a one, feeling unfairly done-to, copes by either refusing to acknowledge troublesome difference or seeking to subdue difference away (see Chapter 8).

It is from Winnicott's *Playing and Reality* that I have drawn the notions of illusion and disillusionment. Winnicott differentiated two co-inhabited maternal positions: the "environment mother" and the "object mother" (in Bollas, 1993, p. 401). We could say that, in dyadic relating, the environment mother (in effect, the holding environment) "will be appreciated . . . by her unobtrusive support of the infant's developing subjectivity" (p. 401). In triadic relations, an object – it world comes into play. On this matter, and speaking for Winnicott, Bollas writes, "The . . . mother presents objects to the baby, and we might say that the most important 'object' she presents is herself" (1993, p. 401).

I heretofore investigate the emergence of the intrapsychic self as nestled first in the holding environment of dyadic relations. Next, I consider triadic relations and an emerging dilemma for the child: a world in my head, a world out there, and a mediating pedagogue in both. The intersubjective realm bequeaths intrapsychic meaning and shapes unconscious desire, even as it delimits and defines the force and manner of desire's outward expression. In the matter of education, one of the most significant intersubjective lessons on intrapsychic being will involve a capacity to tolerate and play in a Winnicottean transitional space with the illusions *made* in mind and the disillusionments *given* from without.

Dyadic relations: ways–of–being–with

The infant mind, immersed in primary attachment relationships from birth, will organise familiar experiences with newly accruing ones. The nascent mind – brain *quite literally* is physically organised by experience – or more aptly put, in a dialectics that sees the infusion of newly given experiences into what can and is made of them (Daniel Stern, 2000). Accordingly, internal objects begin as those mental construals realised "from repeated, relatively small interactive patterns" (Stern, p. xv). Though they are about people, they "are not people; nor are they parts or aspects of others. Rather, they are constructed from the patterned experience of self in interaction with another: What is inside (i.e., represented internally) comprises interactive experiences" (p. xv) associated with the people that matter most in early life. In such interaction, the attuned recognising and recognisable other serves as critical witness and arbiter of what to notice in the world (Carpendale & Lewis, 2006).

Primary attachment figures and their infants co-create subtle, significant, and complex patterns of relatedness (Beebe & Lachmann, 2014). By age one, these patterns have congealed in degrees of security that predict ways of experiencing close relations in adulthood (Beebe & Lachmann, 2014, p. xviii). Over the second year, the toddler – with newly emerging mind, already predisposed to particular patterns of interpreting and reacting – will want to exercise his independence while sorting out: what he knows from what he "makes up;" what happens from what he "makes happen;" what others might know, imagine, and make happen; and what everyone knows.

A discourse in attachment

Freud identified "two components in the etiology of acquired psychopathology: constitutional . . . predispositions and early experiential factors" (Kandel, 1999/2005, p. 79). Traditional psychoanalysis emphasised constitutional predispositions. In a radical departure, influenced by Piaget's cognitive psychology (Wallin, 2007, p. 27), John Bowlby studied the "early experiential factors" beginning with the homeless and orphaned children of World War II. In the doing, he pioneered attachment theory.

For Bowlby, childhood behaviour arose in answer to the immediacy of early close worlds of experience. In later and broader contexts the same adaptive behaviour could prove variably adaptive or maladaptive. Across a 40-year collaboration, he and Mary Ainsworth (Wallin, 2007) developed a metric called the "Strange Situation" for parsing attachment security according to the observed responses of one-year-old children, across varying scenarios, to a primary caregiver's presence and absence. The paradigm led to four constellations of attachment behaviour: one tending to *security*; two that represented opposite adaptations to the problem of insecurity – either an *avoidant* rejection of emotional connection altogether or an insatiable, yet *anxiously ambivalent*, need for it; and a fourth rare cluster (documented by Ainsworth's student, Mary Main) of *disoriented-disorganised* behaviours found in children for whom the caregiver was source of both comfort and distress (Wallin, 2007). The patterns proved traceable from the one-year-old infant, to the five-year-old child, and into early adulthood as per Main's "Adult Attachment Interview" (Wallin, 2007). It has more recently gained popular currency in a complementary line of research on attachment styles in intimate adult relating (e.g., Brennan, Clark, & Shaver, in Shaver & Mikulincer, 2004).

Rejected for decades by the psychoanalytic community, for both its empiricist methods (Fonagy & Target, 2007) and the danger of opening the mother to blame (Mitchell & Black, 1995/2016, p. 114), attachment theory has more recently surfaced in a complement of literatures in child development and contemporary psychoanalytic thought (see, e.g., Banai, Mikulincer, & Shaver, 2005; Cassidy, 2008; Cozolino, 2010; Kernberg & Caligor, 2005, p. 128; Laible & Thompson's, 2000; Meyer & Pilkonis, 2005; Daniel Stern, 2004; Sandler, 1995). For example, functional neuroimaging studies suggest that attachment classifications reflect differences in underlying neuroendocrine brain systems involved in affiliation and reward systems and that these differences, manifesting behaviourally and psychologically, emerge as a function of early caregiving experience (Strathearn, 2007). Fonagy and Target (2007) position the theory at a promising hub of mind science and psychoanalysis with the potential to re-establish psychoanalysis' "position as the premier neuroscience of subjectivity" (p. 446). In their esteem, "attachment immediately takes center stage once we recognize the physical origins of thought" (p. 428).

Initially, attachment research rendered a bleak picture for those tending to insecurity: Deep disturbances in early parent – child relationships spawned insecure attachment and risk for later psychopathologies (Leckman, Feldman, Swain, & Mayes, 2007, p. 104). Moreover, transgenerational studies suggested a pattern whereby the quality of caregiver-to-infant responsiveness traced to the caregiver's own childhood history and attachment-related experiences (Leckman, Feldman, Swain, & Mayes, 2007, p. 104). Unexpected breaks to transgenerational insecurity was effectuated only by an able few who, for unknown reasons, rallied mindfulness and mentalisation (thinking about thinking) to "right" difficult beginnings (Target & Fonagy, 1996). Conversely, an early relationship with a caring attuned adult conferred, even onto otherwise high-risk perinatal infants, a degree of resiliency and protection against such future psychopathologies (Leckman et al., 2007, p. 104).

The difficulty here lies in the very nature of categories and the theory's potential for their entrenchment, skewing what we look for and limiting what we can find. As attachment theory enters public and educational discourses, its fixed categorisations offer newest ways for measuring and treating children and their teachers. Care with these constructs is in order. All the while, appreciating the seminal importance of degrees of attachment security – these being far more mutable than originally thought – we can pick up from the rich body of the last two decades wherein attachment theory, in a more nuanced form, joins contemporary psychoanalytic studies of childhood development.

Primary intersubjectivity

A father took his 8-day-old, fussing, infant into his arms. In frame-by-frame microanalysis, the following was seen to ensue.

> The father glanced down momentarily at the baby's face. Strangely enough, in the same frames, the infant looked up at the father's face. Then the infant's left arm, which had been hanging down over the father's left arm, began to move upward. Miraculously, in the same frame, the father's right arm, which had been hanging down at his side, began moving upward. Frame by frame the baby's hand and the father's hand moved upward simultaneously. Finally they met over the baby's tummy. The baby's left hand grasped the little finger of the father's right hand. At that moment the infant's eyes closed and she fell asleep, while the father continued talking, apparently totally unaware of the little miracle of specificity in time, place, and movement that had taken place in his arms.
>
> *(Sanders, in Clement, 2014, pp. 159–160)*

The foregoing description details an interlude of joint co-ordination between a father and his newborn child. Fascinatingly, it is not particularly unique. Numerous studies have charted the intricate choreographies whereby "neonatal selves coordinate the rhythms of their movements and senses . . . engag[ing] in intimate and seductive precision with other persons' movements, sensing their purposes and feelings" (p. 119). In such moment-to-moment co-ordination – rapid, subtle, co-constructed, and generally out of awareness – infants come to know themselves, to feel known, and to know another (Beebe & Lachman, 2014, p. xix). As it turns out,

> We are born to generate shifting states of self-awareness, to show them to other persons, and to provoke interest and affectionate responses from them. . . . It seems that cultural intelligence itself is motivated at every stage by the kind of powers of innate intersubjective sympathy that an alert infant can show shortly after birth.
>
> *(Trevarthen, 2011, p. 119)*

By the second month, the major emotional peaks and valleys of social life occur outside activities of physiological regulation (e.g., feeding) in affectively exciting interactions that directly serve cognitive function (Daniel Stern, 1985/2000, p. 75). While infants, at this point, are not "able to recognise a number of basic categorical emotions of others (see Gergely, 2007; Nelson, 1987) mothers will certainly react to these emotions if their child expresses them" (Fonagy, Gergely, & Target, 2007, p. 293). This kind of "teaching and learning about minds and states of mind is mostly a mundane process within the attachment relationship . . . inaccessible to reflection or modification" (Fonagy et al., 2007, p. 312). The uniqueness of individual caregiving turns on the rhythm of these caretaking responses, their contingency on the infant's instinctual behavioural biases and emerging subjectivity, and the synchronicity of micro-level matching and moderating of the child's affective states and levels of arousal (Leckman et al., 2007, p. 87). "Affect regulation at the earliest stages . . . [occurs] as the caregiver, reading the infant's automatic behavioural emotion expressions, reacts to them with appropriate affect-modulating interactions and emotion displays"

(Gergely, 2007, p. 58). Degrees of wellness emerge in accordance with the tenor of this pedagogy of interactive caregiving (Damasio, 2003; Gergely, 2007; Klin & Jones, 2007, pp. 10 & 12; Donnel Stern, 2003). In an infant-attuned attachment environment, social reactions reflecting the infant's internal states prime the development of their subjective sense and awareness (Gergely, 2007, p. 60). Critically, such matching, even at the young age of four months, portends a secure parent-child attachment relationship at one year (Beebe & Lachmann, 2014).

Remarkably, in one extended study of 84 mother-infant pairings, just 2.5 minutes of face-to-face interaction at four months predicted the trajectory of infant attachment patterns at one year (Beebe & Lachmann, 2014). "By 4 months infants are already 'dialogic,' entering into exquisitely sensitive reciprocal bi-directional exchanges with their social partners" (p. 139). These dialogical exchanges when analysed according to fine-grained, second-by-second, implicit procedural communication show revealing patterns of attention, emotion, orientation, and touch.

When infant – caregiver recognition is reciprocal (though not identical), it supports the health of the relationship. "While maternal behaviours may act to promote infant development, infant cues (e.g., suckling, auditory, and visual stimuli) may also stimulate maternal care, even modifying pre-existing behaviour patterns" (Strathearn, 2007, p. 121). For their part, mothers of secure infants are "more responsive, and 'sensitive,' more consistent and prompt in response to infant distress, more likely to hold their infants, less intrusive, and less tense and irritable, than mothers of insecure infants" (Beebe & Lachmann, 2014, p. 99). At the same time, secure infants are "more responsive in face-to-face play, better able to elicit responsive caretaking, more positive, and more able to express distress" (p. 99).

Myriad mitigating factors will influence the integrity of this caregiver-infant relationship, including: differences in temperament, socio-economic and environmental factors, reduced parental attention (as a result of, e.g., mother-infant separation, maternal depression, or substance abuse), and dysregulation in the baby, as in cases of extreme prematurity, illness, or birth defects (Strathearn, 2007, pp. 121–122). In other words, the caregiver – infant relationship is vulnerable to the vicissitudes of daily life in the contexts of a wider world – a reality that renders critical the social networks holding the primary caregiver's capacity to be present to the infant in relationship.

Affective contours

Caregivers rock, touch, soothe, talk, sing, and make noises and faces, most often in response to infant behaviours that are also mainly social, such as crying, fretting, smiling, grimacing, and gazing (Daniel Stern, 1985/2000, p. 43). These acts follow characteristic activation contours that speak to and with the infants own vital bodily states, doing so in degrees of comfort- and pleasure-inducing synchronies. The familiar and unfamiliar way things – like feeding, swaddling, and bathing – are done shape strong feelings and important representations, including a growing sense of intersubjective knowing and being known.

94 A dialectic theory of learning

According to Daniel Stern (2000), the infant subjectively experiences the parents' regulatory acts and the resulting altered self-states as a "small but coherent chunk of lived experiences" (p. 95) – a memorable aggregate of sensations clumped together with, and rendering valence to, "perceptions, actions, thoughts, affects, and goals" (p. 95). The recurrence of such episodes amalgamates in nonverbal memory into known ways-of-being-with another and thus acquire a prototypical character to the infant, the likes of: "This is what an episode of diaper changing feels like." Prototypical episodes are what permit the "indexing and reindexing and the organizing and reorganizing of memorial events about self-invariants (or other invariants) in a fluid and dynamic fashion . . . resulting in a growing and integrating network of organized self-experience" (pp. 98–99).

There are two consequences of these processes: They enable the emergent sense of major self-invariants of agency, coherence, and continuity (as figured in the model) to become swiftly and sufficiently integrated early in life. And since the episodic memories consist of sensations integrated into events with accompanying affect, cognitions, and/or actions, then it comes to pass that, for humans "*there are never emotions without a perceptual context. There are never cognitions without some affect fluctuations* [emphasis added]" (p. 95). This realisation alone calls for a theory of learning that attests to affect and intersubjectivity as always and everywhere critical in the intrapsychic embodiment of cognition – even if the things learned seem entirely removed from the personal.

Primary ways-of-being-with the other

Stern distinguishes, in the infant, three emerging ways-of-being-with the caregiver: *resonating-with* the other, the *other as self-regulating*, and oneself *in-the-presence-of* the other (Stern, 2000, pp. xii–xxiii). For the teacher as pedagogue who also cares for students, these same three modes of primary intersubjectivity underwrite and coexist with secondary intersubjective forms, and become critical capacities for monitoring classroom dynamics in inclusive ways (see Part III). Importantly, what was learned early is not left behind. Major developmental shifts in self experience are incorporated as revisions that elaborate and enrich the self-capacities that came before.

Beebe and Lachmann (2014) detail the bidirectional affective and attentional matching that Stern described as *self-resonating-with-another.* Mutual resonance and reciprocal understanding function according to a kind of interactive contingency of split-second co-ordinated shifts, outside conscious awareness. Each other's actions and affects are predictive of the other's. If the infant could speak, he might communicate the following:

> I can count on you to share my state, to go up with me as I get excited and happy, and to come down with me as I become sober or distressed. I can influence you to follow me and join me. I can count on you to "get" what I feel. I feel known by you. I know how your face goes, I know you. . . . I know I can influence you to touch me more tenderly when I need it.
>
> *(Beebe & Lachman, 2014, pp. 100 and 103)*

On the mother's side, a verbalised version might be as follows:

> I know that when I touch you more affectionately, you will look at me and smile more. I know that moving forward and looming in is hard for you, and you orient away. I know that when I move back, you come back to me.
>
> *(p. 103)*

The sense of a *self-regulating-other*, leans on the symmetry and complementarity of resonating symmetry, but is not itself symmetrical. It is for the parent to assist the baby with her self-regulation, not the other way around. The parent regulates the baby by sufficiently mirroring (see *affect attunement*) the baby's affect in ways responsive to the baby's cues and in a direction to acknowledge and appropriately moderate the baby. In this way, the infant develops a capacity for affective self-regulation. "In principle the dyadic relationship is symmetrical. . . . It is not symmetrical in practice" (Daniel Stern, 1985/2000, p. 119). It could not be, quite simply, because the parent brings a great deal more personal history into each experience.

The manner by which the caregiver serves in the capacity of self-regulating-other – to strongly influence "security, attachment, arousal, activation, pleasure, unpleasure, physiological gratification, self-esteem, and so on" (Daniel Stern, 2000, pp. xxii–xxiii) – have been long-studied. Classically, we see a style of exaggerated adult communication, including the "baby talk" (motherese) of repetition, simplified syntax, and raised pitch, accompanied by animated, fuller, facial expressions, at a focal distance approximating an ideal for the child (Leckman et al., 2007, p. 105; Daniel Stern, 1985/2000, pp. 72–73). These behaviours work to keep "the infant's level of arousal and excitation within a tolerable range" (p. 74). The secure infant responds in manner to regulate his own level of excitation by either averting his gaze or using gaze and facial behaviours to seek out and invite new or higher levels. For appropriate regulation, the parent notices and responds to maintain comfortable levels in the ebb and flow of infant excitation.

These forms of regulation are thought to take advantage of the various neurological capacities of mirror neurons and adaptive oscillators such that the parent's nervous system, in a sense, meets the infant's affective state where he is and then entrains affect in directions to maintain optimal states (Stern, 2000, p. xxi). Indeed, studies in attachment research have documented a parent's early capacity to "entrain the infant's biological rhythms . . . providing a 'resonance'. . . . of internal and external experience, self and other, brain and behaviour" (Leckman et al., 2007, p. 105). In providing "external support for the infant's developing bioregulatory abilities . . . [the attuned parent] convey[s] resilience to stress-coping capacities throughout life" (Leckman et al. 2007, p. 105).

In secure enough situations, infants profit from much practice, learning from and internalising the caregiver's function as a regulator of their levels of excitation (Stern, 1985/2000, p. 75). If all goes well, this early form of attunement will progress to lessons in cross-modal matching and affective mirroring as the caregiver establishes his subjectivity as a different centre of being, present as witnessing other to the toddler. Later yet, the child will profit from extended caregivers

96 A dialectic theory of learning

and teachers who, themselves secure enough, can visit these forms of attunement forward. Indeed, these very capacities can serve teachers well in interactions with students and classrooms where affect attunement is critical to reading and shaping the mood of the learning environment (Farmer, McAuliffe Lines, & Hamm, 2011).

Finally, and of further relevance to education, the physical proximity of a trusted caregiver (and pedagogue) is sufficient to, in a sense, guard over the solitude of an infant (or child) who is perceiving, thinking, or acting alone (p. xxiii). In terms of attachment, we could say that the presence of the parent, and later a teacher, as a "secure base" to forage out from and a "safe haven" to return to, as needed, is sufficient to enable independent action in learning. The comfort of physical proximity returns us to Winnicott's notion of the environment mother who creates the sense of a holding environment – a space that the mother gives the child, in trust, appropriately so, and without pressure, so as not to impinge on the child's own processes of self-becoming (Slochower, 2018).

Secondary intersubjectivity

In early life, affects have been "both the primary *medium* and the primary *subject* of communication" (Daniel Stern, 1985/2000, p. 133). What the infant poignantly experienced on the inside could not but be vividly expressed "on the outside." Though a parent might not have known the physiological cause, of say distress, she could recognise it and respond empathically. At the same time, physical dependency was clearly not bidirectional. When it came to burping, rocking, diaper changing, swaddling, bathing, and the like, the caregiver's responsibility was as "doer," while the infant was "done to." In primary intersubjectivity, the infant's experience of the primary caregiver is that person to be counted on, and turned to, as unquestioningly omnipotent and omniscient.

However, as infants begin to have a stronger sense, however nonverbal, of their own mind, they also can begin to appreciate that there is something in them, "in mind," that goes bewilderingly unrecognised and unacknowledged by the other.

> The concept that unifies intersubjective theories of self development is the need for recognition. A person comes to feel that "I am the doer who does, I am the author of my acts," by being with another person who recognizes her acts, her feelings, her intentions, her existence, her independence. Recognition is the essential response, the constant companion of assertion.
>
> *(Benjamin, 1988, p. 21)*

The awareness of difference, together with experiences of recognition (per Benjamin, just above), marks the dawning of a "theory of mind" that calls for intersubjective communication and the possibility that "what is going on in my mind may be similar enough to what is going on in your mind that we can somehow communicate this (without words)" (Stern, p. 124).

And so, while the period from roughly nine to eighteen months is concerned with the developmental tasks of independence, autonomy, and individuation, it is also increasingly attendant to dilemmas of difference and the exploration of a revised intersubjectivity that makes room for joint attention and intention – not only pointing to things in the world but also pointing to potentially shareable "things" "in mind" (Stern, 1985/2000, pp. 128–131). In the dawning of secondary intersubjectivity, these shifts find initial expression in two critical movements: from the entrainment to the attunement of affect and from dyadic to triadic relations. We explore each in turn.

Affect attunement: resonations of difference

The notion of affect attunement, coined by Daniel Stern (1985/2000), has come to connote two aspects of infant – caregiver interaction. In primary intersubjectivity, the caregiver matched the infant's affect in the *same* modality as the infant's. Now, in secondary intersubjectivity, matching is: no longer a faithful rendering, tending to be cross-modal, and imitative of a feeling state and not a behaviour (Daniel Stern, 1985/2000, pp. 141–142). Instances of affect attunement "concern *how* a behavior, *any* behavior, *all* behavior is performed, not *what* behavior is performed" (p. 157).

Whereas 4-month-old infants in secure relating with their mothers (viewed in split-second filming) match smiles that open up together (Beebe & Lachmann, 2014, pp. 8–11), a half-year later affect attunement is not so identical. For example, a 10-month-old girl who, pleased with something she has done, looks to her father with a facial expression that opens and closes in delight. Father's response is a verbal intonation of "Yeah" that shapes a prosodic contour matched to the child's facial-kinetic one (Stern, 1985/2000, pp. 140–141). We see a communion of "intensity, timing, and shape" of affect, but not of the act nor the medium of expression (p. 146). These "behaviors . . . recast the event and shift the focus of attention to what is behind the behavior, to the quality of feeling that is being shared. . . . *Imitation renders form; attunement renders feeling*" (italics added) (p. 142). Per Wittgenstein, "an 'inner process' stands in need of outward criteria" (in Carpendale & Lewis, 2006, p. 241).

In this way, psychic intimacy as well as physical intimacy become possible. What seems to be shareable or not turns on parental choice, mostly beyond conscious awareness, as to which affect (across the full spectrum of expressed vitalities) to attune. There will be untold selective biases that, in their acting out, "create a template for the infant's shareable interpersonal world" (p. 209). "What is ultimately at stake is nothing less than discovering what part of the private world of inner experience is shareable and what part falls outside the pale of commonly recognized human experiences" (Stern, 1985/2000, p. 126). In this way, "the parents' intersubjective responsivity. . . . desires, fears, prohibitions, and fantasies contour the psychic experiences of the child" (p. 208).

98 A dialectic theory of learning

> The communicative power of selective attunement reaches to almost all forms of experience. It determines which overt behaviors fall inside or outside the pale. . . . It includes preferences for people. . . . And it includes degrees or types of internal states that can occur with another person.
>
> *(Stern, 1985/2000, p. 208)*

Extending this work, Fonagy et al. (2007) studied social affect-mirroring where the caregiver, as pedagogue, matches *mimicked*-feeling to the child's *expressed*-feeling. Such mirroring is *contingent, marked*, and *containing*: contingent on the child's affect; marked as imitative and not the adult's real emotion; and containing because it renders the child's affect back in a manageable form – an idea borrowed from Bion (in Mitchell & Black, 1995/2016, pp. 102–106; Wallin, 2007, pp. 48–50).

Consider a 15-month-old boy who, biting into a balloon, finds it removed. Mother receives his disappointment, acknowledging it in facial mimicry and voice inflection, as if to say, "Aw you're sad. I understand." While attentive and concerned, she is not in the same way sad. She notes her son's situation, shows that she feels his affect, and then contains it in a way that encourages confidence that, while he may have influence over mom, he is not held to account for her actions. She is her own centre of being and he can count on her to have his mind in mind. His disappointment, after all, is neither catastrophic nor contagious.

Affect as a containing mock-up that respectfully, and oft-times playfully, though always seriously, acknowledges the child's emotion, returns it as understood and validated. "Contaminants" such as irony, humour, and scepticism are useful markers. They can balance the child's distress while flagging the emotion as "analogous, but not equivalent, to their experience" (Lachmann, 2008, p. 94). Without such contaminants, the caregiver's response might reinforce the child's heightened state. By mirroring the infant's expressed affect (i.e., not the behaviour) in the same feeling register (not cross-modally), but in a way explicitly marked as sympathetic imitation, the adult stops short of the communion of primary intersubjectivity (above). The difference frustrates the infant's "agency" to determine the parent, but in no way diminishes contingency. The infant learns to *expect* to be understood and, at the same time, gains the confidence of not being responsible for the adult's feeling state. *The infant's affect is not frighteningly contagious. And the possibility of a subject–other is born.*

In sum, we have two expressions of affect attunement in secondary intersubjectivity. In each, the caregiver affirms the infant's affect but is not swept away by it. Although the adult continues to acknowledge the child's affect, the manner of response conveys a much more sophisticated message: Where the response is in a different key – for example, matching a baby's crawling with a hand on the backside that jiggles in the same rhythm and intensity of the baby's actions – a caregiver's matched affective essence *communicates an understanding of interior feeling* as opposed to its outward presentation. On the other hand, a face-to-face response that, for example, mirrors the baby's exuberance but intentionally marks it as not belonging to the adult, announces *a different subjective experience – one that the baby can count on as containing.*

Importantly, in secondary subjectivity, we see a beginning separation of the attachment figure, but one that does not invoke desertion. To this effect, the contingency of attunement is "ideally" *just* good enough, in the sense of Winnicott's "good enough mother" (1971/2005). Affective re-renderings are not 100 per cent contingent on the child's emotional and cognitive states. Instead, the caregiver mitigates contingency to suit the child's emerging independence. In *just so* absences, given the reliable experience of the caregiver's reassuring and affirming return, the child develops a budding capacity for self-reliance. A recognising and moderating caregiver can thus promote "the integration of discrete, articulated emotions . . . [and] makes the having of feelings less anxiety producing . . . expand[ing] the 'window of affect tolerance'" (Benjamin, 2018, p. 80). If all goes well, across repeated scenarios, the child will begin to internalise these vital regulating functions such that, in later life, she can find the "parent-within" as calming internal-object.

In all of these subtle and critical ways, the secure child begins to develop a sense of her own mind both because of and in contention with a growing sense of both the other's sameness and difference. In the manner of Wittgenstein (earlier), the inner process of the baby becomes real by way of its outward expressed acknowledgement. If it can be shared, it returns as known. On the other hand (as will be explored in Chapter 8), if affective expressions are too often misattuned, or not rendered at all, then that can "undermine the [future] appropriate 'labelling' of internal states (i.e., the establishment of introspectively accessible second-order representations for them), which may, in turn, remain confusing, experienced as unsymbolised and hard to regulate" (Fonagy et al., 2007, p. 309). As teachers, there will be students in our classrooms who have had varying access to primary caregivers as calming internal-objects. In contrast to the currently popular "affect regulation" as a learnable technique, we will want to understand and respond to such students with a much deeper understanding in mind.

Secondary intersubjectivity recasts the mutuality of primary modes of relating into an unavoidable tension – a paradox really of the child needing the other's separate existence in order that there be someone to recognise her own. The push-pull struggles of the second year of life – to know and be known, to be confronted with another's difference yet to need that difference against which to know oneself, and to begin to do for oneself yet not quite be able or permitted to – all make of this both a precarious and exhilarating developmental period.

Triadic relations: introducing objects

In the first few months of life, infants orient to the perfect contingencies of self-generated events. Approaching three months and continuing until six, the high but imperfect contingencies of human interaction seem to have the strongest allure (Daniel Stern, 2000, p. xxi). During this period, infants enjoy a relatively intense and almost exclusive sociability with their caregivers. Thereafter, providing that physiological and affective states are in sufficient equilibrium, "an interest in inanimate

100 A dialectic theory of learning

objects sweeps the field" (Stern, 1985/2000, p. 72). As part of a growing repertoire of attentions, intentions, and actions, a tangible world of objects comes into view. Caregivers participate by enthusiastically encouraging and applauding agency, especially, locomotion, eating, eliminating, imitating sounds, and manipulating things.

With the advent of reachable objects, toward which and upon which an infant can act, an "it" world emerges somewhere between "I-you" experiences. Once there are objective "it" things, out there and in mind, then all known things, people, the self, and even the family dog, can be an "it" too. Knowing a parent is like knowing a thing. Both the parent and the rattle, for instance, have aspects of predictability. Indeed, for there to be an experience of familiarity with the rattle or the parent, there needs to have coalesced generalised memories of like experiences. Across time, the infant's mind has been busy shaping itself and consolidating working models to represent ways-of-being-with significant others. By the first birthday, the child will have developed robust internal-objects, steeped in histories of affective meaning, each with unique, pivotal status. There is at the same time likely to emerge a treasured proxy for those critical object-others – something, almost sacrosanct, that can serve, if only temporarily, in the occasional absences of caregivers. The familiar scent and texture of, say, a blanket or maybe a favourite stuffed animal can serve as external representation, providing soothing security somewhere transitional between the physical object and the mental object-other.

With the advent of objects in mind and an emergent imaginative capacity for make-believe, conflations will become a matter of course. Even inanimate things can take on animate qualities. The housecoat on the hook may become a moving phantom in the dark, just as the experienced world can be a destabilising affront to one's internal-object representations. For example, whereas, in the child's mind, the caregiver has known, is supposed to know, and therefore should know everything, the real parent might actually not know what the child has in mind – a situation most frustrating to the toddler!

We have seen how a pedagogy of affect attunement renders the child back to herself. Insofar as she sees herself in the parental mirror, then she is both subject and object of knowing. The interaction between self and reflected-self implies a budding "I-it" dyadic relation. The budding "it" world of conceptualised (pointed-to) physical objects portends perceiving self and others as objects too. In an "it" world, one can take an imaginative view of oneself from outside oneself, as object not only reflected in a physical mirror but also seen through the eyes of witnessing others. In the turnabout of a reflexive gaze from I to me, we see the rudiments of mentalisation's possibility, but also a capacity to "objectively" distance oneself from oneself and from one's emotions about oneself.

In brief, when objects enter dyadic relations they come in three capacities: as physical objects in the world, as object-others in mind, and the infant as object to herself. All known objects will exist as much in the world as in the mind. Critically, they will have entered the infant's experience in the context of, and through meanings imbued by, primary dyadic relations, and these are intersubjective. In this sense, *the object is known through the subject*. Across development, worldly things become increasingly infused into the shared relational space of child and caregiver. It is a space destined to swell, all the more in schooling, such that it comes to include all emerging conceptualisations, engulfing, as it were, those of the original dyads.

Physical objects

In contradistinction to the environment mother – in principle, unobstrusively guarding over the child's idiosyncratic being – Winnicott's object mother is responder and initiator. Yet as Bollas writes, "her 'provision' of an object – even a new one – will be felt by the infant to be a response to his desire or need, insofar as he lives for a few months within an illusion that those objects that show up ready for use do so as a result of his wishes" (Bollas on Winnicott, 1993, p. 403). That is, child – world interactions initially appear to be dyadic and not yet referential: child with other, child with object (Carpendale & Lewis, 2004, p. 84). In time, children "discover . . . [that] different patterns of activity are possible with people as compared to with objects" (Carpendale & Lewis, 2004, p. 87). Given the experience of people not always responding in predictable ways and given the occasional refusal to comply with the child's expectations or wants, "infants begin to regard people as independent 'centers of causality'" (Piaget, 1967/1971) (p. 87).

By the latter part of the first year, the infant is already embedded in triadic interactions between self, caregiver, and objects (Carpendale & Lewis, 2004). That said, acts of joint attention seem not to begin as such. Rather, the infant mimics parental action and vice versa such that, where the parent looks the child appears to look and where the child looks the parent looks. At this point the external object has not entered into the dyad. Beginning at about nine months, infants will follow an adult's gaze, but they do so without expectation or awareness of communicative intent (Carpendale & Lewis, 2004, p. 86). They are merely mimicking behaviour. The expectation of something to be learned or seen is, in effect, learned in the doing.

By twelve months, children's pointing is more likely to establish joint attention and enhance interaction; that is, they point when a parent is looking at them (Carpendale & Lewis, 2004, p. 86) or to an object over which they have no direct interest (Fonagy et al., 2007, pp. 292–293). Experiences of co-ordinated attention occur "before infants understand much about attention . . . The infant becomes embedded in interaction with some success and only through the experience develops a more complete understanding" (Carpendale & Lewis, 2004, p. 86). By fifteen months, the infant no longer simply points. He also checks that the caregiver is looking (Carpendale & Lewis, 2004, p. 86). There begins communicative intent, maturing by the second year, when acts of pointing, "eye direction information . . . [and] head turn[ing] achieve joint visual attention" (p. 86). An epistemic triangle of primary pedagogue, toddler, and worldly object is thus born (Carpendale & Lewis, 2006, pp. 236–237). Drawing on the connection of primary intersubjectivity, the caregiver increasingly assumes the role of interlocutor moderating "knowledge" to the child. Significantly, these objects include not only "things" in the world but

102 A dialectic theory of learning

also collections and classes of things – and not only these but also other beings and collections (and classes) of beings, especially the being that is the child mediated to herself (Carpendale & Lewis, 2006, pp. 236–237).

Csibra and Gergely describe what they designate a natural human pedagogy whereby children are predisposed "to learn, from trusted adults . . . the technological, social, conventional and institutional knowledge and skills that are necessary for survival in their culture" (Csibra & Gergely, 2011, p. 1105). In the first phase of the pedagogical moment, the caregiver alerts the child by enacting universal ostensive cues: eye contact with, for example, a raised eyebrow, a broadened gaze, wry smile, or an inflected voice that entices as it communicates, "Get ready. Watch what I'm about to show you." Then the caregiver directs the child's attention by singling out an object for knowing or by performing an act for mimicking. What is communicated is a way of perceiving, being with, and acting upon the world. Following ostensive cues, infants pay special attention to generalisable features of objects shown, infer intentions of actors in demonstrations, and take expressed preferences for certain elements to be qualities of those items. "These and other findings suggest that preverbal human infants are prepared to receive culturally relevant knowledge from benevolent adults who are, in turn, spontaneously inclined to provide it" (Csibra & Gergely, 2011, p. 1105)

Defended as a human-specific communicative pattern meant to "efficiently convey knowledge with opaque content to others in a single act of demonstration" this natural pedagogy succeeds

> not only because the recipient is prepared to recognise . . . [ensuing] actions as communicative demonstrations, but also because the addressee has the default expectation that the content of the demonstration represents shared cultural knowledge and is generalisable along some relevant dimension to other objects, other occasions or other individuals.
>
> *(Csibra & Gergely, 2011, p. 1105)*

Significantly, however, the success of such pedagogical moments depends on established relationships of trust between infant and caregiver. In such a relationship, ostensive cues "mark not only the possibility of physical security but also the likely veracity of information communicated by that individual" (Fonagy et al., 2007, p. 313). *Thus, the child turns to a trusted adult, not only for rendering a safe world but also for communicating a knowable one.*

Object– and subject–others

For at least the first year of life, the infant has been reality-tester extraordinaire (Daniel Stern, 1985/2000, pp. 11 & 42). Experiences have congealed into familiar templates against which to contrast variance and invariance, present and past, self and other. The forming and testing of hypotheses on sameness and difference has produced a rapidly categorised physical and social world. Assuming all has gone well, the

Becoming self **103**

baby enters the second year of life with fairly stable representations of interactions with others, things, and her own self. This is the point that Winnicott (1971/2005) makes when he writes, that the caregiver's "adaptation to the infant's needs, when good enough, gives the infant the *illusion* that there is an external reality that corresponds to the infant's own capacity to create" (p. 16).

Assuming the child's mental representations, formed of prior ways-of-being-with, have proven predictive enough of future ones, she has no reason to doubt their reliability. Too, from the beginning, the baby's significant others have had all the answers, been able to do anything, and have done *for* the infant what she could not do for herself. All of these "realities" are about to be challenged.

When a two-year-old insists "no" or bursts forth in a tantrum at a non-compliant parent, that child is contending with the reach of who she is and with conundrums like: If I think a thought and it happens, I must have caused it. I count on you to know me, to have my mind in mind. You are supposed to be, as I know you, in my head. The world I conceive falls apart when you are not. As Winnicott puts it,

> If the use of the [maternal] object by the baby builds up into anything . . .
> then there must be . . . an image of the object. But the mental representation
> in the inner world . . . is kept alive, by the reinforcement . . . of the external
> separated-off and actual mother.
>
> *(1971/2005, pp. 130–131)*

When that external separated-off actual mother (or caregiving other) behaves in ways unanticipated by the child's internal representations of her, there is cause for frustration. "The toddler is confronting the increased awareness of separateness and, consequently, of vulnerability" (Benjamin, 1988, p. 34). These significant others, who have applauded and encouraged his growing capacity to take matters into his own hands (and mouth), now behaviourally "move away" by restricting his newfound agency. All the while, the child's unruly, creative, and nimble neurons are metaphorically strapping experiences together. In a perfect storm, newer creative "mades" can be imagined, fantasised, and dreamt. It is becoming decidedly difficult for the child to discern between that which was given as real by the world and that which she can now make up to be real in her mind – especially since these two were once one and the same. What to do? Continued agency seems dependent on the child taking control of her adults.

In "Playing with reality," Fonagy and Target (1996, 2006), and Target and Fonagy (1996), introduce and theorise upon modes of psychological experience in the confusion between internal and external realities. The toddler, confronted with the "reality" of her own creative mind and the "reality" of the world, is caught in a beginning confusion of *psychic equivalence* – the belief that intrapsychic experiences are equivalent to external ones: "If I think something, then it must be real. And if I know it, then everyone must." To work these things out, the child uses a pretend space of bracketed reality where, for example, a special blanket (never to be washed) can afford security as transitionally both fantasy (caregiver) and reality (blanket). The

104 A dialectic theory of learning

transitional space and its objects, as per Winnicott (1971/2005) are critical to the creative working of learning about self and world. If all goes well, by the fourth year, a now-mentalising child has a twinkle in her eye when she knows something that someone else does not know. She plays with perspective and has a budding theory of other minds as different from hers. She can begin to account for and hold those other minds in mind – a capacity to be developed across a lifetime. But, for now, our toddler begins and must contend with psychic equivalence.

Imagine that toddler in a state of anger because her dad, the real one "outside her head," is not complying with her idea of him. Maybe that idea is someone supposed to applaud her newfound skill of pulling electric cords out of outlets. She is frustrated, *disillusioned*, with the way he is not conforming to the image, the *illusion*, she has of him. In a tantrum, she strikes out to destroy his different existence "out there in the world." She does this, almost desperately, in the name of preserving the world she knows and her own budding independence. Critical to her psychic well-being, the illusion, upon which she insists, must be the thing to suffer disillusionment. And it is the real father, the one in the world, who must survive destruction. He will need to hold his ground in a way that sidesteps the power struggle, and that also recognises the child, without retaliating or withdrawing. Only in this way can he continue to emerge as not some*thing*, but some*one*, a subject, beyond and exceeding the object in his child's head. She will need the strength of his survival, as enigmatically separate, never fully knowable, yet trustworthy other.

As teachers, we will want to better understand psychic survival during this developmental phase – that we might appreciate the dilemmas of those students we teach. We will want to understand what it might mean for a parent to survive or to conversely retaliate or withdraw (see especially Benjamin, 1988, pp. 31–36; 2018, pp. 71–90) – that we as teachers better appreciate our students and their parents, and so that we can be present to students who call forth re-enactments of all-too-familiar struggles transferred to the classroom. For surely, the crisis for the child is also a crisis for the caregiver.

> What the mother feels during rapprochement and how she works this out will be colored by her ability to deal straightforwardly with aggression and dependence, her sense of herself as entitled to a separate existence, and her confidence in her child's wholeness and ability to survive conflict, loss, and imperfection.
>
> *(Benjamin, 1988, p. 35)*

Benjamin (1988, 1995), following Winnicott, describes, on the one hand, a mother who might be characteristically intolerant of the child's emerging independence. Such a parent might retaliate in response to the child's self-assertion. In social affect-mirroring, she would not typically acknowledge or value the child's affect. Her returned expression might be one of dismissiveness or outright anger. Either way, the child would not encounter his reflection mirrored to him, only the imposition of a parent's will, denying that of the child's. If the pattern is one of being locked

Becoming self **105**

into an unpredictable doer/done-to complementarity where ultimately only one can survive, it will be the parent's omnipotence who will "win." And the win will be, of course, a loss for both. For the child, the price for parental approval and protection can be compliance, a forfeiting of agency, and a frightful vigilance of the parent's affect.

On the other hand, again as developed by Benjamin (1988, 1995), were the mother to withdraw and submit to the child's will, the converse (in principle) plays out. By submission, the mother enacts a self-obliteration as permissive parent who dares not set boundaries. In this scenario, the child retains omnipotence and the mother becomes his extension. He finds neither subjective difference nor reassuring containment in her eyes. That which is mirrored is too thoroughly saturated with his own affect for there to be any room for her difference as subject–other. Instead, he is in charge of her. As extension of himself, he is left without an other, empty and alone. The price of his power is disconnection and a desperate vigilance over keeping control.

> In both cases the sense of omnipotence survives, projected onto the other or assumed by the self; in neither case can we say that the other is recognized, or, more modestly (given the child's age), that the process of recognition has begun.
>
> *(Benjamin, 1988, p. 36)*

This drama of destruction and survival, beginning in rapprochement, will play out across many micro-moments of interaction – each episode, if all goes well enough, re-inaugurating the caregiver as a real subject–other, present to witness the child as a subject. It will take each subject's survival to recover an intersubjectivity that is mutual. Relapses, into and out of connection, disruption and repair, will be common. "Repair" teaches us to expect reconnection, trust its arrival, and recognise its departure. The lesson, *this lesson*, is critical too for teachers. The classroom and its individuals, like the child in rapprochement will vie for authority (to depend or be independent) and the teacher will need to likewise survive, without retaliating or withdrawing. She will want the capacity to sidestep the power struggle – to enable the preservation of dignity of both parties by "surrendering" into a position of *being-with* (as opposed to submitting or forcing submission, to one or the other side of doer or done-to) – and in the being and doing, teach that disruptive disconnection is the means to revitalising reconnection.

As Winnicott put it, "[T]his matter of illusion [and disillusionment] is one that belongs inherently to human beings and that no individual finally solves for himself or herself" (1971/2005, p. 17). What is at stake is nothing less than, paradoxical individuation-through-belonging and belonging-through-individuation, as the unavoidable human condition of singular-plural-being (Nancy, 1996/2000). Benjamin, drawing from Hegel, summarises the point: "The need for recognition entails this fundamental paradox: *at the very moment of realizing our own independence, we are dependent on another to recognize it* [italics added]" (Benjamin, 1988, p. 33).

106 A dialectic theory of learning

Symbols for objects

A great deal changes with the introduction of language. What happens to affective meaning and intersubjectivity as a person's lexicon evolves from the matching of affective contours in early life, to the sophisticated abstractions of symbol systems that give rise to objectifying distance? That is, in the developmental shift from affective resonance, through gesture and gestural tracings (as in dance, art, and diagram; see de Freitas & Sinclair, 2012) to symbolic specificity, where do affective meanings go? Do they remain remembered by the body but unnameable by the conscious mind or are they reserved for and funnelled into only the most intimate, and vulnerable, of encounters?

Language's origins run deep into early affective conversations, connected there through imitation, analogue, and metaphor (Daniel Stern, 1985/2000, p. 161). "There is a word available nearly always when the concept has matured" (Tolstoy in Vygotsky, 1934/1986, p. 8). Through affectively meaningful language, the spontaneous knowing of children moves from word to thought and, in pedagogical encounters, meets the abstract nonspontaneous knowledge of generation's past. The learning of a language is also powerfully about learning "how to do things with words" (Austin, in Bruner, 1990, pp. 70–71). At the same time, language limits and constrains what can be done. The picture worth a thousand words comes into view through the conceptual lens of world-defining, symbol systems, even as particular elements of being elude their very translation into words. In the "slippage between personal world knowledge and official or socialized world knowledge as encoded in language. . . . reality and fantasy can begin to diverge" (Daniel Stern, 1985/2000, p. 178). As language's documentable specificity comes to trump difficult-to-capture affective experience, a false objectivity can cast its negating shadow over the visceral, leaving us out of touch with our unconscious intersubjective beginnings and the very meanings that drive us in the first place.

> What is said and what is meant have a complicated relationship in the interpersonal domain. . . . When two messages, usually verbal and nonverbal, clash in the extreme . . . [i]t is usually the case that the nonverbal message is the one that is meant, and the verbal message is the one of "record." The "on-record" message is the one we are officially accountable for.
>
> *(Daniel Stern, p. 181)*

Yet if neuroscientific studies are any indication, it would seem that affect underpins all reason. Quite literally, individuals "who have lost the capacity to be emotionally engaged cannot reason appropriately about social and moral issues. That is they cannot choose appropriate ends for themselves and cannot carry out the means to those ends" (as per Damasio, in Lakoff & Johnson, 1999, p. 514). Contrary to how things feel, reason is "not disembodied. . . . mostly unconscious. . . . largely metaphorical and imaginative. . . . [and] emotionally engaged" (p. 4). Multiple research paradigms converge on the point that "we can only form concepts through the body. . . . [and]

because our ideas are framed in terms of our unconscious embodied conceptual systems, truth and knowledge depend on embodied understanding" (p. 555).

Braiding human imitative proclivities into linguistic expression – from inherited mirror neurons (as biological gateway into metaphorically attuned affect) to inherited words (as social gateway into fully symbolic language) – there is the common fabric of gesture. George Herbert Mead writes, "The field of the operation of gestures is the field within which the rise and development of human intelligence has taken place" (1934/2015, pp. 13–14, n. 9). Language is an "implement" to pick out and organise the contents of experiences that once preceded words (Mead, p. 13).

From gestures to words, language, and conscious thought

Protolinguistic patterns of communication develop into "conversations of gestures" not unlike Mead's example of two dogs meeting with "each dog adjusting the mood and acts of the other" (1934/2015, pp. 42–43). To use words and be understood requires that there *first* be sufficient agreement over meaning. If the gesture signals intention, then its meaning derives from its capacity to call out the response of the other (Mead, p. 146). Once we have words and structure, we can use them to layer meaning upon meaning – and/or to distance meaning from abstracted thought.

In a rudimentary way, this is the case for many non-humans as well. My dog has effectively taught me that the message of my sigh, after several hours at the computer, has come to mean ensuing attention. Hearing that sigh triggers her immediate joy and excitement as she bounds into my office. Similarly, the word ball, to her and therefore between us, means a game of fetch. Now that we have this language, I have to be careful when using it, so as not to mislead and therefore disappoint. In like manner, if every time a baby cries, the parent's response is to soothe with a feeding, then has the parent taught, and might the infant internalise, that the meaning of distress is the need to eat?

A communicating gesture both directs another's attention and has a dynamic affective contour. One can point enthusiastically or distractedly. Emotion is present even when affective vitality appears flat – flatness being a quality of affect. Gestures – classically facial, but all gestures – express affect. In the same way that we "do not sense the quality of the air, a particular scent, or a certain sound if they are present all the time" (Marton, 2014, p. xi), in the move from gesture to symbol, the very familiarity of affect may not be consciously discerned even though it underwrites our very thoughts. Words, as shorthand for gestural communication, thus embody affect. "The emergence and evolution of a symbol is tied to actions of adaptation, which in turn are immersed in a context of somatosensory experiences, salience, and perceptually guided actions" (Klin & Jones, 2007, p. 37). The symbol serves as proxy for these elements of action. Thus, *"when we uphold and manipulate symbols in our mind . . . we are also evoking a network of experiences resulting from a life history of actions associated with that symbol"* (italics added, Klin & Jones, 2007, p. 37).

Mead's idea that the meaning of a gesture is in the response of the other, applies to the second aspect of communication, that of pointing attention in acts that evolve, as

108 A dialectic theory of learning

we have seen, out of mimicry. The move from dyadic to triadic relations is troubled by the reliability of directing the mental intentionality of another. Words, as simple as ball and mother, come with myriad associations that elicit affective resonances unique to individuals.

Thus, common generalisable definitions – necessary if we are going to have any symbolic communication at all – strip words from experience. Still, symbolic meaning remains the crucible of conscious thought itself. We realise unthought knowns through their articulation into words. We think as though we are communicating *to* someone. When you or I are saying anything, we are saying to ourselves what we say to others; otherwise we cannot know what we are talking about (Mead, 1934/2015, p. 147).

> The same procedure which is responsible for the genesis and existence of mind or consciousness – namely, *the taking of the attitude of the other toward one's self*, or toward one's own behavior – also necessarily involves the genesis and existence at the same time of significant symbols, or significant gestures.
> *(emphasis added pp. 47–48)*

The bifurcating force of the symbolic: the accountable and the deniable in experience

Language comes as a gift, "potent in the service of union and togetherness" (Stern, 1985/2000, p. 172). Yet on the necessity of universality, language "divides experience into the accountable and the deniable" (p. 181). As I write, I am both constrained and enabled by the universality of symbols.

As gesture mutates to words, groups of words, and a hierarchy of communicable thought, in increasing symbolic representation, distancing abstraction threatens to "override" affective roots – that is, in qualified ways: Language develops according to categories and the generalised episode – not everyday nuanced exception (Stern, p. 179). In the life-world of the toddler, words best communicate, not memorable episodes, but protypical averages (Daniel Stern, 1985/2000, pp. 174–182). The child who repeatedly says, "eat," has in mind something specific. The caregiver may go through several items before arriving at the cookie the infant intended.

In service of union, for instance, a mother's intonation when marking a word does not simply raise "the infant's attention nonspecifically; she is imbuing one particular word with human magic by making it a person-thing for the moment" (Stern, 1985/2000, p. 122, n. 8). The person-thing is a personified object imbued with temporary value insofar as it recalls an episodic memory of its interactive use. It resonates according to the idea that, "We played with this and now it means more, that is, for a while, until I lose interest." As the child matures, words take on even more critical value as gifts, in a sense, points of connection between the caregiver's world and the child's. Like security blankets, words belong to both the child's imagination and the world of real things. Words open the door to cultural objects to be explored, played with, and through which to foster new forms of connection and belonging.

> The word is given to the infant from the outside, by mother, but there exists a thought for it to be given to. In this sense *the word, as a transitional phenomenon, does not truly belong to the self, nor does it truly belong to the other.* It occupies a midway position between the infant's subjectivity and the mother's objectivity. . . . It is this deeper sense that language is a union experience.
>
> *(italics added, Stern, 1985/2000, p. 172)*

Yet language can serve symbolic distance. Unique and specific episodes do not lend themselves well to wording. Dimensional, gradient, and analogue features of experience are ill-suited to verbalisation. In the "slippage between experience and words" (p. 181) we lose the "ineluctable" (p. 182) and the ineffable sense of, for example, the connection one feels in a mutual gaze into another's eyes, the play of a patch of sunlight, and the surprise experience of tasting sour milk. The inability to word these well can distance personal communicable knowing from lived experience. And oddly, when we do try to communicate deeply felt experiences, words generally fail us, leaving a lingering sense of inadequacy and loss. Better, it would seem, to turn to the arts, and if one is fortunate, the intimate presence of someone with whom to quietly feel.

With language, the magical door to conscious cognition, shared cultural objects, and mentalisation opens. Meanwhile, another door – the one depended upon for affective meaning, intrapsychic awareness, and intersubjective connection – slips into increasing obscurity. As language enables new forms of communication it also creates its shadow side of things uncommunicable and therefore deniable. The teacher who speaks kind words to a student but in a tone saturated with contempt, will be held accountable for the words and not the tone. On this point, it is well worth quoting Stern at length.

> One of the consequences of this inevitable division into the accountable and the deniable is that what is deniable to others becomes more and more deniable to oneself. The path into the unconscious . . . is being well laid by language. Prior to language, all of one's behaviors have equal status as far as "ownership" is concerned. With the advent of language, some behaviors now have a privileged status with regard to one having to own [up to] them. The many messages in many channels are being fragmented by language into a hierarchy of accountability/deniability.
>
> *(1985/2000, p. 181)*

Over the course of 30 years in education, I have witnessed teachers increasingly called to document their daily interactions with students. A compelling paper trail has become the mandate for any sort of action – or defence. Only categorical information, nothing interpretive, can qualify in such accounts. This is the world of

110 A dialectic theory of learning

mistrust seeping into schooling and underwriting contexts where legislated control is given to ensure order. This becomes a world of choosing sides as doer or done-to. It is the world we turn to when intersubjective connection erodes.

The collection of these effects seems to prod an evolution in the use of language. Whereas words seem to initially function as proxies for things (including the self), their usage recalls originary affective meanings given by the other, even as their experience is to "it-ify" the thing named. Thus, their apparent objective usage renders affective meanings and associations out-of-(conscious)-mind. The things they purport to signify (for which they are proxy) and the things they do signify (their value, rendered intersubjectively) are not the same. They become a means for reifying conceptions into perceptions (as in projection), even as they relegate beings into things. By overlaying the symbolic atop experience, words also reify perception into conception to create objects – and then the words become themselves the objects.

In narrative capacity, creativity

The arrival of words at roughly 18 months, bourgeons into narrative capacity at about 36 months. Atop life-as-experienced, comes life-as-storied – typically co-constructed with others (parents and siblings) and making its way into official family lore (Stern, 2000). Accompanying life as accountable and re-countable, language also gives force to a new kind of experience: A life of fantasy, magic, and illusion.

> How much the act of making an autobiographical narrative reflects or necessarily alters the lived experiences that become the personal story is an open question. . . . With the advent of language and symbolic thinking, children now have the tools to distort and transcend reality. . . . for good or ill.
>
> *(Daniel Stern, 1985/2000, p. 182)*

With its privileged status and its facilitation of thought, language changes everything. It downplays the *lived* experience in favour of the *represented* one, even as it reshapes that which is *real and lived*. It struggles to grasp the richness of a present moment, the subjective experience that we encounter of a piece (as in the Greek term for the opportune moment, *kairos*). Taken to mathematics and the sciences, symbol systems come to prioritise metronomic chronos, a more objective, sanitised view of time, as the sequencing of infinitely small points, each fleeting, accessible only in hindsight, but adjoined as if to "live the lie" of the conceptual continuity of experience (Stern, 2004).

For good, language opens entirely new vistas: For the first time, children can share personal experiences with others and play at reality. The imaginative capacity of words makes it possible to extract and reorder bits of the real to see how they might fit, importantly without a judging presence. This play happens absent a preconceived plan. It is more an emerging path of connecting thoughts laid in walking – a bit like the experience of losing one's keys or forgetting a name: Once the mind loosens its conscious search, the freed-capacity-within works the sought-after

Becoming self **111**

memory into awareness. In the same way, creative spaces, free of the urgency to know, allow for sense to come on its own time.

We arrive, yet again, to Winnicott's transitional space, as a kind of holding environment, this time languaged, between a given intersubjective world of shareable reality and a made inner world of intrapsychic creation. The learner will want to indulge the experience of kairos in both centrifugal and centripetal moments; that is, in the courage and excitement to inquire anew, to experience "as if" for the first time, to risk the construals one has made against a possibly disillusioning world, and then to dare conjoin the ambiguous into newly conceived revisions on sense.

Teachers as mentors and cultural interlocutors across an expanse of 12-plus years of near-daily schooling are uniquely positioned to affect the lives of many. How learning proceeds and what a pedagogue might do to both provoke and support it, in counterbalancing measure, are the subjects of Part III. Teachers will want to appreciate the foregoing developmental and relational concepts as they introduce curricular objects into the classroom space. They will want the recursive movement of learning, to be neither too fast nor too slow, neither too sweeping nor too constricted, and conceived in terms fitted to the learner's needs, experiences, and tolerable possibilities. In short, we are talking about a pedagogical capacity for affective reading and attunement to what meanings a learner or a community of learners bring to the classroom and what they can dare, alone and in community.

Let me close with a brief summary of takeaway items, infused with provocation and implication for teaching. These we will revisit in Part III.

1 Teachers and their students arrive, all, with different attachment histories and degrees of security such that techniques in "classroom management" and "behavioural supports" are hardly what makes the difference in creating inclusive schooling spaces.

2 Early relationships condition ways of relating in later ones. Just as relational understandings help parents, and developmental understandings help psychoanalytic work, so too can classroom practice benefit from a beginning appreciation of the relational implications of development that play out in the pedagogical relations of teaching and learning.

3 Attunement involving affect mirroring that is contingent to the mood of the classroom and its individuals, marked with useful contaminants, such as irony, humour, and scepticism, and containing the affect of the room, all, are useful understandings to carry teachers forward.

4 Like Winnicott's environment mother who supports the play of objects in mind and Winnicott's object mother who provokes disillusionment by insisting on an external world and other, the teacher can think of the classroom space as a type of holding environment into which she infuses curriculum.

5 Students know their learning selves through the eyes of a pedagogical witness. To be a witness, requires presence as a recognised and recognising centre of being.

6 Just as infant-centred parenting, when it becomes self-effacing, does a disservice to the rapprochement–child by denying the opportunity of a recognising

112 A dialectic theory of learning

disillusioning other, so too might learner-centred education contribute to the difficulties presenting as entitlement and anxiety in learners.

7 Words and objects are imbued with affective meanings and, for their resistance to linguistic formulation, these embodied meanings are largely unconscious.

8 The move to language and the symbolic splits experience into that which is accountable and that which is deniable. Insofar as symbol usage effectuates a distancing remove from subjective experience, it feigns neutrality and strips away meaning.

9 Meaningful sense-making occurs in a transitional space of playing with reality.

10 Teachers, *in loco parentis*, are interlocutors between the world out there and the one in the minds of students.

11 Curricular objects fall into the class of cultural objects and are transitional phenomenon, created in and through language, and grappled with in a space somewhere between individual intrapsychic worlds and a shared intersubjective one.

With these consideration at the ready, especially for their uptake in Part III, we now turn to Chapter 7 and the theories of learning that have influenced pedagogical practice from early twentieth-century schooling to the present moment. I position the present theory as continuous with this trajectory.

7

THEORISING LEARNING

Philosophies, understandings, and perspectives over the years

A theory of how people learn implicates a definition of what it means to know. On the question of knowledge, I take a pragmatic perspective that "drops the notion of truth as correspondence with reality altogether" (Rorty in von Glasersfeld, 1989, p. 3). On pragmatic terms, even modern science has no privileged access to reality. It "does not enable us to cope because it corresponds, it just enables us to cope" (p. 3). Accepting that the world we experience is the only reality to which we humans have access, scientific or humanistic, then anyone's learning becomes *an interpretive act of taking impressions from the given world-of-one's-experience and assuming those impressions into self-revisions* – per one's knowing of that world, with that world, and of oneself as partially comprising it.

Moreover, we generally conceive of learning as adaptive – but on whose terms? *In principle and in the spirit self-enhancement* vis-à-vis *the world-as-understood, an individual undertakes the self-revisions of learning so as to bolster self-viability and vitality with/in the world*. From the side of the collective, *such revisions are also judged according to the perceived enhancement they confer to individual and collective function, and to the ongoing viability and vitality of the larger system.* The very questions of curriculum and what counts in and as learning entangle in these interpretations. The self (or other), who names any such revisions learning, endorses them as having been adaptive, either on the individual's terms and/or in terms of an expectant world.

Acknowledging that "no subject is its own point of departure" (Butler, 1992, p. 9), the self and the understandings any person might make cannot be divested from what the world, literally, makes (and has made) of that person and from what his or her very existence reflexively contributes (and has contributed) to composing the world. We fashion ourselves in answer to and in degrees of accordance with a world that pre-emptively constitutes us, a unique world of our lived experience, and our own evolving perception of, and being in, that world. This adaptive self-making is learning in its broadest sense, though not always in the sense of any or every observer.

114 A dialectic theory of learning

Both individual/singular and collective/plural learning entangle in these fundamental paradoxes at the centre of Jean-Luc Nancy's singular-plural-being (1996/2000) and articulated by Butler (1992, 2005): that though I might experience myself as the agent of my own being, I clearly did not "preside over the positions that . . . constituted me. . . . The 'I' who would select between them is always already constituted by them" (1992, p. 9). We assume our histories and contexts (in all the meanings of "assume"). They constitute us, reinstalling themselves uniquely through us, individually and collectively. Following Piaget and Vygotsky (per Lourenço, 2012), we are as much singular autonomous beings as we are plural heteronomous ones.

Piaget and Vygotsky

Singular autonomous yet plural heteronomous being

Piaget and Vygotsky (both né 1896, Piaget outliving Vygotsky by a near half century) underwrite that which is pervasive, monumental, and voluminous in educational and developmental psychology today. Both recognise the continuous interaction of individual and socio-cultural development, yet both concentrate on one at the expense of the other (Glassman, 1994, p. 212). Whereas Piaget orients to an autonomous subject confronting a physical and social world, Vygostky "appeals almost always to a heteronomous individual . . . [whose] development depends heavily on . . . existing diverse social structures" (Lourençon, 2012, p. 284). That is, "contrary to Vygotsky's (1978) thinking, Piaget (1965) valued mutual respect, autonomy, and social relationships *among* equal *peers* more than unilateral respect, heteronomy, and authority-based relationships" (italics added) (2012, p. 284).

Twenty years ago, Schoenfeld (1999) lamented the absence of good theoretical candidates for unravelling the nature of the learning process. The situation has not much changed. Theorists attribute the problem to a cognitive/social split and the fundamental incompatibility of a Piagetian cognitive theory that positions "the individual as meaning-maker" and a Vygotskian socially grounded theory with "meaning as first sociocultural" (Lerman, 1996, p. 147). Glassman (1994) describes "the combination of ontological [individual] development and cultural development into a single developmental paradigm" as "a daunting task . . . easier said than done" (p. 212). I believe the task is doable, providing "affect" as the missing connective thread and relational psychoanalysis as that thread's weaver.

In this chapter, I follow the perspectives on learning and development through the twentieth century and into the present day. I intend a sufficient, though hardly exhaustive, rendering. My goal is more and less modest: to consider how a relationally informed theory might offer a coherence that follows from and enfolds the various understandings accrued for over a century of philosophical study and empirical research in learning. Indeed, the history of learning theories, with all their shifts, paradigmatic and not – as per Kuhn's periods of normal and revolutionary science (1962/1996) – is, I submit, an exemplar of the process of learning itself; that is, insofar as we admit that societies and schools of thought, as dynamic adaptive forms, do learn.

On spontaneous knowledge and nonspontaneous concept development

Both Vygotsky and Piaget studied children's development from spontaneously conceived structures/schema to the nonspontaneous concepts of higher learning (Piaget, 1962/2000; Vygotsky, 1934/1986). Whereas Piaget stressed the quantity of everyday knowledge and the contributions of peer interactions, Vygotsky stressed the quality of conscious thought and concentrated on child–teacher interactions (Glassman, 1994, p. 206). Both emphasised physical experience and experimentation but in different contexts: as independently conceived among peers, for Piaget, and as intentionally learned with knowledgeable adults, for Vygotsky.

It took a half-century before Vygotsky's works would be translated to English and find Western audiences. Until then, "no theory . . . had greater impact on developmental psychology than that of Jean Piaget" (Lourenço & Machado, 1996, p. 143). His meticulous mapping of children's spontaneous conceptual understanding across the various ages and stages of development continues to be refined and revised in neo-Piagetian work today (see especially Case, 1987). Piaget seeded the field for constructivist principles when he posited learning as a process of *equilibration* whereby the learner *assimilates* new ideas into existing conceptual *schema* and adaptively *accommodates* changes in those schema as needed (Piaget, 1967/1971). Critiquing Piagetian constructivism, Vygotsky would layer vital socio-cultural principles, figuring them central to learning from knowledgeable others.

Both Piaget and Vygotsky were interested in the new intelligence tests of the early twentieth century (Gredler, 2012). Whereas Piaget (1967/1971) charted children's unmediated knowledge, Vygotsky (1934/1986) asked what children might arrive at knowing, if given appropriate prompts. That is, seeing IQ as a dynamic function, Vygotsky posited a region between what a child already knew and what that child could readily grasp if given opportunity. In principle, this *zone of proximal development* (ZPD) represented the child's functional learning capacity in any given context (Vygotsky, 1934/1986, pp. 186–196).

Jerome Bruner introduced the notion of *folk psychology* as "a culture's account of what makes human beings tick" (Bruner, 1990, p. 13). In Vygotskyan terms, Bruner's folk psychology could be interpreted as the spontaneous knowledge of a culture. For teachers-as-learners, ZPD names the distance between a folk psychology of popular, peer-supported spontaneous knowledge for teaching and what teachers might learn in the presence of knowledgeable mentors working in regions within teacher's grasp. Else practice resists change (Coburn, 2004; Kennedy, 2005; Opfer & Pedder, 2011) and teachers become better skilled at fitting to emergent circumstances the very folk psychologies / spontaneous knowledge with which they entered teaching. Even in collaboration with peers, practice makes but practice (Britzman, 2003).

116 A dialectic theory of learning

Vygotsky in the twenty-first century

One cannot but be struck by the foresight of Vygotsky's work. Writing 85 years ago, his descriptions of concepts and systems of concepts as networked, hierarchical structures, with a "systematization based on the relations of generality between [subsidiary] concepts" (Vygotsky, 1934/1986, p. 174) are stunningly prescient of today's *non-linear dynamic systems theory* (complexity science) in education (e.g., Davis & Renert, 2014; Davis & Sumara, 2006). When Vygotsky writes that "the process of concept formation . . . seen in all its complexity, . . . appears as a *movement* of thought within the pyramid of concepts, constantly alternating between two directions: from the particular to the general, and from the general to the particular" (1934/1986, pp. 142–143) – or in today's terms bottom-up and top-down – he invests conceptual thought with the twenty-first-century idea of fractal-like nested structures of networks of networks.

Vygotsky's prescience includes a deep appreciation of language and mind in culture. He anticipates Bruner's call for cultural psychology (1990, pp. 12–30) together with twenty-first-century developmental theory and psychoanalytic understanding of mind (as per Chapter 6) writing, "thought is not merely expressed in words; it comes into existence through them" (1934/1986, p. 218). He charts the increased abstraction of word use and meaning from social encounters, through private speech, to inner speech, mental thought, and written discourse (pp. 210–256). He writes of how sophisticated language marks and moves the evolution of interpretation, and how a personalised lexicon emerges and gives meaning to the categories of things that words and clusters of words come to evoke. Finally, his "principle of the relations of generality" anticipates variation theory (see also Chapter 11), especially in his dealings with words as generalisations on categorical concepts (e.g., flower and furniture being a generalisation above rose and chair). He infuses this understanding of language into his study of conceptual development whereby children learn to discern the features that make a category a category – an evolution from clusters of happenstance congeries, to loosely and/or inconsistently connected complexes, through pseudoconcepts, to concepts proper (pp. 110–119).

If ever there were the beginnings of a coherence across theories of learning, that potential lies in Vygotsky's work. Consider a small snippet:

> One must turn from a study of concepts as isolated entities to a study of the "fabric" made of concepts. . . . [T]he connections between concepts are neither associative nor structural . . . but are based on the *principle of the relations of generality*. Really productive thought is based on "insight." . . . [T]o transfer an object or thought from structure A to structure B, one must transcend the given structural bonds, and this, as our studies show, requires shifting to a plane of greater generality, to a concept subsuming and governing both A and B. . . . [T]he *absence of a system* is the cardinal psychological difference distinguishing spontaneous from scientific [nonspontaneous] concepts.
>
> *(1934/1986, pp. 204–205)*

Yet when it comes to theories of learning to guide education, in the absence of a coherence derived of connection across theoretical concepts in a given plane (per Vygotsky, above), the teacher-perceiver is at a loss to develop a functionally dynamic understanding that can nimbly work from general to particular and back again, connecting across the pyramid of concepts, principles, and theories in teaching. Instead, each concept, principle, or theory seems confined within a like cluster such that, for example, the teacher draws from the educational psychology textbook's behavioural chapter to organise rewards for students, the emotions chapter to help students in their affect regulation, the cognition chapter to have a sense of what might be theoretically appropriate for students to learn (although mandated programs seem to pre-empt such decision-making), and the instructional strategies chapter (together with online sources) for lesson ideas – all the while drawing on folk psychology as governing principle in the near relations of classroom life. This is the state of education today.

A search for theories of learning returns two genres: *compendial collections* and *historical narratives*. Compendial collections tend to see a practical place for each historically conceived theory. Explicitly designed for teachers, these works present a manifold field commensurable to folk psychology, socio-political agenda, and cultural expectation. In contrast, historical narratives, less explicit about practical application, trace the thread of ideas as theories evolve and societies change. The assumed arrow of time typically goes to progressively getting theory right. Neither are these accounts immune to personal desires, socio-political agendas, and cultural expectations.

Compendial collections about learning theories

L'embarrass du choix

In any professional program in education, prospective teachers will take at least one survey course in learning theories. The course will be supported by any one of a plethora of introductory texts on the market today – each one a quintessential compendium of psychological perspectives on learning, updated over the years with qualifying critiques on former views and incorporating those trends finding new traction in ivory towers. Any mention of psychoanalysis will be an anomaly – little more than a nod to Freud (Shedler, 2010; Park & Auchincloss, 2006; Redmond & Shulman, 2008). These courses typically emphasise the practical implications of educational learning theory, purportedly translated into research-informed technique. All the while, "there is little in any pedagogy that is either wholly necessitated or wholly ruled out by . . . any learning theory" (Ernest, 2006, p. 6). The state of affairs, thus described, seemed the case when I began teaching in 1978. It still applies today.

Yet surely an understanding of learning ought to speak to schooling and teaching practice. I believe that the theory I propose does; that is, if not misconstrued as technique. Insofar as theories of learning remain reductionist, piecemeal, and

118 A dialectic theory of learning

undiscerning of their socio-political entanglements, then the strange disparity between conversations about learning and conversations about teaching will continue. There is simply too much disconnection and too-eager slippage from *emphases that are foregrounded by, but do not follow logically from, theories* (Ernest, 2006, p. 6) to *practices reflecting the current socio-cultural* zeitgeist *on a trajectory of historico-political will.*

An online search of learning theories returns perspectives, models, and paradigms, sometimes counting over a hundred at any one site (e.g., www.learning-theories. com & www.brookes.ac.uk/services/ocsld/resources/theories.html). Acknowledging that "it is easier to assimilate a thousand new facts in any field than to assimilate a new point of view of a few already known facts" (Vygotsky, cited in Gredler, 2012, p. 128), there is a functional limit to what any teacher can mentally maintain and access, as viable coherence, at the ready for application in the throes of teaching. Given an as-yet-to-be-pruned overgrown garden of theories (Schoenfeld in Sriraman & English, 2005, p. 453), we might forgive teachers for aligning their practice with persistent folk psychologies detailing not only "how things are but . . . how they should be" (Bruner, 1990, pp. 39–40). "People anticipate and judge one another . . . draw[ing] conclusions about the worthwhileness of their lives" (p. 15) according to folk psychology. Its categories provide "the very means by which culture shapes human beings to its requirements" (pp. 14–15) – schools being a core cultural instrument of that shaping.

While scientific psychology seeks to explain human action from "a point of view that is outside human subjectivity" (Bruner, 1990, p. 14), folk psychology deals with "the nature, causes, and consequences of human . . . beliefs, desires, intentions, commitments" (p. 14) – matters at the heart of lived experience. For these reasons, folk psychology, rather than science, prevails in the interpretation and practical implementation of theory (Bruner, 1990, pp. 33–66) – and as we will see in Chapter 8, folk psychology can provide the means and the support for dissociation and learning's refusal.

Folk psychology works its logic through the "natural vehicle" (p. 52) of narrative, using it to mediate "between the canonical world of culture and the more idiosyncratic world of beliefs, desires, and hopes" (p. 52). "When things 'are as they should be,' the narratives of folk psychology are unnecessary" (p. 40), but when the exceptional threatens, then the stories of folk psychology keep the uncanny at bay by threading the exceptional into more familiar narrative lines (p. 52). Indeed, in any school staffroom, one sees such storying in the collaborative tales that teachers tell to make reassuring sense of disconcerting aspects of student, classroom, and school life. At the same time, folk psychology reiterates and reinforces societal norms, doing so "without being didactic . . . without confrontation . . . [and at times] even teach[ing], conserv[ing] memory, or alter[ing] the past" (p. 52). On all of these counts, it would be a mistake to underappreciate folk psychology's normative work in schools.

Without a philosophy conversant with a cultural psychology of human "beliefs, desires, intentions, and commitments" (Bruner, 1990, p. 14) – the spontaneous knowledge of folk psychology has every reason to prevail in teaching practice.

Theorising learning **119**

If we aspire to move beyond normatively enforced practices in education, then teachers will need access to study, and make second nature, the "nonspontaneous knowledge" (Vygotsky, 1934/1986) of a coherent general philosophy of learning that aptly connects lived experience and theory. Otherwise, we suffer a repeating predicament of psychosocial norms underwriting folk psychologies that, in turn, underwrite schooling practice and render innovation as nothing more than repackaged versions of a curriculum–pendulum swinging across a limited spectrum of unquestioned beliefs.

A typical compendium

Educational psychologists authoring these books take the view that "different theories of learning offer more or less useful explanations depending on what is to be explained" (per Hoy, Davis, & Anderman, 2013, p. 9). Accordingly, they endorse a plethora of techniques for translating disparate theories into useful practice. Moreover, despite current understandings that hold the "study of consciousness, as well as of perception, memory, and cognition . . . [as] inseparable from the study of emotion and motivation," virtually every such textbook (per a comprehensive review by Park & Auchincloss, 2006) adheres "to a traditional format of devoting a separate chapter to each of these areas of investigation, *as if they were completely separate areas of study*" (italics added, p. 1377). They explain: "The psychoanalytic imperative that we search for the motivated aspects of all mental life presents a threat to this traditional division of intellectual territory within the field of psychology" (p. 1377).

To lend a clearer sense of the introductory field of educational psychology (e.g., Berk, 2000; Ormrod, Saklofske, Schewean, Andrews, & Shore, 2010; Santrock, Woloshyn, Gallagher, Di Petta, & Marini, 2004), I close this section with a representative list of discrete, disparate, units of study, commonly comprising compendial collections for beginning teachers. Most resources will have some version of all of the following topical sections:

1   Development: Here prospective teachers will encounter theories in cognitive development (Piaget's stage theory, Case's neo-Piagetian theory, Vygotsky's social theory, featuring ZPD and language), language development, moral development (Kohlberg's stage theory and possibly Gilligan's critique) and socio-emotional development (e.g., Bronfenbrenner's ecological theory and Erikson's lifespan development theory). Affect will not play a part in this discussion, nor likely will attachment theory.

2   Cognition: Here we find information processing, the rudiments of attention and memory (short- and long-term, storage and retrieval), and possibly meta-cognition, but neither mentalisation nor theory of mind (see Chapter 6). The computer metaphor remains pervasive, eclipsing neuroscientific and connectionist understandings of brain/mind functioning. The brain's affective systems (limbic and subcortical) influencing attention, memory, and thought will probably be but a footnote. The unconscious will be hardly addressed, if at all.

120 A dialectic theory of learning

There are increased efforts to redress popular myths of brain-based practices. The mention of cultural psychology (per Bruner, 1990) is more likely to be taken up and translated through the lens of the learning sciences, as for example, distributed cognition, communities of practice, legitimate peripheral participation, and situated learning theory (see Lave & Wenger, 1991).

3   Knowledge construction: Here sections will address student readiness and appropriate stepwise progressions to meet learners in their ZPD (a misinterpretation of Vygotsky's intent as described earlier, see Gredler, 2012). There will be a general emphasis on dialogical knowledge construction, higher-level thinking, authentic activities, rich learning tasks, and design-based approaches to problem-solving (see Chapter 3 for a critique). Again, affect will not be part of the conversation. There may be a section on embodied cognition. Concept development in a Vygotskian or Piagetian sense will be touched upon topically and not engaged in any deep exploratory way. The material in this section, along with the section on instructional processes, is usually revisited in at least one subject-specific curriculum and instruction course.

4   Individual variation: This section will introduce various theories of intelligence and creativity, and include an overview of students with exceptionalities. Some texts may continue to advance the discredited, however popular, rhetoric of learning styles (see Chapters 3 and Part III). Prospective teachers will learn about the relevant government coding systems for individuals with special emotional and/or cognitive needs and the various strategical supports for rendering classrooms inclusive (see Part III, sections on *inclusion*).

5   Diversity: Here texts emphasise the criticality of recognising, welcoming, and supporting, in principle, all students regardless of differences of, for instance, culture, ethnicity, language, religion, familial environment, socio-economic status, gender identity, and sexual orientation. These topics are usually explored in greater depth in at least one social justice course.

6   Motivation: Students will learn about Maslow's hierarchy of basic needs, intrinsic and extrinsic motivation, the effect of teacher expectations, and goal setting and attribution theory (the things students tell themselves about why they succeed or fail). Again, there is unlikely to be a section on early attachment and its implications for security in learning. They will also encounter theories on self-esteem, self-concept, self-efficacy, and self-regulation – possibly delving into mindfulness and meditation practices. More than likely, they will encounter Dweck's theory of growth- and fixed-mindedness (2006/2016) along with any number of emergent theories in positive psychology (see Chapter 3 critique).

7   Classroom dynamics: Today, classroom management typically circulates under a different heading. Following a behaviourist paradigm and under such rubrics as "functional behavioral assessment, positive behavior supports (Soodak, 2003), and, to a certain extent, deliberate practice" (Hoy et al., 2013, p. 10), future teachers learn principles and techniques for conditioning "desirable" student behaviour. From Pavlov and Watson to Skinner, the behaviourist tradition relies on that which is directly observable and measurable. By definition, it studies

those things sanitised of happenings within the so-called black box of mind, including affect and even cognition. As supplement to behaviourism, such a chapter might also introduce the self-regulation of behaviour, Bandura's social cognitive theory, and (though unlikely) Noddings's theory of care.

8 Instruction: Here the focus turns to teaching strategies, uses of technology, and the logistics of organising the classroom space and establishing effective procedures and routines. Practices will orient around folk psychologies about establishing trustworthy engaging environments with sufficient control of learning. There will be little attention to current theorising of these constructs especially with respect to systems' thinking (as per, e.g., Möllering, 2005, 2006, see Part III). Principles of differentiated instruction and universal designs for learning will be invoked as panaceas for ensuring inclusive classrooms (again, see Chapter 3 and Part III for the challenges of translating principle to practice).

9 Assessment: Students learn about standardised assessment tools, reliability and validity, purposes of assessment, dealing with student difficulties with assessment, and various strategies for assessment. A conversation about assessment for and as learning may be included. Education students typically have at least one course focusing on assessment itself, however, explicit attention to assessment at a fault line between societal expectation and learning principles rarely enters the conversation. Rather, these sections tend to be about understanding the terms of discussion, becoming familiar with the different forms of assessment available, practice at creating them, and general guidelines for using them.

Theories of learning historicised

While compendial collections parse an expansive field into packets of disparate information offering à la carte strategies for teachers, historical accounts of theories of learning tend to present a more-or-less coherent through-line of progress, albeit through vying paradigms.

Variations on a story

Bruner writes how "from the latter nineteenth century until a decade after World War II . . . rival paradigms came into existence and . . . research soon became a war of would-be paradigms" (2004, p. 14). Still, the theories riding highest in any era continue to be those most reflective of that era's historically shaped ethos and socio-political and cultural climate.

From nineteenth-century brain physiology to early twenty-first-century cognitivism, psycholinguistics, and cultural psychology

In the emergent brain science of the nineteenth century, studies in brain physiology gave rise to two divergent views on brain functioning: *associationism* and *holism* (Bruner, 2004; Deacon, 1989). By World War II, these came to be near-warring

122 A dialectic theory of learning

factions in America (p. 18). Associationists held the bottom-up, parts-make-the-whole view at the conceptual core of Pavlov's operant conditioning, Watson's drill and practice, and Skinner's behaviourism. Meanwhile adherents to holistic views held a top-down view of the whole as greater than the sum of its parts – a view that gave rise to Gestalt theory and Tolman's theory of cognitive maps.

By the 1960s, the cognitive revolution and a turn to language (precipitated by the linguist Chomsky) began to eclipse these more classical renderings of mind. The cognitivist's computer metaphor had, by the twenty-first century, shown extraordinary staying power, leaving psycholinguistics and cultural psychologists with but the promise of disruption (Bruner, 2004, pp. 19–20). Expressing his constructivist leanings in cultural psychology, Bruner laments, "You cannot strip learning of its content, nor study it in a 'neutral' context. It is always situated, always related to some ongoing enterprise" (p. 20).

Learning theories as pillars for teaching

Bruner's account contrasts with more practically oriented interpretations. In their 2013 review of fifty years of learning theories in the journal *Theory to Practice* (*TIP*), Hoy, Davis, & Anderman trace a non-conflicting story of new perspectives filling in the missing bits in an ever-burgeoning compendium of useful practices – no culling necessary.

There is no lack of research aimed at translating theory to practice. Sadly such research is necessarily shackled by the empirical mandate of operationalising theoretical constructs into observable and measurable forms suitable for study – a process limited only by the ingenuity and imagination of the particular researchers. Such studies, nuanced as they are, have a habit of multiplying exponentially, each building on the other, accruing findings into massive aggregates of information, yet without providing much in the way of new understanding, insight, or wisdom.

Emphasising the practical, and commenting on the historical progression of learning theories from "behavioral to cognitive to constructivist to sociocultural," the *TIP* reviewers position all four paradigms as complementary "pillars for teaching" (Hoy et al., 2013, p. 10):

> Students must first understand and make sense of the material (constructivist); then they must remember what they have understood (cognitive – information processing); and then they must practice and apply their new skills and understanding to make them more fluid and automatic, and a permanent part of their repertoire (behavioral). All of these processes are embedded in social and cultural settings.
>
> *(Hoy et al., 2013, p. 10)*

Their chronology begins with "Skinner's (1950) operant conditioning" (p. 9) as the basis for current-day teacher tools, such as *functional behavioural assessments* to determine student goals in problem behaviours and then *positive behavioural supports*

Theorising learning **123**

to encourage new actions to better serve those same goals (p. 13). The behaviourist assumption – that observing student's overt behaviours is sufficient to inferring their goals and systematically redirecting behaviour – problematically leaves unaddressed the child's motivating embodied affective and relational history.

When cognitivism and constructivism enter the scene, the definition of learning in *TIP* broadens from training habits and skills, to progressive ideals and constructivist concerns for internal processes – for instance, "pattern-finding . . . discovery and creativity" (p. 14). As the story goes, the cognitivism of the 1970s and 1980s computer revolution, makes short-lived a 1960s resurgence of progressivism, forcing it underground to percolate while educational psychology focuses on strategies for better storing, representing, and retrieving knowledge in/from mind (p. 14). Hoy, Davis, and Anderman describe that legacy as leading to valuable cognitive techniques today for teaching student decision-making, problem-solving, knowledge acquisition, metacognition, and self-regulation – from a psychoanalytic perspective, all suspect as naïvely superficial (see Chapter 3 and Part III).

When progressivism and constructivism resurface, they retrospectively produce a through-line from early twentieth-century Dewey and Montessori through the personal, social, and cultural emphases of, respectively, Piaget, Vygotsky, and Bruner. Hoy, Davis, and Anderman describe constructivists as a different group of scholars: ones dedicated to "scrutinizing the extent to which the pedagogies advocated by learning theorists fit the developmental needs of children . . . [and] the qualitatively different ways in which children understood tasks and made meaning" (p. 15). This segues to their fourth socio-cultural pillar – an unusual amalgam of social constructivist theories (usually attributed to Vygotsky) infused with themes of inclusive education and the political and social justice concerns of critical theory (rooted in the work of Paulo Freire, 1970/2000).

In general, one finds an unsurprising correspondence between the *Theory to Practice* journal (per Hoy, Davis, & Anderson's review) and introductory psychology texts for teachers. Both ring starkly true to slippages in theory as it is made to accommodate socio-political intent and folk psychology. Ernest (2006) summarises a troublingly reduction of constructivism to agreement "that pre-existing knowledge and understandings are the basis for virtually all subsequent learning" (p. 3). In teaching, this becomes: Find out what the learner knows and teach him accordingly. A hardly ground-breaking directive. Too, per the 2013 *TIP* review, the radical constructivism of von Glasersfeld and the enactivist understandings of Maturana and Varela (both developed below) had not yet made their way to practice. This remains the case.

Consider, however, what is articulated: that the past 50 years – having generated critical attention to identity politics, social injustice, illegitimate privilege, and the rights of individual citizens – was an era ripe for a particular skew to constructivism. This is constructivism politicised. It espouses the uniqueness of every child and the importance of community – both rhetorics dealing in the optics of attention to rising concerns for individual difference in the public consciousness of increasingly diverse societies. It follows that *TIP* presented constructivist learning theories as endorsing such popular teaching practices as: differentiated instruction; child-centred classrooms; learning tasks designed with different student interests and motivations in mind; greater student freedom in the way of, for example, student choice, discovery learning, and independent study; and emphasis on inclusive practices and collaborative classroom settings.

Whereas such progressive practices offer valuable correctives to traditionalist extremes, any re-centring seems more political and ideologically driven than arising out of a logic of constructivism. Quite simply, a viable learning theory must account for learning *regardless of the circumstances within which that learning is found to occur*. A learning theory does not a particular practice make. As a theory, constructivism should make sense of, *not only* learning in situations deemed constructivist but *also* learning in more conventional settings – the likes of, for example, highly structured environments and programs, about things that are not immediately or necessarily relevant to students, and sometimes involving following directions or listening to a lecture.

Moreover, so-called constructivist teaching rose in conjunction with the entrenchment of "No child left behind" in American legislature (U.S. Department of Education, 2002), and "Every student succeeds" in 2015 (Hirschfeld Davis, 2015). These moves justified today's strong-arming of educational reforms via regulation, assessment, and accountability (D'Amour, 2011; Grumet, 2010). While the situation in the United States is perhaps most notorious (see, e.g., Gartner, 2017), we in Canada and to a certain degree abroad cannot but feel its reverberations – our literatures enmeshed as they are. The point is an ironic one: While constructivist theories inspire increasing *recognition of student individuality and agency* in learning, legislature *increasingly exercises constraint on teacher individuality and agency* in learning and honing their practice. In other words, what is good for students as learners cannot be good for teachers as such. This incongruity points to a fundamental confusion between a theory of learning relevant to teaching and favoured pedagogical practices.

Sorting out constructivism

Several authors are quick to point out the many "variants" or "forms" of constructivism (Bächtold, 2013, p. 2479). To what are they attending?

Personal constructivism

What is understood as personal constructivism typically moves through and includes Deweyian progressivism (Dewey, 1938/1997), Piaget's cognitive theories of learning (1967/1971), and von Glasersfeld's radical constructivism (1989). Whereas Deweyan progressivism emphasises active experience in the classroom, an important caveat follows from Piagetian constructivism: that "knowledge construction implies activity of the mind but not necessarily activity of the body" (Bächtold, 2013, p. 2478). Note too that Piagetian constructivism and most cognitive theories of learning, leastwise as they are taken up, are built on a premise that we can get our knowing right about the world, that what's in our head should match what's true out there, and "that true representations of the empirical and experiential worlds are possible" (Ernest, 2006, p. 4). Radical constructivism differs. It asserts that cognition, as an adaptive mechanism, organises the world-as-experienced. It does not discover any objective world-as-reality (Sriraman & English, 2005, p. 453). Instead, as per my opening definition of learning, the "'real' is what we need to posit conceptually in order to be realistic, that is, in order to function successfully to survive, to achieve ends, and to arrive at workable understandings of the situations we are in (Lakoff & Johnson, 1999, p. 109).

Thus, to reiterate, learning is as *an interpretive act of taking impressions from the given world-of-one's-experience and assuming those impressions into a revised self – as per one's knowing of that world, with that world, and of oneself as partially comprising it.* But of course, the point of the previous two chapters, and the point of Vygotsky's understanding of the role of language is that we do not take such impressions in isolation. This brings us to social constructivism and a commonly conceived "schism between 'fundamentally cognitive' and 'fundamentally social' studies of human thought and action" (Schoenfeld, 1999, p. 5).

On the either-or distinction, Ernest clarifies:

> In . . . [individual construction] a learner constructs their knowledge and understanding internally based on their personal interpretation of their experiences and their pre-existing knowledge. . . . [In contrasting] social construction . . . the learning and knowledge construction takes place in the social arena, in the "space between people," even if its end products are appropriated and internalized by those persons individually.
>
> *(2006, p. 3)*

> Social constructivism regards individual learners and the realm of the social as indissolubly interconnected. . . . [T]here is no underlying model for the socially isolated individual mind. Instead, the underlying metaphor is dialogical or "persons-in-conversation."
>
> *(p. 5)*

Social constructivism

Bächtold takes the distinction articulated by Ernest (earlier) and reminds us of Piagetian versus Vygotskyan differences:

> Piaget's description of the development of spontaneous concepts . . . assigns a major role to the interaction of the learner *with her/his material environment* [italics added], and extends it so as to make sense of the development of scientific concepts. In contrast, . . . Vygotsky's description of the development of scientific concepts . . . puts special emphasis on the role of the interaction of the learner *with her/his social environment by means of language.*
>
> *(italics added, Bächtold, 2013, p. 2495)*

126 A dialectic theory of learning

Interestingly enough, although Vygotsky is widely (and Piaget rarely) associated with social constructivism, it is actually a Piagetian version that currently prevails. In a nutshell, whereas Piaget focused on *co-operation* and spontaneous knowledge, Vygotsky focused on *enculturation* and nonspontaneous, scientific knowledge (Bächtold, 2013, p. 2479). Importantly, neither Piaget nor Vygotsky make the case for the effective development of nonspontaneous concepts through peer interactions. Nonetheless, this *is* the most common interpretation advocated in their names.

Recall that Piaget saw children as developing understandings when working co-operatively *with one another* in a spontaneous manner – that is, a manner unfettered by adults. For Piaget, "social interactions among children have a strong influence on the construction of their respective individual cognitive structures" (p. 2487). Vygotsky would not disagree. However, Vygotsky emphasised the socialisation of children *by adults* – or, more broadly, of novices by experts. Appreciating that children and adults are highly unlikely to come to the complex nonspontaneous understandings of scientific culture on their own (i.e., neither individually nor in groups), he emphasised the critical role of teaching. For Vygotsky, "learning involves both a 'personal' construction process on the part of the students and guidance by the teacher. . . . [such that] students come to 'appropriate' (i.e., understand and master) . . . models or theories" (p. 2488). Taken to adult learning and the learning of societal systems, Vygotsky is describing a dialectic learning process that benefits from (processes of enfolding, reacting to, and synthesising) knowledge beyond one's current knowing – either the knowing of those who have gone before or who have thought differently. That is, it includes not only study with teachers and mentors but also reading across authoritative texts.

To reiterate, the thoughts and perspectives most championed in the present schooling moment are less Vygotskian, more Piagetian (though rarely named as such) and decidedly Deweyan. For example, differentiated instruction and hands-on learning, both, recognise the actively construing learner – practices that follow from both Piaget's individual constructivism and Dewey's ideas on *Experience and Education* (1938/1997), but that also, uncoincidentally, suit a widely promoted, twenty-first-century agenda for creative technological innovation and advancement. At the same time, inclusive classrooms and collaborative practices emphasise a Piagetian regard for peer-to-peer collaboration that is consistent with Dewey's *Democracy and Education* (1916/2004) while serving a twenty-first-century emphasis on people who can work in collaborative teams, especially as per the technologies of design thinking and design protocol.

At least three additional factors, unrelated to learning theory, create a perfect storm of conspicuous explanations giving rise to these present-day schooling preferences: (1) Postmodernism – having surfaced the social construction of knowledge, the falsity of absolute truths, and the collusion of power and privilege in determining whose knowledge is of most worth – has challenged traditional authority and elevated situated local knowledge; (2) in conjunction with postmodern influences, geopolitical migration has dramatically increased the cultural and linguistic diversity in the classrooms of destination societies, and these two forces have pressed a healthy celebration of difference and an ethics of inclusivity; and (3), second-generation cognitive science has reconceived learning in terms of dynamic systems such that we now speak of participatory collectives (e.g., the classroom itself) as the learning body – where the knowing that a group can generate, as a whole, is thought to better occasion the learning of each participant.

Doubtless, the idea of learners freely collaborating to solve real-life, hands-on, rich problems fitted to their learning needs might seem promising – that is, were it not for a society whose conventions, social structure, and economic viability is strictly symbiotic with Western values and ways of knowing, gone global. The fault lines are most clearly drawn through standards, accountability, and assessment. On the one hand, students are products of an innovation-oriented schooling system that teaches them that their knowledge is as valuable as anyone else's, including their teachers and other intellectual authorities. On the other hand (as critical theory is quick to point out), these same students must contend with their cultural capital and earning power being a function of preset conventions on what counts as knowledge and whose knowledge is of most worth. They will inevitably run headlong into the realities of a meritocracy – where coming from power and privilege begets power and privilege and where finding one's place entails fashioning oneself in accordance with prevailing politico-economic and socio-cultural norms.

Acknowledging value in both Piagetian co-operation and Vygotskyan enculturation as educative principles, I believe we run into difficulties when we favour one over the other. We would benefit from a model of learning that is less headstrong (one way or the other), is not shackled by an us/them mentality, and allows for the possibility of something *other than* what generally happens when two tectonic plates collide – that is, where one subducts under, only to raise up, the other. In the final section of this book, we will consider these questions in earnest. For now, we turn to cognitivism and a third way of understanding the history of constructivist learning theories – an approach that, while converging with relational psychoanalytic thinking, takes us up to the present moment.

Cognitivism: from first-generation computer metaphors to second-generation embodiment

A third way of looking at the development of constructivist principles is through cognitive theory. As we have seen, first-generation cognitivism relies on the computer metaphor of information processing still holding sway today. Problematically, its implicit assumptions are that (1) thought is purely symbolic computation, (2) mental processes work like abstract computer programs, and (3) the mind is analogous to software running on, but not affecting, the hardware that is the physical brain (Lakoff & Johnson, 1999, pp. 74–78). In so saying, the computer metaphor splits mind-and-consciousness (software) from brain-and-body (hardware) – a modern spin on Descartes' Enlightenment view "that reason is transcendental, universal, disembodied" (Lakoff & Johnson, 1999, p. 75) and above base bodily being (Bernstein, 1983, pp. 115–118).

128 A dialectic theory of learning

While "the computer metaphor makes [of] Meaning – or how something means something to someone – an inscrutable mystery" (Klin & Jones, 2007, p. 6), "a second-generation cognitive neuroscience seeks neurobiologically plausible accounts" to link brain and body with mental experience and consciousness (Fonagy & Target, 2007, p. 411) – where these processes are increasingly understood as "embodied," that is, as "emerging from or serving the needs of a physical being located in a specific time, place, and social context" (p. 411). Under the scrutiny of second-generation neuroscientific research, the computer metaphor simply does not stand up. Instead we find "a strong dependence of concepts and reason upon the body" (Lakoff & Johnson, 1999, p. 77) and upon such "imaginative processes" of sense-making as "metaphor, imagery, metonymy, prototypes, frames, mental spaces, and radial categories" (p. 77).

To understand what embodied cognition entails, consider the expression "grasping an idea." To make sense of such a phrase a person relies on (and abstracts from) bodily experiences of, actually, "grasping things." Whereas, prior experience-in-action *makes possible* thought; thought *recalls and depends upon* prior experience-in-action. Such recall is rarely conscious. The knowing is rather writ in our automatic nonconscious and unconscious being. Quite literally, *both* the thought and its related action draw on the same motor and premotor areas in the brain (Boulenger, Shtyrov, & Pulvermüller, 2011; Lindgren & Johnson-Glenberg, 2013). We build conceptual meaning, *literally*, upon bodily experience – and those experiences come with associated affective weights, some more salient than others.

Concepts and language derive their meaning from viscerally understood, interpersonally mediated, encounters – beginning from birth (Chapter 6). *We cannot tease apart meaningful experience from bodily experience.* This does not deny that language construes upon itself, exceeding in consciousness the imaginative encounters and thought experiments of its embodied roots. It does say that the things that matter to us have affective salience; and the affective salience of any given moment and context is a function of our socio-affective-bodily histories. Regardless of whether we are aware, language and symbolic thought return us to "a foundation of gestures and actions . . . profoundly influenced by the experience of early physical interaction with [our first significant others]" (Fonagy & Target, 2007, p. 411).

The implication is that, where learners are stuck or where attention wavers (assuming a healthy non-fatigued brain), teachers are wise to begin to question the strength of the link between personal meaning and what comes to a student as an obscure abstract impersonal idea – or worse yet, one that runs counter to the learner's present conceptual schema. The teacher will want to reconnect that which is abstract to that which is visceral. The body-in-relation – be it physical (with a material world), social (storied in an intersubjective world), and/or affective (felt in an intrapsychic world) – is at the heart of meaningful sense-making. Notwithstanding the physiological value of movement (sitting all day is hardly conducive to an alert mind), notice how this idea of embodiment, as a constructivist theory of learning, relates to, but differs drastically from a general emphasis on activity per se. Notice, too, the contrasting implications between, on the one hand, using this deep

Theorising learning **129**

understanding of meaning to dialectically and dialogically guide one's teaching and, on the other hand, teaching as selecting from a menu of techniques purported to engage students and manage classrooms. The distinction, critical to teacher development, echoes the proverb (playfully feminised): "Give a woman a fish and you feed her for a day. Teach a woman to fish and you feed her for a lifetime."

The inseparable how and why of learning in life systems

The constructivist through-line of cognition – flowing across the personal, the social, and the embodied – is a story primarily about understanding "how" people learn, but one largely indifferent to "why" they do (or don't). The tacit assumption has been that "why" and "how" are sufficiently separate phenomena as to warrant independent study. Educational psychology has been content to suppose how-people-learn as the proper subject of cognitive theory and why-people-learn as the better subject of a variety of parsed literatures, such as the study of *motives* (e.g., goal-setting), *motivations* (e.g., intrinsic vs. extrinsic), and *emotions* (e.g., anxiety), to name a few. Yet all the way down, cognitions are ultimately meaning-driven life processes. To these research and methodological inclinations, Vygotsky's advice holds as much today as in yesteryear when he writes, "Psychology which aims at a study of complex holistic systems, must replace the method of *analysis into elements* with the method of *analysis into units*" (italics added, 1934/1986, p. 5).

One cannot productively strip the affective "why" from behaviour and from a divided cognition (be it personal, social, or embodied), for the purposes of controlled study, and then expect to assemble the lot back together again in any consequential way. In other words, the problem of meaning in theories of learning is a likely artefact of reductive empirical research. It is a problem that concerned Vygotsky.

> When we approach the problem of the interrelation between thought and language and other aspects of mind, the first question that arises is that of intellect and affect. Their separation as subjects of study is a major weakness of traditional psychology, since it makes the thought process appear as an autonomous flow for "thoughts thinking themselves," segregated from the fullness of life, from the personal needs and interests, the inclinations and impulses of the thinker.
>
> *(Vygotsky, 1934/1986, p. 10)*

And it remains a concern of contemporary thinkers.

> Although emotions often are not explicitly cognitive in the sense portrayed by traditional cognitive theories, they are indeed thoroughly bound up with and inseparable from cognition. This is because emotions are essentially how minded beings like us care – how we care about objects, events, states of affairs, each other, our own lives, and even our own caring.
>
> *(Maiese, 2014, p. 514)*

130 A dialectic theory of learning

> The more I knew about learning, the less I seemed to know about (the real issues of) learning. The more I learned about learning research, the more I have come to understand that our theories are no more adequate than those that we have had some decades ago. . . . [R]ather than asking questions such as "What . . .?" or "How . . .?," I am asking questions about the *origins* of intentions, perceptions, discourses, and conceptions. . . . [L]earning researchers currently have no answers to these more fundamental questions.
>
> *(Roth, 2011, p. ix)*

A near century ago, Vygotsky began *Thought and Language* by recognising that, for "complex holistic systems," the proper unit of analysis is the indivisible whole. He framed his approach to thought and language by asking first, *"What is the unit of verbal thought that is further unanalyzable and yet retains the properties of the whole?"* (italics added) (1934/1986, p. 5). Through a similar logic, two Chilean biologists, Humberto Maturana and Francisco Varela, ushered forth a paradigm shift to reframe life systems as "feeling" systems that learn. Maturana framed it succinctly when he wrote: "The greatest hindrance in the understanding of the living organization lies in the impossibility of accounting for it by the enumeration of its properties; it must be understood as a unity" (1970, p. 6).

A fundamental unity

Those of us familiar with school biology are accustomed to defining living organisms according to constituent parts and the vital capacities they each serve (e.g., growth/development, response to stimuli, and reproduction). Instead, substituting "cognition" for "verbal thought" in Vygotsky's question (earlier), we might ask, *What is the unit of meaningful cognition that is further unanalysable yet retains the properties of the whole?*

As it turns out, that question has already been asked and answered. Maturana and Varela observed that "overemphasis of isolated parts" (Varela, Maturana, & Uribe, 1974) has obscured the organisational dynamics subsuming all life and meaning. They asked: What do we recognise when we experience something (including ourselves) as a "whole, autonomous unity that is alive" (Varela et al., 1974, p. 187)? In other words: What is the structural organisation necessary and sufficient to life (Varela et al., 1974, p. 187) and out of which life elaborates itself into more complex emergent and dynamic forms?

To this end, in 1970, Maturana launched a theory of cognition with the self-producing (autopoietic) character of living systems at its core – that paper later anchoring *Autopoiesis and Cognition: The realization of the living* (Maturana & Varela, 1972/1980). Together, these thinkers developed and popularised an approach to understanding embodied cognition that, in 1986, Varela termed "the enactive approach" (in Thompson, 2007, p. 444 n. 9).

The genius of Maturana and Varela was to take the philosophical understanding of embodied cognition (especially as developed by Merleau-Ponty, 1945/1962) and apply it biologically to the smallest undivided life unity. Then following a principle of life systems as *self-determining material unities inextricably coupled to their milieus* (i.e., singular-plural-beings), they elaborated from individual cells to the cases of the nervous system, conscious beings, and discursive systems. In the process, they rendered a biology to reframe, in a resolvable way, the apparent paradox of singular autonomous and plural heteronomous being at the crux of the personal/social constructivist divide.

Beginning from the smallest unit and "meaning" of life as self-producing (auto-poietic), they brought together biological and phenomenological understandings of experience – accounting for humans as both first-person (phenomenological) experiencers *in* life and third-person (scientific) observers *of* life (including recursive observations of the self by the self). Moreover, by entailing the (humanities-oriented) *phenomenological question of experience* in the (science-oriented) *material question of being*, in a mutually reinforcing way, they explicitly addressed the unhelpful schisms between the sciences and the humanities (Maturana & Varela, 1998; Maturana with Verden-Zöller, 2008; Varela, 1999; Varela, Thompson, & Rosch, 1991) and roundly put to rest the stubborn Cartesian mind–body divide (Thom, D'Amour, Preciado, & Davis, 2015, p. 70).

The thinking of Maturana and Varela sparked a flurry of conceptual work in multiple fields, under related names, including *complexity theory/science/thinking* in education (Davis & Sumara, 2006) and both *nonlinear dynamic systems theory* (NLDS) (Lewis & Granic, 2000; Teicholz, 2009) and *field theory* (Stern, 2015) in contemporary psychoanalysis. When they argued that "for a system to have the phenomenology of a living system it suffices that its organization be autopoietic" (Varela et al., 1974, p. 189), they not only coined the term autopoiesis and developed the notion of autopoietic organisation but also prompted a paradigm shift that would redefine the quintessential character of life, knowing, and learning. Bruner reminds us that "it is natural enough that scientists would want somehow to simplify what we mean by 'studying learning.' And, of course, the standard way of doing that is to agree on some paradigm" (2006, p. 14).

The ramifications of Maturana and Varela's reconceptualisations may be as paradigmatic as those of the Copernican revolution when a likewise shift in perception – from the sun revolving around the earth, to the earth revolving around the sun – changed everything (Kuhn, 1962/1996).

Autopoiesis and the autopoietic organisation

In 1970, Humberto Maturana asked "What is it to know? . . . How do we know?" . . . "How does the living organization give rise to cognition in general and to self-cognition in particular?" (p. 6).

In the spirit of Maturana and Varela, the theory I am proposing could indeed be termed a theory grounded in autopoietic understandings. It is therefore useful to explore these authors thinking, beginning with a definition drawn from multiple works (Maturana, 1970; Maturana & Varela, 1972/1980; Thompson, 2007,

132 A dialectic theory of learning

pp. 91–127; Thompson & Stapleton, 2009): In brief, a system is alive, and therefore cognitive and learning, if it is organised autopoietically – satisfying the following conditions:

1   The system physically comprises, both, a semipermeable boundary separating it from its milieu, and a distinct internal reaction network circumscribed by that boundary.
2   The system is recursively self-producing; that is, the internal reaction network regenerates both itself and the boundary.
3   The system secures its continuance by adaptive self-regulation, where "adaptation is a relation of operational congruence between the changing organism and the changing medium in which it lives."

(Maturana with Verden-Zöller, 2008, p. 1)

The first of these criteria puts the system in a physical space and renders it materially existent, observable, and therefore alive in our reckoning; the second describes self-producing recursion – the peculiar circular interdependence of components that define a living system as a closed unit of internal interactions that work to reproduce themselves; and the third, by virtue of the first two, leads to a much more generalised and embodied definition of cognition than we have thus seen.

It follows from these three points that an autopoietic system – being operationally closed, selectively permeable, and therefore subject to the flux of dynamically changing milieus within and without – needs some adaptive way of maintaining vitality (staying alive). That is, given that the materials and energy used by the internal reaction network come to it from its external *niche* – the aspect of the milieu to which the organism is coupled and upon which it depends – then shifts in that external milieu will necessarily affect the substance and character of the recursively produced components within, in turn altering the internal reactions that those components serve. As such, in the flow, predictable and not, of a necessarily changing environment, a system *stays alive and retains its identity* (Maturana, 1970, p. 9) while undergoing inevitable *structural drift* as consequence of recursive processes. In brief, owing to the *coupling* of organism and niche, external dynamics affect internal dynamics and the replications of replicating components are never quite exact. Insofar as structural drift serves ongoing organismic viability and vitality, it is adaptive. At its most fundamental level, this is learning.

From knowing, being, and doing: to language and thought

We see the foregoing understandings already articulated in Merleau-Ponty's prescient philosophy.

[For him,] sensory perception was not a channel that separated, but a membrane that connected. Perception, he argued, is an integral part of cognition. . . . [and] a key element of action-in-the-world. For him, action was not a reflection of knowing; it was an aspect of knowing. The body was not a vessel for knowledge; it was a knowing system.

(Thom et al., 2015, p. 70)

To put these criteria of autopoietic organisation into context, imagine a simple organism, a cell, defined by a boundary, perhaps a membrane. Notice that materials pass in and out of the cell through this selective membrane, doing so along a gradient of shifting internal states, those shifts being a consequence of life doing what life does – that is, maintaining its dynamic viability. There is a kind of intelligence to this. *The cell "knows" what to do, and its knowing is entirely a function of its structural being.* This is embodied cognition in its simplest form. It captures the deep meaning behind the enactivist saying: *"knowing is being is doing."*

In the same way, my hands on the keyboard know (where knowing is doing) that which, in this case, my mind has structured them to know through training. But knowing need not come into being through thought – indeed most of our non-conscious and unconscious knowing is of a less obvious genre. The infant knows as a condition of its being and acting, even and especially before the possibilities of thought through language.

There is a leap to be made from the embodied cognition of a non-thinking cell to that of a human. That leap goes through language and has been well addressed by Maturana and Varela. However, space does not allow its explication here. Suffice it to say that what we have seen in previous chapters is consistent with enactivist understandings.

To reiterate the key points: Language makes possible thought's formulation, even as it constrains it. Language renders tangible and communicable modes for knowing ourselves, connecting with others, and making sense of our world. Maturana with Verden-Zöller (2008, pp. 30–35) describes the recursive processes of thought and meaning as a co-ordination of co-ordinations that are sufficiently consensual for communication across humans. As for Vygotsky, we have seen language figure centrally in the teacher-mediated shift of locally developed, spontaneous, student knowing into culturally and historically construed, nonspontaneous conventions and systems of understanding and perceiving. In return, new nonspontaneous scientific knowing has a way of retrospectively shedding light on prior "old" spontaneous understandings (Vygotsky, 1934/1986, pp. 195–197). Word and thought – as per all of: Vygotsky (earlier), Daniel Stern (Chapter 5 & 6), Donnel Stern (Chapter 8 ahead), and Maturana and Varela – are a function of conceptual linguistic formulations, begun in the affectively contoured co-ordinations of infant-caregiver relations, and evolved through gesture, sound, and word into entire language symbol systems of conceptual meanings and relations, including relations of relations of concepts where concepts themselves are generalisations on experience (Vygotsky, 1934/1986, pp. 197–208). Moreover, insofar as two adages – "The consequences of choices sediment" (Juarrero, 1999/2002) and "We lay our path in walking" (Thompson, 2007, Chapter 6) – are understood in enactivist terms, we can conceive of memory, in language and in body, as entailing system change qua biological action.

134 A dialectic theory of learning

Emphasising the social, and adding affect (as per Daniel Stern), I leave the last word on these matters to Maturana with Verden-Zöller:

> Language is a manner of living in recurrent interactions in a flow of coordinations of coordinations of consensual behaviors. . . . When we speak of "languaging" as a verb, we are referring to the recursive flow of consensual coordinations of behaviors. Furthermore, we human beings exist in the braiding of languaging and emotioning. . . . [that w]e call . . . *conversation.* . . . [And] the particular configurations of sounds, gestures, or marks that we call words are operational nodes in the network of consensual coordinations of coordinations of behaviors that we live as languaging beings.
>
> *(2008, pp. 30–31)*

Autopoiesis, cognition, and learning

Maturana introduced autopoeisis with the following daring claim:

> A cognitive system is a system whose organization defines a domain of interactions in which it can act with relevance to the maintenance of itself. *Living systems are cognitive systems, and living as a process is a process of cognition.* This statement is valid for all organisms with and without a nervous system.
>
> *(1970, pp. 12–13)*

Of euglena, amoeba, and pond

The very cognition of a system – that is, the knowing of the organism – and its possibility for learning is embodied in its unique structure. At the same time, we must also contend with the fact that

> living systems are units of interactions; they exist in an ambience. From a purely biological point of view they cannot be understood independently of that part of the ambience with which they interact: the niche; nor can the niche be defined independently of the living system that specifies it.
>
> *(Maturana, 1970, p. 9)*

To begin to get a sense of what this could mean, consider a euglena and an amoeba living in a pond. A euglena is a mobile unicellular organism that has a light-sensing eyespot and, uncoincidentally, photosynthetic capacity. The eyespot can "notice" light and trigger a series of ensuing internal dynamics such that the euglena, both, uses its flagellum to swim toward the light and "makes sense" of the light by "formulating" it into its own recursive self-making. In contrast, the unicellular amoeba engulfs smaller organisms for energy. It has neither eyespot nor photosynthetic capacity. Therefore, *to the amoeba, the truth of the world is that there is no such thing as light.* The amoeba has no biology with which to "know" light or even notice light.

(Recall, in the model that the centrifugal and centripetal moments of learning are about noticing and formulating, respectively.) For the amoeba, light is neither *given* by the world nor can it be taken and *made* into the amoeba by the amoeba. In this respect, the amoeba cannot learn/do/make itself into a difference (self-produce) by "incorporating" sunlight – whereas the euglena can.

Moreover, from our observer perspective the sunlight is a factor of the environment of the pond for *both* organisms, yet it exists *only* to the euglena – to be specific: as part of its *niche*. Sunlight is not part of the amoeba's experienced niche. By virtue of their different structures, the amoeba and the euglena are each *differently coupled* to their milieu. Owing to this coupling, changes in their niches (e.g., the availability and quality of sunlight for the euglena and of smaller organisms for the amoeba) will necessarily install changes in these organisms which, in turn, will change the entire environment. Notice too that we could not say that the environment *caused* the euglena to swim a particular way. Rather the environment occasioned that possibility and it was up to the organism, as determined by its structure, to behave in accordance with its possibility. This is what Maturana and Varela mean when they describe a particular organism's activity and learning as *structure-determined*.

Accepting that any organism can notice only in terms of itself, we must also agree that what-is-available-for-noticing turns on the constitution of its milieu. This is as true for the unicellular organism as it is for the classroom learner. Like the simplest life forms, so too for the most complex: Learning is *determined by the learner* and *dependent on the milieu*. However, a critical difference to make all the difference is, of course, language and a teacher. The teacher can use "linguistic interactions [to] orient the listener within his cognitive domain, but . . . [she can]not specify the course of his ensuing action" (Maturana, 1970, p. 50). Thus, in reference to our model, the teacher can orient the learner's attention to notice dissonance and to formulate resonance, but she cannot "make" him learn. The zone within which the teacher has to work is the learner's niche – an area akin to Vygotsky's zone of proximal development (see earlier and 1934/1986, pp. 186–196).

Motivation and desire

Prior to the burgeoning field of complex adaptive systems, the Aristotelian principle "that nothing, strictly speaking, can move, cause, or act on itself in the same respect . . . remained unchallenged" (Juarrero, 1999/2002, p. 2). From a dynamic-systems perspective we now understand life forms as "typically characterized by positive feedback processes in which the product of the process is necessary for the process itself. [T]his circular type of causality *is* a form of self-cause" (p. 5). The admission of self-cause, as pre-eminent principle of life forms, changes everything – especially educational research bent on finding the holy grail of evidence-based cause-effect relationships between operationalised pedagogical action and observable student outcome.

Given self-cause, we can reconceive learning and its motivation by connecting three ideas at once, and then applying them in more abstract ways: (1) the idea of the

136 A dialectic theory of learning

organism's structural coupling with its milieu, (2) the recognition that the organism's milieu is always in flux, and (3) the appreciation that, in order to remain viable, the organism needs to maintain its autopoietic organisation, and that this directly depends upon maintaining biochemical homeostasis. That is, the organism needs just the right conditions (temperature, pH, etc.) and resources (matter and energy) for it to continue doing what it knows to do.

Learning involves taking note of differences that matter (or can matter) to the self in terms of the self, admitting those differences through one's self-defining boundary, and then recovering and reconstituting a revised self out of any ensuing disequilibrium. Indeed, this very principle describes the way our body's immune system learns from vaccines. In the case of either incremental or cascading change, for learning to occur, the self will need to sufficiently deal with potential breaches to its boundaries, either by fortifying its boundary (altering its permeability) or by assimilating admitted differences and accommodating internal schema/structure accordingly (to use Piaget's words). Here the governing rule is that of sufficiency. That is, whatever changes happen, they must be sufficient enough to ensure *viability* in the immediacy of each next moment.

Cognition and motivation are inseparable across the spectrum of life systems. In the universal tendency of life toward ongoing viability even a single cell "thinks" and experiences "desire." But if the cell embodies cognition and knows such desire, it is only in its being as the doing of its aliveness, not in any conscious, much less self-reflective, thought. The intrinsic autopoietic movement of life to go on, is a primary condition defining the possibility of its existence. Else, life would not exist. Yet any such "desire" (named as such by the viewer) is nothing more than the logic of a reaction network dynamically monitoring homeostatic conditions and, via positive and negative feedback loops, "knowing" to amplify desirable states (in humans, neurochemically instantiated "pleasures") and diminish undesirable ones (in humans, neurochemically instantiated "displeasures"), always to the ends of viability and always within the context of the perceivably possible. We, as any other living form, are subject to these biologies. They are fundamental to our experience of emotion, and to the feelings that we recursively construe through language and thought upon emotion – the two, emotion and feeling, together comprising the affect that fuels cognition (Damasio, 2003, 2018; Panksepp & Biven, 2012).

Disequilibrium states are necessary and unavoidable consequences of life's dynamic existence in, and interdependence with, a shifting immediate world. Life forms must adjust according to the materials produced and exchanged with the very near-worlds of their existence – milieus in which they are embedded, and out of which they are made. In humans, to be sure, linguistic and digital worlds widely expand the range across which we can selectively create our niches.

The drift of recursive restructuring and the successful recovery from cascading system changes shapes and reshapes a cell and a self's knowing and thus constitutes its learning. Such learning is always within the limits of the life form's structure-determined capacity at any given moment in time. Where capacity is exceeded, structural breakdown ensues at some level. A single cell may disintegrate. A student may suffer diminished senses of coherence, continuity, and/or agency, and ultimately a loss of trust. In the model, swinging too far out into dissonance may mean the inability to recover oneself anew in resolution. Thus, in the face of shifting dynamics, motivation to learn becomes a twin function ultimately connected to the need to recuperate vital homeostatic conditions and a capacity to do so. Thus, for example, anxiety relates to both the biology and the phenomenology of diminished trust in the possibility of "surviving" perturbations (see Chapter 8). To protect *viability* in the immediacy of a moment, the cost may involve compromised *vitality*.

Nested systems

Our evolutionary story is one of life forms scaling up. Organisms have a tendency, over their singular and plural histories, to form collectives according to varying degrees of entrainment, co-ordination, and integration. Examples run the gamut from temporary to enduring: collectives of like forms (e.g., compare a flock of geese and bundles of nerve or muscle fibres); colonies of either co-operating organisms or symbiotically integrated ones (e.g., respectively, an ant colony & a Portuguese man-of-war); networks of tightly coupled like-forms (e.g., the brain's reticular formations and rhizomatous networks in plants), and finally multicellular organisms.

Any "particular self-referring system may have the circular organization of a living system or partake functionally of the circular organization of its components, or both" (Maturana, 1970, p. 11). Maturana offers honey bee colonies as third-order self-referring systems: The entire society has a circular organisation "superimposed" on the bees; the bees have a circular organisation "superimposed" on each of their cells; and the cells have a circular organisation. This tiered phenomenon characterises human societies giving a nested quality such that the systems at each level "are subordinated both to the maintenance of themselves and to the maintenance of the others" (p. 11).

Nesting arises spontaneously and is sustained according to its survival advantage. The result, over evolutionary time, is a characteristic self-similar, fractal-like organisation of life systems, with smaller totalities nested in and collectively composing larger ones, these larger ones themselves being nested in and forming larger, more comprehensive ones yet, and so on. Riding atop all of this, bootstrapped to biology, is our discursive world of thought, likewise self-sustaining, autopoietically so, and conditioning the social as that entanglement of our individual and collective, conjoined conjuring.

It is for living well amid such entanglements, that a science of autopoietic systems joins a psychoanalysis of relations and a humanist philosophy, per Jean-Luc Nancy, who names "plural singularity . . . the origin . . . [that] we reach. . . . to the extent that we are in touch with *ourselves* and in touch with the rest of beings" (1996/2000, p. 12) for, "if Being is being-with, then it is . . . the 'with' that constitutes Being. . . . *the 'with' is at the heart of Being*" (italics added, p. 30).

138 A dialectic theory of learning

Paradox

Two paths – one humanist, the other scientific – arrive to the same intrapsychic–intersubjective paradox. Of life forms and, in particular, humans, Maturana (with Verden-Zöller) writes that we "exist as part of the medium for each other. . . . [In a]ny relation between two human beings . . . both beings change congruently together, as long as they impinge on each other recursively" (2008, p. 29). Nancy (1996/2000) seems to echo these same sensibilities when he writes of nothing existing but in a condition of singular-plural coexistence where all life shares co-originary impingement.

Importantly, whereas the phenomenology of autonomy characterises autopoietic systems (Varela et al., 1974, p. 192), it redefines autonomy in terms of each of us with and because of one another. That is, agency, as autonomy to act on one's own behalf, is paradoxically as much a function of the organism as it is a function of the organism's milieu – a milieu to which it is coupled, yet from which it is distinct; and a milieu in which it is co-embedded with other forms, and of which it is composed. We can argue that we are self-causing, autonomous living forms, but this does nothing to deny our coexistence in states of interdependence according to that which is availed to us from our milieu and to which we must adapt to stay viable.

Put differently, as with all life forms, we necessarily operate in at least two domains of existence at once: the domain of operation of the elements that compose and constitute us (our biologically sustained *intrapsychic* selves) and the domain within which we exist and operate as a part of a larger totality (the worlds of *intersubjective* being) (Maturana with Verden-Zöller, 2008, pp. 22–30). We are simultaneously individuals who learn, and partialities of larger systems that likewise learn. The milieu of this learning is a geopolitically, culturally, and ideologically coloured social world. And each knower's knowing is a viable enough *interpretation* (for that knower on that knower's terms) of the knowledge of the larger system within which that self is embedded and out of which that self emerges. At the same time, each self is co-implicated and partially complicit in the conditions of the whole and of the milieu that is the space of their intersectionality.

The paradox of autopoietic organisation returns us to the learning model's depiction of the expansion of a learner's consciousness of self and world as that learner undergoes a dialectic process of enfolding aspects of the external milieu into revised coherences in the internal one. It is the autopoietic organisation that makes of learning a necessarily dialectic tacking, centrifugally and centripetally, noticing and formulating into the self, what we may from the world. Insofar as we can do this and succeed without fragmenting – indeed while augmenting our sense of coherence, continuity, and agency (literally our integrity) – viability and vitality strengthen, not only for us but also for the world we comprise. The gift of such an education is security – enough to appropriately mitigate trust in self and others, to learn again. Yet we find ourselves in a historical moment of conspiracy theories, denialism, and rampant distrust.

Critical to vitality in human interaction is the "braiding of languaging and emotioning" (Maturana with Verden-Zöller, 2008, p. 30) in conversation. But as conversations ramp up, on the auspices of technological innovation, are we sacrificing bodily connection in favour of proliferating interactions with bodies-multiple-times-removed? If *learning is the quintessential dynamic by which autopoietic systems maintain their viability* in their milieu, and we our coupled to a strangely distant yet ever-near virtual other, what is our niche? In an age of far too much information, enclaves can too readily form as people selectively design their own worlds, absent much sense of any larger collective. Indeed, the rate of proliferation may well have exceeded our capacity to keep up, to sustain a viable sense of any whole and so we cherry pick. In societies dependent upon a sustainable and sustaining material world, hiding in our virtual ones, does nothing to address encroaching forces that threaten to compromise our human vitality on multiple fronts.

Embodied life forms as we are, we cannot escape the fact that our medium of connection and disconnection remains language and the reading of bodies writ large – from affective vitalities through gestural and verbal utterances (that we perform and that perform us), through massive reticular networks of discursive practices, to virtual worlds that increasingly bring fantasy and imagination to digital life. The promise of learning – to broaden inward-reaching and outward-searching consciousness, advancing both individuation and belonging in a "with" of being and becoming – expresses a need, none so dire, as today.

A theory of learning applicable across systems

If meaning (emotion), mind (cognition), and body (behaviour) can be understood at the level of the most fundamental autopoietic organisation, then we have a basis upon which to think about learning as it occurs in multiple implicated domains at once (biological, personal, familial, educational, and socio-cultural). I thus propose the model of learning developed in Chapters 4 through 8, to be relevant across all levels of emergence. It represents a dialectic relationship between the learning body (the self) and its external milieu (represented as "difference . . . world . . . otherness" in the model). Its utility owes to the fact that the self who learns is as much:

- a single cell in one's body, where the milieu of its world is its immediate surroundings and a function of its broader surroundings;
- a whole human self who learns, within the context of the human and the more-than-human world;
- a collective of humans, such as a classroom, within the larger context of a school, school district, community, culture, society, and so forth;
- a discursive system or subject discipline, bootstrapped to a human collective, that learns in relation to other disciplines and schools of thought circulating within the world at large.

(to paraphrase Maturana with Verden-Zöller, 2008, pp. 27 & 158–173)

140 A dialectic theory of learning

In summary, at each level of emergence, witness an individual embodied self, embedded in its social milieu, enfolding and interpreting aspects of its milieu into itself, even as it effectuates changes in that milieu. Each self interacts and maintains viability recursively, within the limits of its own possibility and in answer to its felt needs – in humans, these feelings rooted in primary affective relationships and their continued elaboration from infancy forward.

At least for the moment, the classrooms of children are not yet wholly virtual spaces. The teacher's agency in prompting student learning in such spaces resides in the relational dynamics of multiple fields at once. Just as autopoietic systems theory has made its way into learning theory, it also shows up in contemporary psychoanalysis to deepen insights in regards the relational field (see especially Donnel Stern, 2015). We will want those insights in the pages ahead, especially in considerations of not learning.

Indeed, to understand the refusal to learn we will want to remember that whenever there is self-change in the offing, it puts a present self in jeopardy. At stake are identity and trust in one's capacity to recover oneself on the other side of change. Sometimes early adaptations are maladaptive as circumstances change and sometimes learning must be foreclosed in favour of coping. We will want to understand this about ourselves, about our students, and about the socio-cultural and political worlds that contain us. Dialectics arrested is the subject of Chapter 8. It will hold us well for Part III on how we might differently proceed.

8

DIALECTICS ARRESTED

On learning's refusal

The legacy of the Enlightenment per E. O. Wilson, could be considered a prescription for learning's refusal: It is "the belief that entirely on our own we can know, and in knowing, understand, and in understanding, choose wisely" (Wilson, 1998, p. 325).

We approach the end of Part II having introduced and developed a theory that is consistent with both a third-person account of learning – that is, the view from the sciences, to describe life systems as autopoietic – and a first-person account – the view from the humanities, that looks at life through its felt experience (phenomenology). Both are interpretive renderings. Freud, in a letter to Einstein, once said as much, writing "All this may give you the impression that our [psychoanalytic] theories amount to [a] species of mythology. . . . But does not every natural science lead ultimately to this – a sort of mythology?" (Freud, 1932).

And so, with Freud, I reiterate: Both "objective" and "experiential" accounts on "reality" are interpretive. This is so, even though science interprets *as if* it had uncontested access to the "real," while phenomenology understands that all we can know of any "real" is through interpretive experience. Having different perspectival starting positions and following different rules of formulation, the power of these perspectives is in their convergence. When different, widely endorsed, interpretive programs converge onto a new coherence, then we come closer to an understanding that, practically speaking, seems more promising – if only on principles of fit and consistency.

In 1997, Donnel Stern first introduced two forms of dissociation, weak and strong: *narrative rigidity* and *not-spelling-out*, respectively. These concepts – completing our model ahead (Figure 8.1) – play well into and with the theory of autopoiesis, especially, as autopoiesis is taken up and elaborated by Alicia Juarrero in *Dynamics in Action: Intentional Behavior as a Complex System* (1999/2002). Both Juarrero and Stern devote large tracts of their books to Hans-Georg Gadamer and his

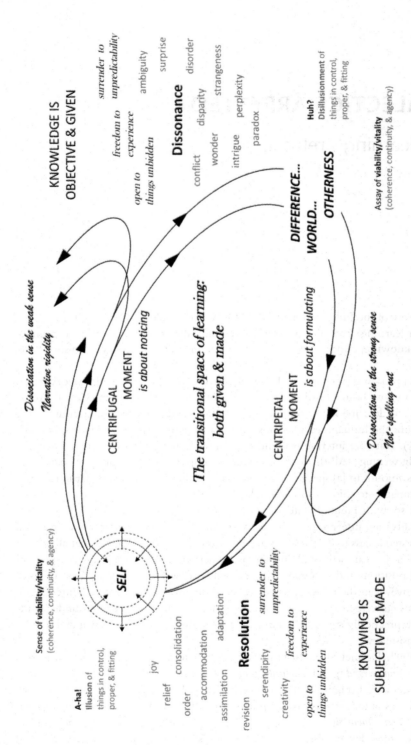

FIGURE 8.1 A dialectic model of learning and of learning's refusal

hermeneutics of understanding as "the adoption of an interpretive perspective" (Stern, 1997/2003, p. xiii) that is "always and inevitably dialogic" (p. xii) – as individual as it is social. Of the hermeneutic "circle," represented in the recursive dialectic cycling of the model, Juarrero writes that its interlevel (i.e., part-whole, individual-collective, self-world) "tacking . . . reproduces the self-organization of complex dynamical process . . . [making] hermeneutic narratives . . . uniquely suited as the logic of explanation" (1999/2002, p. 223). The resonances are no coincidence. Both thinkers and the different discourses they represent are steeped in later-maturing twentieth-century philosophical understandings. Stern and Juarrero – writing from relational psychoanalytic and dynamic systems theory respectively – share a common historical and contextual moment. Though I very much doubt these authors know of each other, their understandings fit like Escher's *Drawing Hands*, each scribing the other.

In this chapter, I knit both discourses into the model in a way to account, not only for learning but also for learning "going off the rails" when potential learners feel the threat of irresolvable chaos. Both Stern and Juarrero concern themselves with how the structures that creatively order and maintain interpretive life do so by drawing from a wellspring of as-yet-uninterpreted, unsettling but often familiar, chaos within and without – for Stern, the chaos of the unconscious; for Juarrero, the chaos of dissipative systems, those spontaneous emergences and orderly synchronicities (e.g., neuronal patterns) that render life's possibility. While Stern focuses on the role of language in formulating newly noticed experience into consciousness, Juarrero's gaze is toward the neurophysiology of such linguistic formulation. In short, both writers come at the same phenomena through entirely different conceptual schools to arrive at mutually reinforcing narratives. We do well to take note.

Recapitulating Part II's convergences

We have visited twentieth-century learning theories and have addressed the unresolved dispute between the personal constructivism (classically Piagetian) of an intrapsychic self and the social constructivism (classically Vygotskyan) of an intersubjective self. We can conceive of that dispute as evidence of our grappling to live well in the paradoxical singular-plural biology of our being and the phenomenology it entails.

We have likewise seen an ongoing disagreement between progressivists and traditionalists on schooling regimes. Critiquing the progressivist's constructivist argument, we pointed out that constructivism would need to account for learning, period, regardless of educational circumstance. We recast these schooling wars as evidence of our grappling in the paradox of the given and made, where learning happens with one foot in the familiar structures of what we and any culture think we know (the *objectively given world out there*) and the other foot in the conjuring world of our imaginative sense-making bodies (a *subjectively made world in mind*) – Winnicott's *transitional space* (1971/2005) and Taussig's "real and the really made-up" when he writes that "the strange thing about this silly if not desperate place

144 A dialectic theory of learning

between the real and the really made-up is that it appears to be where most of us spend most of our time" (1993, p. xvii).

Critical to the theory is the idea of discernible difference – a permissible puzzlement, new-to-awareness but not so foreign as to go unseen. Such difference both entices and provokes learning's movement. In autopoietic terms, when dynamic changes in the external milieus of biological organisms trigger noticeable internal shifts, the noticing is a call to assess, address, and deal with the new difference in manner as to re-equilibrate system integrity. Learning's mitigation thus entangles in the selective permeability of boundaries, in what gets noticed, and in the capacity to resolve differences admitted. And of course, what gets in and what we make of it turns on prior lessons retained as memory.

When the mind brings memory to bear on the now, it takes past interpretations and generalisations on experience and applies them to make present contextual sense. Memory lives in variably accessible and interrelated unconscious, nonconscious, and conscious aspects of self – each differently comprising the sediments of prior experiences, according to a biology of neuronal behaviour. Neurons, for their part, are those strangely networked organisms whose lives span our own and whose collaborative connective litheness and responsivity afford the means by which we story and re-story who we are to ourselves and others. The associative habits of neurons and their responsivity to affective/neurochemical salience make possible our recognition of symbols as proxies for original experiences and their meanings. In turn, symbol systems birth thought, according to the way concepts assemble into networked, tiered, organisational structures. Learning involves the making of such structures. Thoughts, and the words expressing them, are historically meaningful according to the way they connect back to feeling states and habits learned in primary attachment relationships, what was important then, and how secure we felt. In this way, our very being is storied in relationality and steeped in affect.

Learning as adaptive self-change involves a dialectic intrapsychic–intersubjective, self–world, tacking as depicted in Figure 8.1. In the outreaching centrifugal movement, we look to a world beyond our knowing, in terms of our knowing, and find, if providence will have it, the confounding but alluring dissonance of a newest ambiguity: the "huh?" – a "violation of expectation" in psychoanalytic terms, a "perturbation" in constructivist/autopoietic ones. The admission of dissonance places us at the door of a centripetal return to self. Dissonance's meaningful resolution percolates out of conscious awareness, emerging (when ready) as the "a-ha" of a newly realised sense. Though we can encourage the percolation, we cannot force the realisation. Should successful articulation (as shareable thought) ensue then it promises a sliver of revised coherence as our newest familiar for greeting the world again.

A deficiency in capacity, trust, or meaning can halt the movement of learning (developed further in Part III). When learning is not an option yet we feel the pressure to learn, then dissociation affords a means of coping. In this chapter, we will complete the model with two added components, each representing a potential dissociative moment. Before developing these further, acknowledging that learning is

Dialectics arrested **145**

mitigated by boundary permeability and by what we can do with what gets in, then the milieus within and without any system merit our attention.

Milieus and their refusals

There are milieus outside and within the self – some consciously known, others less so, most not at all. What our bodies know, we are typically at a loss to say to ourselves. My hands know the keyboard; my mind could no longer tell you its configuration. In trying to word the knowing that does reach conscious awareness, we often stumble on the sense we felt we had. When it comes to conceptual understandings, if we are lucky, and more than a bit fearless, this can prove a usefully compelling and creative exercise in coherence-making – as much world-making as it is story-making and sense-making. But sometimes we know enough not to "go there." Recall that "the folk psychology of ordinary people is not *just* a set of self-assuaging illusions, but the culture's beliefs and working hypotheses about what makes it possible and fulfilling for people to live together" (Bruner, 1990, p. 32). Sometimes folk psychology comes to our aid, providing rigid cover stories to justify our avoiding the uncomfortable things.

For learning to occur, the difference outside that spawns a responsive difference within needs symbolic articulation to be consciously known. If only for biological efficiency, most of what we experience does not get past unconscious and nonconscious processes. Our consciousness, even its very composition, depends on this. *What I am talking about is an inside that is like an outside.*

If these unarticulated bits are potent and can neither be extricated nor functionally incorporated – that is, if no bodily sense can be made of them – then they can either accrue into rich dynamic reservoirs of possibility or they can fester there, threatening havoc if loosened. Accrue and fester (like plastic debris wreaking havoc in the bodies of sea organisms). We cannot incorporate something into conscious awareness if we cannot make a workable coherence of it on our terms and in terms of the world we know and that knows us. This is what I mean when I say something does not make sense. The inability to make sense, when sense is needed, can prompt dissociation.

We surely entertain experiences that begin harmlessly enough, but that escalate in unforeseeable ways, becoming so disturbing as to exceed our capacity to sit well with them. How do we make sense of someone saying they love us in a voice that bespeaks indifference? The unspoken indifference can resist formulation, existing as an unregistered-but-registered shard of something salient, vaguely rememberable yet untenable. We cope by refusing its acknowledgement, refusing to spell it out, and dissociating our conscious self from that discomfort. Yet we will surely be changed by this thing we cannot "know," not to mention drained by the psychic effort of maintaining a safe distance. In fact, we are likely to weave rigid explanatory narratives as protective boundaries to keep difficult interpretations at bay.

To see how this might play out in learning, consider the example of the mathematical construct, pi (revisited in Chapter 12). To a classroom of young teens, "pi" is often experienced and later remembered, not as any useful idea, but as an intangible given. The learner is hard-pressed to make sense of this unreasonably irrational

146 A dialectic theory of learning

number and its strange signifier, "π." It's digits can't even be fully written out. It calls into question everything one thought one knew about numbers as counting things – standing among those bewildering ideas commonly associated with mathematics. Almost emblematic, pi can trigger a host of anxieties that begin in mathematics, but land in other places – or is it the other way around? One's felt incompetence in making "pi" one's own, can implicate how one knows oneself and one's agency to do things like learn, please the teacher, be seen well by peers, belong to the classroom community, and/or live up to both one's expectations and those of the people one values. These kinds of experiences chart the compromising of trust in learning, trust in oneself, trust in a world that makes sense, and trust in those we thought we could count on to help. Pi is not unlike a robe on a hook in the dark – for although we can rationalise it as a harmless housecoat, this does little to stop the haunting feeling with which it threatens.

In working with prospective and practicing elementary-school teachers, the mere mention of pi will strike visible fear in at least a quarter of any such group. Would that I had exaggerated or misread my students! I am not, and I have not (see, e.g., McAnallen, 2010; Novak & Tassel, 2017). There seems no shortage of targets to blame for debilitating anxiety in learning. We have pointed the finger at management, diversity, textbooks, effort, attitude, parents, teachers, assessment, technique, gender, biology, stereotype, tracking, and mismatched styles. Mathematics may well be a canary-in-the-coalmine of systemic insecurities whose roots go much deeper, begin much earlier, and persist much longer than we generally appreciate – often across lifetimes, intergenerationally so.

From autopoietic implications for learning *to* dialectics-arrested, failures in trust, and dissociation as coping

Per Donnel Stern,

> We develop those articulations that we believe we can tolerate, or that further our purpose, or those that promise a feeling of safety, satisfaction, and the good things in life; we dissociate the meanings that we believe we will not be able to tolerate, that frighten us and seem to threaten the fulfillment of our deepest intentions.
>
> *(1997/2003, p. 128)*

To broach not-learning, we reconsider learning and the character of learning systems, this time asking: How might learning conditions go awry and how might dissociation – as a reasonable solution to the unreasonable situation of not knowing how to make the sense one should make – become the devil to sabotage future learning?

We set the stage, by revisiting the implications of life as autopoietic and structured-determined. The unknown known exists as the embodied residue of experiences and the unprocessed elements of internal milieus. It can threaten to ambush

Dialectics arrested **147**

or promise to enlighten us, either way emerging through the cracks to call into question that which we thought we knew. Echoing across the unconsciousness of an individual life and the disavowed components of collective life, the unexpected stands always at the ready to turn topsy-turvy the structures we know. To borrow Donnel Stern's terms (1997/2003), while the unknown known is the "familiar chaos" threatening demise, it is also the "creative disorder" of life's self-renewing possibility. These principles set the contexts for dialectics-arrested and for dissociation as learning's refusal.

When life is structure-determined: implications for learning

From the materially grounded, autopoietic understanding of embodied cognition, we can parse six implications for learning, where the fifth gives clues about difficult learning and the sixth presents dissociation as coping mechanism to forestall that difficulty. These implications are as relevant to physically perceived life systems (per the view through science) as to relationally conceived thinking systems – including of course individual minds, collective minds, and the connecting conceptual-symbolic systems that make any kind of human interpretive sense possible in the first place. A healthy dose of imagination will help us traverse the broad example space of life forms.

As a first implication, an autopoietic premise situates learning as part of life's teleology toward ongoing viability according to a *principle of sufficiency* as good enough. That is, for any life form (as bounded, relationally connected, system), *to remain viable means self-regenerating in functional enough accordance with its milieu.* Systems can learn only what their milieus avail to them via provocative enough invitation, and only in terms of what their being permits them to notice. "Safety lies in familiarity. . . . [T]he self system . . . perpetuates itself. . . . [W]e avoid anxiety by searching out the familiar in experience and throwing away the rest" (Donnel Stern, 1997/2003, pp. 55–56). Moreover, just as the amoeba cannot "see" light, while the euglena can (Chapter 7); so too can we perceive and understand only "what the language of our time and place allows" (Gadamer, paraphrased in Stern, 1997/2003, p. xi).

Second, self-replication is never exact because internal and external contexts are never identical. The result is drift in autopoietic systems as self-producing/replicating. Drift assumes directionality insofar as shifts in milieus, being not entirely random, move along a gradient. Drift effectuates a kind of substitution that instantiates a revised present and forgets or buries what came before. *Drift is learning as self-change along a relatively passive continuum.* It also explains atrophy: Acknowledging system-specific constraints on viability, we can say that a system passively drifts "up" or "down" in *vitality*, while sustaining sufficient *viability*.

Third, in response to stress that is non-catastrophic (per point four), through processes of positive and negative feedback loops, systems actively self-change and they actively self-regulate in support of that change. This is also learning. For example, assuming non-catastrophic damage, when incrementally strained to carry heavy

148 A dialectic theory of learning

loads, muscle tissue adapts in the direction of upscaling bulk as strength; and, when incrementally stretched beyond usual ranges-of-motion, muscle tissue adapts in the direction of upscaling length as flexibility. *Insofar as change draws the global attention/ intention of the system – in a sense, at the threshold of conscious discernment – we could call such learning active.* In discourses in human development, these notions fall under the rubrics of *effortful and deliberate practice* but also *metacognition and mentalisation* as processes of thinking about thinking.

Fourth, learning consists in some combination of passive up-drift and active self-change, in functional accordance to the provocations of non-catastrophic stress, *provided there are sufficient resources to support such accommodation.* In catastrophic stress, the affected systems, subsystems, and/or component parts either disintegrate or become irreparably dysfunctional and a burden to the greater system. In stress's absence, the affected systems, subsystems, and/or component parts atrophy. If the degree of stress (with respect to the system and its available resources) increments somewhere between these two poles, then *learning proceeds as a process of self-amplification-by-replication through twin structuring inclinations of bundling sameness (mimesis) and creatively coupling difference (poiesis).*

Fifth, learning in its least-threatening, most common, capacity is a process of *scaling up.* However, to remain viable, systemic structures will eventually need to disassemble and reassemble in ways that also preserve self-continuity of the system's co-ordinated relationships – its identity. Nature's solution to the need to disassemble and start anew (but not quite) is procreation.

Scaling up in learning entails somewhat orderly accrual, amenable to degrees of controlled quantifiable metronomic time – what the Greeks called *chronos.* Its primary signature is mimetic growth, leastwise from the perspective of the experiencing organism. But there is a functional limit to scaling up at which point the system (even and especially a conceptual one) becomes so weighty and cumbersome as to lose its responsivity and resilience and become vulnerable to discontinuity. We scale up from and hold firmly to foundational histories within – often increasingly anachronistic with respect to the dynamic flux of shifty milieus. Thus, growth becomes unwieldy, wanting for paradigmatic reconfiguration into more eloquently adapted, relational form.

Inspiration for paradigmatic change rarely comes from the already-made. Rather, inspiration takes shape in the unsurveilled (out-of-sight, out-of-mind) shadows that structures necessarily create, and according to inspiration's own non-metronomic rhythm – a time marked as *kairos* where moments can be fleeting or seem to stand still. Such changes are quintessentially poietic – and not for the faint of heart. If scaling up is a matter of increased Promethean-like potency, then paradigm changes are akin to giving oneself over to the wisdom that can be found in Dionysian-like fecundity. This is as risky as it is promising, and ultimately necessary. The threshold to paradigmatic change is fraught with angst. It is crossed when the present feels so inadequate as to threaten viability in measure exceeding the leap of faith to some unforeseen possibility. Letting go of one trapeze, one hopes the other coming into view materialises as both accessible and worthy.

Finally, where resources are insufficient, and/or stress portends impending catastrophe, and/or needed learning requires impossible self-reorganisation, then the system with nowhere to go and not trusting its capacity to adapt and survive will seek to forestall disaster by "dissociating." In dissociation, the system refuses the dialectic lesson of its milieu and instead rallies its defences either by isolating itself (decreasing boundary permeability), symbiotically affiliating with protective counterparts (coupling), and/or changing milieus. In the material world, these defensive solutions can take the following appearances: In the first instance, boundary-building in unfavourable conditions can look like cocooning, dormancy, or hibernation, for example. Where unfavourable conditions are internal, boundary making can look like a clam coating a grain of sand (from our view making a pearl), scar tissue accruing around an invasive species, or the actual dissociation of parts (a kind of disintegration) in, for example, a Portuguese man-of-war that disperses into a colony of polyps. In the second instance, symbiosis of organic forms can entail various combinations of benefit, indifference, and parasitic exploitation. Finally, changing milieus can look like migration or other forms of relocation (e.g., wildlife on the move with climate change) or it can be about staying put and being an agent of change to one's milieu (e.g., an ant colony acts to alter its milieu). The human as hunter gatherer and as agrarian species demonstrates, par excellence, each of these strategies – until of course the limits of the milieu are reached – in our case, the biosphere.

The processes by which autopoietic systems forestall disaster when learning is not an option – namely isolation, symbiosis, and altered milieus – have, as we will see, their counterparts in human relational experience.

Sometimes learning is not an option

Not-learning

By dialectics-arrested, I mean to say that the reiterative processes of learning represented in Figure 8.1 come to a halt. This is not yet to dissociate. Why might someone not be able to make sense? Why might someone not be able to notice a dissonance or, thus-noticing, not incorporate the rupture's effect into a revised coherence? Note the nuanced difference between not being able to make sense and passing over its opportunity. Maturana with Verden-Zöller writes, "we do not have to live all the realities we may create," nor can we. Stern reminds us that "all unconscious material is unformulated . . . Experience is fundamentally ambiguous" (1997/2003, p. 26) and that "understanding is an act . . . easier, less effortful, not to carry it out than to carry it through" (p. 76). Moreover, "because it is effortful, [it] is the exception and not the rule" (p. 121). To successfully go about our daily lives, almost all opportunities to consciously make a formulated sense must be regularly passed over. The situation is different in schooling where the educational system requires that particular senses be made and on someone else's schedule.

There are human variations in readiness and in openness to the formulations to be had as learning. In many circumstances, the learning demands simply exceed capacity. Much of Vygotsky's and Piaget's work focused on determining what might be within any child's conceptual reach (see Chapter 7). Today, intelligence seems a fallen concept – popular theory having it that most any curriculum is within reach, if rightly approached. But one cannot bring together ideas and/or skills that one has not yet developed and there is the problem of keeping apace. Raw intelligence may be a function of the agility of neurons and the nimbleness with which discernments can be noticed, resolved, and retained. Too much nimbleness and one's imagination can outstrip the world; too little and one cannot keep up. While the demand to keep up can engender a sense of failure for some, there will be others whose identities are built upon a capacity to exceed demand, even effortlessly so. In short order, everyone in the class will know who is who.

These conditions compound much earlier life lessons *vis-à-vis* self, others, and the world. On the one hand, learning is severely compromised when feeling under immediate threat or having assumed a state of constant low-grade vigilance, especially if the requirement to learn is also the source of threat. On the other hand, in situations where school success comes easily, learning can be the escape to soothe away other angst – one's safe symbolic retreat from an affectively dangerous world.

We saw an entire body of developmental research, especially from Daniel Stern through Beebe and others, that included the meticulous documentation of interactive parent–child dyads, with degrees of secure and insecure relational patterns already formed and robust by four months. And we saw how attachment insecurity put self-agency, continuity, and/or coherence in peril and compromised children's ability to navigate learning and life in trust with others. In short, the regular sabotaging of coherence-making, at whatever age, begets affective distress in the anticipation of disruption, especially to one's most cherished knowns.

The cumulative effect of repeated failure-experiences, especially when expectant others seem oblivious to our reality, chips away at self- and other-trust, threatens debilitating anxiety, and creates a sense of being alone, unseen, and misunderstood, even by those purporting to help. In such conditions, when the needs for security and recognition are split "the self also tends to be split between security and recognition. In some instances parts of self must be dissociated, unrecognized, in order to be safe; in others, safety is sacrificed in order to feel known" (Benjamin, 2018, p. 9). The learner unable to keep up can soon be riddled with reasons to dissociate.

How do we know not-learning as failure? Must it be so?

What does a failure-experience in learning look like? How does anyone know that they have not made sense – enough to become anxious about it? Where is the crazy-making that presses rigid cover stories as dissociative solutions? I ask because I have a grandson who is so "cognitively impaired" that, at ten years old, his communicative skills are no more than the sounds of a typical four-month-old. He is, however, affectively attuned. And he is blissfully happy. He does not know the feeling of "supposed-to-know," and has thus no reason for anxiety about his ever-so-limited capacity to learn. In short, he has no need to dissociate.

Dialectics arrested **151**

I ask also because studies in mathematics anxiety show that, in early-year schooling, children can dislike mathematics and know themselves not to be good at it, yet show no signs of related anxiety. This contradicts the consistently reported negative correlations between ability and anxiety in adults (Krinzinger, Kaufmann, & Willmes, 2009). But *those children for whom happiness hinges on performing well, regardless of capacity, are the children who are anxious* (Thomas & Dowker, 2000). Especially for these children, once adults – and for many, long before – emphases on performance and producing finished products according to someone else's criteria will have produced the well-documented downward spiral of mutually reinforcing anxiety and compromised ability (Baldino & Cabral, 2008; Bandura, 1993; Burns, 1998; Dowker, 2005; Hattie, 2009, pp. 49–50). Donnel Stern writes, "To be capable of new experience is to be capable of not knowing what will come next" (p. 88). The felt surveillance of a preoccupied watcher renders "not knowing what will come next" a terrifying omen of continued failures to measure up.

These observations suggest something insidious and grave with schooling. It points to a problem, not of ability, but of relations and expectation. How do we know, in our heart of hearts, when we have made sense? There seems no question of recognising the feeling of a new coherence, an "a-ha," when it happens. The fit immediately surprises and rewards us. "Once seen, a new clarity may seem so inevitable that it is experienced as having 'been there all the time'" (Stern, 1997/2003, p. 69). When we make sense, "we take given experience and make it into something that is our own . . . by avoiding violations of the givens that define what the experience can be" (p. 3). But who chooses which violations must be avoided? Who is the final arbiter on whether any sense we have made is right or good enough? Who endorses it and, in the doing, legitimises the learner and his own experience? In schools, that person is someone other than that learner. The first thing any child wants to know is this: "Did I get it right?" The question suggests a deeper problem: that understanding is not about meaning at all, it is about doing right and having one's rightness affirmed – a prescription not to trust oneself. The most difficult moments in my teaching have been when a student – eyes lit up for having arrived at a new coherence, but for which that coherence relied on flawed premises – asks, "Did I get it right?" In such moments, the child has surely made an invaluable "a-ha" – one to be celebrated for the understanding it does reveal. Yet the request for affirmation is reduced to whether the answer is right. Poorly navigated – witnessed as failure, experienced as failure – it will surely function to further erase the child's sense of self-trust as sense-maker.

Ultimately, an authoritative world has some say in vetting the sense we make. That is, for the resultant sense that is made, to make sense, it must be perceivably strapped to a world taken-as-given, but not on our terms; that is, taken ultimately as culturally authorised others perceive it to be given. Where one's new understanding is inconsistent with pre-existing conclusions or is articulated in ways unrecognisable to established conventions, then "proper" sense has not been made, and this will be the case regardless that the sense-maker's experience says otherwise. Pressed to live these contradictions, assuming they are not resolvable, the sense-maker can

152 A dialectic theory of learning

either deny the other's professed perception or ignore his own self-experience. That is, in the face of an inability to see it their way, said learner either insists on his difference – and risks being called, at best, wrong/misguided, at worst, mad – or he can keep those inadmissible perceptions to himself, even dissociating against their formulation. Is it any wonder that some of our most creative minds drop out of school early?

Dissociation avoids failure-experiences by pre-emptively avoiding the question of learning altogether – and this is true regardless of what is to be learned. It leaves unanswered whether knowing could have been possible in the first place. It is not enough to school someone to parrot "I can." It is not enough for a teacher to insist that the child rally courage to believe it. A defensive "I won't/I can't" simply cannot, by sheer force of will (or to please someone), transform into a true "I can." In the least, when learners say they can't (or when the risk of "can't" hides behind "won't") we will want to bear witness, striving to mitigate conditions such that they ultimately "can" (see Part III). Here we could take our cues from the relational world of psychoanalysis whose theorists have devoted great thought to freeing the relational field to permit the risking of difficult formulations and the noticing of what we are fearful of seeing, lest these reinstate old failures and deepen wounds.

The compounding of defences

The young learner *dissociates from future learning as a solution to past experiences of failures-to-learn.* The material we avoid has a way of compounding upon itself such that the degrees of freedom for finding one's way out of the weighty morass become so constricted as to render some learners extraordinarily debilitated. An example comes immediately to mind of a grade 7 student in a class to which I taught both science and math, in succession. At the start of the year, in science class, this student was engaged. In the next hour, in math class, that same student absolutely refused to even look up from her desk. In a most literal sense, she dissociated from any possibility of noticing dissonance, much less attempting to resolve it. Defensive solutions to learning-arrested become a part of the learner's very identity. The solution was not in forcing her gaze. Her actions were symptoms of something much deeper. Conferencing with her parent, I began to understand the state of this girl's world and how I might proceed.

As we move into adulthood, early difficulties can intensify and go underground, while new challenges surface. Insofar as new knowing requires a paradigmatic restructuring of old knowing, then disassembling might be needed before moving forward – leastwise if one is to stay current with one's milieu. In today's world of information-on-demand, there is pride in proclaiming one's love of learning. But lifelong learning is rarely undertaken in the spirit of disrupting what one thought one knew. Rather, it seems to play out much more as amplifying what one already knows – that is, becoming knowledgeable in fascinating details while leaving one's worldview and self-understanding intact and beyond reconsideration. In a profound sense, old knowing blocks new learning. Stern writes, "The capacity to see the

Dialectics arrested **153**

familiar in the unfamiliar, one of the great achievements of infancy, becomes in adulthood an equally great impediment to thought's growth" (1997/2003, p. 63). At the same time, insofar as adulthood enlarges the geographic if not the socio-cultural reach of one's gaze, it can seem to magnify the differences and dissonances one encounters, making increasingly difficult the task of bridging more egregious human estrangements. Perhaps this is at play in rising populism, and worldwide political shifts of identity politics and nations divided. Meanwhile, our extraordinary societal proclivity to inventive thought lends to conjuring alternative fictions and truths to assist in our dissociative projects. This conjuring can parade as more meaningfully real when caught in that transitional – real and "made up" – cyberspace where the world in one's head materialises as the world out there.

Just as our well-being entangles in the phenomenon of human coupling, through language, into powerful, networked, socio-cultural regimes, these regimes (and ourselves in them) likewise entangle in and are coupled, through capital, to powerful, networked, socio-political ones. To be well with ourselves and the world, we want to feel that we are safe enough in these entanglements. Under such conditions, different learning seems entirely out of the question and amplification of what we already know the only viable option. Indeed, individual well-being, and agency to do or be otherwise, cannot be divested from the regimes that contain us. We cannot extricate ourselves and survive. And so, the regimes themselves must somehow remain viable. In a scaled-up world, affiliation in powerfully subsuming systems seems the only reassurance of survival, yet this does nothing to help us navigate the contradictions of, say, espousing altruistic beliefs (the likes of success for all) while securing competitive advantage. When systems become thusly incoherent, dissociation finds its expression as denialism, not-me, and doer/done-to insistences.

Pathology's signature seems to be rigid cover stories, clung to, however contradictory in nature, as first-line defence of turning a blind eye to discord. Like the child who, with chocolate sputtering in mouth, adamantly insists to have not eaten it, such actions express some version of the frightened refrain "not me." Each denial, meant to smooth incoherence out of sight, presents a façade at odds with experience. The contradiction instrumentalises yet another iteration of incoherence. If conditions allow the unchecked propagation of insidiously denied anxiety-begetting incoherence, then a pathos of historically conditioned socio-cultural angst makes sense.

As adults, we become particularly adept at maintaining self-coherent façades, protecting our psychic selves from the very self-elements most likely to be rejected. We are experienced in enacting a game of "not me" as unspoken, but ever-lived refrain. Some difficulties are best left alone, or so a wisdom of denied affect goes. Too often, feeling ill-positioned to address the difficulty, we opt for letting it fester a little while longer until such time, as might never come, that we could find the fortitude, gumption, and resolve to deal with the inevitability of waking "the sleeping dog that lies." I often wonder to what extent such strategic adult expertise is borne by the young we teach, society's newest citizens.

154 A dialectic theory of learning

Still, the argument I seek to advance is not one of blame, but rather another way of interpreting current predicaments. It is not that we – some or all of us – have been "bad," nor even that we have been "foolish." There is no absolute measure, no threshold against which to call us in error as such – except the ones we construe. When it comes to dissociation, we can only begin to appreciate and live in ways mindful of the litheness by which human mental capacity, individual and collective, serving sophisticated unconscious predisposition has made us highly adept at wielding all three defensive strategies that life forms implement under duress: isolation, symbiosis, changing milieus. We simply seem to be able to accomplish it in astoundingly manifold and exponentially escalating ways.

Psychoanalysis and teaching: a common goal

Stern maintains that *"psychoanalysis is defined by its attempt to expand self-knowledge and widen the range of explicit choice"* (italics added, 1997/2003, p. 24). Dienes formulates the aims of teaching

> under the rather vague heading of *building up personality*. . . . through a process of integration. . . . An integrated person. . . . will try to unite things rather than separate them. He will seek connections rather than differences and – perhaps most important of all – he will have made a good adjustment to his environment by establishing a fundamental identity of interest between himself and his fellows.
>
> *(1960, pp. 24–25)*

Following Stern, I would slightly alter Dienes description of *"building up personality."* I believe education and psychoanalysis share the aim of promoting an *integrating*, rather than *integrated*, psychic structure – one in which the self need not choose between security and recognition, between being accepted or being known.

Given that the claims I am making and the model I am forwarding takes seriously the physical and experiential paradox of the inside as also the outside, then what I am calling learning and what I seek to advance in teaching (if indeed this book does teach) is an education that – per Stern's description of psychoanalysis cited just above – can also be "defined by its attempt to expand self-knowledge and widen the range of explicit choice". Though the rhetoric in schooling seems very much to privilege the learning of content and an outside-in gradient, at the same time, learning proceeds from the inside-out. More aptly put, it is transitionally neither and both, dialectically so. Thus, insofar as the widening of anyone's range of explicit choice, I hope that breadth be not only for each individual person-learner but also for the collectives and collections of life forms and those things learned, all, whose modes of becoming well and wise, must encompass that which is singular and plural, the world in a grain of sand.

In summary, I have presented many possible circumstances that could provoke the arrest of learning's dialectic movement and foreclose learning's possibility. We

Dialectics arrested **155**

first dissociate because we cannot learn; yet we cannot learn because we dissociate. Remembering that learning is what life forms do, indeed must do to stay alive, then, dissociation is the defensive solution to the problem of dialectics-arrested – the problem of the inability to render a coherent self in the face of the intolerably ambiguous strain of unregulatable milieus within and without the self. When, for our sake and the sake of others, we fail to make sufficiently workable coherences out of those dissonances (out of what Stern calls "creative disorder," 1997/2003), dissociation is the way we cope. Dissociation is about not-spelling-out that which we fear we cannot mend; it is about paying no mind to the murmur of dissonance, the "familiar chaos" at our door, and it proceeds from a refusal to look, to an *inability* to see. In dissociation, dialectical learning is unnecessary. In dissociation, "I can't make sense" becomes "There is no sense to be made because the sense I have is not broken," and, as the adage goes: "If it's not broken, don't fix it."

Put in the words of Stern, the "avoidance of formulation is accomplished by means of selective inattention. . . . One simply does not notice what one does not wish to know. . . . Anxiety is prevented of course, but the strategy is equally effective in the prevention of learning" (1997/2003, p. 59).

When trust fails

Garrison mentalities and unassailable walls

After grievous failed attempts at sense-making, we stop trusting that we can. *The gaps that matter to us, but whose bridging prove too elusive, are those ambiguities to trouble us most. They constitute the urgent sense we cannot (but must) make and, thus, the sense we can only refuse to consider.* In dissociation, defensive boundaries mount a selective opaqueness that pre-emptively prohibits the possibility of the very recognition that could open the door to ourselves as sense-makers. The solution of dissociation is a solution of abandoned possibility.

By somehow reconceiving our milieus as to functionally distance ourselves from their compulsion, we split ourselves safely away from any provocations that we believe could potentially shatter our being. We close ourselves off, limiting any forays into worlds that bode strange, within as without. We can neither entertain, much less admit, the difference of the other nor the other's conceptual "curricular" objects – that is, insofar as that other and that understanding is not the echo of our own. Accordingly, there can be no meeting of minds except in commiseration on one or the other side of me/not-me, doer/done-to, us/them positions. And the world splits. We can install and maintain such splits as a matter of near life-or-death consequence.

Following Donnel Stern (1997/2003), we enact our dissociative defences through two modes of neglect: In not-spelling-out we pass over what augurs disquiet within – the things we must not experience for fear of their incomprehensibility and incommensurability. In narrative rigidity, the understanding we adamantly profess occludes from view any other – thus rendering the things we *must* not

156 A dialectic theory of learning

experience into those we *cannot*. And so, as with other life systems, we too manage threat by manipulating boundaries. From an autopoietic perspective the boundaries we manage are between the structure-determined identities we endorse and cling to as self, and the internal and external milieus that beg to differ.

It would be difficult to underestimate the debilitating effects of dissociation.

> Dissociation is an intervention designed, in advance of the fact, to avoid the possibility that a full-bodied meaning will occur. Dissociated meaning is style without substance, the story that accounts for what it addresses but tells us nothing we don't already know, the conversation we can fill in without having to listen. Dissociation is the deletion of imagination.
>
> *(Donnel Stern, 1997/2003, p. 98)*

The understandings coming out of research in early childhood development and attachment relations parallel those arising out of psychoanalytic work with adults. In Chapter 6, we touched on Fonagy and Target's (2007) "theory of external reality rooted in intersubjectivity," wherein they expand upon two modes of primitive intersubjectivity in childhood: "psychic equivalence and pretend" – these predating the more sophisticated versatility of presence and mentalising capacity *vis-à-vis* self, other, and world. "In *psychic equivalence* everything is 'for real'" (p. 927). The ideas in the infant's head feel "tantamount to reality" (p. 927). Consciousness is assumed as shared. Later in *pretend* mode, children can play at make-believe. This reflects an awareness that shared consciousness is by no means a given (p. 928). In make-believe the child casts "as if" imagined scenarios and then plays in them, as to play at reality. Often children devote more time to contriving these scenarios than to their actual play. In essence, both psychic equivalence and pretend modes of intersubjectivity are all about making heads or tails of where I end, and you begin. Make-believe is about "trying on for size" what it might be like to "stand in someone else's shoes." It is still a far cry from living in that other's feet while standing in their shoes. As it turns out, there is a world of difference between "doing onto others as you would have others do onto you" and "doing onto others as they would have you do onto them." But few of us get to that realisation.

The contexts of insecure and disorganised attachment can, from the start, compromise progress through these processes. If unattended, the dissociative solutions to intersubjective insecurities develop around issues of psychic boundary maintenance (and this too is reminiscent of our autopoietic systems). One readily encounters in one's classrooms the extraordinary breadth of boundary permeabilities characterising schoolchildren and youth, these destined to crystallise into adult patterns of relating. In the direction of impermeable boundaries, there are those prone to avoid affect and connection altogether – turning away from anything or anyone who bodes disruptive, and shoring up defences by way of offensive attacks that say, "not me" and if not "me," you. In the direction of indiscriminately porous boundaries, there are those desperately seeking security from without and (in a symbiosis that can never be quite enough) investing themselves wholly in some perceived-to-be-certain other. Culture seems at the ready to supply iconic figures serving just such a purpose.

In terms of doer/done-to relationships, the avoidant individual who rallies a garrison mentality seems better poised to inhabit the "doer" side. A pretence of security, posing as certainty, means refusing to entertain vulnerability: One dare not look inward to spell out what could be there, and one dare not let go of the rigid narratives defining one's unambiguous world. On the complementary "done-to" side of doer/done-to relations, in a kind of bewilderment about self and world, the ambivalent person is more likely to seek to endear themselves to powerful others. Such a one is at the ready to forsake boundaries in willing exchange for worth-and-safety-by-affiliation (and connection as fusion). Going back to the child's imaginative world, the tenuous shadow of a housecoat hanging in the dark can become a spectral apparition. The avoidant solution might entail a stoic insistence on the affectless real, that with a flick of the light ridicules fear and imagination. The ambivalent solution might entail a dire insistence on a night light (or a parental presence) to hold ever-present imaginative construals at bay. The avoidant solution disavows fear and censors imagination; the second solution disallows both.

From the classroom to the world stage

These dissociative processes have a way of playing out in multiple scenes and at multiple levels at once – perhaps no scene so disconcerting as today's populist arenas. Drawing on Foucault's *Discipline and Punish* (1977/1995), Kahn-Harris describes the psychological burden of modernity's explosion of accessible knowledge and with it the "widening chasm between what is speakable and what is done. . . . between private desires and the public language of values" (2018, pp. 74–75). He writes,

> We know more about our past, our future and the material world we live in than ever before. . . . We may do the same destructive things we always did, but now it is almost impossible not to be aware that there will be *consequences* to our actions and that there are always *choices*.
>
> *(pp. 71–72)*

But taken together, the choices we *must* make can feel as though they are no choice at all. Self-improvement being the spirit of the day, we are given to accord with a well-disciplined altruistic society where good citizens co-operate, stay healthy, live gratefully, and continue lifelong learning. The promise is that everyone, who (correctly) tries, succeeds. A rising science of positive psychology is there to help us on our way (see, e.g., Yale's popular "Happiness course," Tremonti, 2018, February 18). And yes, the full coercive force of societal disciplining on the side of the "good" begins early and is sustained across campuses and Western governments. To be blunt and polemic, we are called to atone for the sins of the father – or in the very least to "try harder" while giving up the illegitimate advantages begotten by having just

158 A dialectic theory of learning

such an inheritance. For many, especially those accustomed to privileged inheritances, this is too much.

In the 1990s the expression "politically correct" came to be a pejorative term critiquing the new left. Writing for the New York Times, Richard H. Bernstein contributed to that shift in "The rising hegemony of the politically correct" (October 28). He listed the beliefs that one, then, should stand for on the side of the good: "a powerful environmentalism . . . support for Palestinian self-determination . . . sympathy for third world revolutionaries, particularly those in Central America. Biodegradable garbage bags . . . [and not] Exxon" (p. 2). Today that list has shifted and gotten a great deal longer. Being unable to do all the things we should do, we can either flounder in contradiction or dissociate contradiction out of existence.

> As Nichols and others point out, the solution has seen the pendulum swing to the unabashed privileging of feelings and desires over facts and expertise. Nichols cites Michael Gove, a leader promoting Brexit who argued exactly this point, saying "I think people in this country . . . have had enough of experts." (Gove in Nichols, 2017, p. 209). Here, we see the word "expert" used pejoratively toward those individuals who know what they are talking about. The point is that "people should be free to build gratifying fantasies free from unpleasant facts".
>
> *(Traub in Nichols, 2017, p. 210)*

In describing dissociation, Stern notes that "selective attention [and/as selective inattention] comes to our aid as so suave [a tool] that we are not warned that we have not heard the important thing in the story" (1997/2003, p. 102). And as if in answer, Kahn-Harris writes,

> The language of progressive humanitarianism is often confused with progressive humanitarianism itself. . . . Modernity has seen the emergence of a whole host of institutions and practices, often of labyrinthine complexity, that maintain the ability of humans to inflict suffering on others in ways that are consistent with the requirement to be good, rational and reasonable. *We do what we always did, but in more convoluted ways.*
>
> *(italics added, p. 79)*

It seems that denialism, as a notably pernicious form of dissociation "exemplifies how in modernity we. . . . are all of us caught up in this pretence to some extent – denialists most of all" (Kahn-Harris, 2018, p. 90). As with dissociation, "denialism protects not just the unspeakable, but also the *unthinkable*" (p. 93) – and therein lies its greatest danger.

Schooling's promise, that every child succeed, squarely contradicts the "exceptionally difficult to recognise and justify . . . fact that capitalism requires that some people 'lose'" (Kahn-Harris, p. 81). This narrative has, in escalating proportions, spawned crops of students who – many frustrated at the implicit, if not outright, designation "entitled" – thinking themselves as doing more-or-less as told, find a receding end goal. With increasing anxiety, many arrive at a disillusioning reality:

that the promised vision was a mirage. Thus, it seems no coincidence to find that the predominantly white and male electorate, choosing Trump over Clinton in the 2016 American election, were characterised by an "unfounded sense of persecution. . . . [feeling] threatened, frustrated, and marginalized . . . on an existential level" (Khazan, 2018, April). They did not take kindly to the fact that "losing" was always a possibility; and, that those "others" who had learned this the hard way – while conceivably disadvantaged off the blocks – scrambled harder, longer, and with greater determination, until they left many of their white, male, cis-gendered, heterogenous classmates in the dust.

Yet in this righting of wrongs, something is amiss. Francis Lee's November 23, 2018 essay addresses a problem on the other side when she comments that,

> After years of being in the social justice community, I had fully embraced my identity as a person of colour. I had grown attached to the special underdog comfort it provided me, especially when I found myself in a roomful of progressive white people. And then it hit me – I don't know how to be anymore, without this identity.

In her open letter in the *Harvard Educational Review*, Eve Tuck (2009) writes of a "persistent trend in research on Native communities, city communities, and other disenfranchised communities" (p. 409) of documenting peoples' pain and brokenness – to achieve reparation. Encouraging the rethinking of "damage-centered research . . . [that fails] to consider the long-term repercussions of *thinking of ourselves as broken*" (p. 409) she writes,

> Testifying to damage so that persecutors will be forced to be accountable, is extremely popular in social science research. . . . In educational research this is especially true. . . . It is a powerful idea to think of all of us as litigators, putting the world on trial, but does it actually work? Do the material and political wins come through?
>
> *(pp. 414–415)*

If electoral decisions around the globe (e.g., the UK, Brexit; the US, President Trump; Brazil, the Bolsonaro scandal; Ontario, former Mayor Rob Ford; and Venezuela, Chávez and Maduro) are any indication, any seeming material and political wins may well be short-lived. In the great accounting of centuries, nay across our entire human existence, of devastating and horrific wrongs inflicted by people's in power on those persecuted (historically and in the present moment), societies do again split and denialism and "not-me" run rampant. Kahn-Harris cautions that denialism "threatens to turn democracies . . . into a kind of shadow world where nothing is what it seems" (p. 88). This is because, "for democratic societies to live up to the principles they claim to affirm, they would need to challenge and question the self-interest of dominant groups" (pp. 88–89). In other words, a paradigm change is in order. But can the system learn?

160 A dialectic theory of learning

Conditions exacerbate. We seem now to be stepping past denialism to something Kahn-Harris calls post-denialism – or in psychoanalytic terminology, perhaps post-dissociation. Its most icon image may be that of Donald Trump who – in manner refreshingly liberating for many who, justified or not, feel put upon – brazenly breaks all the rules with proclamations the likes of, "Would I approve waterboarding? You bet your ass I would. . . . It works . . . and if it doesn't work, they deserve it anyway for what they do to us" (Trump in Jacobs, 2015, November 24). Is it any wonder that this man went on to be voted president in 2016?

If pathology entails irresolvable but ever-assaulting ambiguities that put at risk our very capacity to integrate any sense, then the requirement of performing oneself into presence according to the expectations of an invisible everywhere Other would press a retreat to a self-pathology of a kind of minimalist existence (as per *The minimal self: Psychic survival in troubled times*, Lasch, 1984). That is, the retreating self copes with incongruence by denying or annihilating it. The refusal to allow difference is a refusal to learn and it conditions the self-imposed solution of solitude and commiseration in solitude. In a fortified enclave, the barricaded self engenders his own self-imposed siege while unabashedly declaring offence outward. Thus, at the pathological extremes of minimal selfhood, a governing pretence must reign: "I am the world and the world is me." Exercising willpower over that world, such-a-one dismisses breeches of conduct according to a disposing, forcibly extricating logic of it is "not me" who is wrong, or done to, it is you. This grand drama plays out on a world stage no more clearly than these days. Yet we are best to acknowledge that a "not me" is part of all our self-constructions.

In summary, in manner to mirror the solution of life forms under threat, we seem to enact three choices, often in concert. Where threat emanates from the world outside, we tend to circle the wagons by way of impermeable boundaries. Here, the pretence of particular favoured stories affords a narrative rigidity that disavows the imposing presence of anything different. On the other hand, in defence against the world inside, one can simple refuse to "go there." That is, whenever one feels the presence of discomforting possibility, one simply passes over it and changes the subject to oneself. One refuses to spell out, to even consider that there is anything disconcerting worth attending within the self's familiar chaos – the psychic weight to which one has become accustomed. We have also seen how dissociation finds its ally in symbiosis. We can couple ourselves with power; we can turn to and align ourselves with those unassailable others of our experience. And of course, these allegiances also come in paired combinations of benefit, indifference, and exploitation.

And finally, one can cope by either exerting one's influence to change/deny any offending milieu's legitimacy or simply relocating to a milieu more commensurate with one's preferred views. In the unchecked world of digital connection, changing milieus has never been easier. The facileness with which the internet aids and abets dissociation, often under a cloak of self-righteous indignation, is nothing short of frightening. Wireless connection creates a mythical place where illusion laughs in the face of any, and all, disillusioning reals – where doubt can be sown willy-nilly, where false narratives proliferate at exponential rates, where one can readily find others eager to commiserate, and where a blanket of anonymity enables the free proliferation of conspiracies against threats to one's status quo.

With digital technology, we become better poised to make things up – all the while, seeking confirmation for and of the worlds we create, even as we crave both the agency of the power of individuation, and affective resonance as satiating reassurance of belonging. In other words, hooked into the symbolic through our devices, we are prone to greater internal circularity of thought and to finding reinforcement in too-often highly suspect enclaves of fabricated worlds. The effect of these worlds is to ramp up our most cherished beliefs. The shift to digital has the dual effect of exaggerating the virtual while exacerbating deficits in the very visceral connections that Daniel Stern described so well (Chapter 6) that make us whole. And thus, a powerful technology for learning becomes an alluring resource for its refusal. Consider the following workshop description:

> When the words psychoanalysis, technology and innovation are considered together, one might reasonably expect that the innovation then discussed would be a realization of technology's shimmering promise. . . . democratization, continuity, convenience and cost-effectiveness. . . . [S]uch techno-dreams of remote therapy are neither innovative nor a fulfillment of technology's promise. They are yesterday's future and offer illusory gains. Instead, innovation is to be found in the differences between remote therapy and local therapy, between physical co-presence and technologically-mediated presence. . . . [A] vibrant future for psychoanalysis most likely resides in understanding the limitations, illusions and costs of screen relations and then becoming fierce advocates, both clinically and culturally, to protect intimacies that can only be experienced when people are bodies together.
>
> *(Essig, 2018, December, presentation abstract)*

Would that education, in the rush to go online and take advantage of the mass production of bodies in schooling (e.g., via lucrative MOOCs: massive online open courses), could heed Essig's alternative viewpoint (see Chapter 3).

At the confluence of these forces, dissociation finds manifold directions in which to move and, in moving, to indefinitely forestall the difficult look inward where the other resides, the difficult look outward to learn oneself anew, and any capacity to fathom new coherences across experienced differences. In an era when planet-altering human actions exceed and are vulnerable to imagination, dissociation – that age-old protection of "I won't" against the fear of "I can't" – has never been more dangerous.

Where to now?

Both teaching and psychoanalysis concern promoting productive self-change: The near-focus, in the first, is on learning about the world and, in the second, is on learning about the self. In either case, the critical aspect of learning anything entails

162 A dialectic theory of learning

learning oneself into ongoing viability. What happens in the earlier years seem most critical over the long term. Education and psychoanalytic questions increasingly turn on how to encourage far-from-equilibrium states with a high probability of resolving to "improved" system organisation. How much dissonance can any system admit and resolve in any go of the cycle? And what can a teacher, a school, a community, and a society do to support dialectical learning that is radically relational and embodied? These are the questions I address in Part III of this book: "Into practice: A theory for meaningful inclusion."

PART III

Into practice

For meaningful inclusion

9

CAPACITY, TRUST, AND MEANING

One of these things is not like the others,
One of these things just doesn't belong,
Can you tell which thing is not like the others
By the time I finish my song?
> — *Joe Raposo and Bruce Hart, Sesame Street (1969)*

Three of these things belong together
Three of these things are kind of the same
Can you guess which one of these doesn't belong here?
Now it's time to play our game (time to play our game).
> — *Joe Raposo and Jeff Moss, Sesame Street (1970)*

In aligning sameness with belonging, and difference with not-belonging, does the foregoing *Sesame Street* song contribute to a "manner of thinking [that] has caused conflict among diverse groups" ("One of These Things," 2015) or is that reading in the eyes of the beholder? How do we get past inborn human predispositions for discerning difference from sameness and picking out sameness across difference – these being the very capacities upon which are built all of language, communication, and thought?

We emerge as complex, thinking, social beings as consequence of needed discernment and choice – between this way and that, a neural threshold exceeded and another not, a communication made and another foreclosed, inside and outside, inclusion and exclusion, avowal and disavowal, and me and not-me. Much in the way that computer programs build up from on/off decisions to simulated realities and virtual worlds, perhaps we might find our way to better using our imaginative construing minds to resolve differences into an ever-expanding embrace of possibilities

166 Into practice

in being – emerging from a politics of identity, into living inter-sectionalities of rainbow colours, vibrantly insistent against a swirling pull to homogenised grey.

Capacity, trust, and meaning

How does anyone get from the dissonance and contradiction of difference to harmony and resolution across difference? With Benjamin (2005), I am fathoming a resolution of acceptance of the "presence" and "necessity . . . of countervailing forces" – of "living with, not eliminating contradiction" (p. 196).

> Resolution and receptivity, openness and closure – I want them to function like dissonance and harmony, to be mutually enhancing rather than crudely opposite. Union and dispersal, the one and the many – the voice I would like to find would weave between them. It would come from the place of the third. . . . inside, below, in between, from which to experience contradictions (another way of thinking about Winnicott's [1971] transitional experience) that gives us a different relationship to opposites.
>
> *(Benjamin, 2005, pp. 196–197)*

How does anyone even begin to get around the dialectic circle of learning – that is, where learning is the making of physical and/or conceptual discernments of difference and sameness to conceive a next resolution as part of incrementally embodied refinements, in the doing of oneself, in and with world? And how, in so doing, might learning open and broaden inward-reaching and outward-reaching awareness – doing so without losing sight of comprising parts and composing wholes? It's a tall order!

I propose the critical issue is one of negotiating fit between the situation of learning and the capacity, trust, and meaning that anyone can bring to it, iteratively so, from one dissonant and harmonised encounter to the next and the next. In the contexts of the model, I am imagining a functional interrelationship whereby: *trust frees capacity; meaning enlists it; structure focuses it; and anxiety inhibits it.*

In so saying, by *capacity* I mean the resources that anyone can bring to the invitation of a perplexing provocation. *Trust* in things trustworthy – a situation, the persons present to that situation, the processes of sense-making, and oneself as capable sense-maker – makes it possible, indeed pleasurable, to dwell awhile and muck about, as needed, in the play of not-knowing, false starts and so forth, on one's way past disillusionment to that illusive a-ha. And *meaning* names the salient appeal that draws a person to want to do so. To put the matter succinctly – irrespective of who has contributed to generating the circumstances of learning – from the perspective of a learner capacity affirms, "I *can* know," trust says, "I am *open* to knowing," and meaning says, "I *want* to know."

Importantly, because all encounters are relational ones, we can look at these three from the other side: How does the situation of learning, its circumstances – the classroom, the curriculum, the community, and all those interlacing systems containing

Capacity, trust, and meaning **167**

the learner – make capacity, trust, and meaning possible for that learner? It is not that we should say the student has capacity, trust, and meaning, but rather that these three as relational functions operate on and arise out of the inter-contextual space between the self, the dynamics of any learning situation, others present (virtual or otherwise) within and without that self, and the histories that collide, entangle, and co-emerge in the meeting. As such, capacity, trust, and meaning have everything to do with the situation of the encounter between self and world, the two poles of the dialectic model of learning that I have proposed.

Capacity

It will be noticed that capacity goes to equity and access to resources. Keep in mind that even the discourse of brain science, especially as popularised, tends to articulate capacity as intelligence but according to predeterminate "values and lifestyles – the cultural capital – of white, middle-class suburban populations" (Nadesan, 2002, p. 407). The capacity of which I speak, thus deals, not only in ability but also in privilege and necessarily invokes questions of inclusion.

In the interests of framing responsive teaching *vis-à-vis* the model, it might be helpful to think about capacity, less in terms of clinically framed special needs and/ or other categories of inclusion or exclusion by which we code difference (e.g., socio-economic, cultural, linguistic, racial, gender, belief, sexual orientation, and so forth), and more in terms of their lived-out implication *vis-à-vis* two interrelated phenomena: (1) the *prior knowing* that any student brings to the learning context, including especially the degrees of fit between the, historically emerged, present self and what that learning situation "asks" and "expects" that self to do, know, be, or become and (2) the *neural responsivity* that any learner's *current* physiology allows (the emanation of an historic interplay of self and world), including sensitivities to stimuli, stress, distractors, etcetera and the cognitive ability and agility to sustain the coupling and decoupling of categories of sameness and difference so as to conceive networks of functional perceptions and conceptions with and of the world. These are the resources to make dialectic movement possible in the first place.

> We cannot intend learning (about) something if we do not already have the capacity to be affected. This also leads to the fact that learning cannot be administratively planned. . . . The very fact that the thing to be learned is inaccessible to students prevents them from intentionally aiming at it.
>
> *(Roth, 2011, p. 248)*

To say the learner *can* learn, is to name the capacity to intend learning and to thus make, refine, and retain discernments, based largely in analogous thought across qualities of sameness and difference.

In Chapter 11 we will return to capacity to see how we might rethink our approaches to teaching that work with capacity; that is, assuming sufficient trust and meaning.

168 Into practice

Trust

"Whatever matters to human beings, trust is the atmosphere in which it thrives" (Bok, cited in Baier, 1994, p. 95). No matter one's capacity, a deficiency of trust in self or in the situation and the other, can put a quick stop to learning. That said, there are surely times when this is appropriate. "Exploitation and conspiracy, as much as justice and fellowship, thrive better in an atmosphere of trust" (Baier, 1994, p. 95).

A difficulty arises when, in learning, mistrust and distrust inappropriately jeopardise openness to trust again. Teachers will want to be mindful of the confidence they project about what students can or cannot do. On the one hand, too little confidence and too much compensatory structure can bespeak a lack of trust. Deemed untrustworthy, it is difficult to trust ourselves. Apprehension is contagious. On the other hand, too little structure can preclude student success and give reason not to trust either the teacher, the situation, or oneself. Students benefit when teachers can artfully fit learning invitations to learner capacity.

Anxiety and trepidation are physiological reminders of prior lessons in mistrust that are presently going unheeded. In internalised apprehension, quicker-than-thinking nonconscious and unconscious physiologies command the scene, leaving creative attention to learning awash in turbulent affective seas. The anxious learner cannot freely engage the play of learning, cannot relax into a transitional space, in sufficient trust and control, to toggle there between *imaginative construals* and *perceived realities* – what Benjamin might describe, respectively, as the big energy of uncontained possibility tethered to a minding little energy of secure ground (2005).

When *failures-in-learning* – in terms of the perceived expectations of caregivers, teachers, peers, oneself, and/or the norm – are internalised as *failures-of-self* or externalised as *failures-of-others* then mistrust and distrust beget future *failures-in-learning*. If I am surrounded by others who regularly jump to right conclusions, for which I need hours to reach, it will be hard to feel included. I might trade security for recognition or vice versa, either hiding parts of myself to belong or, claiming my reality, calling out the purported reality of others. Likewise for the learning of a physical skill. For example, if, after a group ski lesson, everyone except me seems competent and confident to tackle the hill, then I will trust less in future lessons and/or my capacity to keep up. If imposed upon to believe in myself, to join the group, say on the auspices that an ideal (become ideology)[1] of inclusion trumps my personal experience, then I am much more likely to succumb to anxiety's constraining force and, resisting, assume a fixed-minded attitude.

We trust when we feel embedded in systems that we can rely on to be in sufficient control, whilst having our mind in mind. If a judging and consequential world can be held at bay while everyone, including the teacher, grapples together and differently in some challenge, then I might persevere and gain trust in the doing. Given opportunity, students do rally effort and curiosity to face challenges and arrive at creative accomplishment. Indeed, we are predisposed, from birth, to do just that.

Capacity, trust, and meaning **169**

Trust, control, and autopoietic (structure-determined) systems

Looking at trust through the perspective of autopoietic/life systems (Chapters 7 and 8) we can differently appreciate its relationship with structure and control. A too-loosely organised internal system and/or one poorly bound will dissipate in short order and an anxious petrified system with impenetrable boundaries is one in rigor mortis. Somewhere in between lies functionality and life. Granting this – that life exists between the extremes of too lax and too rigid boundaries and structures – the appropriate degrees of freedom in learning depend upon context.

In observing team acrobatic stunts one becomes keenly aware of the high degrees of both trust and control necessary to avoid injury. In the structuring of such activities, the latitude of permissible movement is necessarily tight and this makes for trust that one is safe to refine the exactness of the act. Control alone is not enough unless it is supported by trust, and trust alone is not enough unless it is supported by control. Something similar needs to happen in the learning of skills that require precision. For example, a child in a Montessori preschool, when tracing the shape of a sandpaper letter, profits from the structure of immediate sensory feedback. She is refining an embodied understanding of a traced movement mapped onto the visual of a cultural artefact. In this way, she comes to know a small, specific piece of an arbitrary writing convention – a knowledge of the letter and a precision about its essential features that she could not construe on her own. But we could not, nor should we force her hand. A paucity of trust cannot be renovated by more control. We trust her to undertake the exercise as imagined.

When, for lack of trust, external forces seek to control the internal workings of a system, then trust and control are at odds with each other and dissociation seems the only viable solution. "Dissociation and recognition . . . [occupy] poles of affect relations – negative and positive poles of connection" (Benjamin, 2018, p. 81). Dissociation enables the doer/done-to dynamics of dominion, surveillance, suppression, submission, deceit, and rebellion. But where there can be co-recognition between actors, bearing witness to each other in a taken-as-shared system, then trust and control serve each other – that is, where actors, including the teacher, understand the space as "in this together" (with the teacher as the learners' strongest ally and advocate), then trust and control assume the mutually reinforcing coexistence described by Möllering (2005, 2006). In such instances, the expectation of trustworthiness has an almost compulsory power but still leaves the freedom to choose. Likewise, when embedded in a system that we trust, then we will want to use our freedom to keep the system intact.

An example, poignant to me, comes immediately to mind: When I was fostered at 15 years old, my new mother made it her business to check my schoolwork and invest herself in its production. I read this as her unwarranted distrust of what I knew of myself, and an infringement on my own agency. I had "made it" through adversity – in all 13 family moves – and still retained a straight-A grade, this time in the Francophone school into which I had been transferred the year previous, despite hardly speaking the language. It took all of my fortitude to not rebel, to grit my

170 Into practice

teeth, and to remind myself that I was learning *for* myself and no amount of forcing my hand to do what I would have done anyway would deter me from being me. *It can be difficult to trust oneself and to become trustworthy, when others do not trust you.*

Assertions one way or the other about the appropriate degrees of freedom in learning contexts (e.g., traditional vs. progressive perspectives, see Chapter 4) overlook the critical question of fit between the expected specificity of a learning outcome and the defining strictures of the learning task. In terms of such fit, the teacher's role becomes one of titrating the structured artifice of a learning task to internally construed structures in the student – these destined to become nonconscious knowing in the service of further thinking and doing. For instance, when learning to ride a bicycle, training wheels operate as an adjunct structure designed to decrease the risk of serious, but importantly not all injury. As the learner gains proficiency in riding, the extra wheels become redundant and a dynamic regulatory system of internal balance takes over in the child. For the redundancy to work, the internal regulatory system must, for the most part, come to operate underneath conscious awareness as nonconscious habit, thus freeing the conscious mind to other more managerial and executive concerns. The child cries out, "By myself. I don't need any help." If teacher titration is effected according to a principle of "good enough" – that is, where there is room for error but the damage is never catastrophic (from the child's perspective, catastrophe being a reason to quit altogether), then the child learns to appropriately trust in both himself and the other. What I am describing is a fascinatingly attuned teacher–learner dynamic that facilitates the movement of trust with control in ways that are, at once, sensitive, responsive, and reliable. Such relational dynamics in teaching cannot be productively reduced to technique.

These same principles apply to the preparation and professional development of teachers. Instead of specifics about how to act in this or that situation, we might do better to give our teacher-students the benefit of various interpretive exemplars – the engagement of which, across a broad example space, could hold promise for fostering a more deeply informed appreciation of the human condition and the nature of learning. In learning to teach, the teacher, like the bicycle rider, will profit from practice with such ideas, in concert with conditions meant to offload other concerns, while honing capacity. It will serve little useful purpose and is likely to be counterproductive to ask the teacher to memorise techniques en route to making them habit. This would be akin to having the child memorise that: when the bicycle tilts one way, you lean the other way and turn the handle bars that way too; and when the bicycle gets wobbly, stand up more, and push harder on the pedals. Now, one could break this down even further, producing an unwieldy checklist, the very kind that we give teachers when we attempt to "train" them. Wouldn't it be infinitely better if we could instead give them the option of training wheels, should they want to use them, as they grapple to find their balance, without worry about falling too hard? The training wheels might come in the form of a virtual experience, say the viewing of a video or the reading of a story with an unfinished ending, that they might complete it in as many ways as they can fathom. Then the class could compare and discuss the various interpretations and the range of possible meanings for going this way or that – importantly doing so not to serve a common sense of folk psychology, but rather to critically deconstruction that "sense" in light of newly learned, psychoanalytically informed, relational principles. Alternatively, the training wheels could entail in micro-instances of teaching, videotaped for the purposes of knowing and interpreting again and differently (as per Critical Race Theorists: Carter, Skiba, Arredondo, & Pollock, 2017, p. 221). And finally, it might help if the teacher of teachers submitted her own teaching to wonderment, musing aloud about instances of lost and regained balance, even "on the fly," and thereby inviting her students into the experience – one with no clear right answer.

In thus understanding the learner, given all that I have written, we will want to remain mindful of the kinds of prior lessons, in trust and control, that we all bring to class – regardless of age and ability. They are these differences that condition notoriously wide discrepancies in learning across any given classroom of learners – differences that can go largely overlooked in discussions about inclusive environments, yet differences that can be among the most challenging teachers face. Just as learners with severe cognitive impairment can be unaware of the risks ahead, those with gifted capacity can fabricate risk at every turn. Trust is a relational function that frees or constrains capacity. And returning to early childhood relations, as Anthony Giddens forcefully puts it, "The suspension [of doubt] that enables trust has to be learned in infancy" (in Möllering, 2006, p. 116). Degrees of trust are early learned and thereafter construed upon and with. It is not a matter of all or none. Teachers have the potential to enact dramatic differences.

Trust, attachment patterns, and dissociation

All of capacity, trust, and meaning in learning turn to some degree on the nature of early attachment relations, paid forward. Each child and youth will have arrived to one's classroom having already grooved a particular preferred solution to the problem of appropriately mitigating trust and control in learning. The solution itself will be a nonconscious habit wedded to an unconscious mitigation of need. How that is negotiated will matter more on the teacher presence to the learner than whatever is being taught.

Regardless of reason, without sufficient trust to risk the free play of physical and/ or conceptual movement, learning cannot but be refused. Dissociation (previous chapter) effects the solution to justify that refusal. In dissociation as the particular attachment solution of anxious *avoidance*, fearing reality's judgement, the learner refuses to put his familiar and favoured understanding to reality's test (the model's centrifugal movement). And in dissociation as the particular attachment solution of anxious *ambivalence*, in the wake of reality's unfavourable judgement, the learner refuses to formulate anew, for fear of getting herself wrong again (the model's centripetal movement). In the first solution, not trusting others, the individual can put up imposing walls, to extricate and diminish others; in the second solution, not trusting self, the individual cannot get enough of an other's reassurance. Both learners are awash in anxiety's neurochemical bath, whether felt or denied. Caught in

172 Into practice

anxiety, these learners are not free to think. Coping generally veers in one of two directions: manufacture offence as the best defence and defiantly deflect shortcomings by inviting a power struggle and/or visiting blame on any convenient target; or seek security in that other who knows and, in overeager desire to get things right, insist on exact instructions and ongoing help. Neither individual can critically think. This is because dissociation is, at bottom,

> the unwillingness to allow oneself freedom of thought. . . . [S]ometimes . . . [it] involve[s] nothing more than the defensive refusal to formulate or interpret. Sometimes . . . [it] is a simple matter of preventing a certain kind of experience or memory altogether. . . . [More commonly] dissociation is the refusal to allow prereflective experience to attain the full-bodied reflective meaning it might have if we left it alone and simply observed the results of our own capacity to create it.
>
> *(Donnel Stern, 1997/2003, pp. 97–98)*

Dissociation is a common occurrence in classrooms – evident in students that simply "tune out," proclaim boredom (a lack of meaning), or distract the teacher and class to other attentions. A teacher will want some means of understanding what is going on, both in the learner and in herself. How does anyone sidestep the power struggle? How does anyone help a desperate other trust himself? To the analyst, Donnel Stern writes, "What we can do . . . is to be sensitive to the evidence of dissociation, which we note as absences, gaps, contradictions, stereotypes, repetitions, and dead spots in the material" (1997/2003, p. 99).

Dead spots, as I interpret them in the educational context, are signalled in those fogs of teaching when things feel cloaked in a haze of distance. The students' faces are zombie-like, unresponsive, some looking at their cell phones, others at the clock, or outside. Even if their gaze is directed *at* you, it feels as though no one is behind that gaze. They are somehow not there and one is suddenly aware of the screaming quiet. These are not moments for pressing through one's agenda toward some externally enforced deadline. They are calls to stop, and note aloud: "Something is not working here. What's up?"

The question of trust cannot be disentangled from those of capacity and meaning. It is a question that wants for deep exploration, conversation, and reflective study, for all teachers, most promisingly, I believe, with a teaching mentor well versed in relational psychoanalytic understandings. We have a very long way to go.

When it comes to prescriptions on how to encourage learners to round the dialectic circle in learning, I resist giving free license to any mandate about best practices on the openness or closure of tasks. The answer is, it depends. How much can any learner, alone or held well in a classroom community, risk leaning out into dissonance and recover herself on the other side? The good enough pedagogue reads capacity against trust *and* meaning to provide just enough structure that students can discover their ability to persevere to resolution "on their own." Success in these terms broadens capacity to aptly trust self-and-situation the next time, to persevere a little longer, and to know that temporary impasses are merely setbacks in the uneven process that is learning.

Meaning

From capacity through trust we come to meaning. That one can learn and that one feels safe doing so is hardly assurance of caring about it. There can be no "meaningful" learning without meaning – and meaning returns us to the "interpersonal event" and a world of coexistence:

> Meaning . . . is an interpersonal event. . . . Any relationship is made of multiple fields, with their corresponding multiple selves, so that at any one moment, it is possible to use language creatively about some things and not about others; and the distribution of those areas of light and darkness changes a moment later.
>
> *(Donnel Stern, 1997/2003, pp. 110–111)*

> A world is not something external to existence; it is not an extrinsic addition to other existences; the world is the coexistence that puts these existences together.
>
> *(Nancy, 1996/2000, p. 29)*

Meaning, with its roots in the primal and the intersubjective, is that which spawns desire to engage learning in the first place and to sustain efforts over the long haul. When there is meaning and movement in learning, one can lose oneself in its flow. It's as if the body with its dopamine-reinforcing reward systems takes over and we happily lose ourselves in immersive doing. This is engagement at its simplest and most exhilarating. But when there is meaning, but movement is frustrated, one will need to rally fortitude, perseverance, and resilience to press through. This is as relevant to the seemingly tedious or mundane task as to the glorified challenge.

A task will be meaningful for any number of manifold reasons; and those reasons, as have been belaboured throughout this book, will always be rooted in the unconscious, always related to the other, and (contrary to current best-practices rhetoric) hardly limited to whether the task is set in a real-life context. Why anything is meaningful or not, engaging or not, is practically inaccessible to consciousness. Meaning is the domain of the unconscious. If pressed to say why one does anything, the tale one can tell, while related to implicit motivation, is not amenable to linear reduction. In particular, the reasons typically given for not-learning are more related to the very defences serving to justify and maintain dissociation in the first place.

Meaning turns on personal value, and personal value turns on how one has come to know oneself as "of value." Storied in relationality, steeped in affect (Chapter 6) meanings take their shape in the unfolding narrative of interpersonal relationships, seeded in and emerging out of early-life possibilities, and what one learned to do, be, and know to sustain ongoing value, self-coherence, self-continuity, and agency.

174 Into practice

Where the task of learning is meaningful to the student, then that student will, in the language of psychology, be intrinsically motivated to persevere – assuming, of course, that he trusts the effort is not futile and trusts that, if by chance success eludes him, he is not the failure – that failures in knowing and/or doing are not failures in being.

On a principle of good enough

Having evolved from its earlier self-esteem and self-efficacy movements (see Jack Martin's 2007 review), educational psychology's present growth-minded literature now emphasises applauding effort over outcome (in performing and producing). Meaning wrapped up in an identity of prestige and personal value tied to easy success and notable productivity (everyone gets a trophy) is a set up for crises when anticipated success does not come so easily. Of course, there are societal contradictions to the alternative emphasis on effort. Achievement is ultimately the success to enable succession into societal positions considered of enviable privilege.

To further complicate matters, much of the literature guiding educational practice forwards the assumption that, with the proper balance of teacher technique, student effort, and engaging activity, everyone can succeed. This is patently false. We will want to look deeper than untenable platitudes about imagination, belief, and capacity with which we cajole students – the likes of, "If you can imagine it, you can do it;" "Believe you can and you will succeed;" and "You can do anything you set your mind to." Belief in self *follows from* experiences of capacity, trust, and meaning, not the other way around.

We return to the psychoanalytic principle of the good enough mother, as the good enough pedagogue, providing neither too excessive nor scant support. In judiciously divesting control to a learner's own incrementally fitting resources, we teach appropriate learner self-trust in a developing capacity to navigate himself in learning the world, with others, while in the world – and thus in facing coexistent challenges with that world. The good enough teacher, like the good enough mother, returns – eventually as that reassuring internal-object presence in the mind of the infant, child, and student. At first the leaving and the returning is a viscerally felt affective attunement that enfolds into, and with, presence and absence of body and mind. At the same time the progression extends, however unevenly, from short absences to longer ones, sustainable for the infant, child, and youth without cause for worry. In this way, the child graduates his proclivity to effectuate movement in learning, on his own, under varying conditions – which is to say taking advantage of internal and external resources to buoy capacity, trust, and meaning as needed.

These three qualities bear a surface similarity to the popular attribution of willpower. What I hope is clear is just how so-called willpower turns on multiple, precursory, circumstantial, relational conditions. Contrary to folk psychology, it is hardly the result of something so simple as "trying hard enough." Becoming the kind of successful learner that I am describing will want the support of a pedagogical presence titrated in appropriate manner so as to encourage continued effort and progressive success. Of course, the world must be so constituted as to also permit, and hopefully encourage, such success – hardly a given, considering socio-cultural disparities that remain legion. If all goes well, the successful learner will be one who finds meaning in ferreting things out on her own, freely playing with ideas and concepts, tapping available resources as warranted (of which the teacher is but one), and conversing about and articulating emergent understandings with self and others.

In sum, the teacher provides the kinds of structures to focus capacity so that learning can take place and so that anxiety need not grow to debilitating proportion. Fuelled by meaning, borne by appropriate trust, and facilitated by increasing capacity, the learner, internalising the affirming teacher, begins to assume the reins of her own learning. While principles of inclusion and differentiation play heavily in this process, the overly generalising prescriptions of the current rhetoric are less than helpful. The "devil is in the details" – that is, in all things human and interactive, nuance carries the day.

Having thus framed the centrality of capacity, trust, and meaning in learning, how do these understandings sit with current educational practice?

In the context of a conviction

I have come to the disconcerting conclusion that, in the quick production of teachers, *faculties of education problematically frame and grossly abbreviate, if not outright neglect, those things that seem to matter most. What schools do well in teaching continues to be reductively interpreted and minimally, if at all, understood.* This owes to several reasons: (1) a human tendency (and the dissociative denial of that tendency) to harness ideology in service of unconscious desire, (2) the complexity of the task, (3) a public appetite for simple answers and immediate solutions, and (4) a market economy that, having thus trained that public, is bent on delivering the goods. My experience with school governance and academic counsel in education brings back a lament my son once had about a summer job. At the time, he was digging ditches according to the dictates of a rather simple-minded, but overly confident, contractor-foreman. One day, quite exasperated he exclaimed, "Mom, it's like I'm playing hockey and everyone's shooting on our own net. Worse yet, the coach is making me do it too." In schooling, either we're shooting on the wrong net, or I am playing a very different game.

Whether teachers and learners succeed seems to have little to do with educational reforms geared toward the production of particular kinds of students. Instead, it has everything to do with the relational field that participants can and do co-create and the dynamic fit between elements of influence in that field. First, there are the people: who the learners are and what they can be, who accompanies them in mind and in physical co-presence, who engages the lessons with them, and the teacher, all that she brings, not the least of which is her own history. Then, there is the political, socio-economic, and cultural climate within which the nested systems of class, school, and community reside and from which they take their cue. Lastly are the tangible things most commonly measured and therefore readily held to account (or discount): the number and age of students; the time, frequency, and duration of

176 Into practice

convening; the nature of supports and resources available and their mode of access; the obligations and responsibilities (e.g., programs of study and codes of conduct); and the actual affordances of the space, including even whether there can or should be sunlight streaming in.

Given the complexity of the relational field - including especially the indirectly accessible and deeply compelling workings of the unconscious at play – considerable ingenuity would be needed to reduce critical components into operationalisable constructs at the ready for evidence-based study. No matter the ingenuity, the leap back from empirical research into contextual application is chasm-spanning. Many a teacher has scratched her head over the latest advice, techniques, and mandates on how to navigate the complex waters of teaching and learning. Notwithstanding curriculum theory, neither holding the reins nor the purse-strings of schooling practice, the educational research having most ideological and technical influence in schooling practice has yet to comprehensively and compellingly address the capacity, trust, and meaning necessary to the intersubjective–intrapsychic dialectic that is learning, including especially developing a substantive scholarship with deep and nuanced appreciation of the relational field of a classroom that supports such learning.

While part of the difficulty surely entails in the complexity of the challenge, it strikes me as no small coincidence that public schooling, as an arm of government, is about (1) pleasing and/or placating the electoral masses (2) maximising conditions so that the "cream" rise to the top and economic viability is maintained, and (3) keeping expenses (and taxes) down. Now the societal cream, no surprise, describes the highly influential, tech- and business-savvy, nouveau bourgeoisie comprising stakeholder groups and filling the ranks of big business, government, and educational research institutions. In Western economies, despite shifting demographics, these institutional structures continue to carry the attitudes and beliefs of the notoriously white, heterosexual, and cisgendered men who built them and the national structures upon which they depend. The ideal school, in today's rendition, bears an uncanny resemblance to the kind of school that just these folks would have liked to have attended and in which they would have thrived – or indeed wherein they did. In the manner of autopoietic systems, the social system replicates itself, performatively and recursively so. But being accomplished affords no privileged access to unconscious proclivities or motivations and little assurance of any critical view on human nature and the socio-political systems that govern the possible. What being accomplished does provide is a distinct advantage in terms of one's continued place and the place of one's offspring in the evolving system that made one's accomplishments possible in the first place.

Yet it would be difficult to deny the grave magnitude of the multiple sociopolitical and economic forces tugging today at the thin fabric of schooling: Global unrest and social migration have made cultural diversity a fact of life, joining special needs education as dominant preoccupations for inclusive practices responsive to and welcoming of students of difference. Global overpopulation and urbanisation, environmental degradation, and digital promiscuity press a dire need for cutting-edge, fiscally sound, technological advancements as governments vie for economic and political security on the world stage. Meanwhile self-same innovative technologies, including artificial intelligence, increasingly encroach on labour, supplanting blue colour jobs and making a tech-savvy entrepreneurial population all the more urgent. And so, the divide between the rich and the poor expands, while schooling practices continue to favour the privileged – for the seeming reason of not really knowing how to do otherwise. We seem to be going about things all wrong and the result is increasingly playing out in nations divided – this despite, and I would argue because of, gross misunderstandings about what it takes to foster equity in teaching and learning. Regrettably, on the near horizon, I do not see any paradigm-shifting disruption to these, our now-global, repetition compulsions.

In these contexts, twenty-first-century orthodoxy holds the ideal student as empowered and engaged, self-actualising, teacher-independent, technologically savvy, and collaborative learner extraordinaire. The archetypes of technocrat and entrepreneur capture cross-pollinating clusters of charismatic citizens with qualities that marry business connoisseurship with inventive design and innovation in the STEM disciplines of science, technology, engineering, and math. Buzzwords and rally cries of "success for all," "everyone can," "everyone included," "everyone unique," "differentiated instruction (and assessment)," "student choice," and "student-centered learning," advertise an even playing field, student rights, and no place for advantage or disadvantage. But these things do not an even and inclusive playing field make. As if to please the masses (fortifying and serving meritocratic beliefs), a pervasive "can-do" rhetoric promulgates myths of self-control, self-empowerment, and self-actualisation so that everyone can be happy and productive. Such practices as "growth-mindedness," "goal-setting," "mindfulness," "presence," "metacognition," "self-reflection," and "self and peer-evaluation" set the purported means by which students will "self-regulate," eat right, exercise right, act right, and think right on their way to individual happiness and success (see Cederström, 2019, & Brinkmann, 2014/2017, for critiques). The result, however, is an ever-escalating set of strictures on "right being" that are the fecund ground for either outright rejection, rebellion, and defiance (for those who are quite fed up) or troubling preoccupations and deeply engrained anxieties as conscientious citizens strive every day to be all that they are told they can be. Clearly the fallout of in-your-face defiance, on the one hand, and anxious preoccupation about doing and being right, on the other, could fairly characterise the extremes of the political landscape in most Western countries today. In the middle, perhaps, are those who know how to play the game to their advantage, often ruthlessly so.

All of the foregoing said, the purported ideal learning environment is, today, more narrowly defined than advertised: Gaming culture and makerspaces epitomise best practices on the way to a holy grail of *ensuring* student engagement.

> A makerspace is a collaborative work space inside a school, library or separate public/private facility for making, learning, exploring and sharing that uses high tech to no tech tools. These spaces are open to kids, adults, and entrepre-

178 Into practice

> neurs and have a variety of maker equipment including 3D printers, laser cut-
> ters, cnc machines, soldering irons and even sewing machines. A makerspace
> however doesn't need to include all of these machines or even any of them
> to be considered a makerspace. If you have cardboard, legos and art supplies
> you're *in business.*
>
> *(italics added, www.makerspaces.com/what-is-a-makerspace/)*

In the makerspace, student-centred learning calls for the collaborative generation of products as solutions to problems that teacher-designers find or create. The best problems are "practical," "real-world," "authentic," and "rich" in terms of possibility for interpretation and address. They allow for the application of those things that the student already knows and can do, without necessarily translating the doing into further conceptual understanding. The approach is interactive, real-time, and high energy. Pride of product is emphasised in showcases for all to see. Meanwhile, gaming, the complement of the makerspace, offers student engagement with high-paced interactive technologies, where students apply, and purportedly hone, their skills for the reward of levelling-up in the game. In gaming and makerspaces, the entertainment value of an activity is extrinsic to the object of learning. Any learning itself is more by-product than by-intention – neither the point, nor the source of joy, in the engagement. In short, the objects of learning are not taken up for their intrinsic cultural value as transitional objects. These incarnations of twenty-first-century learning increasingly erode values and capacities associated with, for example: solitary study; quiet, sustained attention; clear instruction; Socratic dialogue; teacher-directed and curriculum-centred learning; desks in rows; repetition; effortful practice; traditional tests; introversion; and critical thinking.

As it turns out, the child who most succeeds in current contexts is the one who is able to figure things out on his own. It is also the child already schooled in diligence and perseverance, usually at home, and mostly by example – a matter of course, given that the relevant socio-cultural resources are already in place. And finally, the successful child, typically arriving to school already endowed with notable cultural capital, is either unintimidated by and can focus in the fray and/or has developed the charisma to take the lead.

> Advocates move too easily from "complex" to "enriched", where "enriched"
> is very much in the eye of the beholder, often reflecting the beholder's cul-
> tural and class values. Rich, complex environments tend to include what the
> authors value and exclude what they abhor. . . . Complex, enriched environ-
> ments for humans end up having many of the features of upper-middle class,
> urban, and suburban life.
>
> *(Bruer, in Nadesan, 2002, p. 407)*

Thus, as before, privilege begets privilege in the twenty-first-century school. Can we do otherwise? In the pages that follow, I draw on relational psychoanalytic understandings to deconstruct current educational practices, to think through the

Capacity, trust, and meaning **179**

contradictions, and to entertain different, non-prescriptive ways of framing and approaching the challenges we face. Acknowledging the inevitability of categories, I look, in Chapter 10, to trouble popular understandings, beliefs, and practices in relation to ideals the likes of inclusion, meaningful experience, community, character, learner-centred education, and therapeutic, emancipatory, and entrepreneurial schooling projects. How can we rethink twenty-first-century orthodoxy?

Note

1 When I invoke the notion of ideal-become-ideology, this is not to disparage idealism. A distinction might be warranted. I take idealism to be honest about its illusionary qualities. Idealism is about imagination. I consider myself an idealist. The problem with ideology is not its idealism, nor its ideals. Rather ideology seems to be idealism masquerading as realism. Ideology deals in certainty, privileging one imaginative construal over idealisable others, insisting on its objective reality, whilst refusing any disillusioning of a singular view on how things must be. Ideology thus occludes alternative possibilities. It forecloses imagination.

10

RETHINKING TWENTY-FIRST-CENTURY ORTHODOXY

The inclusive ideal

What does anyone mean by inclusive education?

> The term . . . continues to evoke multiple meanings, with some interpretations referring to . . . *students with disabilities* in mainstream settings and others to an education that offers the systemic and structural supports . . . of *all students* in the learning environment.
>
> *(italics added, Naraian, 2011, p. 956)*

Naraian goes on to contextualise "the successful participation of students with disabilities in a general education classroom" (2011, p. 956):

> [It] is premised on the creation of [just] classroom communities that . . . nurture the qualities of equity and care. . . . [are] hospitable to all learners, particularly those whose social histories reflect marginalisation by dominant groups. . . . [and] where subjugated knowledges are honoured and . . . different forms of diversity are valued.
>
> *(p. 956)*

Keeping the ideal of successful participation in mind, consider the shrinking globe, advancing human migration, broadening awareness of marginalisation, and the multiplication of categories of special needs. These conditions have augmented learner diversity and heightened the struggle to realise the inclusive ideal.

The last 30 years have seen radical shifts toward greater legislated inclusion – defined as the physical co-presence of students of difference, especially those with special needs, in everyday classrooms. In 2009, *UNESCO* advocated a "major

Rethinking twenty-first-century orthodoxy **181**

reform of the ordinary [community] school" (p. 7) and prioritised "rights-based, child-friendly schools" (p. 15) offering a "common core curriculum . . . relevant for . . . [all] learner[s]" (p. 18) and flexibly taught using a "range of working methods and individual treatment *to ensure that no child is excluded from companionship and participation* [italics added]" (p. 15). Here again the call for *ensured* inclusion belies what we know about life and learning systems as necessarily autopoietic and relational (see Chapter 7). Legislating ideals, my no means assures their realisation.

While Brown v. Board of Education was a hallmark for racial desegregation in the United States in 1954, co-presence of students of difference in everyday classrooms has proven no guarantee of interactive co-participation, meaningful communication, equal opportunity, or a sense of belonging – especially since the curriculum and those teaching it are likely to embody the norms of the dominant social group (Sleeter, 2017). Inequality in schools and society is simply too many centuries deep (Carter et al., 2017, p. 225). It seems that "social scientists . . . underestimated . . . the rigidity of mind-sets and stereotypical beliefs borne from social segregation" (Carter et al., p. 212).

Moreover, the move toward integrating the wide spectrum of students of special needs into everyday classrooms has created a new set of dilemmas. Insofar as it has disparaged a continuum of services for these students (favouring everyday classroom settings over frowned-upon dedicated schools), it has overlooked the wide disparities in kind and degree of need and what any classroom might practically be able to support. Despite wide contestation in disability studies literature and among advocacy groups (Smith, Polloway, Patton, Dowdy, & McIntyre, 2012, pp. 33–34), the ideal of "all students with exceptionalities, regardless of the severity of the disability, be included full-time in general education classes" (Smith et al., 2012, p. 33) dominates schooling policy and practice. Unsurprisingly, teacher preparation programs have responded by offering inclusive education programs and graduating highly sought-after specialists touting more than the typical fare of one survey course in school psychology (with a component addressing special needs from a clinical perspective) and a separate course in social justice. Still, reaching the ideal of inclusion wants for more than a fleet of newly credentialed "experts" in answer to heightened public consciousness. It remains true, despite all manner of political motivation otherwise that, in delivering inclusion, we flounder on what to do or how to go about doing it (Sleeter, 2017).

What would or should it mean for a classroom and a school to be inclusive? And what would it take to get us there (see, e.g., Qvortrup & Qvortrup, 2018)? Should we prioritise physical co-presence of children of all needs, abilities, and backgrounds or should student belonging and quality of learning take precedence? Can we do both? To appreciate the nuances involved, consider the different attentions called for by the following questions, each located in the unique contexts of the cited authors.

Is an LGBTQ-affirming school [expressly designed to enrol only LGBTQ students] inclusive or untenably segregated (Hope & Hall, 2018)? Would a blind child prefer a school where teachers could read and write braille (Low, 2001)? Is a school for gifted children, with gifted teachers, exclusive or inclusive (D'Amour &

182 Into practice

Markides, 2017)? To what extent can any white teacher, briefly schooled in systemic inequalities, but committed to "celebrating" diversity (Gorski, 2009), appreciate pervasive inequalities, relate to those harmed, and address unconscious personal biases (Sleeter, 2017)? What social stratifications arise when children from all walks of life are assembled and instructed to work nicely together in ways often emphasising compliance, for example: honesty, gratitude, humility (Walsh, 2017), self-discipline, and empathy (Etzioni, 2002)? Are those students, identified and coded in less severe categories of exceptionality (e.g., as mild attention deficit disorder, high-functioning autism, and mild intellectual disability), better off than without such identifiers (Mithaug, 1998; Shakespeare, 2017)? How do categories for inclusion automatically create exclusion (Hilt, 2015; Michailakis & Reich, 2009)? How much equality and flourishing is possible for children who, not speaking the language of instruction, sit among others who are fluent (Adler, 1998)? How included can a child with severe intellectual impairment feel in an all-inclusive classroom of same-aged intellectually abled peers (Kavale & Mostert, 2003; Reid et al., 2018)?

Getting a handle on the field of inclusive education asks for reading across various literatures and considering how these perspectives play into the governance, conduct, and lived experiences of teachers and their students. In this chapter I bring relational psychoanalytic understandings into conversation with disability studies, critical theory, cultural studies, and school psychology to address the question: What fosters and what hinders the development of a lived sentiment of belonging and the promotion of quality learning for all students, regardless of the diversity that political resolve happens to put in any one classroom?

Structuring inclusion or compliance?

The issue of inclusion in education plays into four intersecting categories of concern: (1) the political resolve for equal access to community classrooms for all persons irrespective of (dis)ability, race, creed, class, Indigeneity, gender, and sexual orientation; (2) the felt sense of belonging and the equitable quality of student-appropriate learning opportunities for all such persons; (3) the companion challenges of increased student diversity, increased numbers of students with emotional and behavioural disabilities, and in an inclination to categorise students as particular kinds of learners, each with unique needs; and (4) the tendency for identified categories-of-concern to dominate the discourse, precluding attention to the subtle interplay of personality, temperament, and cultural capital that shape a place of belonging or not belonging in the stratifying socio-political dynamics of classroom, school, and society.

The first of these concerns sets top-down constraints on the remaining three. That is, government fiscal and policy decisions place parameters on local, district-mandated, and school-directed choices with respect to the functional design of, and access to, inclusive facilities and the provision of school and classroom resources. These, in turn, determine the contexts within which teachers are given to make inclusion work.

Rethinking twenty-first-century orthodoxy **183**

While straightforward unambiguous mandates make good political optics, inclusion in schools is an idea and an ideal conceptually mired in definitional ambiguity and practical contradiction. In brief, the concept of "inclusion into regular classes is (and has to be) formally compensated by assignment of a special identity/status that is functionally equivalent . . . to membership in a special class or even school" (Michailakis & Reich, 2009, p. 37). If an exclusion-identifying name is the cost of accommodations and affirmative action so as to permit access to learning in a regular classroom, then all bets are off as to the social repercussions down the way when such a person seeks opportunity as contributing societal member (see Mithaug, 1998). The competitive individualism of capitalist societies does not lend itself to "genuinely inclusive and equitable" principles (Hardy & Woodcock, 2015, p. 144).

Nonetheless, as if the path to genuine experiences of inclusion were clear-cut, governments underwrite guidelines and protocols, conceived according to school psychology, detailing how teachers should proceed. In North America and Europe, the cornerstone of these recommendations is educational psychology's multi-tiered, *Response to Intervention* model for "healthy social-emotional development and the prevention of challenging behaviors" (Fox, Carta, Strain, Dunlap, & Hemmeter, 2010, p. 10). Although designed, tested, and refined for "early childhood education" (p. 10), this approach is deemed suitable for all grades (see, e.g., Bradshaw, Waasdorp, & Leaf, 2012; Hoy et al., 2013). Problematically, support for its effectiveness has primarily depended on teachers in conflict-of-interest positions as both program implementers and reporters of results (Debnam, Pas, Bottiani, Cash, & Bradshaw, 2015). Other challenges have been teacher reticence to buy in, short-lived effects in some studies, and an over-reliance on researcher presence for implementation (Ervin et al., 2001).

The tiered model calls for the triaging of teacher actions from some version of *Positive Behaviour Supports* for classrooms, to more targeted *Functional Behavioural Assessment* for marginal students, and finally, more formally documented intervention protocols for students of greatest risk (Bradshaw et al., 2012; Ervin et al., 2001; Fox et al., 2010; Hoy et al., 2013; e.g., see Mackenzie, 2008; Souveny, 2008). At the level of the entire classroom, Positive Behaviour Supports widely promote popular, but dubiously enacted, principles of differentiated instruction and student-centred learning along with programs of reinforcement based on such oversimplified beliefs that positive reinforcement "for being part of a group" generates belonging and a sense of being "accepted, attached, friendly, intimate, cooperative and trusting with others" (Council for Inclusive Education [CIE], 2017, p. 6).

If this does not work, the next level of intervention focuses on correcting the "inappropriate methods" and "challenging behaviours" that students use when their basic needs, such as belonging, are not met (CIE, p. 6). The intention is to shift "a negative cycle [*in these students*] that, if not corrected, can negatively impact their future success. . . . [as] learners, socially responsible citizens and contributing members of their school and family" (CIE, p. 6). In short, the model approaches inclusion first through behavioural management and reinforcement techniques applied to the whole class and, that failing for some, to individual interventions "based on Applied Behaviour Analysis . . . a set of empirical principles [and techniques] . . .

184 Into practice

for explaining and addressing human behaviour" and "reclaiming" students at risk (CIE, p. 12).

Unfortunately, the devil in the details of these sanitised treatment protocols elides over interpersonal affects in favour of the following assumptions: (1) that student actions are motivated according to discernible precipitating causes and reinforcing effects and that student actions can be manipulated by modifying these causes and/ or effects; (2) that a teacher can objectively record student "challenging behaviours," antecedent environmental conditions, and the reinforcing consequences they elicit, analysing this data to determine the function of the behaviour and how to redirect it (Bain, Fulton, & Sautner, 2017); (3) that maladaptive behaviour belongs to the student with the relational field hardly a consideration; and (4) that tailored resources can appease, overcome, or circumvent obstacles to academic achievement and classroom inclusion. These resources run the gamut from the stationary bicycle and fidget toy for the ADHD child, a daily planner for the forgetful student, a teaching microphone and audio-transcripts for the hearing impaired, a teaching assistant to accompany the oppositional defiant child, and specialist pull-out programs for students as have, for example, dyslexia or dyscalculia or who are second language learners.

The final complement to positive behaviour supports are individualised plans. Here, the teacher takes the lead and, in consultation with others, generates a schedule of stepwise objectives and their related supports. It is, however, up to the student, in consolidation with family members, to realise the prescribed progress. Districts generally require these plans for students with clinically identified specific needs, and advise their use for those at increased risk of formal coding – often in queue for clinical assessment.

The individual plan can be deeply conflicting to the student. Its emergence typically arises when some student-generated deficiency escalates to sufficient proportion to warrant concerted school–caregiver consultation and action. Thoughtful adult attention can engender hope for the learner. It lives in the substance of vague promises, structured plans, and that strange relief of finally having one's struggles aired, given a name, witnessed, and maybe understood. But a strange punishment almost inevitably follows hope, if there is hope. It is self-administered in more-often-than-not iterating reminders of inadequacy as one fails to "try hard enough" to follow the regimes purported to ensure recovery into the mainstream of student flow and ability. Worse, the awful feeling comes delivered with contradictory kindness and concern.

The logistics of creating such plans can seem harmless enough. They begin with *first measuring and documenting what is wrong with the student* and then using these to divine a sequence of steps by which the student, with the consent and support of family, and the close monitoring of the teacher, will progress to goal-attainment by year's end. One can readily see the way these plans follow from the "can-do" twenty-first-century attitude that with clear targets, one can rally self-regulation, self-empowerment, and self-actualisation, to achieve the ends one desires. In practical translation, given the numbers of such students

Rethinking twenty-first-century orthodoxy **185**

in classroom's today, pushing 50 per cent by some accounts (Smith et al., 2012, p. 5), it becomes up to the student to achieve what she precisely cannot, that is to catch up to the others, even as she is moved along, up the grades, feeling increasingly inept, until she can be tracked into a special needs class or a less aggressive academic stream. It is at this point that we say we have done all that we could – the child, on the brink of adulthood, having become cultural sink for what ails a society.

To supplement this tiered government-endorsed path to inclusion, schools purchase highly marketed programs for fostering school spirit, promoting character and healthy habits, and otherwise addressing educational challenges (the likes of bullying and cyberbullying) as these arise. As it turns out, the creation of such programs are lucrative projects for educators-become-entrepreneurs.

Taken together, the foregoing structures and programs describe the field of common practices offered teachers and schools to guide them in fostering a sense of inclusion and belonging in their classrooms today. The grim picture has not gone unnoticed among curriculum studies scholars, especially in the wake of their 1970s reconceptualist movement. However, the tides have yet to turn (Pinar, 2004). Too much continues to be lost in translation when inclusivity-in-principle passes through technique to get to inclusivity-in-practice – and no shortage of medicalised models in the offing. Clinical approaches continue to mesmerise governments and publics who, in turn, hold schools hostage to guidelines and mandated policies, usurping precious attention to differently conceived understandings and ensuing action. In short, current processes, in some way or another, seem bent on standardising that which cannot be standardised: a factory with union employees on a production line that can be none of these things.

Any deep consideration and nuanced development of teacher awareness in and of the interrelationships between the subjects and objects of learning (self, other, collective, and curriculum-as-cultural-object) is generally left unattended – except where there is a complaint and an administrator (or the union) intercedes. Under the auspices of professionalism, the difficult matters-that-matter-most dare not be broached. To do so would crack the thin veneer of adult social convention behind which cloister our childhood vulnerabilities. "Elephants in rooms," the "emperor's new [missing] clothing," and concerns that brush dangerously close to strong emotions are taboo topics. If aired they risk engendering unhelpful judgement, empty assurance, and/or unfitting advice – all reminders of one's aloneness, absent any viable witness. The teacher, knowing too well the expectations on what to do, unable to make that work, wanting to make something work, and finding her circumstances denied, sees little recourse but to suppress her own self-chastisement and/or frustration in favour of denial and collusions on the positive – to no reprieving avail.

In short, classrooms, like families, are sacrosanct intimate spaces and a great deal of injury can happen there without anyone able to admit it. The point, eloquently made by *Carter et al.* (2017) *vis-à-vis* racial difference, applies across the breadth of classroom and school disparities:

186 Into practice

> As in a family that can never discuss its fundamental secrets, our deeply held and often unconscious beliefs, stereotypes, and biases are too rarely brought to the surface, examined, and finally expunged. Yet, as much as we seek to lock them from view, . . . [they] continue to color our interactions, including our disciplinary actions, on a daily, even moment-by-moment basis.
>
> *(p. 225)*

Benevolent collusion and the art of the impossible

Reviewing over 1,300 studies of inclusiveness up to 2005, Lindsay reported little in the way of research support for whether inclusion is a preferable approach in terms of outcomes, or how it should be implemented (2007, p. 16). It seems good intention is not enough. William Blake said as much when he wrote "He who would do good to another must do so in Minute Particulars: General Good is the plea of the scoundrel, hypocrite, and flatterer" (1908).

A study by Stockall and Gartin (2002) coined the term "benevolent collusion" to describe "a tacit form of communicative interaction that was negotiated between educators and [those] students who were academically challenged to create a context of superficial social inclusion" (p. 184). These researchers detailed the tacit collusion between students making the most of unworkable situations and teachers seeing and celebrating only success. Students "generally appeared happy and content with their assignments . . . [and] 'got along well' with others . . . [but also] played a critical part in reducing the visibility of their academic limitations" (pp. 184–185). For their part, teachers met student attempts to communicate any difficulties, not with targeted assistance, but rather with meant-to-be encouraging reassurances. Teachers believed that

> active participation in collaborative or cooperative groups would not only create a context of belonging, it would also address skill deficits for all students. . . . [and] provide students with disabilities a more centralized position within the cultural world of public school.
>
> *(p. 186)*

They were wrong.

A phenomenal belief in the power of peer collaboration grows problematically on the wings of misconstrued constructivist understandings. Constructivism suffers from abbreviated attention in university studies and a naïve reduction of Vygotskyan understandings (see Chapter 7) that puts disproportionate faith in peer collaboration over pedagogical relationships with more learned others. An example, not particularly earth-shattering, might give a better sense of inclusion/exclusion dilemmas.

In one particular year – on this side of the prioritisation of group work, differentiated instruction, and physical co-presence as inclusion, but before documented behavioural supports had become de rigueur – I had a grade 8 mathematics student

Rethinking twenty-first-century orthodoxy **187**

whose severe lack of understanding caught my attention early. Her cumulative records showed an IQ of 80, assessed in grade 2, putting her at the cusp of moderate intellectual disability. The student, her parents, and I hatched a plan, approved by the administrative team, whereby I worked with her, over lunch, twice each week and then quietly gave her modified learning activities and assessments. It was critical to her that she not be singled out in front of her peers.

Meanwhile, she was succeeding in her other courses, even earning As in social studies. Perplexed, her parents petitioned the school psychologist for reassessment. Her scores had not changed. In consultation with other teachers, I learned how her higher grades depended on group work and that she had become so expert at masking challenges and beguiling peers that she could game the system. Yet in working with her, at her level, I watched her vigilance dissipate and confidence grow with each experience of understanding. At year's end, a letter from her parents arrived to the principal, copied to myself and the district superintendent. It praised the difference our work together had made in her life. She now embraced the idea of beginning grade 9 in a Special Needs classroom, a chance for success *vis-à-vis* her classmates, and an environment free of the need for pretence. Whether these things played out as imagined, I can only hope.

Myriad studies and reviews of studies report inclusive intentions, meant for everyday classrooms, gone dismally awry (e.g., Kavale & Mostert, 2003; Michailakis & Reich, 2009; Reid et al., 2018). The notion of inclusion, where physical co-presence in everyday classrooms defines everything good, risks pitting different needs and agendas against each other. One-size-fits-all in education is mythical *and* we can do a much better work of creating inclusive community classrooms. In any case, we have hardly arrived at knowing what to do and having the resources and resolve to do it. As Göransson and Nilholm (2014) put it, "Unless researchers advocating this ideal are able to show how more inclusive practices can be established there is a risk that theorising inclusion will be the 'art of the impossible'" (p. 276).

An ethos of inclusion: what might it take?

In the immediacy of lives lived together in continued daily communal interaction, distal differences can seem unrelated to those more proximally felt. In school classrooms, as in familial environments, we ultimately settle into patterns of individual and collective interactions that order, in predictable enough ways, the capacity to trust, be well with, and value ourselves and others. These are challenges of intrapsychic and intersubjective well-being. The schooling solutions described earlier are inadequate – especially because, owing to power distributions, attention to, responsibility for, and agency to act on what feels right and to intercede when it does not feel right will also be unevenly distributed across persons.

In any given classroom, ways of coping come to define positions in familiar, often stereotypic ways – for instance, Louise, who likes to be in charge; Jasmine, who is always rushing and late; Nagamo, who is forever early and anxious; and

188 Into practice

Mark, who has nice clothes. There will be soft-spoken easy-going Hasan; Jory, the teacher-pleaser; and Alexis, who just likes solving puzzles. Chloe will take your lunch if you're not careful. Basha is sneaky but funny. Faith is sometimes really sad. Talia will be your friend. Mikayla is difficult to understand. Noor will know what to do if you need help. And you can trust Parkeet with your secrets. These descriptors are as applicable across student populations as their "matured" analogues in the world of adults. Though commonplace enough, positive and negative near-interpretations are rarely topics of interest or attention in the study of inclusivity. Yet these are the kinds of differences that can be retrospectively read back onto explicit targets of race, creed, class, Indigeneity, ability, gender, sexual orientation, and so forth.

In my limited Canadian context, where we can be prone to hide our biases – sometimes to ourselves and surely behind politeness and, historically, a distaste for confrontation – those students most at risk of being ostracised are less individuals that others *consciously* intend as explicit targets of difference (according to race, creed, class, Indigeneity, ability, gender, sexual orientation, and so forth), and much more those targeted according to implicit, normative, and "colourblind" judgements on appearance, behaviour, psychological well-being, and approachability. All too typically, "equal" treatment is invoked, playing against inclusivity in its disregard to predisposing histories, current circumstances, differences of heritage, and uniqueness of vantage points.

In curriculum studies, scholars of critical theory especially continue to act for change against the never-ending tides of social injustice. Too often, however, their messages seem to suffer unconscionable distortion from course lecture halls in teacher preparation programs to subsequent teaching enactments. On the watch of the well-intending teacher, learners that are singled out and variably shunned are rarely "done to" *explicitly* according to the categories showing up in education courses. The situation is far more complex than that. Those most on the margins are those who, in coping with something much larger than themselves, live compromised local conditions that cannot but diminish the capacity, trust, and meaning they can bring to any learning situation. What seems to go repeatedly underappreciated is the way that anyone arriving to a learning situation, including those individuals learning to become teachers, has been shaped according to familial histories and human interpretive experiences that both transcend and are constrained at the limits and inter-sectionalities of culture and of cultures in cultures. This realisation is the point of the entire previous section of this book.

Relational psychoanalysis offers a deeper understanding of the way that trauma is visited forward in insidious ways. It dissipates horizontally across societies and into local milieus, just as it settles vertically through societal histories across intimate transgenerational lines. They are these near forces of local milieus and intimate relations – to be sure the sedimentations of grander forces – that will most poignantly shape which available identities suppose anyone into being (see Althusser on interpellation, in Butler, 1997, 1999) and what children do become. The exclusionary treatment of learners in any classroom is most typically enacted as teachers and offending class members react to the reactions of those who have suffered original wounding – back and back. Victims thus live the double injury of the insecurity and vulnerability of their assigned-as-assumed position and an insufficiently dependable world – a deficiency in Benjamin's "lawful world" (2018).

Learners and teachers, despite (and because of) the most idealistic of intentions, can react in marginalising ways, first through blindness to injuries, and second in reaction to the effects of those injuries. In this way, the dissociated material of adult generations comes to wreak further havoc on children already disadvantaged, marking them as unfavourably troubled, in want of clearer disciplinary protocols to bring them in line – for their own sake in a system unlikely to change. The well-meaning unaware teacher, dutifully riding a wave of ideology of inclusion as acceptance, thus struggles to find ways to keep safe those children who, *for no apparent reason*, squirm or fail to respond well to her – our – goodness, when we try to help or hold them. The story of residential schools, for example, can ultimately be rejected by the coloniser offspring, now teacher, as disconcerting call for guilt and atonement for being born into a traumatiser-heritage, still carried. Or, it can be a path to understanding, collective grieving, and communal healing to bear witness and ask how we might help those who unfairly carry the enormous weight for the horrific genocide that one society visited on another.

Whatever the classroom, each student will arrive with their ongoing story with/in and beyond their particular circumstance and place in a familial constellation of relations (that reach into a broader world). They will draw on that self-, world-, and other-knowledge to establish a viable enough place *vis-à-vis* a classroom of differently conjoined constellations of relations. The synergies will decide whether a child belongs. And of course, the teacher, having greatest influence (Farmer et al., 2011) is nowhere immune to her own histories, and the socio-political, cultural, physical, and material differences holding her well, or less so, in classrooms, schools, communities, and districts.

Though rarely central to mainstream definitions of quality teaching, the teachers who students value are those able to "cultivate safe, respectful, culturally sensitive, and responsive learning communities . . . [by] establish[ing] relationships" not just with students but with their families and communities (Sleeter, 2017, p. 163). Why are we not introducing teachers to the relational understandings so central to such relations? Instead, we offer little opportunity in preparatory education programs to hone a nascent wisdom on how to be in or with classrooms and what to notice or do about its developing ethos. Without such opportunity, teachers have little recourse but to apply forward the skills and strategies from all of their own upbringing, prior schooling experiences, mentors over the years and in teaching practicums, and the folk psychologies and platitudes on offer. In short, they will promulgate more of the same.

To understand exclusion and to create countervailing classrooms where all students can feel known and accepted is to appreciate that *prior and obscured-from-view predisposing circumstances hide behind the conceptions and perceptions that anyone holds, and the manifest behaviours through which and to which they react.* The predisposing circumstances for navigating one's own subjectivity are largely unknown to the acting self (Butler, 2005). They lie at a place of intersectionality between (1) those broad homogenising categories by which we cluster people and are thus clustered – according to race, creed, class, Indigeneity, ability, gender, sexual orientation and unnamed others, but also the ways these intersect with normative judgements on appearance, behaviour, psychological well-being, and approachability; (2) the assumptions we make, not knowing we make them, according to our ignorance; (3) the psychic split and degree of denial we invoke in order to live with ourselves; (4) different inborn proclivities of temperament, sensitivity, and intellect to name a few principal ones; and (5) the dire effects of social injustices of war, strife, shame, poverty, and all manner of trauma visited forward, generation to generation, so as to distinguish persons as variably disadvantaged and privileged. Together these five influences, if we could usefully parse them this way, make an unconscionable myth of the kind of proclamations so favoured in Western societies—*you can do anything you set your mind to*. Really?

Psychoanalytic thought, for its very work at the hub of intersectionality, joins critical theory to tell us differently, pointing instead to imposing individual and collective histories that severely limit what anyone, as a living, breathing, heartful being, can do. Nuance matters – with more profundity than it seems we care to acknowledge. Just as one-size-fits-all homogenising benevolence will not do, neither will differentiating teaching suffice. Indeed, differentiation too readily devolves to the student choice and independent self-direction that is well suited to those learners arriving to school with cultural capital and a sense of how to wield it. But those on the wrong side of privilege, already compromised by adverse experiences (Burke-Harris, 2014), are too often left floundering in unfit choices that bespeak abandonment's reiteration.

A word on the "unreachable" ones

In the course of anyone's teaching, there will be the unreachable ones who, one way or the other, opt out while remaining physically present. I am describing a common form of resignation, as disaffection and complacency, rarely addressed in the literature on inclusive practices. Its prevalence creeps up the grades; that is, to the degree that the promises we've made to students don't play out and distrust and disillusionment set in.

Given sufficient time with such students, I have learned the most from and because of them. My sense has been that, to begin with, *they could not trust me and the class with their difference, perhaps their anger, and surely not their pain*. Best to keep the simmering on the inside. If only for the consistency of their world, they could not "be bothered" to breach the banality of it all; which is to say they had learned to refuse to submit their convictions to any public scrutiny. Doing so would only prove futile – again. Indeed, it would mean risking the dissolution of formidable boundaries and rendering themselves vulnerable to hope.

The risk that could not be taken was that the deplorable state of affairs – the one upon whose continued existence they had now staked their being – might be destroyed. As Winnicott first described so well (1971/2005), I am drawing attention to a critical principle of psychic development: In order for there to be the possibility of inter-subjective relating – being with the other rather than being caught in a doer/done-to dynamic – the developing learner will need a recognisable and recognising subject-other (Benjamin, 1988, 2018), different from his desires, expectations, and projections (see Chapter 13). I am speaking of that someone "out there" to count on – the stuff of near-mythical teachers who made a difference – someone who stands firm and genuine, neither retaliating nor withdrawing, and with enough acknowledging grace and presence to emerge whole after the psychic destruction of that other teacher, the student's all-too-familiar anticipated internal-object facsimile that he calls forth and usually "gets." Not trusting these dynamics, such students prefer their familiar chaos over risking reiterating loss.

Now, I will keep returning to this idea because, while being most pivotal to any kind of dialectic understanding of learning, it also strikes me as a difficult concept. Let me put the matter another way: The idea is that sometimes we can be angry at, resentful of, or disappointed in another person so as not to be angry at, resentful of, or disappointed in ourselves. This conundrum exists even though the significant others in our lives, with whom we were first attached, may have had a strong hand in seeding us with those unwanted parts. It's the familiar "if it's not you, then it must be me" conundrum. And so, in essence, we extricate the unwanted parts of ourselves and, in saying "not me," locate those parts in another person. If the projected image of this disappointing other were to be destroyed and a different other, beyond our fathoming, to emerge, then that would mean coming to terms with those unwanted elements in ourselves. The difficulty of resolving just this psychic split between elements of good and bad, in self and in others, is at the heart of a great deal that troubles children, youth, and adults – including teachers, who by and large have a strong desire to be good.

Winnicott tells us that "it takes years for the development in an individual of a capacity to discover in the self the balance of the good and the bad, the hate and the destruction that go with love, within the self. In this sense, maturity belongs to later life" (1971/2005, p. 200). Taking our cue from Winnicott, we might find it in ourselves to render grace inward that we might render it likewise to others.

Milner's insights join Winnicott's:

> It seems that when one can just look at the gap between the ideal and the actuality in oneself, see both the ideal and the failure to live up to it in one moment of vision, without either turning against the ideal and becoming cynical, nor trying to alter oneself to fit it, then the ideal and the actuality seem to enter into relation with each other and produce something new; and the result is nothing to do with self-righteousness or being pleased with oneself for having lived up to the ideal.
>
> *(Milner, 1956/1987, p. 187)*

192 Into practice

Good ideas and their troubling simulacra

Labels do not inclusion make

In 2012, Smith, Polloway, Patton, Dowdy, and McIntyre reported on dire circumstances:

> Approximately 10 percent of school-age children in Canada have a recognized exceptionality. Another undetermined number experience learning and behaviour problems but have not been classified as having a disability. Still another group . . . are those at risk of developing learning and behavioral problems. . . . Such students, plus those who obviously need assistance but do not fit into any distinct group, comprise about half the population of public schools.
>
> *(p. 5)*

As if the foregoing challenges were not enough, in the emphasis on individual uniqueness and the educator's desire to aptly differentiate instruction according to uniqueness, there have sprung forth all manner of categories of students. Indeed, learning styles, inclusion, and differentiated treatment have become firmly grouped in the public lexicon of folk psychologies.

On the point of categories and the language of inclusion, while valuing difference, diversity, individuality, novelty, and uniqueness there seems little room for sameness, redundancy, homogeneity, convention, and tradition. *What is the same about all of us is that we are all so different.* At a personal level, I have begun to notice a peculiar pattern: If ever I describe my family of origin as dysfunctional, I can expect an effort of inclusive reassurance that says, "Didn't I know?" all families are dysfunctional. In this example, we see a tendency to radically reduce difference to sameness. This is inclusion gone awry, ideologically so. Fonagy and Target put the problem more succinctly: "It is not the overvaluing of private knowledge but the undifferentiated experience of shared knowledge that hinders perspective-taking" (2007, p. 922)

Consider another example. The setting was a middle school in which I was conducting research in a participatory ethnographic capacity. One day, I arrived at the school to find the teachers eager to put to use a new tool introduced to them by a guest presenter's half-day workshop on inclusive practices. It was a near 30-page amalgam of all manner of popular self-administered rubrics and inventories on personality type, learning style, and the like. Each set, not unlike the descriptors one finds under astrological signs, returned to the student the kind of person and learner they were. Armed with this information, feeling a little more recognised and unique, the students were then to choose and complete an appropriate learning task from a menu of options and follow with their preferred demonstration of understanding. The missing piece was the actual learning. No matter their style or approach, only a few students could puzzle over the necessary concepts on their

Rethinking twenty-first-century orthodoxy **193**

own and come up understanding. More problematic it has become commonplace for labels, thus-determined, to become self-fulfilling prophecies that justify not-learning in environments falling short of expectations (see entitlement literature, especially Twenge, 2006; Twenge & Campbell, 2009).

In today's inclusive classrooms, the more medicalised are special needs, the more resources any school can legitimately tap. September is the usual month to settle per-student funding based on enrolments and special needs for a term. Would that access to resources be less tied to coding and measurement! Would that teachers and schools have discretionary funds to use as they see fit, judiciously so, without the requirement of labels and endless paper trails. In other words, if the things that students "have" are not of the ilk for documenting and not properly documented – things like a single parent who works night shift, a sibling who suffers from a chronic illness, a radically unique belief/faith system frequently misunderstood, a first language different from that of instruction, a nervousness about tests, a discomfort in groups, a need for quiet, small desks making a child too big, and the list goes on – then the less resources (by way of assistants, teaching materials, class size, preparatory time) and residual attention any teacher is going to have to go around. On the plus side, the student may not know – or, knowing, feel the need to dwell in – his or her difference. With a good teacher, each learner might even feel witnessed nonetheless and even *be* included. The point? Labels do not inclusion make.

Given these dynamics, it is no small wonder that the categories for students (and the accompanying bureaucratic mischief dedicated to measuring them), like rabbits do multiply (Shakespeare, 2017) – as do, uncoincidentally, rampant individual and systemic anxiety. Student categorical differences and the design of engaging experiences, these days go together with differentiation for inclusion. But the revival of a Deweyan notion of experience may be truer to form than we might want. From a psychoanalytic perspective, it shows problematic signs of playing further into anxiety and against capacity, trust, and meaning.

Experience and community

Of community Jean-Luc Nancy writes,

> Cum is an exhibitor, placing us in front of one another, delivering us up to one another, playing us against one another, and delivering us all together to . . . "experience": that which is nothing more than being with. . . . One should certainly not magnify being-together. One of the discretely perverse effects of the recent work on community has been the occasional revival of a certain Christian and humanist emphasis on "sharing," "exchange," or "others."
>
> *(1996/2000, pp. 104–105)*

In almost the same breath, Nancy both defines *experience as nothing more than being with* and cautions against *magnifying being-together as one of the discretely perverse effects of recent work on community.*

194 Into practice

If experience is "nothing more than being with," even a "with" in the absence of a physical other, then it may be at odds with Deweyan revivalism insofar as for Dewey, the interaction-of-note in experience is between the student and his circumstances of doing, alongside and with other doers. In *Experience and Education* (1938/1997), Dewey emphasises *interaction* and *continuity*. That is, in the Deweyan ideal and increasingly today, engaged experience, as that *symptom* of the thing desired, becomes the sign that eclipses meaningful experience itself – where meaningful experience always finds its roots in intrapsychic–intersubjective relating. Just as in group work one can be thoroughly disconnected from each other or a larger world, in solitary study one can be wholly connected.

A common student question, especially in the non-humanitarian disciplines, asks, "Why does this matter?" For some, mathematics and science can matter as escape to an objectified thing-world, safely away from others and affect. For others, it will matter as connection with, and/or power to act on and in, that world – to make something, to produce. And for others yet, it will be the joy of mysteries solved and threaded together in intriguing narrative coherences that give of a sense of connectedness.

For experience to be about being with, it cannot be enough that, as per Dewey, the student *lose himself* in tasks set forth and regulated by the teacher solely to the ends of developing the knowledge, skills, and attitudes of a government-prescribed curriculum (1997/1938, p. 28). For Dewey, the litmus test on the value of experience is whether it engenders *continuity* of learning (pp. 16–17). For Nancy, as for myself, its value turns on continuity with the world, the situated experience to and from a much larger context. In other words, for Dewey, experiences are valuable insofar as they leave experiencers wanting more. Although this is useful, in Nancy's conception, and in the dialectic model I propose, it is surely not enough. Of "interaction" and "continuity" Dewey writes, their "active union . . . provide[s] the measure of the educative significance and value of an experience" (p. 18). As in gaming (a favourite paradigm case in the learning sciences), education is progressive insofar as experience begets further experience (Dewey, p. 40).

My concerns echo those expressed by Matthew Bowker in *Ideologies of Experience* (2016). He offers a politically conscious and psychoanalytically sensitive critique of Deweyan experience, become ideology, in education. Bowker details how Dewey's "model of teaching and learning by experience . . . confuses submission to experience with self-realization . . . [and confuses] self-control with self-development" (p. 99). Indeed, performance and production, as twin schooling preoccupations, eclipse attentions to intersubjective and intrapsychic negotiations of self and, with these *in*attentions, foreclose any "paradigmatic critique of the framework of the experience or the situation or community in which it is embedded" (p. 92). In other words, "the Deweyan student does not question science, itself, but uses the scientific method to enhance experience. He does not question the need for 'economic progress' but applies his experience in producing it" (p. 97). In Bowker's hands, contemporary design-based pedagogies advance Deweyan revisionism when they privilege a meaning of experience that, in the mode of gaming, support (1) a radical fusion of selves to experience's objects, that is, between the unthinking actor-learner and the object upon which the learner acts; (2) reflection restricted to thoughts about how to better accomplish a given task and that, in so doing, distort the very notion of critical thought and reflection in its socio-political and psychoanalytic sense; and (3) psychic splitting as enabled by the provision of engaging distractions, these serving as laudable forms of dissociation that foreclose the development of the capacity to admit and hold dear both desirable and undesirable aspects of self – especially insofar as they lead to reward for innovative entrepreneurial performances and productions (pp. 15 & 83–85).

In overemphasising the engagement potential of any learning activity, we run the risk of underappreciating the engagement capacity of the learner and the possibility of schooling helping that learner develop her own agency for focusing attention and rallying perseverance and patience to stay with an activity of notable pedagogical value. In a digital marketplace designed to feed, amplify, and otherwise play into desires, these skills arise as arguably critical counterpoints to an age of immediate gratification. One would hope that schools not only teach concepts but also broaden learners very capacities to learn and to trust in their ability to find/create meaning in a learning activity – even if that activity is as seemingly mundane as paying attention, entertaining ideas, asking questions, and making notes. Given that engagement is necessary but not sufficient to learning, privileging the so-called intrinsic engagement value of any activity misses on engagement's relational character. Instead, it feeds a condition whereby "engage me" becomes the mantra of a kind of learner who expects the learning environment to cater to favoured modes of thinking and/as doing – essentially amplifying rather than disrupting and/or elaborating who that learner is, what she already knows, and the meanings to which she gravitates.

There is an aphorism in psychoanalytic thought that pathological narcissism compromises learning. Yet pathological or malignant narcissism, as expressed in antisocial personality disorder, psychopathy, and sociopathy, is over-represented in positions of power; that is, among CEOs, lawyers, organisational leaders, and other top executives (Peltokangas, 2015; Reich, 2014/2015). Surely, if these individuals can rise to such positions they must be able to learn. The notion of learning as amplifying one's known versus expanding one's knowable relates to discourses around student entitlement (e.g., Twenge, 2006; Twenge & Campbell, 2009) and this attitude of "engage me." What I am positing as a dialectic model of learning is a broader conception of learning that entails resolving difference, as dissonance and ambiguity, and that invokes the whole of a self, including especially the psychosocial aspects of that self with roots and motivations in affect. This does not preclude the ironic fact that there will be those for whom learning is about amplifying one's known in a way that denies subjectivity, even and especially one's own, even if the thing studied is subjectivity itself.

Put differently, losing oneself in experience with a transitional object of learning – whose transitional status one denies because that part is buried under a belief in the thing's neutral objectivity – can serve as self-aggrandising and intoxicating escape

196 Into practice

from encountering the subject-other and the subject-self hidden in the meaning of that object. That is, sometimes we become enamoured with things and with concepts-as-things because they give us the sense of power, preoccupation, and/or conceptual movement to help us avoid discomfort when it comes to people. The motivation is still people; and the object is still transitional – although, on surface impressions, we would adamantly deny it being so. Bowker writes,

> I define what is meant by "thinking" and "knowing" in a psychoanalytic sense, and argue that the protection or "fortification" of experience against intrusion is actually a defense against the internal threat of thinking.
>
> *(2016, p. 15)*

With Bowker then, the kind of learning that I am advancing in this model, insofar as it is dialectical, is one to advance thinking and knowing that invites intrusion and works to resolve the dissonance thus encountered, doing so in ways that cannot but change the self-who-learns.

Finally, in the problematic notion of experience, ever so popular today, I locate an undercurrent of control that refuses the kind of openness conducive to rethinking and knowing again and differently. Bowker describes "an illusion of freedom" (p. 84) where choice is embedded in structures that go unquestioned and where, although there is "diffusion of the locus of control across the social group" (p. 84), the teacher facilitates the task design such that it gives only *social authority* to the group. Of course, group work fits well with the contention that we all ought to learn to work well together – never mind that the power hierarchies of groups do mirror and reinstall those already existent more broadly. For Dewey however, social control becomes both the means to "teach" self-control (1938/1997, p. 27) and the hinge-point of democracy (p. 22). But in suppressing nascent selfhood to the civilising authority of a purported real-world of group activity, working on adult-like projects (as in the rhetoric of authentic learning, see, e.g., Edelson & Reiser, 2006), these technologies seem to move students in the opposite direction of community, leastwise Nancy's conception of it, and toward more narcissistic self-orientations in a competitive world of entrepreneurial survival.

In these ways, as part of the individualism of an ideology-of-experience, today's schools do emphasise community – arguably doing so, as we have seen, much in the way cautioned against by Nancy. To reiterate, this ideal of community has gone hand-in-hand with problematic incarnations of inclusion as benevolent collusion, the development of highly prized, so-called soft, social skills essential to the twenty-first-century knowledge worker, character education for our youngest "to be good," and for teachers, differentiated instruction as the prima facie tool of inclusion.

At some point we do well to resolve these rhetorical preoccupations – alive for more than several decades now – with present-day divisive politics that are anything but inclusive. Inclusive sentiments when fused to an imperative of being good, do contribute to psychic splitting and a different kind of us/them mentality – one

Rethinking twenty-first-century orthodoxy **197**

echoed in ever-exacerbating left-right extremes pitting the idealistic-good-strawperson and the realistic-bad-strawperson against each other. To what degree are schools cultivating damaging fictions by telling students and teachers that being good means colluding as told and that if they set their mind to it, they all can successfully jump through hoops en route to assured success? What is the relationship between these schooling practices and current political shifts worldwide?

Of prodigal sons and daughters

A part of me has always recoiled in the face of essentialisms – the purported essences, flat and superficial, of community and of experience. Appreciating the critical value of heretofore unheard voices now courageously ricocheting across digital air waves of "hash-tag me-too," those on the wrong*ed* side of long-time social injustices, find new opportunities for solidarity, as they clamour to bring to light grievances too long covered over.

Yet I worry that a world focused on making amends, atoning for the sins of distant wrongs, risks somehow missing the mark. Where do blame and forgiveness go when we understand life systems as infinitely nested and relationally connected? The underlying socio-cultural patterns of distant wrongs, if left unaddressed, will surely continue to wreak their havoc today, but recompense is insufficient to the task. Rather the question is one of making peace and somehow prioritising attention to currently lived wrongs.

Perhaps a story, somewhat allegorical, will help. It relates to a common reaction from the caregivers of my 12- and 13-year-old students when I called – or sometimes, yes, even visited them in their homes – to have a conversation about emerging concerns. Importantly, this was never the first call. That one happened early in the year, as my way to say hello.

> Almost invariably these caregivers wanted a list of missing assignments or perhaps a chance to redo some form of assessment. *They sought opportunity for their child to go back and rewrite a past* – as if it were a simple matter of doing or redoing. But the issue in learning has always been much less about going through the motions of completing a "to-do" list of tasks. Rather for me, it has always been about students learning themselves into their own difference. I devised a way of communicating and enacting this priority. It seemed to work.
>
> First, I pointed out that *there will have been valid reasons for falling behind* and that it would be good to begin there. I asked the caregiver if they wouldn't mind it if I kept their child after school (or in at noon) *to see what we could do to understand what was happening*. I then said that our focus would be on keeping up with present learning, that trying to catch up on past assignments, without any sort of remediation, might be counterproductive to their class participation, and that *a mind is too precious to waste* on practicing what one does not understand or going through the motions of busywork. Their child mattered too much for that.

198 Into practice

I also told them that I would not call them back until their child had suc-
ceeded, for two weeks, to manage present learning. I added that, if I had not
yet called and their child insisted on having had two good weeks, this was
entirely possible. Their child could call me to confirm. Once nascent habits and understandings showed signs of solidifying, then we would pace our
insertion of the bits of learning that had been missed. *We would not work on
"catching up" until we could first "keep up."*

In regards homework, I reiterated my policy: The work was graduated
and students could focus at appropriate levels of difficulty. Moreover, if they
struggled they were to call me. We would cross impasses over the phone
together. Should I not pick up, they were to leave a message. If I failed to call
back, then it was "on me." We would sort things out the next day.

Finally, I emphasised that this entire process ought not infringe negatively
on family time: Family, too, was precious and I could imagine little worse than
a regular dose of evenings fraught with battles over schoolwork. They should
leave these concerns with me. *The responsibility, happily taken, was mine to work
with their child.*

Now, an interesting pattern would happen when I did call after two weeks
of successful effort. I would say, "This is Lissa, so-and-so's teacher." At exactly
that point, I would hear a sigh or an anticipatory silence. I could feel the emotion literally coming through the phone. These caregivers were simply weary
of bad news. When I followed with good news, the effect was transformative.
This for me, in retrospect, was all about community.

Today, I feel the world at the brink of a new wild west of public lynching or perhaps
counter-lynching (e.g., with the inception of "deepfake" videos) that splits wide-
open chasms of infinitely construable fantasy, against any stable real, at the ready
to serve psychic longing. We cannot win this battle. The material effects of digital
lynchings are and will continue to be dire. We may want to attend to what's at play.
How is it that those lynched serve as metonymic stand-ins for all that ails, and has
ailed, a society. On the other hand, who is to say whether current localised vindica-
tions are necessary, if not unavoidable, collateral damage? But where does all this
lead? And how might schools, perhaps arguably and inadvertently complicit, learn
themselves and their participants into a difference?

For all these reasons, I worry and wonder at inclusive schooling practices that,
attendant to the tragedy of societal wrongs committed, also fail to include those on
the wrong side of such doings – the newly excluded "prodigal sons and daughters"
of a society where inclusion is the mantra that nonetheless cannot but entail its
exclusionary other side.

In thinking of inclusion as a kind of circling the wagons, I do want to be on the
inside of goodness. Yet returning to Nancy, I am reminded of his conception of
being-with as being-open. He plays with the notion of being exposed: posed and
dis-posed without – as in outside and beside oneself. And he addresses the tragedy
of humanity's

Rethinking twenty-first-century orthodoxy **199**

> but first of all Europe['s] . . . unsuspected talent for self-destruction, in the
> name of community. . . . talent both on the order of quantity (but to a degree
> that the expressions "extermination" or "mass destruction" convert the num-
> bers into absolutes or infinites) and on the order of ideas or values.
>
> *(Nancy, 1996/2000, p. 102)*

And he asks how

> to say "we" otherwise than as a [generic] "one" (= everyone and no one)
> and otherwise than as an "I" (= a single person, which is still no one)? How
> then to be in common without creating what an entire tradition . . . calls
> a community (a body of identity, an intensity of property, an intimacy of
> nature)?
>
> *(p. 103)*

These questions I intend, also, at the heart of the proposed model of learning – a
model where I hope the agencies of *capacity* and *trust* enable movement to resolve
tensions fuelled by bodily felt and relationally inspired *meaning*. I believe that exis-
tence-that-is-coexistence derives of vital trust-given as viable trust-learned. It conditions the very being of secure enough selfhood – that is, intrapsychic being whose
plural interiority consists in a dynamic "with" of object-others, open and ever-
revised according to inter*personal* encounters that can also be inter*subjective* ones
lived. This is the dialectic I seek to provoke in the model.

To have a mind in mind

There are indeed some programs in schools that show promise. However, too often
in a naïveté antithetic to psychoanalytic wisdom, there are others that at best cause
no further harm, at worst exacerbate the very conditions they seek to ameliorate.
Character education, if taken up as folk psychology's solution to a troubled society,
can fall into the latter categories (Walsh, 2017). Insofar as it indoctrinates children
on the merits of being good and the wrongs of being bad, it disavows recognition of
parts of a self and encourages a psychic split between an acknowledged good self as
"me" and a disavowed bad self as "not me" – pushing shame and resentment underground. Indeed, Carter, Skiba, Arrendondo, and Pollock's call for a conversation
"about race and discipline [that] means talking about what we think automatically
about 'types of children,' even if those thoughts are undesired" (2017, p. 225) is a
conversation to expose our vulnerable "not me" parts – one that few dare risk in a
society that neither promotes psychic health nor even a healthy society. Where the
self splits, so too does the socio-political world – a situation all too pervasive across
the globe today.

Emotional self-regulation is a second example having gained popular momentum –
in some enactments promising, in others troubling. Recall one of the critical points
of the previous chapters on child development: that we learn self-regulation in the

200 Into practice

harmonising presence of a self-regulated and attuning other. When, in the face of distress, a calming adult joins me in my experience to de-escalate it, I learn how to do this for myself. If the housecoat on the hook is frightful phantom in my mind, it may serve little benefit to insist, either on its reality as a housecoat by flicking on and off the light, or to cater to its fantasy as a phantom by always leaving a night light on; better if someone, sensitive to my affect and confident in his own, *walked with me in the dark* to explore this thing that frightens. Similarly, if I am going to write a test, it may serve little benefit for someone to insist, either on a purported reality that everything will (or at least should, if I believe enough) be fine, or to cater to my fantasy by exempting me from all tests; better if that someone *walked with me in my darkness* in preparing for the next test and successively reframing this thing that frightens me. The point is that we learn to self-regulate through a recognising other who is attuned to our own affect but for whom that affect is not contagious. Where affect regulation in schooling understands this, it shows great promise (e.g., Lipsett, 2011).

> Recognition makes action into communication, and this action on both sides is required for the child to be coherent, regulated, to have defined emotions as well as agency, as well as to later think about what is in the mind of the other and her own mind. . . . Affect regulation and mentalization are effects of the caregiver's recognizing action on the growth of the mind, and conversely build the capacity to act in this way with others.
>
> *(Benjamin, 2018, p. 9)*

As for the caregiver, so too for the teacher.

On the other hand, there is a danger that the self-regulation movement translates a problem of a relational field to an individual problem whereby we hand over tools to the child and leave that child alone to use them to self-regulate. Those tools are typically mentalising and mindfulness practices.

Mentalising invokes a thinking, or metacognitive, stance to notice somatic expressions of strong feelings and emotions – accepting, identifying, and talking about them rather than suppressing them. Doing so can enable a calming symbolic distance to settle a self in moments of distress (essential a neocortical override on limbic triggers) while shelving affect for later attention.

Mindfulness practices are those meditative strategies whereby a person brings their focus into the present to interrupt a runaway mind ruminating on future and past. Difficulties persist if the relationally embodied roots of strong emotions remain unaddressed and the thing we try to keep out of mind is the thing, in back of mind, that we must be vigilant about avoiding (Hardt, 2019; Westen, 1998).

In these contexts, affective self-regulation can become problematic insofar as it leaves troubled students to enact mentalising and mindfulness without the benefit of an attuned, attuning, witnessing other. (Recall Daniel Stern's three ways of being with the caregiver: *resonating-with* the other, the *other as self-regulating*, and oneself *in-the-presence-of* the other Chapter 5). In other words, if we leave students to manage themselves on their own – as can often be the case in overcrowded classrooms with more need than teachers and classroom community can possibly meet – then the behaviour modification strategies and individual program plans we give them can feel like withdrawal or retaliation. Students need to know they can count on us as separate centres of being who have their minds in mind. They need this so that they can begin to count on themselves, even enough to rebel against us. To this point, Winnicott insightfully writes, "It is wise to remember that rebellion belongs to the freedom you have given your child by bringing him or her up in such a way that he or she exists in his or her own right" (1971/2005, p. 196).

To these ends, I seek to provoke a psychoanalytic influence that is neither therapeutic nor emancipatory (see Taubman, 2012, for an historic account of these psychoanalytic projects in education). *As motives go, the therapeutic project of healing students (or teaching them to self-sooth and heal themselves) and the emancipatory project of, for instance, encouraging them to rise up for their rights, can skirt dangerously close to being about manipulating them to suit our agenda, our desires, our vision of a new world order – the entrepreneurial technocratic world of knowledge workers.* In so saying, I *do* endorse a particular interpretation of learner-centred education, but an interpretation at seeming odds with the one most advanced – leastwise as it plays out in classrooms. Learner-centred need not mean putting learners in charge, or even letting them think they know all that wants knowing about their learning. They need us in charge, but authentically so, and always with their hopes and desires and the realities of their progress in mind.

Learner–centred education: neither a therapeutic nor an emancipatory project – and hardly an entrepreneurial one

We live in a world that can be far too eager to capitulate to children's desires to take charge and to grow up quickly. Winnicott writes extensively on the problem of adulthood foisted too early on teens – and, these days, I would add on even the youngest of children. It seems a matter of course that some of the grave anxieties we are presently witnessing might ensue (e.g., Baldino & Cabral, 2008; Bandura, 1993; Burns, 1998; D'Amour, 2013; Dowker, 2005; Hattie, 2009, pp. 49–50; Hoy, Davis, & Anderman, 2013).

A fine disillusionment

On the issue of realities, while it does no good to pummel students with a harsh world, holding reality's re-centring disillusionment indefinitely at bay defines a problem in the opposite direction. For instance, many of my student-teachers return from their field experience having learned that when children's work and thinking

202 Into practice

is incorrect, teachers should withhold that information from them, so as not to discourage their self-esteem and sense of self-efficacy. While, I do not advocate a page filled with red x's, I do protest this increasingly common practice on multiple grounds, the most critical being the belief (on the part of the teacher and communicated to the student) that something showing up as an "error" is to be feared, rather than an opportunity from which to learn. Notably, in regards error analysis, I agree with Carol Dweck, 2006/2016, and Jo Boaler, 2016, who seem to have made a small fortune taking this nugget of insight to market, albeit embedded in a larger cluster of more exaggerated claims the likes of "*everyone* can learn math to the highest level" (Boaler et al., n.d.).[1]

In any case, the analysis of the *mistake* – as the relational miscue between what child and teacher have taken to have been communicated – contains the clue to improved connection between persons and ideas. Plus, there is a grand opportunity to make life more interesting for teacher and student(s). For example, the teacher could juxtapose contradictory bits of evidence as invitation for the learner to reconsider, for example, "That makes good sense, however, there is this to also consider. If this is true and this is true, and we change this one thing, well I wonder why that doesn't work out? Can you be detectives and find other places where this happens?" Or, "Oh, I see what everyone did here. Oh dear, I forgot to give you a chance to practice this bit first."

Instead, the practice of letting a particular individual or group understanding go unconsidered, leaves it to sediment. At the same time, in protecting the learner from the knowledge of mistakes, one communicates that mistakes are to be feared, that one must get things right. At the start of every term, my new grade 7 students were reticent to check their answers against those at the back of the book. They told me that that was like cheating. By the end of the same semester, not only were they checking their answers but also they were seeking to analyse any discrepancies between the solutions at the back and the one's they generated. Of course, every now and again, the textbook had it wrong – the finding of which, in my class, came with a fair amount of delight.

The practice of hiding feedback as to whether a student is obliviously ingraining problematic habits is akin to having students practice shooting hoops in basketball without letting them see if any of their shots are going in. Worse yet, it also suggests that knowing you've been missing too-often-for-anyone's-liking is a bad thing. Better not to know. Now if one does keep missing the mark, rather than persist in hopes that the brute force of repetition (e.g., as in more homework) should be enough to change things, such failed attempts flag a problem of fit between the task required and the readiness of the student. The error, if we want to call it that, is relational and in the system. It suggests a time for analysis (see Chapter 11). Perhaps the hoop is too high or too far for the learner; perhaps the technique could use functional adjustment and progressive development; perhaps the student could care less about making the shot; and perhaps this learner's pace of development is nowhere near the vicinity of the assumed norm to which we (problematically) cater. Keeping the learner busy with taking blind shots is hardly helpful. The illusion that all is

Rethinking twenty-first-century orthodoxy 203

well if it is not, while meant to protect the child, simply forestalls the eventuality of disillusionment. When disillusionment does come, and all at once, the experience can be crushing, leaving dissociation and denial as the only viable modes of coping. Eventually, the children we've misled in this way get wise to our false reassurances and simply stop trusting us and/or stop trying altogether. They opt out.

From teacher as object-other to teacher as subject-other

Instead of opting out, we will want our young to embrace idealism – "one of the exciting things about adolescent boys and girls. They have not yet settled down into disillusionment, and the corollary of this is that they are free to formulated ideal plans" (Winnicott, 1971/2005, p. 201). Winnicott insists that

> society needs to be shaken by the aspirations of those who are not responsible. If the adults abdicate, the adolescent becomes prematurely, and by false process, adult. Advice to society could be: for the sake of adolescents . . . do not allow them to step up and attain a false maturity by handing over to them responsibility that is not yet theirs, even though they may fight for it.
>
> *(p. 198)*

To reiterate an earlier point, students need us in charge, authentically so, and always with their hopes and desires and the realities of their progress in mind. This means educational decisions are our responsibility. In the interests of pleasing them, learner-centred education can lose its way. Let me share a small example from an undergraduate course in mathematics methods. One day, I solicited the class for input on their preferences about how we might next proceed. After class, several students pulled me aside, worried that I would put the decision to a student vote – as had apparently happened, to deleterious effect, in another course. Surprised, I reassured them that that was hardly my intention, that the decision was fully my responsibility, and one I would not shirk. I clarified that I had asked for their input to broaden my understanding of the issues and challenges they faced and because I valued their thoughts. Nothing more.

We teachers are surely called to cultivate longer, broader, and deeper views than our students. It is a sad state of affairs when the young have to rise up to shake their quarreling adults into responsibility – the likes of, for example, addressing climate change. In schools, students should be able to count on knowing that their expressed preferences, though valued, do not our teaching mandates make. At the same time, it's worth reiterating Marion Milner's point: That when we disillusion mercifully (1956/1987) our students can trust that impasses in knowing-or-doing are invitations into intrigue and difference. It is in so trusting that they can realise growth in their own tenacity and resilience. This is the kind of good enough pedagogy to engender critical thinking and to ultimately make "rising up" possible, should that be the path they choose.

Our students, even the adult ones, will benefit from our being true to ourselves, holding to that which we know, while modelling curiosity and openness to disillusionment. Put in psychoanalytic terms, they need us to survive their dissatisfaction,

204 Into practice

protestation, and anger when we are other than what they imagine and insist us to be (see especially Benjamin, 1988, 1995, & Winnicott, 1971/2005, in Chapter 6). They benefit when we stand courageously in our imperfect being, to become recognisable and recognising subjects, *not* object-extensions of them or servants to a cultivated student craving for kinds of pedagogical treatment and reassurances of achievement.

Is there not an inherent contradiction, if not outright dishonesty, in learner-centred teaching when it begins first by categorising the child as a kind of learner, thereby prematurely limiting that child's self-conception, and then using a narrative of special treatment to cajole, coddle, if not coerce, that same child into achieving ends other than his own? Better perhaps to keep the child's learning possibilities and natures open, while remaining forthright about what must be, can be, and has been learned. Moreover, acknowledging that the accessible reasons for anyone's action are often but a distant cousin to underlying unconscious motive, *we can say no to students and* not *have to explain ourselves.*

Students benefit from the opportunity to confront and grapple in the incommensurable differences between, as we have seen, the world they have in mind – inclusive of (and represented in) their teacher as internal object-other, whose nature their imagining and enforcing makes – and the world out there – inclusive of (and represented by) their teacher as subject-other whose nature exceeds whatever they might imagine it to be. The former makes for a student alone in his responsibility; the latter is the basis for curiosity and discovery in the possibility of someone beyond the self on whom a learner can depend – someone enough "in charge" and a life enough "in control" to allow the reprieve of unfettered play with ideas.

For another example, the teacher, who uses an "I" statement with her class the likes of, "I feel sad when you do not settle down after recess because I think it means that you do not care about me and your learning," is a teacher using guilt to manipulate a class into behaving well. It is a teacher attempting to make the class responsible for her. To be clear, it is the teacher's role to own the situation, shifting the environment or her expectations in some way, in consideration of the learners, so that learning continues. Instead, her "I" statement shackles the students with that responsibility and, in the doing, bestows upon the students a kind of omnipotent responsibility for their teacher's well-being. This is simply too much power and, when taken to extremes, backfires, conditioning an us/them divide that, among other problems, includes unhealthy narcissistic tendencies associated with entitlement and the like. Winnicott (1971/2005) writes,

> This brings me to my main point, the difficult one of the *immaturity* of the adolescent [and child]. Mature adults must know about this and must believe in their own maturity as never before or after. It will be appreciated that *it is difficult to state this without being misunderstood, since it so easily sounds like a downgrading to talk of immaturity* [italics added]. But this is not intended.
>
> (p. 196)

A child of any age (say six years) may suddenly need to become responsible, perhaps because of the death of a parent or because of the break-up of a family. Such a child must be prematurely old and must lose spontaneity and play and carefree creative impulse. . . . However, it is different when, as a matter of deliberate policy, the adults hand over responsibility; indeed, to do this can be a kind of letting your children down [an abdication] at a critical moment. . . . [T]he adolescent [or child] who wins too early is caught in his own trap. . . . Here is one of the many places where society ignores unconscious motivation at its peril.

(p. 197)

Our students, young and old alike, strike me as too "falsely mature" for their years. In the increasing prevalence, down the school grades, of students who cut themselves, have eating disorders, and suffer extremes of anxiety (to give only a few dire examples), Winnicott's wisdom seems more apt these days than at the time of his writing:

In the psychotherapy of the individual adolescent . . . there is to be found death and personal triumph as something inherent in the process of maturation and in the acquisition of adult status. . . . The unconscious theme may become manifest as the experience of a suicidal impulse, or as actual suicide. . . . The situation lacks its full richness if there is a too easy and successful avoidance of the clash of arms.

(1971/2005, p. 196)

In owning our difference, our students have someone and something to push against.

Old too young

Let me repeat, *as motives go, the therapeutic and emancipatory projects can skirt dangerously close to being about manipulating learners to suit (adult) agendas, desires, and visions of a world order – the entrepreneurial technocratic world of knowledge workers.* To this point, Nadesan writes,

The cultural production of individuals who self-actualize through work and who possess just the right mix of technical/intellectual and social skills seems a formidable project, a project that could not be realized successfully unless the gold-collar entrepreneurial subject was cultivated from his or her earliest moments.

(2002, p. 412)

I do not want, nor seek, to hear my voice through the voices of my students, nor do I expect any fully formed voice emanating from them. Indeed, the heroes and hero-children that Western societies hold up as exemplars of notable talent and

206 Into practice

insight (e.g., Cooper, 2011; see also Nadesan's critique, 2002), strike me as not much different from those winners of the very child beauty pageants that most of us decry. Both bespeak a tragic spectacle of children and youth too old for their years, who as open and willing receptacles, vulnerable to adult ideals, have become other-formed, other-serving, and other-responsible carriers of adult dreams. In bringing those dreams to life, the dreams of their parents, these children earn status and an identity to which they can become enslaved – the more capable the child, the more extraordinary the feats and alluring the status. In these contexts, a quick online search returned myriad examples. I found Cooper's by-line in *Parenting Magazine* to be a most alarming one. It reads, "Get inspired by these 8 kids making a difference in the world with their nonprofits and charity organizations" (2011). On the other hand, Country singer Luke Bryan makes my point much more eloquently and simply when he croons a deeper wisdom of children staying young when they can, of shutting off screens, climbing trees, and getting dirty (David Frasier, Ed Hill, & Josh Kear, 2018).

Just as we educators must stand in our difference as adults, for our students, so too must we allow them to stand in their difference as children. Doing so is critical to rendering even the possibility of co-recognition and genuine intersubjective experience. For there to be any recognition and any intersubjective connection at all, it must be across difference. This is a principle to be cherished when it comes to rethinking the inclusive classroom. There must first be an *other* with whom to contend (as expressed in Elizabeth Ellsworth iconic 1989 piece, "Why doesn't this feel empowering?"), if there is ever going to be any other in whose gaze learners might find themselves known – and this goes both ways, teacher to student and student to teacher. Without the existence of and dialogical encounters with an other beyond one's contrivances, however baffling that other may seem, there can be no possibility of feeling heard or seen and no distinct existing other to hear or see. It is in this sense that giving audience and bearing witness are practices that imply difference, the difference to make connection possible. Therein lies the very paradox of singular-plural-being with which we all must grapple. To be included, we must first be seen. Jessica Benjamin's theorising on co-recognition re-joins that of Donnel Stern when he voices a central principle of relational psychoanalytic thought, that "It takes a witness to become a self" (Stern, 2010, p. xvi) and that witness wanted a witness, and back, and back. These concepts I return to in Chapter 13.

"Nothing more than being with"

If neither emancipatory nor therapeutic, what then *is* my goal in teaching and in writing this book? At a minimum, not unlike the Hippocratic oath, it is "do no harm." Teach from a position of trust in and respect for one's students, as wellsprings of human possibility. But too, teach from a position of responsibility, with trust in and respect for oneself, also as wellspring of human possibility. Aspire to relational freedom in the interpersonal field (as per Stern, 2015) that permits spaces between centres of being and also centre-to-centre connection, without forcing that which

Rethinking twenty-first-century orthodoxy **207**

cannot be forced. And finally teach from a position of joy in the exquisite dialectic processes of learning by which, in the encounter with the other and with cultural meanings beyond the self, new awareness can broaden and deepen experience-as-presence in and with that other and the world. In the words of Jean-Luc Nancy (2010), I believe in and aspire to experiences of experience as "nothing more than being with" (p. 104), where such being with is "the same thing as being-open" (p. 106).

Note

1 As hyperbole goes, the proselytised claims and the waves of enthusiasm and buy-in (quite literally) to the next miracle solution (as per strong elements in Boaler, 2016; Dweck, 2006/2016; and Cozolino, 2010) sometimes bear frightening resemblance to the methods and "successes" of a cult (Koebele & Villines, n.d.).

11

CLASSROOMS AS HOLDING ENVIRONMENTS

Speaking on behalf of Winnicott, Bollas elaborates on two worlds and their healthy nurturance according to each of two overlapping aspects of caregiving: the *"environment mother"* and the *"object mother"* (see Chapter 6): "Between the worlds of stillness, quiet, and intrapsychic unconsciousness . . . and the world of activity, relationship, and consciousness . . . we human beings spend a fair amount of time commuting" (1993, p. 404).

The iconic symbol of the environment mother is a non-impinging parent, cradling an infant. This is the starting point of Winnicott's *"holding environment"* – where one's solitude is guarded over, unobtrusively, in a sanctuary for unfettered intrapsychic being and becoming (Bollas, 1993, p. 404). In contrast, recall the caregiver as object mother: She "is not only . . . a 'responder,' but also an initiator" (p. 403). She invites the child into an external world of relational activity by providing "objects, including herself, for the infant to use" (p. 403). She thus promotes the intrapsychic shaping of a rich robust internal-object world of "things out there."

At first, the infant will be under the *illusion* that "those objects that show up ready for use do so as a result of his wishes" (p. 403). He will soon need the caregiver to disillusion an inevitable misunderstanding: that what-is-in-mind about others and the world *is* (and thus creates) others and that world. In *disillusionment*, the child gains a world of never-quite-knowable subject-others (Winnicott, 1971/2005, pp. 13–18) and the opportunity to belong with those others as co-recognising witnesses (Benjamin, 1988, 2018). Winnicott writes, "The mother's main task (next to providing opportunity for illusion) is disillusionment. This . . . continues as one of the tasks of parents and educators" (p. 18).

Following Winnicott, the remainder of this book looks to the teacher as inheriting these aspects of caregiving pedagogy, doing so with a steady gaze on the inclusive goals of capacity, trust, and meaning for all students. In the present chapter, I reframe inclusivity in terms of a trusted holding environment where students, free

Classrooms as holding environments **209**

from worry and premature judgement, can entertain the messy spaces of meaningful learning. In the next chapter, we take up the teacher as "initiator" who creates capacity by titrating learning provocations, providing new but accessible objects that challenge the illusion of prior knowns and that beg revised dialectic resolution in light of a disillusioning world. In Chapter 13, we locate these elements together in the teacher as witness.

Holding environments and their lesser substitutes

We touch inclusivity to the degree that we create environments where learners, in a spirit of feeling known and accepted, can freely bring capacity, trust, and meaning to the curriculum, to incrementally discern its essential aspects and resolve emergent dissonances (per the model). We have seen that knowledge – neither belonging to construing minds nor to any objectively accessible real – makes of learning an interpretive act of reciprocal enfolding: self into world and world into self. The possibilities of any moment, what matters and why, arise at the meeting place of prior relational stories, where histories converge and inter-sectionalities co-evolve.

A sense's gestation needs freedom from urgency if it is to find its way to awareness and formulation. In this, the stability of the learning environment matters critically. The structures and persons upon which we depend – our trusted familiars – are those to facilitate flex and the judicious apportionment of risk to capacity. In attachment theory – respectively corresponding to Winnicott's environment and object mothers – our trusted familiars become internalised for us as both the *safe haven* of intrapsychic re-centring and the *secure base* from which to venture worldly explorations.

A classroom, school, or district benefiting from an ethos of trust, with predictability enough for individual agency, affords a holding environment of the Winnicottean sort (1971/2005). In forestalling the world's urgencies, it creates time enough and space enough for members to freely press their boundaries in the conceptual work of learning. Lampert approaches this point when she writes,

> When classroom culture is taken into consideration, it becomes clear that teaching is not only about teaching what is conventionally called content. It is also teaching students what a lesson is and how to participate in it. . . . what counts as knowledge and what kind of activities constitute legitimate academic tasks. . . . how what anyone says is to be understood. . . . The teacher has more power over how acts and utterances get interpreted . . . but these interpretations are finally the result of negotiation with students.
>
> *(1990, pp. 34–35)*

In stark contrast, externally imposed, thinly veiled control manoeuvres – of surveillance, behaviour management, and motivational schemes (the carrots and sticks of accountability) – communicate mistrust and erode the agency of selves and collectives up and down systems. They are spirit-negating. In the overwhelm of

210 Into practice

unpredictability-from-without and too much at stake within, it would seem foolish to any learner to divert precious resources or expose vulnerabilities for the sake of undertaking difficult self-revisions in accordance to "power's" imposing agendas. Instead, cocooning oneself within an optics-of-capacity serves a learner better than capacity itself. Coping increasingly depends on vigilance in keeping any dubious self-qualities under wraps, even to the self. In the thick of dissociative enactments, denial deflects criticisms and fortifies defences. This is as true for educators as for their students.

Tricks to get by: fake it till you make it

Lampert describes student's evasive coping strategies when understanding seems illusive and effort at achieving it too risky (1990, pp. 56–57). She captures these strategies in student pronouncements, eerily reminiscent of President Trump, as follows: *My answer is right because that's what he said. This is the rule; I don't need to know why I know, I just know. That's just 'stupid. Ok, let's vote and you'll see I'm right. It's right because it's my way of doing it.* The respective tactics she names are all too common: the invocation of authority as argument, refusal to submit one's thinking to scrutiny, exercising physical or political offence as defence, and stubbornness and face-saving.

The sad state of affairs was, one day, made poignantly clear to me when, as my grade 7 students were filing out of class, I overheard a "veteran" say to a newcomer: "No, this class *really is* different: You have to think." It seems we inadvertently encourage the following strategic student dictums as substitutes for thinking.

> (1) After a given answer, a teacher's hesitation or a continued line of questioning typically signals the answer is wrong. Try again. (2) If you are asked, either to explain what something means or to describe what you notice, it means that you must sufficiently approximate the way your teacher, as authority, would respond on the subject. (3) A teacher explanation or demonstration need not be fully understood. To avoid embarrassment and lengthy, equally confusing, re-explanations, nod in agreement and await further cues. (4) A corollary of three: If what you hear sounds familiar and, by association, vaguely reasonable, then your understanding is sufficient. Wait for the examples. They will offer the details of what you are expected to do. (5) When asked to respond with the name for something or to perform a particular action, use the most recent name or action heard or seen. If your first choice meets hesitation, self-correct and offer the second. This is quicker and less confusing than trying to understand instructions or decipher meaning. (6) Rather than risk a "stupid" response, keep silent, however uncomfortable. This will minimize your embarrassment and heighten the teacher's, prompting him to either move on or offer more clues so that you can better guess at what is expected.
>
> *(D'Amour, 2010, p. 292)*

Service rationing: "getting by" – a meagre survival

Speaking of teachers, Gartner invokes service rationing.

> It is the process workers go through to bridge the everyday divide between the ideal of how they would work if they were free to function to the best of their ability and the reality of how they can work, given the numerous obstacles in their way. . . . It may diminish people's spirits and possibly the quality of their work but . . . without it many people simply couldn't stay in their jobs.
>
> *(Lipsky in Gartner, 2017, p. 202)*

Gartner describes the "systematic oppression" (2017, p. 194) of New York City's teachers during Mayor Bloomberg's autocratic micromanaging. Bloomberg's strategy was to "identify and close 'failing schools'" and implement "high stakes testing . . . [tied to] teachers'. . . performance ratings" (p. 195). We know that, when injuries are experienced as premeditated betrayal, they triggered the psychic distress of complex trauma (Courtois in Gartner, p. 194). Such betrayal was most palpable to those teachers "who believed that connecting emotionally with their students was fundamental" (p. 194). Gartner details the predicament of such teachers, those for whom service rationing was not an option:

> Greg eventually found a way to return to teaching part time. . . . keep[ing] his health insurance, if not his health or self-esteem. Unlike Greg, . . . Cathy described spending even more hours . . . documenting every teaching choice she made, assessing her students repeatedly, using standardized measure even though she could describe in elaborate detail each student's progress without this testing. She was physically and emotionally exhausted.
>
> *(2017, pp. 202–203)*

Most of my 25 years a school teacher, I have been some version of Greg and Cathy. The costs were as demanding as the work was fulfilling. Over the 15 years since, across two Canadian provinces and four universities, including deep and broad transdisciplinary forays into the literature and academic appointments in teacher preparation, professional development, and on-site school research, I can confidently say that the trauma of New York City teachers is hardly anomalous. It increasingly describes the situation of teachers in the United States, Canada, and abroad.

At the risk of oversimplifying, let me gather the complications of inclusion under three headings: the art of the impossible, the optics of solidarity in community, and a false promise of differentiation. The "art of the impossible," characterises classroom circumstances that pit genuine inclusivity against a teacher's balanced life. It presses either service rationing or burnout and hides behind the "optics of solidarity and community" best showcased in highly valued, publicised celebrations of collaborative achievement – as if to reassure potential onlookers that all is well.

212 Into practice

But true solidarity in community is not a defence mechanism. In learning, it derives from interpersonal connection on curricular topics that matter to learners. Else it risks devolving into benevolent collusion and hype. But such interpersonal connection on curricular topics can become a near-insurmountable challenge for learners who come at concepts with drastically different depths of understanding or when they bring vastly different assumptions about the direction to take or how to interact together (Christiansen, 1997). The result can be more like a game of baseball with players who either cannot catch, throw, or bat – or who can, but are either oblivious to the actual play of the game or don't care to play it at all. Compliance, getting along, and good intentions are hardly generative of learning collectives (see below).

The proffered solution is differentiation. But differentiation's promise of bolstering inclusion is contradictory. Insofar as it serves an ideal of commonality by claiming *everyone* different and *everyone* unique, it engages in colour blindness, refusing the uneven ground of difference even as it purports to serve difference. The teacher simply cannot be differently present to all students at the same time. Thus, to differentiate is to give over dialogic student-teacher exchanges (per Vygotsky, 1934/1986, in Chapter 7) to goal-oriented tasks, general enough to suit everyone, that leave the differentiating to learner choice and peer collaboration as per Piaget and Dewey (see Chapters 7 and 10). But leaving the bulk of learning to independent student interaction and choice – at a troubling distance from the teacher (Marton's teaching without pedagogy, 2014) – brings us back, full circle, to the status quo of privilege begetting privilege (see Chapter 10).

An era prone to seek and accentuate "all of us different" is a prescription for teacher burnout. I leave to the next chapter to consider an alternative: titrating fine-grained, dynamically responsive teaching to individual need in manner as to bring students together. For now, suffice it to add that teachers (like all learners) benefit from opportunities to grow their capacity, trust, and meaning for and in learning. Such growth arises of incrementing encounters with aptly expanding example spaces that, in bringing different sets of experiences into conversation, encourage revised and resolved conundrums in an expanding world of understanding. Teachers would benefit from such growth experiences, especially in a teacher curriculum focused on the close back-and-forth reading and negotiation of student understanding (the made) and the curricular landscape (the given). The task of differentiation, if we want to call it that, cannot *but* be one of negotiating dynamic micro-fitted resonances (reminiscent of parent – child attunement, Part II) with one's students in ways that bring the class discourse along together, without neglecting differences in depth and breadth of capacity and concern across the student body.

These challenges bespeak relational psychoanalytic sensibilities as matters of greatest import to education. In understanding otherwise than what we have, new vistas open. Imagining better, I cannot fathom that we would continue as we have, not only in schooling and teaching but also in the research we undertake, value, and, yes, monetise. How might we learn to better walk awhile together, knowing we can never fully grasp what it might mean to be in another's shoes?

Walk with me awhile

Dean Ryan closed his convocation speech to the newest Harvard teacher-graduates by quoting Raymond Carver's *Late Fragments* (1989) – that when all was said and done, to feel oneself beloved would comprise what anyone might want from life. Ryan adds, "I can't help but think that schools, and indeed, the world, would be better places if students didn't simply perform well but also felt beloved – beloved by their teachers and by their fellow classmates" (May 26, 2016). Ryan names a human desire, pervasive across a lifetime: to feel connected, to find oneself beloved. "Starting as small babies, [we] seek other human minds to interact with . . . because we are wired to respond visually to the human face, olfactorily to human smells, auditorily to the human voice, and semiotically to human signs" (Mitchell, 2002, p. 67).

Where we connect

Among the things to hold a people together, a shared history – and the folk psychologies (Bruner, 1990) threading a coherence across that history – may well be the most salient. Common and conflicting human values come alive in archetypal tales addressing and making sense of the toils, trials, and tribulations of antagonists and protagonists alike. In each of any stories' characters, constellations of personality traits gather and congeal to serve and trouble familiar stereotypes. Audiences, as co-participants, can and do mould their identities against pervasive and iconic representations – even as they use them to facilitate the identification and misidentification of others in their midst. Different audiences find themselves variably personified as understood, misunderstood, or glossed over (if not outright erased) across portrayals that run the gamut from multidimensional to flattened and from conspicuously present to inconspicuously disavowed. The young, bringing identities seeded in the contexts of early familial years, are especially likely to refine those identities against the cultural models on offer, even as they serve a shorthand for judging self and other. In myriad ways, iconic tales and their offshoots work universal themes on categories-of-being at the confluence of individual and collective struggles for agency, continuity, coherence . . . and meaning.

The tales that societies tell - supportive of the manifold understandings that citizens seek and need to make - seem to span a finite breadth of universal themes (e.g., about love, betrayal, hardship, loss, kinship, life passages, villains and heroes, the powerful and the vulnerable). They come to us as the time-immemorial subjects of theatre, the arts, and myth. Language – that makes possible thought and social connection across distance – re-members how we know these themes. Language, working and responding to the human social condition, begins from and returns the continual reshaping of categories of perception and conception. In language, universal themes come to span differently conceived yet strangely common species' heritage. And so, though finite – rising out of and defining a sameness – the depth and nuance of interpretation within and across these themes is naught but infinite. Put otherwise, a finite set of storied universal themes are worded translations reaching back to common experiences wrought of inter-visceral connection, before words and the mode of singular-plural-being to make all ensuing being possible. Yet infinite nuances of situated interpretation give rise to experiences and distributions of difference – differences that bend to a human tendency to gathered desirable traits as me and to extricate unwanted parts as adamantly not – finally, serving who gains admission as part of one's clan and who must be on the outside.

Theoretically and conceptually - in the service of our own psychic splitting – there is a convenience to aligning with certain differences of history, visited forward. Still, these – any – culture's narratives, also bespeak common human conundrums that return an originary humanness – however differently shaded from this or that social vantage. In other words, in thinking community and inclusion, I am insisting that human social and biological proclivities manifest commonalities that, if not overtly evident, run underneath constructed stereotypes spanning "me" and "not me." This is the case even though, over time, our shared sensibilities and sensitivities may well become buried under morasses of time-crusted, good enough for here-and-now, anachronistic coping strategies as one's familiar self-protective reflex.

I believe that relational psychoanalytic understanding is about reaching deeply and with grace, past such self-protective habits, to touch the unifying themes of our singular-plural-being and an inclusive plural, a "thirdness," that resists an engulfing oneness – the erasure of the singular, where, what I think, so must you – while reaching across the isolation of disparate twoness. The kinds of spaces I hope for are those where experiences in thirdness happen and, in repeated happening, become sustaining places of promise for the ongoing ebb and flow of connection and reconnection across difference.

Thirdness

Benjamin writes of the third as corresponding "to the locus on the axis of intersubjectivity where we recognize others as separate, equivalent centers of being/feeling rather than as objects, as Thou [for "Thou," see Buber, 1970 (1923)]. [It describes a] position of differentiating without polarizing, connecting without erasing difference" (Benjamin, 2018, pp. 77–78).

This idea of thirdness, pervasive across contemporary psychoanalysis, "designates both a relationship and its organizing principle" (Benjamin, 2018, p. 78). In thirdness are *moments* of finding ourselves anew in the other (and the other in ourselves), of freely construing reality in the play of fantasy (and fantasy in the play of reality), of seeing the given in the made (and the made in the given), and of daring to submit our favoured illusions to a creative but disillusioning world. If we can but taste such moments, I believe we will want to find our way back to them.

Benjamin (2018) distinguishes thirdness as a transitional place of both/and. It incorporates the rhythmic third of attunement – prototypically the amodal matching of affective contours in early unworded "conversations" – with the later-developing differentiating third of affective mirroring that now attunes in a different key, marked with an appreciative translation that says we are not the same (Chapter 6). Together the rhythmic and the differentiating third render what Benjamin describes as a kind of lawfulness, the moral third, of a rightful order of things. In such a world, trust and control exist not as either–or opposites, but rather as Möllering's duality (2006) – where one can trust that things are duly in control; and where, owing to things feel sufficiently in just and ethical control, one can more freely take leaps of faith.

A deep appreciation of universal, yet idiosyncratically lived, human needs, desires, and defences – to individuate, to belong, to move into and out of states of thirdness, and to occasionally succeed in holding the tension of the third, with another, in a shared transitional space – lies at the heart of relational psychoanalytic understanding and stands among its greatest gifts to education. Remembering Chapter 8 on dissociation, we can teach in a way that better renders meaning-making possible *and* that, at once, rethinks inclusion.

I close with a return to the idea of the classroom collective, this time as autopoietic form (per Chapter 8), asking what that view might pivotally contribute.

The classroom as autopoietic life form

Autopoietic theory suggests a different way of looking at inclusion and community, one that speaks connection in terms of collectivity and co-ordinated relationships. Turning here to a discourse in biology we also find the paradoxical singular-plural in a whole that, as a collective, entails but does not obliterate the difference of its parts. Describing the dynamics of such wholes, Juarrero writes, "Coordinated relationships make the system one kind of thing and not another. . . . No one molecule or event, however, serves as coordinator. The organization and coordination are distributed relationships that act as a virtual governor" (1999/2002, p. 125).

Insofar as a collection of learners, say a classroom, can act as a bounded interactive network where all participants contribute in some vital way to the ongoing viability and adaptive self-change of individuals and the whole, then that collection acts as a learning collective. While this is not to presuppose inclusivity or thirdness, I am suggesting that *the possibility of thirdness, inclusivity, and what (in education) complexivists call collectivity entails in a collection of students whose members, all, experience themselves as recognised and recognising participants.* The signatures of such collectives are thought to be: a common feeling of dynamic communal engagement in learning, a developing topic-specific shared vocabulary, and visible signs of students enthusiastically construing upon and with each other's ideas.

All the foregoing said, collectivity is not a sustainable state nor are member contributions equally weighted across time. Rather, not unlike thirdness, individuals and groups move in and out of autopoietic relations according to the ebb and flow of classroom life such that, in any given moment, member contributions and growth are unequally distributed across the parts/members of the system. Over the course of a teaching term, the class, its individuals, and subgroups will drift into and out of collectivity. Where the teacher can hold in mind a consciousness of the collective

216 Into practice

and its component parts, without splitting herself off from that collective or its parts, she becomes most treasured member. Where she sections herself away as external authority, imposing her will upon individuals and/or groups, she jeopardises collectivity and inclusivity and puts a constraining rider to eclipse moments of thirdness.

Coming at inclusivity through systems thinking, Davis and Simmt analysed high-functioning classrooms to arrive at five critical attributes of connectivity: redundancy, internal diversity, neighbouring interactions, organised randomness, and decentralised control (2003). I discuss each in turn.

Redundancy is that sameness across elements of a system to make communication possible. In counterbalancing measure *diversity* promises provocation from within. Whereas redundancy holds a dynamic system together, diversity presses it to learn from itself. For want of redundancy a system fractures; for want of diversity, it does not learn. The two work in conjunction with *neighbouring interactions* such that "agents . . . affect one another's activities" (p. 155). Neighbouring interactions allow students' ideas, hunches, queries, metaphors, words, and other manners of representation to bump up against each other in communicative acts of sense-making (p. 156).

As the classroom lays down its history a shared memory takes shape in a kind of *organised randomness* of tacitly endorsed rules of behaviour. These are enabling constraints that set the trusted and mistrusted aspects of classroom life. Uncoincidentally, per Möllering (2006), we see trust and control in paradoxical duality. The more things cohere into a tacitly agreed order, with appropriate room for flex, the more members can "trust" in that order to mitigate risk.

Finally, the idea of *decentralised control* describes the strangeness of no individual, nor subgroup, in charge. Rather the relational spaces of communicational exchange tug at the system, this way and that, as it morphs in learning. Though the landscape of curricular content may be externally set, the processes of exploring that landscape, including critical touchstones for participants, remain emergent properties of the whole. This is not, however, to undermine the teacher's more influential role and responsibility (per Chapter 10). The effective teacher stands in the group yet not. As consciousness of the collective she attends to those things that play out unconsciously in, and as, the system – relating in manner not unlike the attuned caregiver.

In another sense, again not unlike the parent, she is knowing co-participant and mediator entrusted with negotiations between, at once, the broader educating social system into which the classroom system is nested (her professional obligation) and the classroom at a nexus of intersectionalities with the social system's derivatives that constitute the near-worlds of her students and the classroom collective. In the way that Jessica Benjamin conceptualises co-recognition, such a teacher takes a position of dynamic tension between sameness and difference – enough connected with her students so to be familiar and knowable to them as one-of-us, yet enough different so to be uniquely present as a subject in her own right, exceeding the object-construction that the collective and any subgroups or individual minds might make of her.

Autopoiesis and inclusivity

At this point, it might be clarifying to apply systems' principles to critique carte blanche policies mandating physical co-presence of students of difference in everyday community schools.

In the early 1990s, when inclusion first impacted my school district, Gerald (not his real name), the son of a close friend, saw his life change. A pre-teen with Down's Syndrome, he had been happily learning key life skills, alongside classmates who had become close friends, from teachers and staff whose training and expertise almost exclusively focused on teaching children with moderate to severe cognitive impairments. One day Gerald's world changed. The school he so loved was permanently closed and because of, what seemed a moral and political mandate that he be "included" in a regular classroom, Gerald's place of belonging was dismantled. Indeed, the district saved money. But Gerald, in the new and bewildering environment of his now-regular classroom, never did regain his footing – no matter the good intentions of the teachers there.

We might directly attribute Gerald's distress to his displacement and not to the shift of classroom complexion and dynamics. However, that he never recovered suggests other influences at work. From a systems perspective, we could say that Gerald entered a collective with which he shared limited redundancy and with which there was negligible if any possibility for neighbouring interactions on common curricular topics.

More broadly speaking, when diverse students with a variety of "special needs" converge in a classroom of same age peers to learn a common core curriculum, there is a limit to what any teacher can do. These days, with more students of difference sharing the same environments, the breadth of diversity can stretch system redundancies too thin, compromising the quality of neighbouring interactions that might happen there. Meanwhile, if only to prevent chaos and anarchy, the teacher can enlist any number of strategies of coercion, manipulation, and behaviour management to at least create the facsimile of quietly co-operative worlds. Of course, this does little to address the needs of those students most precariously at the edges of collective possibility (some overwhelmed, others bored, too many left out).

Is there an alternative? Framed in the contexts of systems' principles, just what would it take for all students to have access to appropriate sense-making opportunities in inclusive environments? How might teachers adapt that which they do to make this possible? How does the model fit as much for someone like Gerald (easygoing and mostly unaware of what he does not know), as for gifted students (facile at making quick and nuanced sense, yet who can be anything but easy-going in instances of not-knowing), and the entire gamut of students between or across the various continuums by which we classify and sort them? A closer look at discernment in learning (Chapter 12) and witnessing in teaching (Chapter 13) might help bring us to alternatives.

12

THE PROVISION OF CURRICULAR OBJECTS

Teaching for discernments that matter

Redox: knowledge given and made

We have seen how traditionalism conceives of knowledge as something transmittable, making good teaching about good explaining. In contrast, progressivism has it that knowledge is personally and socially made. It uses the argument of constructivism to disparage the direct "giving" of information, especially if students might arrive at conclusions on their own. Given an economic climate pressing for practical innovation, both traditionalists and progressivists come together on the value of pedagogical strategies grounded in the STEM disciplines of science, technology, engineering, and math, as, for example, in the use of collaborative makerspaces, iterative design, and inquiry activities – traditionalists favouring teamwork for refining and applying things already learned; progressivists emphasising peer collaboration for making sense in the first place.

Trending popular in education is progressivism's conceiving of the learning task as superseding the teacher who shifts from "sage on the stage . . . [to] guide at the side" (Smith, 2017, June 16). For some (e.g., Sawyer, 2006; Laucius, 2019, March 22), the ideal learning task erases the teacher altogether. As "an interface between the learners and the information offered in the learning environment" (Richter, 2012), insofar as it provides "feedback" on performance and "guidance on how to acquire the relevant information" (Richter, 2012) then, in a limited view of the role of the teacher, the learning task serves as teacher. With the availability of advanced digital technologies, the dream is that computer programs will be able to individualise learning prompts on the fly, solving at once the challenges of inclusion, differentiated instruction, and student-centred learning. If artfully designed with relevant, engaging, rich problems, then, so the argument goes, learning task will motivate students to pursue creative self- and peer-directed learning.

Meanwhile, in the reality of everyday classrooms, after many an exciting exploration, progressive-leaning teachers face dilemmas about telling students what they failed to grasp, but need to know, especially "for the test." Whereas traditionalists will have few qualms about teaching directly to standardised assessment outcomes, progressivists can struggle to resolve the traditional "what" of curriculum content with its more progressive "how." Whereas the traditional position unabashedly deals in *givens*; the progressive position admonishes teachers to bring students to those same givens but as student-*made* in and through their own initiative.

These differences and dilemmas live in an era of knowledge-economies whose prized citizens are entrepreneurial innovators. Quite simply, the STEM disciplines outflank the liberal arts in focusing a nation's capital and supporting its fiscal viability, leastwise in the short term. Governments want team players at the ready to contribute to the production of saleable knowledge. In particular, if information and knowledge are power, insofar as the STEM and technosciences promise to generate the information and knowledge needed to keep apace of the accelerating march of societal change, then in the eyes of governments, the longer view of the humanities, dedicated to nuanced understanding of the individual and collective human condition, past into present, will continue to pale in immediate value.

Yet grander forces at play, not the least of which is the wisdom of an electorate, return us to the humanities. My point is not that we forsake ourselves to losing the twenty-first-century knowledge race, but rather that in raising our children we not confuse information with knowledge and cult-like hype with actual practices that matter. *The education wars are embattled over the wrong question.* The point of Winnicott's transitional objects, taken up through relational psychoanalytic thought, is the educational implications of knowledge as, at once, both given *and* made (Donnel Stern, 2003; Winnicott, 1971/2005). In dialectic movement, the knowledge that one made before, in turn, shapes the knowledge that one can know to look for and take into the next given conundrum and the making of new sense. Importantly, *the erasure of the teacher will not do.* Meanings that matter most return us to thirdness (Benjamin, 2018), that provocative intersubjective space of both the intrapsychic world of singular individual knowing and the interpersonal world of plural social knowledge. For thirdness, the teacher is irreplaceable.

In teaching, there will be those (e.g., students, parents, administrators, and stakeholders) who see knowledge as the thing that must be told to learners and who believe that the art of good teaching is to explain well. There will be others who see learners as the arbiters of sense according to their own desires, with the right to their own perspectives, absent the impress to consider otherwise. And there will be those who understand learning as a relational negotiation of functional enough coherence for-and-of self *and* world. One would hope that school people, teachers and administrators alike, and the scholars supporting them tend to the third group.

220 Into practice

Encountering and enfolding the unknown: tracing a sense-making iteration

Wait, what?

Learning as recursive self-change, progresses according to iterative excursions from one's made-known, beginning with a centrifugal reach to the unfamiliar. In this initiating centrifugal movement, the role of the pedagogue and the progression of the learning activities she instantiates is to bring the unanticipated into view. Keeping in mind the "curse of knowledge bias" – where what one knows obscures the coming-into-view of the thing one does not know (Fonagy & Target, 2007) – the learner does not necessarily know to go looking for the novelty. As Roth puts it, "the visible emerges from the previously invisible, and, therefore, the knowable from the unknown" (2011, p. 260).

Still, the unknown must exist within and as against the realm of things discernible to the learner. Marton reminds us that "we cannot understand what 'dry wine' is by drinking dry wine only, we cannot understand what linear equations are by seeing linear equations only and we cannot experience 'flow' if it is flow that we experience all the time" (2014, p. 44).

> [For this reason,] when I point to an object and say "That is a tree," . . . my designation is meaningless unless we also know that this "tree-thing" is not grass, corn, bushes, shrubs, hammers, houses, clouds, and so on. "Green" does not derive its meaning by identification with a particular wavelength of light, but by its difference from turquoise, chartreuse, blue, yellow, and red.
>
> *(Stern, Donnel, 2003, p. 7)*

A new known may be stumbled upon or occasioned by a vexing situation in the world out there or the world in mind. In the pedagogical moment, another's literal or metaphorical pointing prompts noticing (see Chapter 6, especially Csibra & Gergely, 2011). Within the limits of a teacher's own curse of knowledge bias[1] – that is, the tendency to assume that others have the background to understand – she attends to student attentions and mitigates situations that point – offering to students appropriate next provocations and introducing layer upon layer of accessible newness into ever-revised and elaborating versions of the known.

Each newness installs a dissonant ambiguity that wants for the clarity of resolution. Student differences in the encounter can be pronounced. For some, a resolution may happen so swiftly as to seem immediately obvious; for others, ambiguity engenders bewilderment and the frustration of: "I knew this until you made it confusing." Refusal to consider anew or otherwise – in the vernacular, closed-mindedness – forecloses one's ability to look for, and thus find, the unanticipated. It compromises capacity to protect against movement into anticipated discomfort.

To be clear, in speaking of ambiguity and dissonance, I am meaning conflicting representations that leave a person struggling to think things together and wondering: "Do you mean this or that? How can it be both?" The duck–rabbit illusion is ambiguous, as is the paradoxical artistry of Escher. If a child understands "rose" to mean "flower," then she will be confused when daddy calls "roses" tulips. Ambiguity is at the heart of puzzlements and/or fascinations such as: "How can a tiger and my pet both be cats?" "Why doesn't that heavy ball fall faster than the light one?" "How can this person be mean one day and nice another." "When poietic phrasing is literal and figurative, I don't know which meaning to take?" "How can two intelligent people arrive at entirely opposite conclusions about climate change?"

Realising an "a-ha"

The encounter with ambiguity presents a conundrum. It invites looking at the new strangeness from various angles, maybe being annoyed or intrigued by it, comparing aspects, noticing sameness, contrasting difference, or simply toggling between views, practicing seeing them together until a comfortable enough fluency arrives. In these considerations, a teacher can help. The centripetal return involves active play at fitting newness with-and-in an elaborating scheme of things understood. One can see it first-hand in a toddler at play who, part-way through a block construction, encountering a confounding piece, pauses as if to consider: *Wait, what? This doesn't fit.* Then, in the next moment, her face lights up with: *I have a better idea,* and a flurry of directed activity ensues as she approximates in physical form the resolution she had in mind. The sequence repeats from each intrigued, *Wait, what?* to a realisation in mind and its industrious articulation into emergent form. She occasionally steps back to see what has happened and then steps in again.

Inspired by provocative ambiguities, resolutions take their nascence outside the reaches of conscious impulsion. Like a word on the tip of one's tongue, the "a-ha" bubbles into being only when the mind is free from conscious constraint. Its rises from within, as if unbidden, sometimes in a split second, like "getting" a joke, and sometimes after untold oblique contemplations and many sleeps.

To resolve especially difficult ambiguities, learners will want unforced time to muck about, perhaps profiting from what others have to say, and generally holding an open faith in understanding's emergence. The preoccupied surveillance of anxious others is counterproductive, especially when those others take up residence within the self. Even when they do not speak, the silent watcher can be so loud as to drown out the possibility of one's own voice. It seems no coincidence to find sociologist Reginald Bibby charting a rising preoccupation among Canadian teens over the last 40 years and naming the "paramount personal concerns [of millennials] . . . the pressure to do well at school" (Bibby, 2010, p. 42).

The teacher can help by holding contemplative spaces open, highlighting elements a learner might overlook, and presenting ambiguities whose resolutions are interesting and within conceptual reach. In such presentations, the teacher offers two related ideas and, like puzzle pieces that fit in particular ways, invites the students to consider "What do you/we already know about these? and "How might

222 Into practice

they relate to each other?" The overlaying of analogous relations familiar to the learner can further facilitate graded resolutions of micro-ambiguities – often so well that each next new thing hardly seems new at all, it simply follows from and extends what was known before.

The event of a newly formed coherence arrives with its own neurochemically instantiated, feel-good reward. It literally shows on our faces that we enjoy making sense. But the joy of realising a resolution does not complete a sense-making iteration. What follows realisation is its articulation into and with a world of knowns.

Articulating one's new known

In the same way that recounting a dream marks it for retention, so too does the sublime of an "a-ha" need to be marked into and with the conventions and symbols of a network of communicable understandings. Without such articulation, the realised slips back into a hazy sense one thought one knew. Here is the logic behind the adage "By teaching, we learn." It also underpins the value of students explaining, conversing about, and/or journaling their understandings.

Some students balk at the seeming tedium of articulation. Worse yet, the attempt can call into question the very sense they thought they had. Others will protest that they understand but cannot explain. *To articulate requires there to be an internal coherence that fits an external world. To articulate is to make connections tangible.* But if learning has been piecemeal, one might be able to answer a multiple-choice question on a matter without there being coherence enough for containing and indexing this new bit. The inability to render one's new understanding in relation to prior understandings suggests confusion running much deeper. Such students will need help, not to "get by" this task, but rather to revise what it means to make sense and to attend to dropped threads yet to be integrated into a tapestry of interdependent meanings.

And then again, in one's diverse classroom, there will be students who, riding on the inspiring high of realisation will balk at any meddling from others. They will want first dibs on seeing this creative process through. Caught in the flow, they will not want to leave their thinking until a satisfactory formulation comes into detailed view. These students will struggle with a world that increasingly values abbreviated sound bites. They too will need the teacher, in this case to perhaps guard over their solitude.

In all cases, no other person but the experiencing self can suffice as active formulator. Teachers will want to resist the temptation to compose a formal articulation for the student to mime. It is the actual process of formulation that takes the "a-ha" experience and effectuates its distancing remove into recognisable symbolic representation, conscious thought, and the possibility for metacognitive reflection on it. It is formulation that closes the loop of the centripetal return from dissonance's provocation to a newly perceived and accounted-for world, enfolded into a consciously revised knowing self.

Teaching as pointing attention

To learn about anything takes noticing it, whether "it" is inside the self or without. And noticing it means having the capacity to find oneself impinged in manner to physiologically register the impingement. No organism can learn from that which it does not have the means or inclination to seek. For we humans, most of what impinges upon us, and that we discern, happens without our thinking about it – that is, without conscious attention and conscious learning. But when an impingement tugs at conscious awareness and we find reasons to disregard its pull, this is dissociation.

> Most not-knowing that occurs under circumstances in which knowing is at least possible is best described as dissociation, and that dissociation should be defined as the unconscious decision not to interpret experience, to leave it in its unformulated state for defensive reasons.
>
> *(Donnel Stern, 2003, pp. 30–31)*

Discernment and recognition in learning

A consideration of unicellular organisms may give a useful sense of the relationships between discernment, impingement, and recognition in learning. Recall the amoeba. It has no means to discern light – to be impinged by it. Nor should it. Inconsequential to the amoeba's direct survival, light does not exist to it. But for the euglena, a photosynthetic swimmer, light does exist. Its impingement sets off a sequence of internal reactions such that, among other things, the euglena swims toward the light. The euglena uses light-discernment to "know" where to swim. It "learns" of the light, because its eyespot *already* knows to look for it and to recognise it when found. Recognition entails the adjoining of impingement and its anticipation such that, on its own terms, the euglena "knows" how to "take" the impingement. But of course, the euglena neither entertains this in any conscious way nor does it generate a memory to guide future decisions. It does not have a physiology for thinking, remembering, and planning.

In the sense of the euglena, learning requires (and presupposes) discernment as the capacity to register an impingement – to see something. And "seeing something . . . amounts to seeing how it differs from other things. . . . The meaning of colors, of words, of anything, originates from differences. Without differences there can be no meaning at all" (Marton, 2014, p. 48).

Moreover, for any learning to accrue (whether to good or ill-effect), a physical revision of the self, by that self, must ensue from the impingement. This is the point of constructivism. To discern, we need to know enough to look for and see difference in terms of our familiar and to interpret it through the lens of what we know. Moreover, for such discernment to be retained as learning, impingements will need to instantiate embodied changes such that we interpret and respond differently the

224 Into practice

next time. In this way, recursion ensues from embodiment and sets life systems on trajectories of progressive redeterminations of self in relation to dynamic co-evolving worlds. The process is most striking in the early years of child development. It explains how consciousness develops from diffuse lantern-like attentions to more categorical spotlight discernments and how the newborn's keen sensitivity to affective signatures makes possible the early discernment of self from others and world (Chapters 5 and 6).

We use what we know to know differently. The familiar is the portal to encountering and making-sense of the unfamiliar. When we discern something, we note its presence through our familiar. When we recognise something, we perceive it as an instance of that familiar. We grow what we know by discerning the similarities and differences of unfamiliar things in relation to familiar ones and using this information to either enfold the new into our existing conceptual schema, including categories and their relations (Piaget's assimilation), or to rejig those categories and their relations into revised coherences (Piaget's accommodation, see Chapter 7).

All of us grow an understood-world based on variances and invariances that matter and congeal into working conceptual frameworks (i.e., schema or categories) about that world. These in turn render things predictable enough for purposeful action. When things are predictable we can offload discernment – response interactions to nonconscious and unconscious routines. Just as my fingers tap the keyboard as if they "know" my thoughts, our bodies learn to do our bidding without our mind's having to think about it.

Sesame Street's "One of these things is not like the other one" (Raposo & Hart, 1969) – sung with an accompanying representation of, say, four sitting black cats of varying sizes of which three are ceramic and the fourth is a real live cat – captures the essence of discernment. The discernment of the live cat seems to jump out as unexpected recognition. Without any systematic conscious intention, we take in the shared attributes (e.g., all cats, all sitting, all black), disregard the features that make each cat unique (e.g., variations in size and proportion), and stumble into the surprise of one cat, a real live animal. Of course, we will be applying forward our capacity to discern "catness" and "aliveness" as already familiar knowns through which to perceive.

It is associative reasoning that allows us to map meanings from familiar sets of relations to unfamiliar ones. And they are words, serving as symbolic proxies for knowns, that capture meanings to render experiences articulable and relatable. The relations between words – as expressed in simile, metaphor, analogy, allegory, and metonymy (including their corollaries across various other symbol systems, e.g., in mathematics: equivalence relations, substitutions, proportionality, and the calculus of relations of relations) – are those to elaborate meanings into ever co-implicating webs of association. When we say, for example, "They gave her a warm welcome; he was a big part of my life; and I feel very close to my children," we use metaphor to reason analogically from early attachment experiences of warmth, bigness, and closeness to abstract concepts of affection, importance, and emotional intimacy (Lakoff & Johnson, 1999). Words not only shape our disposition to perceive but also carry the residual affective meanings of stories long forgotten and imbue newly perceived instances of a conceptual category with sentiments predating them.

Out of the capacities for the neurological memory of impingement that can be held in mind, comparing and contrasting sameness and difference is made possible, and categories rise to awareness. Out of symbolic representation comes the capacity to hold in mind (the neurological remembering of impingement) and toggle between salient aspects of more than one perceptual–conceptual encounter so as to compare, contrast, and pick out similarities and differences that matter. This is discernment. It allows the seeing of wholes and parts together, experiencing at once the separateness of examples and the common qualities that unite. Discernment follows from the co-tracking of relations that move in parallel or in opposite directions in time and space on one or more graduated aspects. It is fundamental to grasping forwards and backwards, doing and undoing, true and false, the thing and its obverse. We use it to juxtapose past and present, to zoom in and out of tiered conceptual hierarchies of thought, and especially – when, seeing boundaries and transcending them – to assemble, disassemble, and reassemble understanding, and so we reconfigure conception to change perception which feeds back onto conception, and so forth. Not all discernments are created equal. Some require more intellectual aplomb than others. There can be simply too much to hold in mind. Here is where the oral and written conventions allow for the offloading of memory – that we might "see" more at once and, in the doing, make appropriate discernments over broader domains of experience.

Moreover, not any discernment will do. For there to be sufficient verisimilitude in communication, we will need to discern whatever others mean by their pointing. Insofar as one learns the sense that people are making when they speak of categories like "chair," "marriage" and "artwork," for instance, then we can begin to converse with them about these matters. This entails having similar enough answers to such questions as: What features distinguish all chairs (marriages or works of art) from those things almost in the category, or nowhere related? What is prototypical and/or ideal? How far can the concept stretch – for example, are beanbag "chairs," stadium seats, loungers, and stools all chairs? Into what broader classes might each category also fit? In short, discernment is the fundamental sense-making capacity by which we unite (synthesise), tease apart (analyse), and interlock the conceptual categories of language and thought. Through discernment we generate networks of analogous meanings – critically, whose essences and vitalities derive from relational lessons of self, other, and world learned early.

226 Into practice

Attention to questions on the "how" of discernment (but not on the "why" of meaning behind our choices) has been the focus of phenomenography, the study of the "plane of multiple social realities" (Paulston & Liebman, 1994, p. 233). For the phenomenographer, "the 'truth' about a horse . . . is the sum of the observations of the horse-book writer, the jockey, the gambler, the farmer, the teenagegirl [*sic*], the veterinary [and so forth]" (Uljens, 1996, pp. 7–8). In phenomenographic terms, these ways of experiencing horses together define the outcome space of the concept of "horseness." Of particular value to education is the phenomenographic work attendant to the ways that thoughtfully adjudicated examples can serve to progressively help students consolidate concepts while elaborating their meaning possibilities. Of sense-making, it is worth reiterating Vygotsky when he writes,

> Thought structure A exists along with thought structure B; both are the result of experience in the material world, but there is no connection between the two. A point in structure A, for whatever reason, causes a problem in the unrelated structure B. This problem from A cannot enter B because there is no connecting system; they are divorced in the mind of the individual. The individual deals with this tension by creating a new superstructure C, which subordinates the other two structures.
>
> *(in Glassman, 1994, p. 197)*

In relation to the model, sets of examples correspond to presentations of ambiguous or dissonant elements within an example space (Vygotsky's seemingly unrelated A and B structures) whose distinguishing qualities want for resolution into overarching discernment on a new emergent category of experience (Vygotsky's superstructure C). Each recursive loop around the model systematically introduces variations to point students' attention to, and hone discernment on what changes, what stays the same, and what counts.

Importantly, this line of research (while influencing my writing here) does not, thus far, take into account the tacit unconscious and nonconscious meanings that come with these examples, including the situations and processes of such encounters that recall earlier life experiences – either drawing learners into or repelling them from engagement. In other words, such research deals in cognitive movement as its own motivation and overlooks the co-embodiment of unconscious and nonconscious mind–body being in any learning encounter. This last point is critical since all that matters to us, including beliefs and values fundamental to our identities, are embedded right along with our seemingly neutral or even mundane categories for organising ourselves, the world, and our thoughts about either. And all that matters to us is also intricately tied up in these networks of interconnected, tiered, and nested conceptual meanings. The result is that once our mind is made up about anything, we are hardly as free as we might like to think to disentangle ourselves from our embodied histories and change our minds – which is to say, change ourselves.

Learning, always a relational process – a little bit me, a little bit you

Any teacher will tell you that the litheness by which students make, unmake, and remake meaningful connections, including the focus they bring to these processes, varies enormously in any classroom and stands among the greatest challenges to inclusive practice. This makes sense if we consider that "all present growth hinges on past growth. Growth is not a simple function neatly determined by X units of inheritance plus Y units of environment, but is an historical complex which reflects at every stage the past which it incorporates" (Vygotsky, 1934/1986, p. 125). Moreover, because "becoming a person entails self-organisation; no matter how rich and multiplicitous it is, no matter how "true" or authentic, self-structure forecloses and truncates many dimensions of experience . . . [B]oth pathological *and* healthy self-development generate loss" (Mitchell, 2002, p. 85). The very uniqueness of individual life, the historical complex of its generation, including necessary losses in self-organisation, ensure a spectrum of proclivities, in any classroom, for discerning, attending to, and resolving emergent dissonances in ways that might sufficiently accord with mandated curricular conventions.

What people think of as raw intelligence may well entail in the fluency with which one can wield discernments and conceptual connections to hold and/or toggle between multiple views in mind, enough to find coherence. How facile can anyone be at ferreting out what matches and what doesn't, such that categories fluidly converge and diverge, together and apart as needed and at once? How confident can any learner be in their own capacity to recover themselves anew after abandoning, or temporarily holding at bay prior understanding in favour of trying on for size other "as if" scenarios and perspectives? In other words, to what degree can any learner suffer disassembling the very knowing upon which they once depended to make room for other modes of knowing? These questions highlight marked student differences in a typical classroom of diverse learners. They are differences that were of great interest to Vygotsky (1934/1986). Yet they are differences whose address educational research is only beginning to investigate. This will need to change.

Notwithstanding differences of mental acuity and attention, the capacity, trust, and meaning that any learner brings to the educative encounter is necessarily advantaged insofar as that learner's familial environment matches a schooling one conducted in adherence to dominant conventions that privilege themselves against other viable but non-dominant knowledge traditions for navigating oneself well in a conceived–perceived world. Personal predispositions and capacities entangle with and can become indistinguishable from forces at the intersection of family, community, and culture that variously compromise and/or privilege potentialities suited to the expectant hegemonic world of most nation's schools. Together, these entanglements come to distinguish capacities for discernment in learners along a wide continuum in any purportedly inclusive classroom.

Among younger learners, who necessarily have limited facility in the various disciplinary conventions for category-making and communication, the process of

228 Into practice

making personal meaning needs the facilitation of some socially informed actor who can mediate the learner's construction in sufficient accordance to societal expectation – even if, and especially for the purposes of ultimately stretching, deconstructing, and/or altering culturally enforced performatives. The need for such facilitation – to actually be told some things, if one is ever to learn of them – does not disappear with age and independence in learning. As students become better versed in disciplinary scripts, they will wean themselves from reliance on designated teachers and mentors in favour of learning in the contexts of broader social forums where manifold potential interlocutors vie for attention – these days, artfully so. That said, for the duration of anyone's schooling years, the measure of learning and the issuance of certification (as needed for entry into the job market) will continue to be adjudicated, on society's (largely hegemonic) terms, by appointed others.

I say hegemonic because, on these matters, when it comes to choosing from among the cultural stock of available knowledge of age-appropriate objects of learning for schools, that choice falls to governments – most often on the advice of selected educational researchers and, in democracies, inevitably in answer to the majority electorate, especially, key educational stakeholders. It is unlikely for this to change. Thus-informed, governments standardise and legislate the grade-level knowledge, skills, and attitudes that students should develop over the course of their curricular progression. All of this makes, of these curricular documents, politically accepted definitions of the scope and sequence of transitional objects of learning, *given* by a tangible "real" world, yet to be *made* as such in the imaginative worlds of the learners' conceiving.

Progressions in knowing

Vygotsky's descriptions of thought structures (recounted above) capture the essence of the dialectic model of learning that I have been forwarding; that is, where the encounter of a dissonant ambiguity between two thought structures finds its resolution in the realisation and articulation of a newly conceived superstructure. But what is it that makes for a thought structure in the first place and how does a thinking kind of knowing differ from, but relate to, the unthought unformulated knowing of unconscious and nonconscious being? The answer lies in our neurologically evolved mental capacities for symbolic representation.

Symbolic representation, distance, and perspective

Donnel Stern writes, "We know only one means by which we can create critical distance: symbolic representation. It is only our capacity for symbolization that makes possible interpretation and the adoption of perspective. It is only symbolization that makes possible knowable experience" (2003, p. 7). If it is only symbolisation that makes possible knowable experience, then how do we make sense of: a newborn *knowing* to turn toward the scent of mother's milk; my dog *knowing* our routines; my tongue *knowing* an abrasive surface on my back molar; the unicellular euglena *knowing* light? Moreover, does my dog not partake in a symbol system with me? If I put on my boots and say, "I have to go. But I'll be back," her demeanour anticipates my parting. But if I put on my boots and say, "Let's go for a walk," she is clearly beside herself with joy. Does my dog think? Is she conscious of her knowing?

In all these scenarios, we might recognise knowing in an embodied almost-primordial sense, but there being no symbolic representation, there can be no critical distance and therefore none of the kind of knowing to make possible interpretation and perspective – much less interpretation and perspective about interpretation and perspective. Discernments do not make their way into thought except when they are discernments narrated through and according to the organising forms of symbol systems.

Like me, my dog can anticipate, feel anxious, and remember. She cannot entertain what-if scenarios or share these with anyone. She cannot participate in a social network beyond her immediate experience. Her life is not organised according to language's shaping of perception and conception. This is not to deny that her embodied mind holds memories. It does and extraordinarily well. It is not to deny that, in the immediacy of a moment, she can and does make a kind of sense, thereafter remembering the sense that was made. If I give her something new to taste, she is alert to that difference and reacts with a "Wait . . . what?" attitude. She sniffs, testing trusted variables to make her discernments and then to act. *But she does all these things without "thinking" about them, which is to say, without taking conceptual distance from the events. She cannot play with ideas.* We can. But when we do, though we may gain critical distance, we also risk losing the embodied meanings (unconscious and nonconscious) that fuelled our symbolising in the first place – that is, we are prone to misconstrue our abstracted thoughts as bodiless objective facts.

Three modes of discernment for unconscious, nonconscious, and conscious being and knowing

"Our bodies and our cultural creations thoroughly interpenetrate each other – they bring each other to life and also constrain each other" (Mitchell, 2002, p. 68). We could usefully conceive of human development and the interpenetration of bodies and cultural creations in terms of the braiding of three modes of discernment, each strand being construed upon and taking form with the next and ultimately giving rise to, in order, unconscious, nonconscious, and conscious being and knowing.

We have seen how newborns arrive with inborn affective sensitivities, making possible the development of the *unconscious* knowing of limbic and subcortical affective systems that render, in physiological terms, neurochemical value to experience. We all begin life immersed in experiences-of-discernment according to bodies predisposed to feel and register the salience of dynamic aliveness as degrees of pleasure and displeasure, especially with respect to our interactions with/in our own bodies, the people of our world, and its physical elements.

Nonconscious procedural routines are the body – world nonverbal conversations by which we literally co-ordinate perception and action – doing so without thinking

230 Into practice

even as such co-ordination lays down the foundation for conceptual thought. That which once came into view as perceivable (in the world), becomes conceivable (in mind), and thereafter, being sought and found in both places, reinforces itself. For example, when a child shakes a rattle in hand, the rattle's contours are felt even as they contrast against a panorama of things that do not move. The effect is more than improved hand–eye co-ordination; it is perception-making as the child encounters the relative movement of foreground and background and learns to see the rattle as of-a-piece, separate and distinguishable from other parts of the visual scene. Such experiences of sensory engagement with a physical world and the progressive refinement of movement acts, in and on that world, develop from infancy forward. They effect a physical agency (meaningful according to unconsciously mediated reward-systems) even as we come to discern the properties of the world and of ourselves *vis-à-vis* that world. Nonconscious discernment thus underpins the kind of tacit understanding that Piaget charted in the development of young children and that Vygotsky called spontaneous knowledge (see Chapter 7).

Finally, while from birth – at the nexus of the interpersonal and the biophysical – affective salience impregnates unconscious and nonconscious experiences with relational meanings, those meanings will ultimately imbue word usage with salience to fuel and inspire *conscious* thought, the domain of executive neocortical function. The articulation of an unformulated realisation into formulated experience moves what was implicitly felt into the realm of explicit sharable knowledge. But very little of what we know is organised into communicable, thinkable form. Instead, the conscious strand entwines itself with and eventually imposes itself (and the broader worlds that languages carry) upon unconscious and nonconscious knowing, even as the abstracted understandings of consciousness, for reasons of biological functioning, must remain largely oblivious to their rootedness in prior and ongoing unconscious and nonconscious workings. Consciousness would suffer if cluttered with preoccupations about quicker-to-react unconscious and nonconscious doings. Instead it must take these doings for granted. We simply cannot attend to, regulate, and even be aware of all that we unconsciously and nonconsciously do, nor of the ways that these modes of discerning contribute to even our most precious, certain, and seemingly objective understandings.

The symbolic power of language and its implicit underside

We have seen how language, birthed to us in caregiving relationships, comes to capture meanings and organise them in relational thought as symbols synergising with symbols. We do and do not begin in language. We arrive, as if thrown (to borrow a Heideggerian term), into a languaged and languaging world, but language does not undo originary prediscursive selfhood and the viscerally felt affective sensibilities rooted there. Language points attention. "Even creative people cannot anticipate what they want to do until they have a language for doing it" (Roth, 2011, p. 260). In pointing, language configures and picks out the discernible, conferring it with viability and meaning, even as it creates its infinite shadow: that which goes

The provision of curricular objects **231**

undiscerned. Our first caregivers, as pedagogues, come to live in the words we know and the knowing of early years that those words carry forward. Words contain, and subsequently serve as, the pointing pedagogues in whose continued encounter, formulation, and reformulation, we forge, wield, and reshape meaning and, in meaning, the "reality" of our thoughts, imaginations, and experiences.

Organised into and by abstracted linguistic forms, it is consciousness that gifts us with the reach of the self into imaginative and socially configured realms, tugging at and stretching us – even as, in excess, such forms can work to deny intuiting unconscious wisdom or pull to untenable abstraction nonconscious knowing. But *where there are conflicting renditions on reality, the verbal documentable form holds greater legitimacy, casting an offensive shadow that works to supress – sometimes intimidating, sometimes threatening – felt experience* (see Chapter 6 and Daniel Stern, 1985/2000, p. 181). The result can be a self increasingly divided according to that which is permissible and impermissible, understood and baffling. Carrying the power and legitimacy of normative convention – itself arising out of vexed and vexing socio-cultural and political histories – language takes precedence over unconscious and nonconscious being. In particular, the linguistic conventions of the disciplines and their corresponding school curricula hold history's dominant authorities within them. They induct learners into what Vygotsky called nonspontaneous knowledge.

Schooling most overtly deals in the currency of the symbolic as tangible given. But curricular objects are transitional cultural forms whose engagement brings forth a hidden curriculum that is as surely unconscious and nonconscious as it is sociopolitical. The privileging of formal modes of thought promotes a falsely disembodied objectivity that *disregards intuitive unformulated sense, discounts embodied knowing, subdues unruly emotion, and ignores imaginative fantasies.* A disconnect between first order bodily knowing (unconscious and nonconscious) and conscious rationality, especially when exaggerated and enforced, can compromise a felt sense of grounded integrity (as ease of self-cohesion), depth in learning, and the trust needed to face new ambiguities. Even something as seemingly benign as the sliding, rotating, and flipping of geometric figures will depend on prior explorations in physically rolling and rotating oneself, and rolling and rotating external objects (Thom et al., 2015), including all the pleasures and displeasures that may have accompanied those experiences. When students seem to struggle, the teacher will do well to find her way back to the points of disconnection to linger there awhile.

Summarising thus far, we can say that the path to formal thought begins with early affective discernments and the salience of experiences that together shape what matters most. Affect gives and takes further meaning in active explorations of one's own capacity in one's world. Accordingly, the unconscious comes to house the re-memorable remnants of unformulated experiences that gave meaning to our physically experienced world, including the nonconscious habits we developed for fluidly moving and being in and with that world. Together entwined, the unconscious–nonconscious self serves as rich repository of possibility and limitation on that which can be conceived into conscious knowing. Approached from the other side, language comes from a world that likewise enables as it constrains.

232 Into practice

Whereas conscious thought depends upon socio-linguistic structures, unconscious–nonconscious knowing is the ferment of unstructured, free-floating, connected and disconnected, embodied habits of acting in and interpreting one's near-world. While the unconscious can gift creativity or threaten chaos and the nonconscious can reassure with familiar habit or foreclose on possibility with those same habits, it is what makes its way to conscious awareness that has the freeing potential for bridging intrapsychic and intersubjective well-being in a more-than-human world.

Categories

On categories, Lakoff and Johnson write,

> Living systems must categorize. Since we are neural beings, our categories are formed through our embodiment. . . . [T]he categories we form are *part of our experience!* They are the structures that differentiate aspects of our experience into discernible kinds. Categorization is. . . . part of what our bodies and brains are constantly engaged in. We cannot . . . "get beyond" our categories. . . . Neural beings cannot do that.
>
> *(1999, p. 19)*

Concepts and language: categorically in or out?

We learn the words and the conventions of language mostly to capture the things we have already come to tacitly know, according to visceral agreements on rules of discernment that graduate into categories of experience. "There is a word available nearly always when the concept has matured" (Tolstoy, 1903, in Vygotsky, 1934/1986, p. 8). Per Vygotsky, "Thought is not merely expressed in words; it comes into existence through them" (1934/1986, p. 218). We get from neural beings to socially connected ones on the wings of words, precisely because words mark conceptual categories. That is, rather than referring to a single object, a word refers "to a group or to a class of objects. Each word is therefore already a generalization" (Vygotsky, 1934/1986, p. 6).

In time, we will learn about definitions and shifting meanings as we participate in the strangeness of language, the flourishing of conceptual categories, and the way that words multiply and trip over themselves in trying to capture the uncanny. "The process of concept formation . . . seen in all its complexity, . . . appears as a *movement* of thought within the pyramid of concepts" (Vygotsky, 1934/1986, pp. 142–143). From first words, the toddler will exercise language, birthing known experiences into more agile and agentive conscious forms and generating new knowns in a sphere of broadening and deepening discourse. The process will gain sophistication across social encounters from private speech (talking/babbling aloud in the presence of others), through inner speech and mental thought, to written discourse (pp. 210–256). As such we hone our ability to think in categories and to extend and abstract our thoughts through them. From the other side, language works us and our meanings through those same categories. Indeed, our very neural habits of patterned excitation will lay down selfhood as a proclivity to particular modes of thinking, always, with, in, and as the categories that avail the world to us and ourselves in that world and that seem most conducive to supporting our own coherent-, continuous-, and agentive-enough identity.

We would do well to be mindful of the creative and largely unconscious force of categories. "Though we learn new categories regularly, we cannot make massive changes in our category systems through conscious acts of recategorization. . . . We do not, and cannot, have full conscious control over how we categorize" (Lakoff & Johnson, 1999, p. 18). For example, for me, the meaning of 6:00 PM contains all those experiences in my life that have converged upon that time. In a 24-hour clock, my thinking is shackled to a cumbersome need for subtracting 12 hours from 18h00, if ever I am going to call up any meaningful associations. 1800 hours to 6:00 PM. Likewise, though I adamantly oppose my own inclination, I cannot seem to shake the way my mind wants to gender doctor as "he" and nurse as "she" – so ingrained is that habit from many decades when it was reliably the case. Our earliest and most familiar conceptions prime us to seek and find their affirmation. On occasion, the unexpected surprises us, but insofar as we encounter it as exception, we remain unmoved to change. A good teacher can help us to re-mind ourselves, breaking old habits to open alternative vistas, that we might veer down different paths and see different worlds.

We are thus wise to be careful, more careful than we have been, in our instating and wielding of categories, especially insofar as we use them to simplify, structure, and reduce the way we think about ourselves and others. Indeed, no matter how we parse them, drawn as they must be from the cultural stock of available ordered meanings, categories constrain and enable how we can make and know anything and anyone. They smudge away lines of difference within, while thickening those that separate one category from another and its milieu. The very creation of categories generates their outsides, the tangible thing and its intangible shadow, both, come into being at the same time. The birthplace of new categories – new ways of thinking and new possibilities in being – take their inception not from what has been admitted to the self, the known of one's categorical world. Rather, the excluded outside of our favoured conceptual structures are the repositories of provocative difference – of thinking otherwise. As from time immemorial, life's structures and the orders of life's emergence, rare and fleeting, continue to ebb from and flow back into a universe of discordant chaos. Life exists in the flux between order and chaos.

We will want to be humble in the face of our unavoidable ignorance of unformulated, conflictual, partitioned, and refused bodily knowing – ours and our students. In those moments when we find ourselves baffled – perceiving our students' seeming unwillingness or inability to make the sense that seems obvious – we might profit from reconsidering our own assumptions and our blindness to theirs. We will also want to ask after our students' previous tacit experiences. What missing "a-ha's" might want attention? What prior knowing do they have, including especially knowing how to know? What here-and-now experience might kindle the re-minding of selves – again, ours and theirs?

234 Into practice

Teachers can profit from an intimate appreciation and understanding of the natures of discernment, category making and unmaking, and the coupling and decoupling of meanings within a discipline. A developed skill in teaching, if one has opportunity (in time and resources) to work at it, entails in adjudicating encounters with the object of learning and reconciling progressive variations in difference and sameness across an example space – all to suit the discerning tendencies of students. This skill is only just emerging as a theme in educational research, mostly in mathematics learning, and seems virtually non-existence in most teacher preparation programs. Indeed, with but few exceptions (see, e.g., Jump Math, https://jumpmath. org), teaching resources evidence a gross inadequacy in understanding the ways that minds, all minds, make sense. This too will need to change.

We will also want to be wary of elements about the anticipated experience that relate to a student's experienced history in learning and schooling that puts them in the mode of risk. Might they be dealing with the kind of threat that requires constant vigilance – however out-of-mind though that vigilance might be? That is, even as a mind in denial might refuse its sense of threat, there will be psychic vigilance to hold at bay what cannot come to mind (see, e.g., Benedek, Jauk, Sommer, Arendasy, & Neubauer, 2014, on cognitive control). How can we help shift prior lessons-learned and the anticipation of personal harm into promising safe experiences exploring fascinating conundrums, entertaining invigorating intrigue, and finding rewarding understanding on the other side?

The takeaway here is not that teachers should be therapists. That is not our role. However, it is to say that teaching practice would do well to benefit from the deep appreciation of what is at play behind the scenes of conscious awareness in teaching and learning (see especially Chapter 13) – in the least, to question behaviourist sensibilities still dominating the field. In all our wonderings and all our doings as teachers, we will want to remember that people do things for reasons, that most of those reasons are unknowable, and that, however unknown, they are justified and valid according to personal, societally conditioned, histories. As teachers, it is our teacher-work to *allow space for those reasons* and to adjust our teaching accordingly and with sensitivity in the spirit of learning as self- and world-making.

The self as category, given yet made

The very biological and social terms of the meeting of self and world predate our bodily being. They have been set over time immemorial according to material and discursive realms of possibility. That is, we come into ever-evolving being (by doing ourselves differently) according to discursively mediated relational "pointing" on what and how to notice in a world that makes increasing sense to (and of) us, with others.

The categories through which we are first taught to perceive and conceive the world are the self-same categories that have constructed us and that we have at our disposal for coming to know ourselves. Schooling furthers these tendencies insofar as it necessarily participates in the initiation of citizens into the dominant

The provision of curricular objects **235**

discourses – the discourses belonging to and wielded on behalf of power. On this Butler (1997) has written extensively – of our having been installed through language by power and then, in a turn of events, coming to wield it for ourselves. In a sense, power inscribes itself on our bodies, calling us into particular performances of being, beginning with first utterances, "it's a girl/boy," and then policing those interpellations (Butler, 1990, 1999). Yet the transitivity of power entails in its re-appropriation by the subject that it enacts into being (Butler, 1997). Thus, while subjection enables mastery, agency becomes "the assumption of a purpose *unintended* by power" (1997, p. 15).

Naming, as in the assignment of a category, defines and endorses a mode of being – for example, girl or boy. Moreover, to name thusly is to construct the ideal as, in this example, strictly girl or boy and nothing other. Put differently, the construction of the prototypical and the ideal in humanness, at the same time, constructs its outside: the inhuman, the less-than-human, the humanly unthinkable, and various other versions of abject "otherhood." To construct what *can be* is also to demarcate the boundaries of what *cannot*.

If symbolic representation is the ground of thought, then knowing oneself as subject entails the adoption of a linguistic code and occupying various subject-category positions within that code. One's internally conceived self (as object of permissible being) becomes the place-holding structure of one's formation *and* this category co-emerges at the same time as one comes to know and become oneself as individual, bathed in visceral experiences of being. Butler foregrounds the body's unintelligibility outside language but also acknowledges "the permanent difficulty of determining where the biological, the psychic, the discursive, the social begin and end" (2004, p. 185). The crucial point is the linguistic connection forged, from the beginning, between a vital and meaningfully felt self and its possibility as formally recognisable and performatively instated social construction. Who we know ourselves to be "enjoy[s] intelligibility only to the extent that they [elements of self] are, as it were, first established in language" (1997, p. 11).

Thus, when we speak, we enact beyond the utterance of sounds and beyond ourselves (Butler, 2004). In speech, we act upon others and convey meanings – citations of past performative acts – of which we are not consciously privy. Language is that cultural vehicle that, working through us, is of us and not of us. Yet language falters in its writing on the body. There is an inevitable idiosyncrasy that can only be dispensed in a specific way on a particular body at a given instance in time. "The body carries its own signs, its own signifiers, in ways that remain largely unconscious" (2004, p. 198). Thus the recurrence of a linguistic term – for example, (dis)abled, gay, black – indexes "the way in which the social articulation of the term depends upon its repetition. . . . [Such] terms . . . are thus never settled once and for all but are constantly in the process of being remade" (Butler, 2004, p. 10).

In the stumbling spaces, subversive difference becomes possible. In a strange sort of unanticipated interpretation, the language of DNA's genetic speech, owing to epigenetic conditions, stumbles in its writing *into* bodies. As such, the meeting of

236 Into practice

language and genetics seems rife with emergent possibilities of infinite variation. The self, construed at the intersection of structuring forces, bottom up (genetically speaking) and top down (collectively speaking), and never fully proper nor transparent to itself, is nonetheless typically met, understood, experienced, and *largely held to be accountable for itself.* Schools clearly participate in this process. Indeed, in many ways this is their social purpose.

Under the invocation of inclusion, it seems to fall to teachers to, in some way, make spaces that prevent doors from slamming shut, that children and youth in halls of learning have access to viable thriving positions and, having been installed by power, can find their way to claiming agency in such a world. To this end, teachers have a tall order indeed: How might they engage students with the cultural objects of curriculum in ways that enable ownership of these objects yet sustain students in wielding them in manner even remotely approaching that of Richard Rorty's "strong poet"?

> We shall see the conscious need of the strong poet to *demonstrate* that he is not a replica as merely a special form of an unconscious need everyone has: the need to come to terms with the blind impress which chance has given him, to make a self for himself by redescribing that impress in terms which are, if only marginally, his own.
>
> *(Rorty, 1989, p. 43)*

All our educative goals are troubled (and rendered naïve) by the problem that Butler raises: Who or what is this person who makes personal sense if not the one made as such by the world? Recognising that the self is the very one made pliable in the kiln of human relations and then forged into selfhood according to the forces of linguistic performative utterances, how does anyone (student and teacher alike) come to deconstruct the very conditions of their formation without also disassembling the self that those forces made possible?

Categories and culture

The summer before I first taught grade 6 science, I studied the celestial universe and practiced identifying the trees of southern Alberta. I have never since looked at the sky without the constellations coming into view through a lens conceived in ancient Greece, nor have I looked at trees since without also "seeing" their species' story through a Western taxonomy attentive to the pattern of bark, the shape of foliage, the design of leaves, etcetera, and not, for example, the relational role of the tree in the forest. My preparation that summer did not ask anything of me that I did not already have. I could see stars before; I had long developed the tendency to connect dots; and none of the images embedded in the constellations were images of anything foreign to my experience. In this, I was already privileged to learn "well." Newness only entailed in the bringing together of these things into a distinct symbolic representation that reorganised the randomness of stars and, in

The provision of curricular objects **237**

similar fashion, of trees. I engaged in meaning-making according to what Donnel Stern describes:

> To grasp or interpret (or construct or know) experience requires that symbols be related to one another. A symbol unrelated to other symbols . . . would not be a symbol. It would be a thing . . . without meaning. . . . Meaning depends on the relations and differences between symbols, not on fixed identifications of symbols with entities.
>
> *(2003, p. 7)*

Symbolic representations and their relations contain and transmit the idiosyncratic conceptions of socio-cultural ways of perceiving and conceiving. In revising perception and conception, I extended the reach of my knowing beyond the limits of my own singular being through a particular plurality of, in this case, Western perspectives. The effect distanced me from cultures who learn to perceive and conceive these things according to different stories, even as it also broadened my power by connecting me to hegemonic Western cultural sensibilities. In other words, in learning to wield the discourses of power, I gain some mastery but only in terms of that power. I am unlikely to succeed at shifting myself again and differently without some sort of embedded alternative experience. The degree to which I might come to underwrite my own acts, as from a centre of self-authorship, might in these terms seem exceedingly limited. Freedom, within and because of constraints, turns on the breadth and depth of the varied experiences I can make in the world and out of which I might fashion choice.

That we humans make any sense at all speaks to the extraordinary reach of language and the manner in which, in its ongoing formulation we wield and construe understanding and, with it, the world of our personal and shared experience. With great conceptual imagination, riding on the symbol systems of our own socio-cultural endowments and evolutionary history, we implicate ourselves in the world, and the world in us. We conduct this serious imaginative play via the configuring and reconfiguring of mental connections, interconnections, and connections of connections of symbols, bringing along the categories they name, each with their associated tacit meanings. Across history, that imagination has been buoyed by extraordinary technologies, beginning with the written word (Donald, 2001), that extend human capacities for retaining, re-inscribing, recreating, and dynamically connecting memory in and with the present.

From one generation to the next, a "natural human pedagogy" (Csibra & Gergely, 2011) seems to oversee the conferral of particular endowments forward – begun in familial contexts, as we have seen, with discernments about self and other. Then, in schools, teachers take up the mantle, or rather critically supplement it on behalf of society and according to government mandates and socio-cultural ideals about the relationship between the citizen and a society; that is, where, in the systems' interests of bottom-up and top-down vitality and viability (as continuity, coherence, and agency), the citizen serves society and society serves the citizen.

238 Into practice

Given the enormity of the educational undertaking and its inevitable socio-cultural biases, we teachers will want to proceed gently, with inspiration, and some humility, aware that we are inducting our newest initiates, through schooling, into a decidedly messy intersectional cultural space. We will want to recognise that the gateway to that space is through fluency in the use of symbolic conventions, including the symbol systems that call up, trigger, and sometimes fuse viscerally felt, embodied meanings into socially communicable forms of acceptable knowledge. From a perspective of relational psychoanalytic understanding we will also want to remember that we do not live in language; we live in bodies. But these, our, bodies are intimately shaped via language into and with the social.

Into havens of rationality: categorical thought, split from feeling

Our bodies learn. Having fought off a pathogen we develop an immunity. Having suffered frequent respiratory irritation, we can develop heightened allergic sensitivities. If the withholding of caregiver affection unpredictably follows from a child's behaviour, the child's body learns vigilance and the anxious anticipation of loss. In general, in response to impingements that our bodies experience, they learn – which is to say, anticipate like-challenges by developing such capacities as quickened discernment and targeted reactions. Our bodies scan for and dynamically re-equilibrate themselves in response to learned environmental dangers and internal homeostatic variation. For the most part fine-grained physiological responses happen outside the reaches of conscious awareness. While our bodies are becoming "wiser for the doing," we can be haplessly bracketing uncomfortable feelings from conscious mind. This does not mean that we have gotten away from the fact that our bodies do know to seek and, in seeking, discern and remember lessons-learned.

We could say that this kind of bodily knowing and knowing-how-to-know represents evolutions of genetically bestowed wisdom directing the uptake and interconnection of body lessons across a lifetime. These lessons have a way of accruing below awareness in repositories of visceral habit, sensitivity, and predilection. Predisposing us to particular choices, they guide the direction of our lives in tacit ways. Important to school learning, if my body is already taxed by homeostatic concerns and if, at a physiological level, matters have indeed "gotten out of hand" – threateningly so, say as the consequence of emotional dysregulation – then, I will be hard-pressed to focus on or even think about, much less engage at any symbolic distance, those not-here-in-the-moment abstract concepts that are the substance of other-prescribed curricula. A teacher will want to be attuned to the expression of these markers and responsively react in supportive and accepting ways.

Yet some children cope with affective distress by denying it – literally blocking it from mind and turning instead to an almost-soothing predictable object world (Lachmann, 2008). *The symbolic world of categories can serve as retreat from unprocessed affect.* If I can become adept at using abstract concepts to create distance from the things that make me uncomfortable; if I can channel my angst to drive accomplishments in a symbolic world, even as I dissociate from discomfort; and/or, if I can come at the things that disturb me through the safe, unimplicating distance of reason, objectivity, and fact, then immersion in a curriculum sanitised of deep meaning and affective connection will seem to serve me well. It is no coincidence that these sorts of preferences and capacities congregate in milieus where "thinking" objectively is the rigueur du jour: classically, the sciences and the law; definitional in today's knowledge workers; and more generally in those individuals most adept at construing facts as categories for taming away messy human entanglement.

Dan Heyman's anti-apartheid song "Weeping" (1987) is an allegory of a man proclaiming the existence of a threatening but covert monster (affect) and his own reasonable use of steel, fire, and guns to contain it. Yet sounds in the night challenge the man. He thinks:

> As long as peace and order reign
> I'll be damned if I can see a reason to explain
> Why the fear and the fire and the guns remain

Meanwhile, the chorus tells not of a monster roaring in the night, but of one who is weeping.

Perhaps the most challenging and critical ambiguity wanting human resolution is bringing thinking and feeling in close enough conversation, without one obliterating the other, so that the wisdom of each serves to temper and elaborate the other.

Humans have shown great ingenuity in using language to exaggerate the distance between living forms as objects of thought and as subjects of being. In the military, targets are neutralised; in medicine, patients are stabilised; and in education – borrowing language from both the military and medicine – schools undertake disciplinary measures and capitalise on spirit-rousing motivational rhetoric, while teachers work in the trenches managing classrooms and triaging behavioural interventions according to a medicalised model for diagnosing and therapeutically treating learning and students. In the military, the dehumanising effects of these strategies are blatant and intentional. In medical practice the deleterious effects of dehumanising practices presents a well-documented challenge (e.g., Haque & Waytz, 2012). Yet the collective of so-called learning sciences invoke these very approaches for schooling – even as words and symbols can serve to erase the human in the child and in the child's encounter with the world. Indeed, the Age of Reason rose on precisely the capacity to think and write clearly in ways strategically free of emotional contaminants, as if to cut out the human from the very actions that humans undertook in the name of science.

On a personal level, I know how easily one can become engrossed in making progress toward the ends of solving a puzzle of some sort. Hot on the heels of an anticipated "a-ha," we are biochemically rewarded in the doing (Panksepp & Biven, 2012). At the same time, our conscious minds are given reprieve from ruminations as might arise unbidden from an unconscious wellspring. The thinking that we are doing, assuming some measure of success in the doing, when sufficiently abstracted and consuming, can feel wonderfully neutral, logical, objective, and safe.

240 Into practice

Now for many students, especially those who can find soothing respite in the world of hypothetical ideas, this is "meaning" enough. For many others, have we perhaps become too preoccupied with enticements to hold their attention and might this preoccupation have distracted us from addressing the multiple roots of meaning and distress in the first place?

Resolving the *poietics* of the made and the *mimetics* of the given: a difference of perspective

In Chapter 8, I introduced mimesis and poiesis, as the twin structuring inclinations of bundling sameness (mimesis) and creatively coupling difference (poiesis). In this section, we return to these ideas. in *Mimesis and Alterity*, Taussig admits to "often [being] caught musing as to whether the wonder of the magic in mimesis could reinvigorate the once-unsettling observation that most of what seems important in life is made up" (1993, p. xv). Taking our cue from Taussig, we can say that, whereas poiesis is about making things up, mimesis is reproducing that which was once made and is now given. Whereas poiesis posits a new real; mimesis seems to endorse it.

In discourses bringing autopoietic thinking into educational contexts (e.g., Trueit, 2005), poiesis garners higher regard for its association with creativity, the emergent spark of insight, and the spawning of difference. It is poiesis when: An engineer designs a new prototype; a craftsman creates an original product; a caterpillar morphs into a butterfly; a spider spins a unique web; an infant enacts a new movement; neurons connect in unpredicted ways to spawn the surprise of new thought–paths; and, encountering a puzzling ambiguity, we sleep on it and awake with a revised view the next morning. Poiesis is associated with creative coupling, convergence, and emergence. On the other hand, mimesis is, today, the humbler of the two. Its deals in mimicry, repetition, and the accrual and bundling of sameness. It is mimesis when: New neighbourhoods spring out of the replication of near-identical home-designs; factories mass-produce identical products; fireflies come to flicker in unison; birds assemble into flocks; muscles bulk up muscle fibre, neurons bundle into nerve fibres; and we seek what we know for the purpose of fortifying the things we already believe – often to the detriment of noticing anything otherwise. Mimesis is associated with replication, duplication, and mimicry. Yet a phenomenon of biological degeneracy (basically the functional interchangeability of structurally dissimilar biological parts) creates drift in a biological system such that replications are never quite the same. This is important.

To re-join the opening section of this chapter, we find the terms poiesis and mimesis having emerged in timely service to progressive and traditional lines of educational thought, respectively (e.g., in Bausch, 2001; Taussig, 1993; Trueit, 2005). That is, poiesis aligns with progressively framed inquiry learning that emphasises knowledge as personally made; mimesis is associated with so-called traditional practices that emphasise knowledge as given. In a world that changes swiftly, unexpected poietic emergences promise the inventiveness to help us find our way. In the

The provision of curricular objects **241**

slower-paced world of yesteryear, poiesis may well have been the thing to call into question the stability that a society, a culture, and a family held dear. Poiesis is relevant insofar as we seek and value innovation, diversity, and finding new possibility in the unfamiliar. Mimesis calls up the different priorities of convention, uniformity, and refining and strengthening the familiar. Whereas mimesis engenders the security and safety of things predictable, linear, and reliable, poiesis can overwhelm or intrigue with its uncertainty, nonlinearity, and spontaneity. Poiesis asks "How far can you bend and recover yourself anew?" Mimesis asks, "How well can you hold together sustaining yourself against the forces that would break you?" Both are implicated in complementary relations of trust and control (Möllering, 2006). Both are critical to teaching as provoking and supporting learning.

Returning again to the model, we can now layer in mimesis and poiesis, imagining mimesis as tight iterations around the loop with only small and incremental differences being introduced each time, but that, in recursive repetition, accrue to notable shifts in conceptual understanding. And we can imagine poietic excursions around the loop to be broader and lengthier recursions through more drastic differences to perplex and challenge the learner. In other words, although mimesis and poiesis are typically contrasted as opposites, both follow a principle of the centrifugal "huh?" in the encounter with unforeseen ambiguity and the centripetal return to self as the "a-ha" of resolution. But in mimesis, the change does not happen all at once and can feel less intimidating to some learners while less intriguing to others. The important point is that we want to maintain conceptual movement and avoid the arrest of learning when some students "bite off more difference than they can chew" and other students bite off so little that they forget to chew at all. This is what I mean when I speak of the teacher titrating experiences according to student capacities for discernment. If we can mitigate "violations of expectation" so as to hit the sweet spot of enjoyment, as in that surprise of peek-a-boo, somewhere between the frightening shock of "boo" and the boredom of everything predictable, then we can support conditions of dynamic movement in learning.

In discussing violations of expectations, Lachman describes creativity and humour in terms of the creator's use of "optimal operative perversity" to deviate from and to contradict a "previously held principle of organisation" (2008, pp. 133–136). In a cosmopolitan world of accelerating change what seemed perverse yesterday is more likely to be assimilated into today's newly created "normal." We may well be in an era to value would-be violators for the maverick contributions they make in perturbing a system to grow quickly – and, then again, perhaps so quickly as to jeopardise system integrity. In any case, the emphasis on innovation has the effect of placing flexibility ahead of strength, poiesis ahead of mimesis, uniqueness above conformity, distinction before belonging, the extrovert over the introvert.

While today's fast-paced urgencies press schools to deliver on creativity, creativity pushes back. It can neither be forced nor coerced into being. Meanwhile, the emphasis on creativity disparages development of the very conventions upon which creativity works its redesigns. *Paradoxically, the creativity of poiesis could not come into view without some mimetic amplification to bring dissonance forward.* We cannot address

242 Into practice

what we do not discern and discernment is as much a function of difference and sameness as it is of scale. New patterns only come into awareness if they have had a chance to grow (to entrain and replicate) enough to be visible in the perceiving system's scale of time and space.

The tipping point on how much difference or sameness is enough to be discernible – for any student, classroom, or school – may well be a function of relative perspective and scale. What one learner experiences in a given context as irresolvable difference, another cannot tease apart. What one learner experiences as entirely new, another sees more of the same. And what one observer deems a resolution of poietic proportions another sees as a mimetic repetition with hardly a difference. *In teaching that appreciates such interpretive variations, we alter how grand or subtle is the centrifugal swing into dissonance – enough to keep things interesting, not so much as to overwhelm and foreclose resolution.* Who adjudicates whether an event of learning is a fundamental paradigm shift for the learner or merely an elaboration of the same kind of thing? Might poietic emergence, upon close examination, look more like mimetic entrainment? How much a person zooms in or out to discern and resolve a perceived dissonance may well set the distance between ambiguous takes on a concept and the degree of conceptual resolution (whether as small or large leap) needed to bridge the distance.

To approach teaching in manner to promote student discernment of new conundrums and their emergent resolution, the notions of poiesis and mimesis may be better thought, not as absolutes, but rather as relational properties between the learner and the aspect of knowing to be conceived. Thinking in terms of conceptual distances to be discerned and resolved and what any teacher can do about helping students bridge that distance, the notion of "ribboning" (Metz, Preciado-Babb, Sabbaghan, Davis, & Ashebira, 2017) may be helpful. To ribbon a lesson is to view its videotaped recording and code the stretch of time with different coloured bands "according to whether a selected moment involves instruction, assessment, or practice" (p. 181). In their work with elementary school mathematics learning, Metz *et al.* found that "effective lessons typically resulted in narrow bands of colour that resemble ribbons" (p. 181).

> These lessons alternated frequently between drawing attention to important discernments and checking whether students made the intended discernments. This may be contrasted with lessons in which large chunks of information are clustered, either in large instructional chunks or in problems that involve multiple new ideas.
>
> (p. 181)

Taken to the model, we might say that this visible marker of responsive, frequently alternating, teacher–student interaction reflects the teacher's micro-attuned titration of learning provocations, couched in a likewise affectively attuned sensibility as if to say: "If that works, then what do you think about this? And how is this the same and/or not?" The attentive teacher adapts to student differences by

The provision of curricular objects **243**

appropriately fitting pedagogical queries within a conceptual domain: For students who need more practice, the teacher provides prompts in the thick of the concept's example space; for students who thirst for challenges she provides prompts that push its boundaries.

This kind of attuned teaching recalls and is continuous with the affective micro-conversations of parent-infant interactions that have been studied by attachment theorists. The effect is to draw students into shared meaningfully engagement as they discern and resolve newness in a progressively elaborating example space of a concept – importantly, with the depth and breadth of address adjusted to fit individual student proclivities. This, we might call differentiation. Each recursive iteration invites students to revise their understanding along a dynamic procession of tasks, micro-fitted to be familiar and unfamiliar enough for discernment and resolution, thus strengthening emergent sense, even as a next "twist" presses conceptual intrigue. These dialogical exchanges do best when teachers have easy access to the ongoing play of student thought – for example, as when learners convey their thinking on readily visible personal mini-whiteboards. With a clear view of student expressions of knowing, the teacher can respond on the fly by incrementally adapting appropriate challenges to emerging individual and collective understandings.

While this kind of dialogical unfolding is indeed remarkable to observe, it does not follow that all learning is best approached according to tightly fitted micro-recursions. Students can and do in myriad other instances profit from free and explorative play, group collaboration, and all manner of pedagogical acts. The point is that thinking about these acts in terms of recursive cycles (however broad or constrained) – of centrifugal "huh?" to centripetal "a-ha!" – can help teachers reimagine the way they respond to student diversity across capacity, meaning, and trust in learning.

Finally, just as between-student differences matter, there is a critical trajectory of within-student differences that creeps in over the school years and into adulthood. Initially learners are unaware of the processes of coming to know; they just find themselves knowing. The swiftness with which young learners can seem to make sense may well owe to both our inattention to the concentrated work of early childhood and their as-yet-to-be-developed ability to think about their own thinking. But as learners advance in any discipline, the space between ambiguous elements will widen and become more notable, making resolution a more effortful and sometimes intimidating task. Eventually, learners unsupported in knowing their own autopoietic capacities, and unable to immediately "see an answer" can find themselves falling into a confounding abyss.

The more one can leap to sense without having had to grapple in the process, the greater can be one's impatience and/or threat with the process. The more that the sense to be made comes as immediately and practically obvious, the greater can be one's frustration with hypothetical musing. One learns to expect and then need quick answers that promise certainty in a neutral unambiguous, rightfully given, world. If push comes to shove, where the demand for quick-to-mind clear-cut

244 Into practice

knowing fails, then defences ensue as some variant of: "It just makes no sense," or "I understood it until I got this bad teacher." In other words, the self-narrative of "not me" can seem the only plausible explanation for events that challenge one's sense of self-continuity as a capable learner.

Final examples

These days problem solving, critical thinking, and creativity are highly lauded attributes. The great irony of popular approaches to their development may well inhere in the folk psychology that "practice makes perfect" – that students will develop these qualities by simply exercising them. But one does not become expert in higher-level thinking without having developed the concepts with which to think. This is because the learning that can be availed in a space of sense-making turns on prior habits of thought and discernment with respect to conceptual categories, their relations to each other, the narratives threading categorical complexes together, the contexts within and to which they fit, and the examples that concepts bring to mind and through which they have been birthed.

Innumerable examples would bring to life the concepts presented in this chapter. I refer the reader to Ference Marton (1981, 1986, 1996, 2000, 2014) for phenomenological elaborations, the investigations of Anne Watson and John Mason (2005) for their application to variation theory in learning, and JUMP Math (https://jumpmath.org) as exemplar of micro-iterations (see the Student Assessment & Practice books) and macro-problem sequences (see the Teachers Manual). I leave to a future book the formulation of an example space more broadly useful for teachers. For now, suffice it to offer two examples, both taken from mathematics pedagogy. The first addresses the idea of number in the example of 24. The second contrasts two approaches to the meaning of pi.

The meaning and sense of 24 and the concept of 24ness

I have made a habit of introducing concept study to teachers in mathematics education by inviting ways of imagining *the idea of 24ness*. This throws people off. Unlike, say, happiness where we are accustomed to a conceptual space of happiness, including, for example, being glad or ecstatic, 24 seems invariant as a concept. Rarely does anyone imagine 24 beyond an idea of enumeration – as in 24 years old and 24 hours in a day. But there are many ways to "know" the concept of 24ness that go beyond counting things.

To offer a sense of the fullness of the conceptual space of 24, I have parsed it into a non-exhaustive list of interrelated progressive ways of thinking about it. Notice that counting is only the first.

1 24 discreet objects *counted off one at a time*;
2 A *distance* that marks 24 equal increments from zero;
3 A *position* on a number line;
4 A *multiple* of each of 1, 2, 3, 4, 6, 8, 12, and 24;

The provision of curricular objects **245**

5   A *place-value representation* (assumed to name *powers of 10*); symbolically: $2 \times 10^1 + 4 \times 10^0$;

6   In *base five*, a place-value representation of *powers of 5*; symbolically: $2 \times 5^1 + 4 \times 5^0$;

7   A *two-dimensional space* depicted as, for example:

- a *difference of squares* – literally a *5-by-5 square* with a *1-by-1* corner cut out; symbolically: $5^2 - 1^2$
- six two-*squares*; symbolically $2^2 + 2^2 + 2^2 + 2^2 + 2^2 + 2^2$ or $6(2)^2$;

8   A *three-dimensional space* depicted as, for example, 3 two-*cubes*; symbolically: $2^3 + 2^3 + 2^3$ or $3(2)^3$;

9   In *modulus* 12, like our clocks, it is also 0; symbolically: $24(\mathrm{mod}\ 12) = 0$.

Together, in the phenomenographic sense, all these categories are part of a conceptual suprastructure of 24ness. Note how this list necessarily transects other conceptual categories in a network of mathematical meanings that I have italicised (e.g., distance, position, multiple, place-value, dimensionality). It takes years of engagement in instances of number to arrive at the foregoing extensive conceptual list. Encountering it all at once would be intimidating. Each category is built up from a specific set of encounters that calls for and develops a unique class of discernments. Each category relates a different way of experiencing 24 with its symbolic representation.

For instance, enumeration is hardly trivial. It involves mapping *counting up* onto *accounting for*, one element at a time. Learning to do so grows from an example space that superimposes and eventually merges, two different concepts: rhyming off a sequence of number in order and matching this to elements in a set one item at a time. An example space for making such a connection might include walking on stepping stones while counting aloud; counting beads added to a bucket; and sliding items, one at a time, across an interactive whiteboard.

It takes movement through progressively elaborating example spaces for a student to develop the fluidity of nonconscious knowing (the kind we take for granted) as might be readily accessed about number (and 24) in order to apply these understandings. The facility to problem solve and think creatively and critically with respect to 24ness grows as a function of facileness of movement between categories for conceiving and perceiving as these relate to experiences in the world.

Just as it is not possible to isolate 24ness from other things mathematical, neither is it helpful to isolate 24ness from meanings grounded in experiences in the world. Losing sight of these connections risks losing the transitional quality of thought as living in both an illusory "made" mind and a disillusioning "given" world. To appreciate what I mean in so saying, we turn to a discussion of "pi."

Approaching "pi"

How might we teach so as to introduce and tether the symbolic to embodied experience and tangible meaning? Consider two approaches to the concept of "pi," the first built up from the symbolic, the second weaving new experience and symbolic representation together.

246 Into practice

Losing students in abstractions

A common inquiry activity for teaching "pi" has students measuring the circumferences (C) and diameters (d) of various circles and cylindrical objects and entering table values under the headings: C, d, and C ÷ d. After some time, the teacher draws the class's attention to how the values in the third category hover at a little over 3. The students, having no conception of what the number "3.14 . . ." enumerates or signifies, learn that this is "pi," and its decimal representation cannot be fully written out. As a practical application, teachers have students use the formulae C = 2πr and C = πd to calculate missing values from given ones. For fun, students might even go outside and measure tree circumferences to calculate their diameters.

But meanings lie not in such activities. Most adults who, having encountered "pi" in similar ways, will answer the question "What is pi?" with "about 3.14" and "it has something to do with circles" – if they can answer at all. Missing are meanings that strap symbolic representation to lived experience.

Pi as transitional object: in mind and in world

How might we imagine experiences of "pi" to support fluency and meaning central to both practical worldly application and the theoretical constructs of higher-level thinking? We could begin with introductory lessons about circles so as to get to know their dynamic properties – for example, by swirling objects on strings, watching ripples spread in water, twirling lights in the dark, videotaping and viewing a flipping coin, and rolling prisms that progress from few sides (triangular prisms) to more sides (octagonal) to infinite sides (cylinders).

We will find "pi" in the answer to the pedagogical questions: *How shall we experience this thing we call a circle? What qualities are we discerning when we know it as circular?* Specifically, to draw attention to pi is to explore the relationship between the circumference of a circle and the longest distance across it – and to perceive that relationship as a constant property of all circles. Using division to get to that ratio problematically and unnecessarily depends upon a robust student understanding of the meaning of division. Instead, the related meanings of ratio and division can be enhanced in an activity that has students explore the questions: *How many across-the-circles does it take to go around it? Is it the same answer with all circles? Why would anyone care?*

Student can address the first question by estimating and then using their resources to try to arrive at more accurate determinations. A vibrant Socratic dialogue might ensue as students undertake a fair bit of trial-and-error, teamwork, and brain storming. Importantly, the experience of pi as the number of diameters it takes to go around a circle supports a broader category of proportional reasoning. Pi emerges as a constant that is the measure of a relationship and functionally linked to meaningful action on the world in tangible shared experiences. Lessons could follow on pi as a human construct, the problem of accuracy in determining it, what humans have done about it, whether it seems reasonable (rational), who it mattered to, and why. Students would initially work in manner to develop their spontaneous

The provision of curricular objects **247**

knowledge from the affordances of the task. Interwoven individual and group dialogues with the teacher, as knowing other, would be invaluable in bringing shared thoughts and experiences forward and into conversation with the nonspontaneous knowledge of mathematics, even as students enter these broader discourses as valued co-participants.

Pi seems inherently difficult insofar as its meaning is divorced from experience. The approach through symbols moves from number as enumeration to number as relationship and, in that shift, we lose many a student. Importantly, in the second approach, we do not *give* students the value of pi as the outcome of an abstract function. Rather, we first create meaning in experience and then we invoke social convention to name it. We invite students to notice a regularity, resolve a relationship, and then to use it. When the meaning has matured, the time is ripest for words and signifiers to abstract into the symbolic that which is already embodied.

Such lessons have an elastic capacity to extend meaning where students will take it. For instance, comparisons might be made to other regular shapes as students stumble upon an observation that the circle seems most economical in the sense of an edge subtending the greatest interior. They could entertain questions of why some goods are packaged in cylindrical cans and others in boxes. The teacher oversees the movement across an ever-elaborating suprastructure so as to weave a network of interconnected embodied ideas. The so-called concrete thus embeds itself in the abstraction that implicitly names and contains it.

But pi introduced in the first way, leaves students more likely to feel the meaninglessness of the activity, while relishing an opportunity to move around and socialise. They are unlikely to connect their action to the knowing they are supposed to have. They will not realise that spontaneous concepts, when explored with a mentoring other, can lead to intriguing nonspontaneous relationships that turn out to be powerful. What they will likely experience instead is a distancing and fracturing from a broader world of human convention, interpretation, and understanding, and an entire set of associations that can provoke anxiety or simply prove one's adeptness at "getting it." Either way, something hardly worth doing stands in the stead of vital activities in being, doing, knowing, and becoming.

Last words to Donnel Stern

Donnel Stern writes that "what analysts actually set out to do . . . remains the grasp of the nonverbal in words, or the retelling in new words of earlier worded experience" (2003, p. 24). This too, I contend, is the work of teaching. Accordingly, let me close by giving him the last word, applicable as much to teaching as to psychoanalytic work.

> [Language is] most important when it . . . [is] revelatory. . . . Imagination brings thoughts alive. It is important . . . that one be able to say them to someone else, of course, but that comes with the territory. . . . The capacity to say one's thoughts to oneself . . . is what spells the defeat of dissociation. . . .

248 Into practice

Communication is always the eventual point. . . . [b]ut there is no reason that it should always be easy. To communicate about a matter of substance is liable to be difficult. Maybe it even *should* be difficult, because, after all, the thought hasn't been spoken before.

(2003, pp. 100–101)

Note

1 "We assume that everyone has the same knowledge that we do, because most of our beliefs about the world were someone else's before we made them our own" (Fonagy & Target, 2007, p. 922).

13

SELVES AND WITNESSES

Teacher know your story

We approach the book's end with a chapter on the teaching self. It rides upon key understandings developed thus far: that the unconscious and nonconscious self, being central to the capacity, trust, and meaning in learning, cannot remain outside discourses about teaching and learning; and that language, as cultural vehicle of our collective histories, makes possible conscious thought even as it constrains the thinkable and sets the limits of what anyone can be.

Authenticity and presence

Those literatures with the greatest influence in schooling have yet to make a shift that Lewis Aron once described for relational theory as "from the classical idea that it is the patient's mind that is being studied . . . to the relational notion that mind is inherently dyadic, social, interactional, and interpersonal" (1996, p. x).

One need not go far for a current exemplar of the persistent trend to discount the relational in favour of the isolated individual. *The It Factor: What Makes a Teacher Great* (Thornton, 2018) stands as a next likely candidate for operationalising and technologising desired teacher qualities. Not only do we continue to separate teaching and learning selves from their conditioning contexts, but also we continue to privilege empirical studies of observable behaviour, conscious assertions, and measurable achievements of individuals – these conducing to evidence-based techniques to remediate whatever is defined to ail them. Together, measurables and certified technique, however mercurially defined over the years, serve governments in reassuring publics of the proper accreditation and regulation of school personnel (see Cruikshank & Haefele, 2001, on a century of measuring teacher practice).

Meanwhile, when it comes to "knowing" one's story - however naïvely that possibility might go believed for educators – the limited discourses have, over the years, highlighted authenticity (Kreber, Klampfleitner, McCune, Bayne, & Knottenbelt, 2007; Thompson, 2015) and presence (Noddings, 2003; Palmer, 1997) as

250 Into practice

difference-making qualities in teachers, and trustworthiness (Tschannen-Moran, Hoy, & Hoy, 2000) and "withitness" (visible emotional – social intelligence in teaching, Kounin, 1970) as their related measurables. Though these qualities garner respect, their encouragement in education seems dependent on "a specious assumption that these ways of relating to oneself and others are relatively straightforward" (Bialystok & Kukar, 2018, p. 34).

> [Yet,] the process of telling one's own life story – at least as long as it is authentic and not merely "made up" or forced – is not volitional in any simple way, any more than is our construction of dreams. . . . [L]ike our dreams our deepest intentions inform and shape our stories.
>
> *(Donnel Stern, 1997/2003, p. 65)*

When translated through twenty-first-century individualism, the call for authenticity and presence reduces to a dictum of being true to oneself and unconditionally accepting others. Absent appreciation of the opacity of the self to the self, such mandates present an almost laissez faire attitude to self- and other-understanding. At the same time, blind to unconscious motivation, they also leave us to believe that societal improvement follows from the indoctrination of moral values: appealing to the correctness of right behaviour; expecting the desire to be good to prevail; and using punishment to deter those less-good. Psychoanalytic theory, now backed by neuroscience, shows all these beliefs problematic and their approaches more likely to backfire, provoking denial and dissociation (see, e.g., Dobbin & Kalev, 2016).

It is at our peril that we continue to disregard the force of the unconscious, the social construction of the self, and the parts of the self that one would rather not admit – indeed, that, as a dutiful teacher in the current era, one cannot admit. Instead, those disavowed self-parts, the ones we must reject as "not me," become the self-same undesirable traits that we are most likely to situate in the other – if not overtly, then surely subliminally. Such uninterrogated interiorities seem prescriptive of anything but inclusivity and acceptance.

In this chapter, I implicate relational psychoanalytic understandings to differently and more productively think about ourselves in the context of our relational work in schooling. I begin by revisiting contexts that set the terms of the task.

On co-recognition – in want of a witness

Martin Buber's *I and Thou* (1926/1970) captures the essence of co-recognition. He writes,

> Man [*sic*] becomes an I through a You. . . . The man who has acquired an I and says I-It assumes a position before things but does not confront them in the current of reciprocity. He bends down to examine particulars under the objectifying magnifying glass of close scrutiny, or he uses the objectifying telescope of distant vision to arrange them as mere scenery.
>
> *(pp. 80–81)*

Systemic pathologies

New parental designations, including helicopter (cosseting), free-range, and snow-plough (bulldozer) parents[1] and the "tiger mother" (Chau, 2011) suggest troubled relationships between caregivers, students, schools, and their teachers. Popular catchphrases of "alternative facts/truths," "everyone can," "a nation at risk," and the insistence that "no child be left behind" become titles for legislative documents bespeaking conflicted and contested perspectives in the politics of schooling, entitlement to success, and the legitimacy of particular forms of knowledge.

Positioned in the throes of such confliction, and told to rely on evidence-based practices as those techniques that are going to work, the teacher's noble and ethical mandate is to deliver on every student's inalienable right to success. But like Michael Eigen, "Whenever I hear someone say they've found something that's going to work, it makes me scared" (in Peay, 2015, December 10, p. 12).

In the meantime, directly and indirectly, a learner feels as much the weight of a nation looking over his shoulder for guarantees of its prosperous future, as the weight of his adults looking over his shoulder for guarantees of having done enough to ensure him a place in that prosperous future. Caught in a situation coextensive with multiple anxious watchers, *each watcher owning a piece of the student's success, almost as if it was her own,* the learner turns to the teacher and says, "Engage me" and "Do it in my preferred style" (see, e.g., National College for School Leadership video, 2008, December 16) – a phrase marking depletion of much ownership of, and agency in, his own learning. As Adam Curtis developed so compellingly, these children have been birthed out of *The Century of the Self* (2002) where "preferences have become the object of social engineering" (Crawford, 2015, p. 18). Confusions are indeed rife between you, me, and not me.

Teachers are called to manage ever-untenable numbers of individualised programs for cognitively, affectively, and behaviourally challenged students, whilst teaching a curriculum – every bit the favoured conceptual child of Western colonisers – in ways to make it amenable to diverse populations (see, e.g., Alberta Education, 2014, 2015; The Alberta Teachers' Association, 2009, 2015). Meanwhile, a responsive industry of educational research ramps up "tried and true" medical models in the "certain" prevention, assessment, and symptom-based treatment of documentable afflictions – ultimately producing revised protocols to align with this or that new research-driven insight. In the admix of newest and potentially useful understandings, the research domain of social and emotional learning (SEL) (Schonert-Reichl, Kitil, & Hanson-Peterson, 2017) retains a stubborn cultural premise that, with proper technique and motivation, we can rally willpower and habit to subdue and regulate away disruptive emotions (see the critique by Bialystok & Kukar, 2018). *To the degree that such research advances techniques in self-censorship and the discounting of the unconscious and situated context, as the right things to do, we brush dangerously close to exacerbating the very challenges that have rendered many learners, their teachers, and their school environments unwell in the first place.* Self-parts that go denied and unattended have an uncanny habit of wreaking exacerbating havoc (Benjamin, 2018, p. 17).

252 Into practice

Taken together, present conditions define a genre of systemic pathology that seems implicated in a conflicted mêlée of anxiety (Collishaw, Maughan, Natarajan, & Pickles, 2010; Mackenzie et al., 2011; Tone, 2009) and entitlement (Lasch, 1984; Twenge & Campbell, 2009) nagging at the spirit of far too many *Kids These Days* (Harris, 2017) and their teachers (Gartner, 2017). In answer to the question: "What can schools do about it?" a psychoanalytic perspective asks that we consider how to better support pedagogues in their unavoidably relational roles – that they might undertake them as attuned-enough caregiving others (Fonagy et al., 2007; Leckman et al., 2007), neither too preoccupied with, nor too dismissing of, learners to serve as their recognising witnesses. In so saying, we understand that such teacher capacities are a function of their own relational histories, the contexts within which they find themselves, and whether together these are enough to hold them well in visiting security forward.

A childhood bountiful in witnessing makes possible the growth of autonomy and self-acceptance, including the enfoldment of even the not-so-terrible terrible "not me" self-parts. In the sense that Buber wrote (1926/1970), the very authenticity of such individuals – as teachers able to acknowledge and give grace to their own, seemingly less reputable, parts – can work to derail objectification rendered them in the eyes of others, including their students, even as it serves to encourage the authenticity of those budding citizens in their care. Moreover, in measure to counter human tendencies to take everyone and everything as a potential extension of self (or tendencies to fear being thus taken), the recognising of other's recognisability pulls in an opposite direction, toward self-other-affirming "I-You" co-recognising experiences of mutuality.

In this idea of co-recognition lies a fundamental paradox: Independence and dependence require each other; that is, *the capacity to know and stand among others in one's independence depends upon the other's recognised separateness – that separateness in turn being the condition to make a different kind of connection possible.* Before there can be connection and before we can know ourselves, there has to be admitted the existence of a separate confounding other, in whose presence, and because of whose presence, one is yet safe – this, though that other's very self-insistence might work against what we anticipate or think him to be.

What's in a diaper change?

To appreciate these understandings, imagine a scene: A father is changing the diaper of his 15-month-old son. The son is arching his back and protesting because at this very moment he does not want to comply with a diaper-change. He takes issue with his father's actions not only because they are at odds with his wishes but also because they are at odds with his idea of father. For most of his wee life father has met his needs and desires unconditionally and often pre-emptively – as if his desire and its solution co-occurred. Now, given his growing sense of agency, father seems not to co-operate. The inconsolable tantrum arises out of father's refusal to accede to his son's idea of him – someone who continues to do and be according to his

Selves and witnesses **253**

will. Inexplicably, his dad is no longer an extension of himself – and this will simply not do. The child's world is rendered topsy-turvy as he comes face-to-face with an incomprehensible other who defies the self-same other he has in mind.

Now, under these conditions (and at the risk of oversimplifying), the father might withdraw his presence and concede to his son's desire – in effect, agreeing to be "done unto" by his son, either giving up for now or finding some form of coercion or manipulation to succeed with the diaper change. Alternatively, father might override and negate his son's desire, essentially "doing unto" his son by, for example, forcibly strapping the son down while discounting his protests. In either of these cases, the child is potentially thrust, as co-participant, into *a doer/done-to dynamic – a struggle for power where only one can survive.* But there is yet a third choice: Dad could, recognising his son's angst, mirror it back in manner marked as not his own affect, all the while containing the child's frustration in a caring demeanour that radiates: "I see, acknowledge, and accept that you are frustrated. I witness how hard this is for you. *Even so,* I am fine with this. Your frightening feelings are not contagious. You can trust me to have your mind in mind and to make decisions in your interest. With care and recognition, I am changing your diaper, all the while loving you." In the first two instances, the son loses the opportunity to encounter, find, and know security and trust in a witnessing other for whom he is not responsible. In the last instance, the son encounters an other who is functionally distinct and recognising, yet never fully knowable. Importantly the marked and containing response works to defuse angst. The child need not, for his part, learn to manage by either assuming the complementary role of doer (where father copes by submission) or done-to (where father copes by dominating).

Importantly, in the denial of his father's or his own difference, where only one wins, the other is demoted to "fused" appendage: Either the son becomes extension of his father or the father becomes extension of his son. In fusion, no other is visible. There can be no co-recognition. One is invisible by virtue of non-existence except in terms of service to the other. Or, in the dominant determining position, there is no surviving–other in whose eyes to find oneself visible. Though the doer/done-to dynamic can and often does shift polarity, it eclipses mutuality's possibility. When the world is all about manipulation, domination, and regulation, then one is either served or in-service, done-to or doer. There is no such thing as being with another and not losing oneself. Where complementarity is the governing assumption of classrooms, schooling systems, and societies, inclusivity can be nothing but a mirage. In the absence of a discernible other there can be no witness, no one to validate one's own independent existence, no other with whom to feel oneself included.

How then does a person cope? "Not me, but you" expresses a frustrated refrain by which one dumps one's disavowed parts into the disturbingly unco-operative child or parent, student or teacher, progressivist or traditionalist, humanist or scientist, conservative or liberal, and so forth – as the world divides. These relational dynamics are not new. What may be new is the way in which systemic pathologies, bespeaking inchoate states of individual and collective being, increasingly (and digitally) converge into conflicting positions of near tectonic proportions with critical

254 Into practice

fault lines running through our most fundamental institutions, education being one. It is in this context especially, as per this book's title, that relational psychoanalysis, at the heart of teaching and learning, matters now.

Hurt people hurt other people

On August 5, 2012, "a white-supremacist gunman stormed into the Sikh Temple of Wisconsin and opened fire" (Purdon & Palleja, 2019). In search of an explanation for the murder of his father, Pardeep Singh Kaleka contacted Arno Michaelis, a former white supremacist and asked "Why did the shooting happen?" Arno's simple answer, "hurt people hurt other people" (Kaleka, cited in Purdon & Palleja, 2019), is at the centre of relational psychoanalytic understanding and my own passion for writing this book. And so, when Bowlby exclaims that there is such a thing as a bad mother and I add that there is such a thing as a bad teacher, I search for how we can be viable enough witnesses to help heal the hurt and limit its reach so that well-being visits itself forward instead.

In writing about authenticity, Thompson (2015) describes "two types of knowledgeable teachers: teachers who display an instructional ease reflective of the respectful connection they have with themselves, and teachers who demonstrate an instructional artificiality reflective of the disconnect they have with themselves and their students" (p. 604). I want to add a third group: those who bring a knack for "running" an effective classroom, with personalities adept at rallying positivity (often with the difficult-to-see-past, other-negating, charm of a sales-person) and who are particularly adept at leaving work at work. These are the teachers who parents refer to when they think of education as a cushy nine-to-three job with summers and holidays off. Finding it easier to let slide, out of worry or concern, those students less served by the system, such individuals are far less likely to suffer burnout in present schooling conditions. In other words, they can "service ration" (Gartner, 2017). In my observation, a technical approach to one's practice better serves the desires of these teachers, and perhaps this is the direction that we are going as we increasingly move the teacher out of the picture. It is this movement that I protest.

Now, it seems to me that Thompson's second kind of knowledgeable teacher is unlikely to survive long in teaching without some alternative means of managing students. Just as apparently self-made teachers bring a kind of instinctual know-how that eludes clear articulation, there are those who come to teaching rather "beside" themselves, as not present, in practice. What they lack, technique cannot renovate. Technique does not speak to the self. Where struggles of this type are more than beginning nerves, they continue; and if the student does graduate into teaching and they don't fall to either being present or exerting effective manipulation, their life there will likely be short-lived.

But there are those who do resort to manipulation. These are the sorts of unofficial strategies that I suspect we have all come across as students. They include the use of power, shame, and approval to compel student compliance generally, while leaving others to slip through the cracks. The following teacher comments, as a whole, suggest that such a dynamic is at play: "Jory, no one wants to be friends with

Selves and witnesses **255**

someone who is always complaining." "See everyone? Michael did well because he worked hard." "Don't even try those questions, they are for the smarter kids." "See what you did. Now the whole class will have to miss recess." "How many times have I told you?" "You couldn't have been listening or you'd have understood." "Nonsense, you know how to do this," said to a child who does not know. "If I didn't care about you, I wouldn't have scolded you." "What is wrong with you?"

The degree to which the coercive force of dominant–submissive paradigms work to keep students "in line" in schools is the degree to which schools affirm and reinstall the oppressive socio-political regimes that Foucault best outlined in *Discipline and Punish* (1975/1995). There is no scholarly discourse sufficient to address these issues and no legal cause to deter such a person from becoming a teacher. This is especially true when the strategies we observe are only questionably injurious and exist as the seeming sole recourse for making sure classrooms behave civilly enough so that students, who purportedly "want" to, can learn.

A meeting of minds: intersubjective recognition theory

Donnel Stern writes, "Patients listen to themselves as they imagine their analysts hear them and in this way create new narrative freedom" (2010, pp. xvi–xvii). Referencing Benjamin (1988, 1995) he adds,

> We need a witness if we are to grasp, know, and feel what we have experienced . . . Someone else, even if that someone is another part of ourselves, must know what we have gone through, must be able to feel it with us. We must be recognized by an other.
>
> *(2015, pp. 127–138)*

The witness within – the self, attentive to itself – models its attention after a history of external witnesses, from infancy forward, including teachers. The narrative freedom of which Stern speaks is the freedom to formulate unconscious experience into conscious awareness without foreclosure on important and troubling parts of one's story and oneself. Being *held* and *beheld* well in the heart and mind of a witnessing other, we learn trust in our own holding and beholding, which in turn frees constraints we might have on our stories.

It is in the containing countenance and acknowledging recognition of a reliable, responsive, yet psychically separate other that children and youth can come to experience themselves as autonomous agents and distinct centres of being who belong (Benjamin, 2018; Stern, 2015). A key relational insight on the paradox of human singular-plural-being (Nancy, 1996/2000) is just this: "*At the very moment of realizing our own independence, we are dependent on another to recognize it*" (Benjamin, 1988, p. 33). Put differently and to suggest a telling example in student-centred teaching paradigms gone awry, educators can do a disservice to learners if, in the name of student-centred learning, the educator either loses herself or seeks to manipulate, and so to lose, her students, in the process.

256 Into practice

The gift given and received in witnessing and feeling freely held and beheld in the understanding eyes of a responsible other is the gift of psychic being and belonging. When a teacher can bear witness in ways to loosen the classroom's intersubjective field from such constraints as feeling misunderstood or isolated, then an energy of shared curiosity can take hold and the surprise of a different kind of knowing becomes permissible.

It is common to think of the successful teacher as having inborn core traits that render authenticity and presence possible. Yet all of what we know – from neuroscience, child development, and psychoanalytic theory – suggests otherwise. The apparent second nature by which some individuals can readily learn to read a room, bring students on board, attune to individuals and situational needs, and respond in ways that appear to work – if not over the long-term, then certainly in the moment – begs the question: If not inborn traits, what alchemy of biological proclivities and worldly interactions have shaped a person thus? Where and how did they learn what they tacitly seem to know so well? In addressing these questions, relational psychoanalytic theory points helpfully in rethinking how we might proceed to help teachers and our understanding of teaching along.

Using an approach grounded in neither qualitative nor quantitative study, psychoanalytic discourses take unique advantage of the contextualised examples of storied vignettes to further the field and to teach (Stern, 2015). Vignettes serve to deepen analysts' appreciation of their role in the making and breaking of impasses that can either lock a relational field (Stern, 2010, 2015) in complementary doer/done-to positions (Benjamin, 2018), or open it (Stern, 2010, 2015) to co-recognition – the sense of being with the other in mutuality (Benjamin, 2018). They can do as much for teaching.

The practice of using vignettes is not unfamiliar to curriculum theory in education, however, it has not made substantive inroads with the powers that govern teaching and learning today, nor has it been used to bring the foregoing critical understandings into teaching.

Heeding what teachers worry about

Over the years, I have made it my habit to listening to the concerns of practicing and prospective teachers. For teacher candidates, it boils down to "making it" – as in, not being overrun by their students. Practicing teachers, on the other hand, struggle with the misfit between rigid programs of study and flexible inclusive classrooms with untenable ranges and distributions of student capacities.

I have dedicated this third section of the book to addressing these concerns, especially the challenges of diversity and inclusion. In this chapter, I am rounding out those considerations by going to the heart of what it might take to "make it" as a teacher. If making it in teaching is about being with classrooms so that participants can be well with themselves and others in learning, then it has everything to do with negotiating rupture and repair, growing through impasses, and profiting from moments of witnessing, co-recognition, mutuality, and thirdness. To be clear, with Benjamin, I am talking about intersubjectivity as defined "in terms of a relationship of mutual recognition – a relation in which each person experiences the other as a "like subject," another mind who can be "felt with," yet has a distinct, separate center of feeling and perception" (Benjamin, 2004, p. 5).

To these ends, in the spirit of the vignette, I offer snippets from my own stories in teaching – not to define any right way, produce the definitive account, or launch a detailed analysis. Rather, I simply lay forth my own lived experiences that they be windows for fecund imagining beyond where we are now. Donnel Stern writes,

> My vignette is written like a story; it is not verbatim clinical process. . . . The story format works well for my purpose, because interpersonal and relational analysts are convinced that our own experience is just as important as the patient's in understanding what happens in treatment.
>
> *(2015, p. 157)*

For the analyst, so too for the teacher.

Rupture and repair in the classroom: a vignette

In the capacities of student, teacher, professor, and researcher, I have come to know well the impasses of classroom life. Not unlike psychoanalytic descriptions (Benjamin, 2018; Stern, 2015), impasses feels as a deadening of the relational field – as if the collective is commiserating in a prolonged dissociative moment, biding time while going through the motions of schooling. Ruptures swell up from underneath such impasses and threaten the way things are. As such, their demand for attention is also a bid for repair. One way or the other, in subduing a rupture or submitting to it, a teacher participates in reinstating a doer/done-to (Benjamin, 2018) status quo of disconnection. However, in surrendering to what it signals, like the psychoanalyst (Benjamin, 2018), that teacher and the class might find their way to repair, reconnection, and renewed meaning.

For prospective teachers, forever-impasses, fraught with rupture and no hope of repair, are the things most feared. From their student years, they know it as marking the teacher as adversarial other in the doer/done-to complementarity. Twice, early in my career, I inherited classrooms, mid-year, from teachers whose students boasted having driven them "crazy." These recall my own silent sadness, as grade 11 student, at the spectacle of the near-daily lynching of our soft-spoken physics teacher who, one day in desperation, resorted to a loudspeaker to talk over a class refusing him voice. Years later, I learned of his suicide.

The strategies offered me for making it as a teacher spanned the usual gamut of unhelpful advice on managing classrooms – rationalised on practical, therapeutic, or emancipatory terms (see Taubman, 2012, on psychoanalysis in twentieth-century school reform). One could: point to "agreed" class rules and enforce them with greater verve and determination; remain stern, even avoiding smiling, for at least the first month; practice behaviour management – names and check marks on the board, graduated consequences, and reinforcement schedules; use humour – unofficially,

258 Into practice

with deprecation – to make exemplars of problem students; and, resort to "the talk," typically about good behaviour and some sort of "or else" accounting on near and far horizons. On these approaches students often took sides for and against what I would now call the normative functions of schools and the peers who dared violate those norms. That said, there has been a 40-year student trend to increasingly justify peer-collaboration in cheating a system seen as demanding it (Bibby, 2011). As if to commiserate with students who have substituted *succession* up the grades for a sense of *success* in learning, teachers can give up too – defaulting to the tried-and-true classroom movie and a martini once home.

Once I began teaching, though enjoying healthy collegial relations, I also found myself grappling with a disturbing underside of professional solidarity: a collective blind eye to the relational damage that could happen in classrooms. It seemed we could prioritise saving face for the adults at the expense of students. Like Bowlby's protestations "But, there *is* such a thing as a bad mother" (in Mitchell & Black, 1995/2016, p. 114, see Chapter 2) so too with teachers. We are, all of us, responsible – union or not – to reach those teachers (and their students) who struggle.

And so, from the get-go, I found teaching advice mostly disheartening and I vowed to have none of it. *I had a strong sense of what not to do, but little clarity on what else to put there.* I would have to feel my way along. I imagined teaching as "not manipulation of 'motivation' but a subjectively animated intellectual engagement with others over specific texts, a 'characterological enactment' (Anderson, 2006, p. 3) of passion in the public service" (Pinar, 2009, p. 11). An incorrigibly curious and passionate soul myself, I had thought the enticement, solace, and playful reverie of intellectual engagement would be enough. I was wrong.

In my second year, whilst teaching a biology class whose content I naïvely thought would carry the day, a particularly bold Grade 9 student kept finding a way to bring the class to near chaos. He had charisma, charm, and more power than I could ever wield. One day, in frustration, that "f" word, uncommon anywhere in my life, burst from my lips. Stunned by my own reaction, I directed him outside to wait by the classroom door for me and then I hushed the already hushed class. I stepped outside, still shaken, half expecting him to have left. He had not. Relieved, I looked at him and spoke the only thing I could: an apology – something about my poor reaction and a request as to how we might work together. I remember well his change in demeanour – surprised, it seemed, at my sincerity instead of chastisement. This was the incident that marked a shift in the entire classroom dynamic that year. I believe it can be most insightfully understood in relational psychoanalytic terms: I somehow managed to neither lose myself nor my student, to have his mind-in-mind and to return to the care of us and the classroom collective. In short, I responded to the rupture with the humbling realisation that my fascination with biology was simply not that contagious. I would do better to think and feel more with my students.

Stern (2010) reminds us that "much of relatedness is on 'automatic pilot,' . . . [I]t is this automaticity that is responsible for a large portion of what we never perceive" (p. 11). I have worked to shift my automatic pilot. In time, when the classroom mood

Selves and witnesses **259**

drifted to an unproductive state, instead of persisting with my agenda, there emerged in me a different reaction. I remember well when I finally could hear the exasperation in my own voice, heightened in urgency, pitch, and volume – pushing through. It was in such budding self-awareness that I could catch myself and, noticing for the first time, say as much to myself as to the students, "Wait. Something is wrong. How are you doing?" These critical moments grew into lessons in habits changing and the breaking of impasses – specifically, of noticing my own absence, and returning to the possibility of holding my students' minds in mind. I was learning that it did little good to analyse them, report about them, manage them, and do onto them. I needed to be *with* them, to find a way to disentangle myself from a script that could lock us in a frozen complementarity, students and teacher, feeling the other doing this or that to them to make matters worse. Importantly, and not unlike my conversation in the hall with the "disruptive" student, *the impasse broke not because of submission, but rather through surrender to the relational field* (Benjamin, 2018). I had evolved my practice in the direction of teaching and learning relationally. *I was neither student-centred nor me- or content-centred. I was us-centred and the curriculum represented the cultural transitional object we shared together. The difference was and is powerful.*

For witnessing

Donnel Stern reminds us that

> Our best choices and decisions about how to speak about ourselves and one another – our most effective self-reflections – are not under our control. They . . . have their own life. Yet we know we can encourage them. We can do our best to occupy the kind of existence in which spontaneous, generative understanding becomes most likely. . . . the opportunity to lead examined lives.
>
> *(1997/2003, p. 25)*

His words, "We need a witness to become a self" (2010, p. xvi), are at the centre of what I imagine for teaching. If this relational maxim is true, and assuming that such a witness must indeed also be a self, then we can say that the witness needed a witness, who needed a witness, and so on, back and back. Granting that our most critical witnesses are the significant others of our early years, it is also true that teachers – as secondary attachment figures and cultural mediators for some 12-plus years – surely count among the most critical witnessing influences, both directly and indirectly, for each generation of children.

> To state an obvious fact in behavioral, phenomenological, and dynamic terms: the more secure a person is regarding his own acceptability, the more certain his sense of who he is, and the more safely internalized his system of values – the more self-confidently and effectively will he be able to offer his love without undue fear of rejection and humiliation.
>
> *(Heinz Kohut, 1971/2009, pp. 297–298)*

260 Into practice

We cannot assume that all who become teachers, by virtue of being adults, have themselves had a goodly measure of witnessing presence, enough to visit such a gift forward. Degrees of insecurity or security, in oneself and with others, are not inborn proclivities. They are qualities first made possible or foreclosed in the primary contexts of attachment relations (Daniel Stern, 1985/2000). Just as "feeling states are contagious" so too are degrees of anxiety (Sullivan, in Mitchell & Black, 1995/2000, p. 67) and ultimately, security and insecurity – especially from caregiver to child and teacher to student. In these terms, *authenticity* relates to security insofar as it expresses a capacity of non-fragmented being – where interiority is sufficiently in conversation with exteriority so as to permit ease and trust in being oneself. In teaching, the tacit ability to be in synchrony with a classroom – to assume a *presence* that is attuned and *"with it"* – evinces security as *trustworthiness* visited forward. Thus, the issue of the teaching self, just as that of the parenting self, becomes also a transgenerational one.

The imperative "teacher know your story" comes in the context of an invitation to recognise that we do not, to live humbly in that realisation, and to do our best to lead examined lives, as per Donnel Stern (earlier). It is an appeal to seek the other within, to experience the co-implication of selves, and perchance to find grace that can be directed, as much inward as outward. It behooves us, especially who work with teachers, to dedicate concerted attention to our own selfhoods, and neither in any prescriptive way, nor engaging a mindless exercise of reflection absent insightful provocation. Instead, taking a page or two from relational psychoanalytic theory, we might make some of these ideas our own. Perhaps by catching ourselves locked in doer/done-to complementarities with our students, we can find our way to: interrogating our assumptions and asking why; reconsidering the stories that storied us; and finding, refining, and redefining ourselves, what we know, and what we think we know – that we might emerge more quietly present as witnessing pedagogues visiting that presence to the learners in our care.

Toward jargon-free relational insights for teachers

In our preoccupation with knowledge mobilisation as the hoped-for solution to human difficult, a critical aspect of teacher preparation goes under-considered, if considered at all: the modelling role of the teachers of teachers. If one has never experienced it on a receiving end, it is difficult to imagine, from the perspective of an education student, how to be *with* one's class or school in the ways in which I have been describing. Senge, Scharmer, Jaworski, and Flowers in their book on *Presence* tell how they began to appreciate it "as deep listening, of being open beyond one's preconceptions. . . . of letting go of old identities. . . . [and] as leading to a state of 'letting come'" (2004, p. 11). This is what I mean. From the receiving side of another's presence, or lack thereof, what Butler writes captures the learner's predicament.

If I have no "you" to address, then I have lost "myself". . . . [O]ne can tell an autobiography only to an other, and one can reference an "I" only in relation to a "you": without the "you," my own story becomes impossible.

(2005, p. 91)

To give a practical sense of how, at a minimum, particular kinds of psychoanalytic understandings might find a way into our work with prospective teachers, I offer edited excerpts from my own efforts. Written between the lines of this work are my conscious intentions at enacting that presence, to – in the words of Butler – be a "you" who made possible the "narratisable" student-"I," even as I provoked these students, that they might carry witnessing forward.

In this spirit, I offer three of many individualised responses sent to students. On this occasion, just two months into their teacher education program, I was giving feedback on papers connecting their first practicum experience with course readings. I was striving for jargon-free language, undergirded by relational understandings, to prompt student attention to (among other things) the pervasive cultural fiction that, through force of will, with proper technique and motivation, anyone can and should exercise conscious self-control to successfully subdue and/or negate disruptive and undesirable affects bubbling up. In the following, I have replaced students' names with pseudonyms.

Dear Josée

We can think of a positive attitude as an expression of healthy coherent being – a symptom really. On the other hand, where there is less emotional health we see more fragmented being. In fragmentation, a person's sense of well-being depends upon not knowing there are any denied aspects of self. In such individuals, fragmentation . . . can show up to others as baffling . . . contradiction. . . . We see it when someone clearly looks angry but believes and insists they are not. . . .

When we distract a child from their emotions or coach them to put on a brave and cheerful face, as the right thing to do . . . this can work against emotional wellness. . . . [F]or children to develop a sense of security and trust in themselves and their world, to risk themselves in exploring something perplexing, they need to first know their feelings are valid (even if those feelings seem misplaced to the teacher) and that a separate grown up can have their mind in mind. . . . [T]he distraction might teach the child that the best way to cope is to focus on ignoring those things that make her uncomfortable. This is like teaching people to refuse to admit aspects of themselves to themselves. Here then is both the hidden site and the fuel for bias and prejudice. . . . It's the "stiff upper lip" of a person keeping themselves "in line" by monitoring themselves and decrying anyone else who fails to comply with the rules of a world that demands such self-censorship – all in the name of civility.

And this brings me to connect the first part of your essay with the second. If we are going to get to Truth and Reconciliation, then I hope we do not hold children to a

262 Into practice

positive attitude "anytime . . . [they are feeling] upset or frustrated" (p. 2). I hope that we instead support them — not by running away from discomfort but by recognising it as legitimate and then "holding" them, metaphorically, until they are well. To be strong together is to bend with the wind, not to resist it or pretend it is not blowing.

You are right Josée about the need for Aboriginal learning leaders and greater understanding of shared histories. . . . I am thinking of your Great Aunt especially and smiling. There is such a proud legacy in her and others for you to take up.

Hello Marco

Ah, yes to knowing oneself! But not any kind of self-reflection will do. While a tendency to avoidance when it comes to emotions can restrict reflection to questions of what to do next, the tendency to preoccupation with the self can make for circular reflection mired in emotions that lead nowhere. What to do? Let's talk in class.

You speak of aligning core values with those of the school. Yes, that can be critical. This does not however need to imply that one should change one's values in order to fit those of the school. Rather, in a healthy school community (as in a healthy mind) there is acceptance of all the parts. It's in the humanness — in the imperfections we find in ourselves and that we don't hide away — that we learn to better hold ourselves and each other well. And when we work in a place where we can do that, then it's the students who benefit most.

Yue

Oh, but I would love to communicate to the world this line of yours: "The reality is much deeper than what anyone thinks or sees." Yes! You also wrote, "To be an effective teacher, you must put your true identity into your work". . . . I wonder what a singular "true" identity would mean for a person. . . . perhaps a healthy enough integration across all the self-states that a person feels. If there isn't such a coherence to refer to, then being genuine (as in "true" to it) might just not be in the cards. . . . Maybe what you are talking about has to do with personal integration that comes with self-acceptance — the things we often recognise as integrity and presence. . . . [T]he parts of oneself from which a person disconnects arise from a kind of dissociation where a person just refuses to "go there," to even consider a feeling or a thought. Here is yet another reason to interrogate our own histories for the roots of our strongest emotional reactions and our dearest convictions. These reactions and convictions are valuable clues to the very things in ourselves against which we are defending, signatures of lessons learned earlier from situations that may have gone awry.

Following anxieties

Harry Stack Sullivan's words echo behind the foregoing excerpts. He writes,

> Each of us moves through life exquisitely sensitive to rising anxiety, developing complex, extremely rapid, covert security operations to steer us from

Selves and witnesses **263**

points of anxiety back to familiar footing. . . . [T]o increase awareness of the[se] operations . . . [one asks] questions and encourag[es] self-reflection, so that crucial, rapid sequences can be observed, understood, and, through understanding, gradually altered.

(in Mitchell & Black, 1995/2000, p. 71)

To broach the kinds of worries foremost in our future teacher's minds, we do not need to wait until they find themselves stalemated in the throes of a teaching impasse. We can probe their imagination first to create and then to consider instances where such impasses might occur. As per variation theory (Chapter 12), in conjunction with students' questions and concerns, we can engage them in activities meant to expand their relational example-space as they prepare for the field.

The following draws from an activity in which I engage students with example scenarios as discussion points. I compose these scenarios after the students' expressed questions and concerns. As such, they already broach the transitional – at once imaginings in the mind and situations in the "real" world. In my practice, future teachers have voiced apprehension most about the likes of: managing student emotions in ways that do not cause harm but that allow for productivity; protecting children from a sense of failing while encouraging them to risk; fear of student suicide, depression, and tragedy in students' lives and how to help; working with dissatisfied and overly criticising parents; convincing students that you like them, yet holding them to academic account; and coping with power, gender, and identity issues.

In brief, here is one excerpted and abbreviated example for exploring a scenario to begin to address teacher disquiet.

> *For the following scenario, imagine that you are the teacher. Then consider the questions that follow. Silently compose, in writing, any responses that come to mind. Once you have had a chance to quietly explore your own thoughts, we will follow-up with paired and group discussion.*
>
> *Scenario: You are a grade 6 teacher. It's the end of September and already you've had 3 conversations with Shaya's mom about how Shaya is doing. Shaya is a quiet attentive diligent student of average ability. She often checks with you to see if she is doing things properly. If she makes a mistake she is very hard on herself. She worries when she doesn't know exactly what is expected of her. Any time work goes home, she does it with her mom and returns to school very proud of their accomplishments. Shaya's mom has criticised your open-ended activities and insists that you send homework with clear instructions for her daughter.*
>
> *Reflection questions: Imagining this scenario, fill in the missing bits to complete the picture. What is your gut reaction? What do you want to do? What might you actually do? Put yourself in the shoes of Shaya's mom. What do you think might be motivating her actions? Hypothesise on the connection between her beliefs, underlying emotions, and past experiences. Hypothesise on the connection between your beliefs, underlying emotions, and past experiences in responding as you have. Have you run into anything like this before? In what way?*

264 Into practice

After several of these priming exercises and follow-up discussions, I end the class by having students generate their own narratives but with various endings – one of the points being that there are no definitive answers. I then can gather their submissions and harvest a deepening appreciation of where we might go next, what theoretical understandings might be pertinent, what histories they bring, and how we can lean on both the knowing in the classroom space and various scholarly works to better imagine self-negotiations in the anticipation of teaching challenges.

Mutuality and relational asymmetry

Benjamin writes that

> Psychoanalysis must be based on understanding the process of development by which human beings become more capable of mutuality, more able to recognize the other. This development ideally is associated with more vitality, agency and ability to balance dependency with independence.
>
> *(2018, p. 73)*

For these same reasons, schooling, too, "must be based on understanding the process of development by which human beings become more capable of mutuality."

In his 1996 book, *A Meeting of Minds: Mutuality in Psychoanalysis*, Aron detailed the relational approach and its implications. His work marked the growing convergence of contemporary psychoanalytic thought with emerging consensus across research fields on the criticality of interpersonal relations in infant and child development. Aron identified mutuality – an interaction of "reciprocation, community, and unity through interchange" – as "most central and unique" (p. x) in the relational turn. In this turn, the relevance of psychoanalytic understandings for inclusive teaching grew exponentially.

For presence: a particular kind of disillusionment

Aron's mutuality recalls primary caregiver – infant relationships and the Winnicottean notion of the good enough mother. At the hub of mutuality in parenting and therapeutic action (and, I contend, in teaching), Aron locates an *asymmetry of responsibility: It falls to the caregiver, therapist, and teacher to create the space where minds might meet.* Mutuality with asymmetrical responsibility thus steps beyond the unconditional caregiving acts of early infancy, but it is not yet adult mutuality.

In the mutuality of adult–child relating, the caregiver bears the responsibility of disillusionment. Disillusionment names the destruction of the child's illusion that his mental impressions of the people he knows (his internal-objects) are true representations of those people – that, in a sense, she fully determines them. The adult's insistence of an alternative presence, different from the one in the child's mind, presses disillusionment. The destruction of the illusion of the other (as object in mind) opens the possibility of meeting a subject in the world, and the gift of a life not lived in solitude.

Whereas in early life, the responsible-one's consistency supported the child's construing, the later caregiver introduces and is part of the disillusioning world with which the child must contend and, in whose encounter, she might find reason for imagining anew. The tension between our illusory creations and their disillusioning counterparts stretches us. Even so, these are delicate matters. Milner, an analyst and a Montessori-trained teacher (1987, Introduction), cautions us to remember to disillusion mercifully (1956/1987).

Problematising Western notions of care

The terms relational asymmetry and mutuality already circulate in educational discourses, but with decidedly different meanings – problematically so. Introduced by Nel Noddings in her "Ethics of Care," relational asymmetry refers to the positioning of responsibilities in caring relationships in education between the "one cared for" and the "caring one" (2005). In Noddings's conceiving, relational asymmetry persists in mature relating with the *alternating* of "carer/cared-for" positions (2005, p. 17) – a kind of flipping of turn taking. This is what Noddings calls mutuality. But "care" is a signifier-chameleon entangled in Western Christian notions of martyrdom and lending itself to confusions of co-dependency, servitude, and self-sacrifice. As such, the purported ideal of carer/cared-for relationships brushes dangerously close to advocating a special case of "doer/done-to" enactments where the carer is the "good" doer and the cared-for is the should-be-grateful one done-to.

From a psychoanalytic perspective, alternating carer/cared-for responsibilities suggests a complementarity at play – the very obverse of mutuality. Complementarity consists of flipping between *subject–doer* and *object–done-to* positions, whereas mutuality describes *two subjects being with* each other in *co-recognition* – a kind of reciprocal giving of audience, and an unsustainable condition that must ebb and flow with the rhythms of rupture and repair, of subject-object and subject-subject relating.

Thirdness, surrender, and "being with"

Aron addresses the paradox of mutuality and asymmetry at the heart of relational understanding (Aron, 1996). Without mutuality, there is no meeting of minds. Yet without the separating difference of autonomy, mutuality degenerates into merger and there are no separate minds to meet (Aron, 1996, pp. x–xi) – and surely none to bear witness.

As we have seen, Benjamin (2018) expands upon mutuality, exploring its loss and recovery in terms of the rupture and repair of co-recognition. Co-recognition names subject-to-subject encounters of the *I–Thou* kind (Buber, 1923/1970). Its loss, in rupture, reduces a dyad into complementary doer/done-to, submissive/dominant relating – as if caught in a paradox of co-dependence that seeks merged *oneness*

266 Into practice

to erase the other, but enacts singular self-insistences from either side of incommensurable *twoness*. Elaborating on *thirdness*, Benjamin describes a tension that calls for
surrender (as per Ghent, 1990), not submission, on the part of the responsible one.
Surrender implies a shift to thirdness (see foregoing vignette) whereas submission of
either party reinstates doer/done-to complementarity.

To bear witness well is to take responsibility in surrendering to thirdness without losing oneself. It is to legitimately foster another's trust that they are being
genuinely and generously heard. When the threat of shame or dread of alternative
self-understandings can be safely entrusted to a caring resilient–enough other, who
returns it to us with grace, then freedom opens to dare different tales about the self
and the world. As such, our "worth" and "goodness," as seen through our own eyes,
derive from being seen well and accepted through the eyes of others in whose witnessing we can trust. It does not arise out of concerted efforts to expunge all things
"bad" in ourselves: That is a path to denial and dissociation.

Yet I walk elementary school halls adorned with displays admonishing children
to exemplify this or that core virtue – and to exercise self-control and prove themselves on these terms, as if to say: "You will not be seen well, if you fail at these
things." And I understand these would-be achievers as potential Type As at risk of
their own anxieties and preoccupations while distancing themselves as best they can
from those lesser others, miles back, stumbling in the dust, outcasts even unto themselves. We become our goodness by feeling witnessed in our wholeness and still
being found worthy. We learn it through experiences of good enough attunement,
in the presence of others who are their "own persons," and who bring us along
into our own agency, resonating with theirs. And we learn to be and feel good by
recognising others as centres of their own being and not the projection of what we
imagine them to be.

What now? School people, their stories, and
the reach of curriculum studies

William Pinar emphasises that

> A certain solitude . . . is a prerequisite for that "complicated conversation"
> with oneself without which one disappears onto the social surface, into the
> maelstrom that is the public world. Without a private life, without an ongo-
> ing project of autobiographical understanding, one's intellectual "practice"
> too often tends toward the miming of what is fashionable or profitable.
>
> *(2004, pp. 22–23)*

The 1970s reconceptualist movement that redefined curriculum studies as "the
interdisciplinary study of educational experience" (Pinar, 2004, p. 2) distinguished
itself from two other disciplinary clusters: one whose origins derived from and continued in affiliation with the social sciences, and a second preoccupied with decid-
ing which citizen competencies ought to be learned in school and how learners,

teachers and schools should be managed (Pinar, 1978, pp. 206–208). The former cluster sought to smooth out the nicks in the system – essentially how to understand, treat, and remediate symptoms that arose. The latter cluster focused on the delivery of content and management of schooling personnel who would, in turn, generate productive citizens.

We have seen how, in contradistinction, and from its inception as an intellectual phenomenon sympathetic to phenomenology and critical theory, the reconceptualist movement concerned itself with the historico-political contexts of societies and, within societies, the shaping of education and the role of schools. In its commitment to theory development as part of a comprehensive critique of social structures, it refused to "plug into" the extant social order and it consciously abandoned the "technician's mentality" (Pinar, 1978, pp. 210–211). It follows that reconceptualist considerations have spoken less directly to "school people" (Pinar, 1978, p. 210), having, in its beginning moments, conceded that ground to the school-subject specialists and those experts in organisational leadership, and their faith in the social sciences.

Meanwhile, they are curriculum theorists who have been most concerned with questions germane to this chapter – questions of self-knowledge in historical and cultural contexts, the stories we tell, and the ways we come to know ourselves and others. The call to know one's story aligns with curriculum studies in: the method of *currere* (Pinar, 1975) as "a reflexive cycle in which thought bends back upon itself and thus recovers its volition" (Grumet, 1976/2006, pp. 130–131), *autobiography* as considerations in the "architecture of self" (Pinar, 1985/1994), *autoethnography* as "a rewriting of the self and the social" (Reed-Danahay in Hughes, 2008, p. 77), *conscientisation* as "learning to perceive social, political, and economic contradictions, and to take action against the oppressive elements of reality" (Freire, 1970/2000, p. 35), *participatory action research* as that which "values knowledge produced from lived experience as equal to that produced in the academy" (Torre, 2014, p. 1), and *reflective practice and narrative inquiry* (e.g., Hayler & Moriarty, eds., 2017).

Curriculum studies has been a critical force in bringing democratic principles and social justice practices into public consciousness and education. However, despite foundational work at seeding difference into the socio-cultural fodder of schooling, it has, as yet, been relatively unsuccessful in changing the extant structure of educational systems – a tragedy expounded upon as the "nightmare of the present" by Pinar himself (2004, Part I). Indeed, whereas curriculum studies now holds an established place in most graduate programs in education, its principles too often live as ideological footnotes in undergraduate programs. In these programs, it has been my experience that mindful intentions too quickly reduce to politically correct rhetoric, spoken with emphatic force to the next generation of teachers as means to justify an implicit mandate: that these "school people" must somehow compensate for an extant social order not about to change any time soon.

And so, for all these reasons, I close by turning from theory to further suggest how we might do differently. In the spirit of the previous chapter, I seek here to *broaden the example space*. But before I do, let me emphasise my own reticence: In the reach for quick solutions, examples can be too often taken up and translated

268 Into practice

into new prescriptive categories for the technical treatment of teachers and students. In the same spirit with which relational psychoanalysis advances itself, this is not my intention. What I hope is to further a conversation about the self and to do it in a way imaginable for "school people" and for those who work with such people.

Beyond doer and done-to

In hopeful conceiving and with all the naïveté of my own unavoidable self-opacity, I imagine prospective teachers in programs of education on quests into aspects of self- and other-understanding and the conundrum of singular-plural-being. Would-be educators would benefit from provocations to consider their favoured narratives and what lies underneath and beyond them. Per Bialystok and Kukar, "when one's strongest convictions and experiences are called into question by the demands of difference, something has to give" (2018, p. 32). And indeed, this is the place of self-exploration. It "takes place within the messiness of comforts and tensions, alignments and misalignments, stabilities and uncertainties that come with real life" (Thompson, 2015, pp. 614–615)

I fathom undergraduates who, having brought their subjectivity into conversation with scholarly works, enter teaching practice with at least a working appreciation of the historical and social construction of persons. I conceive such undertakings as having gone hand-in-hand with the exploration of relational constructs that obtain in the classroom space and the development of a rudimentary familiarity with the language and concepts of relational psychoanalysis.

Categories, as the unavoidable inheritance of language and social meaning, would also figure centrally – especially in terms of the categories we don and the false recognition they promise "in which uniqueness . . . disappears. . . . [and t]he comfort of similarity wins out over the relational status of distinction" (Cavarero, 1997/2000, p. 91). We would pause long enough to consider how terms like "gifted," "gay," "kinesthetic learner," and "First Nations," when tossed into a rhetoric of inclusion, can effect a kind of blind-eyed seeing that reduces persons to homogenised designations. And we would work to find ways for doing better.

I hope for our own presence with teacher-candidates, that we witness them well in all their manifold riches and peculiarities. I wish for a capacity to draw on the interactive wisdom of the classroom collective to powerfully assist that work. And just as psychoanalysis proceeds through the slippages, inconsistencies, and felt transferences of the therapeutic encounter, so too might our work profit from attentions to the uncanny. In thus imagining and for the purposes of taking awkward steps forward, I return again to the narrative to fathom how such work might begin.

Autobiography approached sideways

Of the stories that have shaped us, many forgotten, most never known, Maturana (with Verden-Zöller) writes

Selves and witnesses **269**

> Nothing that we live is trivial, regardless of whether we are conscious or not. . . . Parents know that their children develop in one way or another according to the emotioning that they live, regardless of whether what they live is real or virtual, true or false. . . . Whatever our children do, or whatever happens to and through them, will depend on the psychic existence that they lead with us during their growth.
>
> *(2008, pp. 212–213)*

Teacher know your story is an invocation to inquire into the shaping of selves and to begin to appreciate how in the uniqueness of one's story are the elements of everyone's story and in everyone's story are the elements of one's own. With Benjamin, I advocate "the argument for finding oneself by going out into the not-self and returning to a now different and altered self (marked by the alterity it has encountered) points toward the underlying movement of intersubjectivity" (2018, p. 12).

Questions the likes of, "What brought you here? How many stories lead you to now? How far back does your story begin? How far forward? And how does it look from outside yourself?" can prompt explorations in perspective-taking and perspective-making.

In one variation, I begin a course by asking students to consider the life forces, motivations, people, and events that may have moved them to arrive at this place, in this time, and then, to tell a story about how they got here. After they have written enough to feel satisfied, I repeat the question, this time asking them to tell a different tale to the same outcome. The point is to press the example space of the possible. For some groups, I have taken the exercise to a third repetition. I collect these narratives and pour over them to learn my students and to prepare our next convening.

Our ensuing lesson begins with the return of their narratives, with post-it notes affixed offering all manner of invitations to converse. Sitting in the round, I use these to begin an improvised script inspired by the emergent themes of life-writings in the room. I might say, for example, "Several of you spoke of wanting to make a difference. Can we talk about that? Those of you who entertained this topic, you'll see that I've added comment. Might you share something from what you wrote or thought?" In this way, I open a space whereby all members feel themselves invited to contribute, but with the freedom to choose. As differences and inter-sectionalities meet along lines of interest and concern, these encounters take on meaning and direction, setting a tone of community and inclusivity that invites ever-deepening considerations throughout the term.

In these kinds of exercises, students have opportunity to come to their story sideways, through its echo and reverberation in the stories that others give, and then to think multiple stories together. For example, in response to: "What brought you to teaching?" and, "Why do you want to be a teacher?" students' themed responses might congeal into such oft-*un*questioned givens as: "I want to be like (or not like) this teacher; I have always enjoyed children; and I love learning." Students rarely will have considered, why, and so I ask – gently working at the blurring and the creative revisioning of each "so-called autobiographical truth" (Saul, 2006, p. 5).

270 Into practice

In other instances, I might have students call up a remembered scene and then work with others at writing the story of that scene through the eyes of different participants. Such practices invoke the notion of the *biotext* – a participatory genre of life writing that seeks "to displace the idea of a single, unified . . . autobiographical subject" (Saul, 2006, p. 4). Despite a preference for a single narrative and an after-the-fact construal of continuity, students discover a rich reservoir of raw unworded, unformulated experience. They begin to rethink the expectation of a single definitive tale in favour of a more hermeneutically open one with its multiple, asynchronous, micro-storied snippets, that overlap, interact, and are not-done-yet.

To write one's story is to seek a tale of presence through a fusion of horizons (Gadamer, 1975/2004) of variably conceivable pasts that project into untold futures. Assuming a culturally and linguistically orchestrated and genetically predisposed dance of unfolding, how then might the teacher-learner interaction create spaces for possibility in self-narration? In tentative answer, I have supposed the following: Insert yourself into what might feel strange. Follow discomfort. Follow fractures. Entertain "as if." Listen for intuition, but resist following with blind faith, instead use intuition to explore "what if" and "maybe." Pay attention to the body's messages. Resist foreclosing judgement. Bear witness. Stay humble.

Transference–countertransference

Donnel Stern describes the interpersonal field as including "the influences on each participant of the entire nexus of affects, motives and intentions, thoughts, proto-thoughts, meaningful behaviors, metaphors, and phantasies that come into being when two people are involved with one another" (2015, p. 111). How much more rife with possibility is such a field when it is composed of a classroom of participants!

In relational psychoanalytic terms, freedom in an interpersonal field refers to the latitude that participants "have to relate to one another without the kinds of constraints introduced by unconscious defensive purposes" (Stern, 2015, p. 111). Transference–countertransference enactments are forms of relating rife with unconscious defences that recall the past to hijack the present, importantly without our realising it. In transference, we attribute our feelings to actions done to us in the now, but the impasses and ruptures we experience bespeak the affective strength of a past transferred into the present and calling out a particular countertransference in the other (Stern, 2015; Milner, 1956/1987).

Put differently, in transference, a person relates to someone now as though they were proxy for some significant past. The transference enactment presses different actors into old scripts so as to evoke a countertransference. In countertransference, one finds oneself caught responding, as if "done to" by the other, and at pains to decipher what is going on. As such, for the analyst, the conundrum of the felt countertransference is shot through with clues to be explored for understanding the original scene that the analysand is re-enacting. Acknowledging that therapeutic action is not the purview (nor should it be) of the teacher, understanding transference – countertransference enactments in teacher – student relating can be invaluable.

Transference–countertransference enactments (in schooling relations as in therapeutic ones) replicate and reinforce prior modes of relating that, in turn, severely constrain the present relational field and potentially jeopardise future interactions. At the extreme, Stern has described such enactments as "'the interpersonalization of dissociation'. . . a rigidity in the field, an impasse or 'deadlock', a single-mindedness that allows no alternatives" (2015, pp. 111–112). In dissociative enactments participants are deadlocked in a single-mindedness of "not me" and "it's *you*." In the defensive mode of adamantly denying parts of self in order to preserve self-identity, there can be no recognition. Thus, the cost of jettisoning aspects of self from awareness is a constriction of the relational field that prevents any free and spontaneous formulation of unconscious experience.

In their daily work, teachers (as well as analysts) navigate many such day-to-day constrictions. In the example that follows, I recount how my reading of a student message, as transference-provocation, triggered my own "not me" experiences and put a stranglehold on my capacity for presence and bearing witness. I believe that the exploration of such examples with future teachers can help deepen their understanding of and appreciation for the relevance of psychoanalytic thought in teaching. This is especially true as they learn to recognise and search their own dissociative moments for clues that deepen understanding of their own stories and those of their students.

The incident happened during a time when I was lab co-ordinator, supporting a new young hire as lecturer, in a course for some 550 education undergraduates in learning theory – my area of expertise and one peripheral to the instructor's expertise in performance-based assessment. For what seemed (to me) political reasons, and owing in part to the marginalisation of psychoanalytic theory in education, I had felt myself respectfully relegated to behind-the-scenes support and guest lecturer. My official role was to design engaging laboratory activities for bringing lecture material into practical classroom life, provide the instructor team with the lessons and related resources to ensure sufficient uniformity across sections, bring the team up to speed on the content of the lectures, and coach them on the principles and intentions undergirding each lesson. Myself a curriculum theorist, this meant liaising with the instructor on course design and content while overseeing 16 sections of weekly 50-minute labs taught by a notable team of mostly doctoral candidates in school and applied psychology. While bringing valuable expertise in the clinical diagnosis and treatment of students with special needs, the team had little relevant school-teaching experience and, to my surprise, seemingly less knowledge about psycho-neurobiology, attachment theory, affective neuroscience, intersubjective theories, embodied cognition, and the unconscious – nonconscious mind.

After the second set of course labs, I received this message, forwarded to me from a graduate assistant:

> *Our lab today was very chaotic at the end of class, it ran over time and most people began to pack up at 10:50 (the scheduled end time) as many of us have class immediately following our lab across campus. During this muddle, our lab instructor continued*

272 Into practice

> *to speak about information that she previously mentioned would be on the midterm, and the lab co-ordinator then also chimed in about flagging something. As it was nearly impossible to ascertain what was said, I was wondering if the lab co-ordinator or the instructor could please touch on this tomorrow during lecture. Additionally, it would be greatly appreciated if our labs could end on time. Thank you.*

My feeling reaction was coloured by the following back story: As per the team's agreed protocol, I had been circulating to as many sections as possible to collaborate with instructors, infuse teaching contexts into conversations, and serve as a medium of course connectivity. In the spirit of dialogue, I would on rare occasion interject supportive commentary for these purposes. Given that I was also the person "in charge," I was aware and concerned with the awkwardness of my position and strived to communicate in a spirit of collegiality and support. In the lab in question, I had arrived to the classroom 12 minutes before its end hoping to interject a small detail that had emerged elsewhere and to which the instructor was not yet privy. However, she was engrossed in a narrative and no opening was forthcoming. This left me to either forego comment or "steal" a minute at the end of class. I chose the latter, and immediately set about to worry for having done so.

The email arrived at close to midnight. Reading it through my own personal frustrations and insecurities, I was immediately flooded with emotion congealing into barely suppressible anger: "What? The time had not eluded me, I noticed all too well the students packing up early and the instructor's persistence in talking through the disruption. Why had this student not approached me personally on our walked back to the education building? Was I not approachable? Did she not realise that her concern with petty details paled to the value of considerations on offer for teaching? How dare she pen a message with the trappings of civility and self-righteousness and in condescension invoke the words "chaotic," "muddled," and the one who "chimed in" to describe the situation. Underneath my lividness, fuelling it, I grieved that her complaint bore truths. Of course, I knew that she was not the projection of my own thoughts, her priorities not mine; but I could not force my heart to know better.

These thoughts recount my strongly felt emotional countertransference. In the throes of my indignation, I could not entertain anything but the idea that I was being unjustly "done to." I rallied resentment, silently protesting the trivialising of my heart's efforts putting in countless hours to be the good person. The truth of the matter is that I may well have lost track of time – because I was so urgently wanting things to be perfect, because I wanted to be the good caring one, and because I had counted too much on my passion (dangerously close to insensitive tactlessness) to carry the day. So, there I was, at midnight, facing the self I could not be, the self-part I most hated to be: insensitive and tactless.

The force of this dissociative "not me" came not from this moment, but from a terrified past it called out in me. The battle in me, waged daily, that I had been winning, had surfaced again. I could not be like my horrific abusive family of origin. I fought against the residue in me of any hint of the insensitivity and tactlessness that characterised that family and against which, my whole life, I had fashioned myself not to be. Alone, in this dissociative state, I could hardly be authentic, present, or "with" myself, so I surely could not be that *for* an other. I was stalemated. It did not help that I could argue with myself that this student likewise had her own life stories and her own hurt and fear moving her accusatory message. It would have been a struggle for me to formulate an appropriate witnessing response. Indeed, had we not had the distance of email, I can just imagine how my strong countertransference would have frozen me into a feigned calmness as false as her civility. We would have found ourselves unsatisfactorily locked in an immutable unproductive field.

Instead, the course instructor, having been copied on the message, had offered to respond on my behalf. In relief, I accepted. My colleague's response diffused the situation, bore witness and "contained" the student's underlying fears, those things that most wanted attention. She accomplished these things by a simple thank you for the feedback and suggestions, a reiteration of the intent of the labs, and the promise of a practice midterm to assuage angst over missed material. In the process, she sidestepped the "doer/done-to" complementarity (Benjamin, 2018) invited by the transference and legitimised the student's concerns by stating that "ending our labs on time will be a goal for us." She demonstrated an attuned sensibility to the student's distress by agreeing that the room location was not ideal, and described actions taken with the undergraduate office in recognition of the problem. Finally, neither preoccupied nor dismissive, after down-regulating the student's angst, she held her ground as a separate, independent presence, available to the student, by inviting her to a conversation before or after lecture or to join her in a meeting "outside regularly scheduled office hours." It is worth reiterating Marion Milner (1956/1987):

> Good teachers understand . . . that their task is to help the children with their hate, help them to accept it, recognize it, not shut it away so that it becomes a hidden Satan; which means that the teachers have come to terms with their own hate, so that, although disillusioners, they are also merciful.
>
> *(p. 188)*

The refusal to open oneself to the pain of one's disavowed parts is a refusal to learn, regardless if one is the teacher or the student. Over time, it conditions the self-imposed solution of solitude. At the pathological extremes of minimal selfhood, lone presence-as-absence clings to a governing pretence: "I am my world and the world is as I see it" – and, exercising will and power over that world, liberally uses the disposing, dismissing, forcibly extricating logic of "not me." It is in this way that, as we have seen, "hurt people hurt other people." There is a little bit of "not me" in all of us.

These days where exchanges can happen digitally, as in the foregoing example, we can more freely wield our object-constructions of the other onto those others and feel ourselves justified. When the space between persons is a vacuum inclined to suck whatever we have loosed there, then disillusionment and coming to terms

274 Into practice

with our own hate, I suspect, is going to become an ever-increasing challenge. For my part, I would likely still struggle to send an appropriate response – challenged as I was by so many meanings overdetermining the concise wording of a digital exchange. And I will continue to struggle with aspects of my being, of my own hate, with which I have yet to come to terms, indeed, to grieve and to give grace. It is a journey into ever-freeing horizons.

In 1932, Einstein sent a letter to Freud asking, "Is there any way of delivering mankind (*sic*) from the menace of war? . . . [Y]ou, I am convinced, will be able to suggest educative methods." If we are ever going to get on with making the world a better place, with fewer people hurting others because of fewer people themselves hurting, then – especially in the losses of intimate connection (across physically and virtually crowded worlds) rendering us oddly more viscerally singular and aggregately plural – we will need the interpretive richness of relational psychoanalytic thought to find our way back to the other and from the other to ourselves.

Note

1 Helicopter or cossetting parents, preoccupied with their children's success, are ever-present and hovering over them (Peters, 2009, June 8). Free-range parenting represents the counter position of trusting that children are too infrequently left to their own devices (Pinarski, 2014, March 28). Snowplough and bulldozer parents obsessively race ahead of the child to pre-emptively clear away foreseeable obstacles (Waverman, 2015, January 14).

EPILOGUE

Through angst and grace, in this together

To be educated

We left the last chapter with Einstein asking Freud for an educational solution to delivering humanity from the menace of war (1932). What would "being educated" mean, were education to succeed in such deliverance? Ted Aoki answers with a vision: "To be educated is to be ever open to the call of what it is to be deeply human, and heeding the call to walk with others in life's ventures" (in Pinar & Irwin, 2015, p. 365). For myself, parented by a WWII Hong Kong prisoner-of-war veteran and his autistic wife, the question of how to get to this vision has been my life's pursuit. The erudition I sought in graduate studies I found scattered across camps skewed along modern – postmodern divides. Sitting somewhere in a middle region, steeped in humanist sensibilities, this book is also a political endeavour joining curriculum theory in pushing back on modernity's stronghold in schooling – as per current allegiances between business, government, STEM, and the learning sciences.

I have presented a theory of learning wrought at an emerging convergence of third-person scientific and first-person phenomenological accounts of human experience. I have argued for relational psychoanalytic theory – that contemporary psychoanalytic development most conversant at this nexus and starkly absent in educational discourses – as our current best bet for reimagining teaching and learning.

The mysteries of life, mind, learning, and learning systems, that once eluded our capacity to make fecund and productive sense, no longer do as they did. This renders untenable the never-ending panoply of school reforms. Under the duress of societies increasingly divided, diminishing planetary resources, and certain ecological disasters, today's exigencies ask for human wisdom far beyond what has been our collective habit. We will want to grapple more wholly and courageously with all that we are and are not – that we might find our way past doer/done-to positions into the kind of co-recognition that gifts integral selfhood, with others, and life, here on the planet.

Drawing inspiration from relational psychoanalytic insight, the theory of learning on offer is continuous with cognitive theories to the present, consistent with the breadth of research literature on the nature of human development, and relevant across life systems from unicellular organisms to socially evolved collectives. I have offered it schematically (aspiring to clarity and not reduction) as a rudimentary framework to anchor an interpretive attitude in teaching and learning that checks the tendency to separate physical visceral bodies, affective meanings, and symbolic systems of thought.

The essence of inclusivity

Not unlike others in education, I have echoed the call for inclusivity, but I have spoken against programs intent on enjoining people into particular forms of thought and behaviour on the admonishment that this is the right way to be a person. Instead, in the humbling awareness of the opacity of ourselves to ourselves and to the stories that have storied us, I am advocating for grace rendered as much inward as outward. This, I am calling the essence of inclusivity.

What would it shift in us to realise: that the scripts for the moments of anyone's lives have been fashioned out of much earlier and older pre-places; that who we are has been written into and as our bodies; and that they have been the particularities of experience, nuanced and subtle, that have over time veered us on seemingly self-chosen paths to difference?

We have followed the story of each human's becoming. As individual possibility thrown into collective possibility, we arrived ripe for the world's moulding according to such gossamer beginnings as, if we were lucky, the melody of a caregiver's voice, a reassuring scent, the warmth of an embrace, the languish of suckling, and an expanse of affectively contoured experiences beyond. Our infant bodies, instinctually primed as was their genius, partook in exchanges to strap and bundle originary, chaotic, perceiving sensitivities into ordered, languaged, conceiving sensibilities. The course of our early years, thus, came to settle the rudiments of our physical possibility – literally as the patterned firings of neural networks and the feeling of being and knowing that is our brain's learned interpretation of experience carried forward. From the other side, we have explored autopoiesis as the way that our self-fashionings are also our own, though less consciously than we think. Prompted by something "out there" our biologies chose their responses, making a self in the way that each self's body knew to do, recursively and therefore never identically across time, but yet sufficiently self-similar to enable a sense of continuity, agency, and coherence in being.

I am daring to dream of a collective movement to inclusivity riding on the insights of such understandings. If learners and their teachers can often enough find themselves generously and justly heard and seen, then we may be on our way. Importantly, I am fathoming the most important lessons of inclusivity framed in the subtexts shading our engagement with others through the transitional objects that compose the curriculum. Though predetermined in the contexts of the dominant culture, these curricular objects can still be addressed in a language permitting of a transitional encounter with something given by the world *yet* made anew by each learning subject. In this attitude, we grow together.

The model depicts learning as one part illusory world-making and other part world-enfolding. Illusion and disillusionment are Winnicottean notions associated with the holding and object mothers. On the one hand, "holding" captures the sense of teacher-as-unobtrusive-other, safely securing learners from a pressing world whilst they grapple, much like cubs at play assuming roles in that world. In this way, the holding teacher permits the unfettered percolation of an "a-ha" into conscious realisation and formulation. On the other hand, the object-mother inserts disillusioning objects from the world, beginning with herself as not quite what the learner had in mind. As such, the teacher titrates student encounters with difference and sameness so as to permit the discernment of disconcerting ambiguities and to beckon revised sense.

A Hippocratic Oath for education: first do no harm

Modernity's illusion is that, for any understanding (traditional or progressive) to matter, it must be reconfigured into an actionable research product guaranteed to practically manage away difficulty, one challenge at a time. Yet such products have had a notorious history of failing to deliver on promised outcomes and/or, in fixing something in the immediacy, leaving long-term underlying issues to fester (Coburn, 2004; Kennedy, 2005; Opfer & Pedder, 2011). In short, despite paradigm shifts of understanding, our practices remain caught in an unabating twentieth-century quarrel over what schools and school people ought to accomplish and what interventions should be done to whom in order to make that happen. These are impasses of an "extant order" that, itself, wants for rupture and repair in ways to prompt a "fundamental structural change in the culture" (Pinar, 1978, p. 210). Meanwhile, on the other side of modernity, postmodernity seems to afford no solution at all, only the questioning of foundational truths. In a world where alternative facts have entered the public lexicon, the critical disillusioning function of the postmodern position leaves a sense of nowhere to go.

The missed point of both modernity and postmodernity has been that life systems, whether individual or collective, must undergo the movement of self-change in order to remain viable. To idle in our favourite illusions or dwell in disillusionment is to fail to learn. Learning calls for movement from the experience of having foundational truths, to the disillusionment of those truths, to the forging of foundations more fitted to a changing world. Learning – as the enfolding of, adapting to, and co-evolving with difference – is about dialectic movement. *There are no infinitely right answers. Yet we need the conviction of our current premises,* for their traction and their orienting capacity, as we push away from and press into new ways of thinking and being.

278 Into practice

Finally, the trick to learning, if there be a trick, is to effectuate the movement of self-change all the while sustaining continuity, agency, and coherence sufficient to viability as a life form – else the learning entity fractures. Individuals and collectives change in response to shifting worlds of experience – worlds governed neither by any particular self, nor by any particular other, but according to a field of interacting relational parts, including their subtended and subtending wholes. The gravitational field of relations and their histories give any system its constitutional character, bracing it in dynamic tension as parts pull and tug for change. When the pace of life, as in today's world, compromises the capacity for systems to maintain viability across self-revisions, then certain forms of violence will be imposed upon the system, as if to force the centre to hold (see Adorno in Butler, 2005). To forestall the fracturing of the field, have we taken to generating contemporary Frankenstein's monsters (as in the example of compendial collections of theories for teachers, Chapter 8), where teachers are given incommensurable parts, forcibly stitched together, and then charged with jolting the assemblage into life with the electricity of hype?

In the throes of radical planetary upheavals that call for paradigmatic changes in our very ways of being together with the planet, to what degree does our clinging to modernity's illusions of control over the planet endanger all life as we know it? Have normative beliefs about the practical management of living systems, including ecological ones, grown anachronistic? And does their insistence upon the present perform a kind of violence there? A great deal of harm seems to be performed in the name of forcing a centre to hold. Perhaps in education, we might adopt our own version of the Hippocratic Oath: First do no harm.

And still, resources and support are hardly forthcoming for veering differently. In the public sphere, appetites for practical certainty invariably reinforce and drive a swift distillation from useful insights to prescribed techniques, typically for getting the next generation to know content deemed most important from the viewpoint of stakeholders with their one foot in the past and the other in their present. As long as placebo effects run rampant in education, and as long as teacher preparation and practice is dictated to by such stakeholders, then any revolution of a Kuhnian sort will be a long time coming. Yet riding on desire, hope, and belief, I dare to forward an ambitious project where capacity, trust, and meaning in learning might come to characterise what we are about in schooling. Let me close with a metaphor.

One fathomable small theatre

I am seeking your help if only by having an audience. Call it help through visibility. Everyone ought to have the gift of an audience.

> – *Lissa D'Amour, an email to my doctoral supervisor, Brent Davis*
> *(D'Amour, personal communication, August 26, 2012)*

Pretend, not pretence, is the proper context for sense-making. The metaphor of a theatre captures many of the characteristics I imagine in an inclusive learning setting. The play is of the real world yet safely not. It is a transitional space. Students read, interpret, and try-on-for-size cultural scripts in a kind of sanctuary of grace given for the striving of individual and collaborative processes. There are moments for memorising, improvisation, and eventual script-writing. Public viewing is ultimately meted in a healthy rhythm fitted to refining the work as warranted and supported against the sometimes-mercurial edges of a judging world.

In time, buttressing walls can be progressively dismantled and the play taken to the streets and, through the graduates, enter into various institutional structures. In an inversion, the "real world" that once infused itself in mitigated portions into the theatre of play, the theatre of play now comes to be infused in mitigated portions into the real world. Actors, secure enough in such histories can continue the work of making poets of themselves and, profiting from having been found visible, can visit presence, audience, and witnessing forward.

To be clear these are utopian imaginings and the devil is in the details addressed in Section III. Any realisation turns on the presence of bona fide witnessing others – pedagogues, schools, societies whose centres-of-being survive beyond the figment of each learner's own imaginative projecting. Winnicott put present concerns succinctly.

> I have chosen to look at society *in terms of its healthiness* . . . out of the health of its psychiatrically healthy members. I say this even though I do not know that at times the proportion of psychiatrically unhealthy members in a group may be too high, so that the healthy elements even in their aggregate of health cannot carry them. Then the social unit becomes itself a psychiatric casualty.
>
> *(1971/2005, p. 190)*

What is at stake is nothing short of societies' health or psychiatric casualty and the cascading effects that reverberate either way across the biosphere. The situation could not be more dire. It is for all of these reasons that relational psychoanalytic theory at the heart of teaching and learning matters now more than ever.

REFERENCES

Adler, J. (1998). A language of teaching dilemmas: Unlocking the complex multilingual secondary mathematics classroom. *For the Learning of Mathematics, 18*(1), 24–33.

Akerman, D. B. (2003, January). Taproots for a new century: Tapping the best of traditional and progressive education. *Phi Delta Kappan,* 344–349.

Alberta Education. (2011). *Framework for student learning: Competencies for engaged thinkers and ethical citizens with an entrepreneurial spirit.* Edmonton, AB: Author. Retrieved from https://open.alberta.ca/publications/9780778596479

Alberta Education. (2014). *How are our young children doing?* Final report of the Early Child Development Mapping Project Alberta (ECMap). Edmonton, AB: Author.

Alberta Education. (2015). *How are our young children doing? Children with special needs in Alberta.* Final report of the Early Child Development Mapping Project Alberta (ECMap). Edmonton, AB: Author.

Alberta Education. (2018). *Positive behaviour supports.* Edmonton, AB: Author. Retrieved from https://education.alberta.ca/positive-behaviour-supports/overview/?searchMode=3

The Alberta Teachers' Association. (2009). *Success for all: The teaching profession's views on the future of special education in Alberta.* Edmonton, AB: Author.

Alberta Teachers' Association. (2015). *The state of inclusion in Alberta schools.* Edmonton, AB: Author. Retrieved from www.teachers.ab.ca/SiteCollectionDocuments/ATA/Publications/Research/COOR-101-5%20The%20State%20of%20Inclusion%20in%20Alberta%20Schools.pdf

American Psychology Association Division 39: Psychoanalysis. *About.* Retrieved October 21, 2016 from www.apadivisions.org/division-39/about/index.aspx

Ammaniti, M., & Ferrari, P. (2013). Vitality affects in Daniel Stern's thinking – A psychological and neurobiological perspective. *Infant Mental Health Journal, 34*(5), 367–375.

Ansari, D. (2015, September 29). No more math wars. *EdCan Network.* Retrieved from www.edcan.ca/articles

Appel, S. (1996). *Positioning subjects: Psychoanalysis and critical educational studies.* Westport, CT: Bergin & Garvey.

Aron, L. (1990). One person and two person psychologies and the method of psychoanalysis. *Psychoanalytic Psychology, 7*(4), 475–485. doi:10.1037/0736-9735.7.4.475

References **281**

Aron, L. (1996). *A meeting of minds: Mutuality in psychoanalysis*. Hillsdale, NJ: Analytic Press.

Aron, L. (2010). Response to Rachel B. Blass' paper about the value of attempting to define the limits of psychoanalysis. *International Journal of Psychoanalysis, 91*, 1279–1280.

Association of Universities and Colleges of Canada. (1988, May). *Statement on academic freedom*. Retrieved from www.aasua.ca/wp-content/uploads/2015/01/AUCC1988.pdf

Association of Universities and Colleges of Canada. (2011, October). *Statement on academic freedom*. Retrieved from www.univcan.ca/media-room/media-releases/statement-on-academic-freedom/Baier, A. C. (1994). Trust and antitrust. In *Moral prejudices: Essays on ethics* (pp. 95–129). Cambridge, MA: Harvard University Press.

Bächtold, M. (2013). What do students 'construct' according to constructivism in science education. *Research in Science Education, 43*, 2477–2496.

Bain, K., Fulton, D., & Sautner, B. (2017). *Behaviour observation assessment teaching strategies (BOATS)* (3rd ed.). Edmonton, AB: Council for Inclusive Education, Alberta Teachers' Association.

Bainbridge, A., & West, L. (2012). *Psychoanalysis and education: Minding a gap*. London, UK: Karnac Books.

Baldino, R. R., & Cabral, T. C. B. (2008). I love maths anxiety. In T. Brown (Ed.), *The psychology of mathematics education: A psychoanalytic displacement* (pp. 61–92). Rotterdam, The Netherlands: Sense Publishers.

Banai, E., Mikulincer, M., & Shaver, P. R. (2005). "Selfobject" needs in Kohut's self psychology: Links with attachment, self-cohesion, affect regulation, and adjustment. *Psychoanalytic Psychology, 22*(2), 224–260. doi:10.1037/0736-9735.22.2.224

Bandura, A. (1993). Perceived self-efficacy in cognitive development and functioning. *Educational Psychologist, 28*(2), 117–148.

Basen, I. (Producer). (2014, September 07). *Class struggle* [Audio podcast]. Retrieved from www.cbc.ca/radio/thesundayedition/class-struggle-documentary-1.2756899

Bass, T., Ipp, H., & Seligman, S. (Eds.) (December, 2014). Email announcement from the editors of *Pyschoanalytic Dialogues* to the members of The International Association for Relational Psychoanalysis and Psychotherapy.

Bausch, K. C. (2001). *The emerging consensus in social systems theory*. New York, NY: Kluwer Academic/Plenum Publishers. doi:10.1007/978-1-4615-1263-9

Beebe, B., & Lachmann, F. M. (2014). *The origins of attachment: Infant research and adult treatment*. New York, NY: Routledge.

Benedek, M., Jauk, E., Sommer, M., Arendasy, M., & Neubauer, A. C. (2014). Intelligence, creativity, and cognitive control: The common and differential involvement of executive functions in intelligence and creativity. *Intelligence, 43*, 73–83.

Benen, S. (2016, October 21). Souter warned of a Trump-like candidate in prescient remarks. *MSNBC*. Retrieved from http://www.msnbc.com/rachel-maddow-show/souter-warned-trump-candidate-prescient-remarks

Benjamin, J. (1988). *The bonds of love: Psychoanalysis, feminism, and the problem of domination*. New York, NY: Pantheon Books.

Benjamin, J. (1995). *Like subjects, love objects: Essays on recognition and sexual difference*. New Haven, CT: Yale University Press.

Benjamin, J. (1999). Recognition and destruction: An outline of intersubjectivity. In S. Mitchell & L. Aron (Eds.), *Relational psychoanalysis: The emergence of a tradition* (pp. 181–210). Hillsdale, NJ: Analytic Press. (Original work published 1990)

Benjamin, J. (2004). Beyond doer and done to: An intersubjective view of thirdness. *Psychoanalytic Quarterly, LXXIII*, 5–46.

Benjamin, J. (2005). From many into one: Attention, energy, and the containing of multitudes. *Psychoanalytic Dialogues, 15*(2), 185–201.

282 References

Benjamin, J. (2016). Intersubjectivity. In A. Elliott & J. Prage (Eds.), *The Routledge handbook of psychoanalysis in the social sciences and humanities* (pp. 149–168). London, UK: Routledge.

Benjamin, J. (2018). *Beyond doer and done to: Recognition theory, intersubjectivity and the Third*. New York, NY: Routledge.

Berger, P. L., & Luckmann, T. (1966). *The social construction of reality: A treatise in the sociology of knowledge*. New York, NY: Anchor Books.

Berk, L. E. (2000). *Child development* (5th ed.). Needham Heights, MA: Pearson Education.

Berkowitz, P. (2011, November 23). AUCC sets out five commitments to Canadians. *University Affairs*. Retrieved from www.universityaffairs.ca/news/news-article/aucc-sets-out-five-commitments-to-canadians/

Berman, E. (1997). Relational psychoanalysis: A historical background. *American Journal of Psychotherapy, 51*(2), 185–203.

Berman, E. (2001). Obituary: Stephen A. Mitchell (1946–2000). *International Journal of Psychoanalysis, 82*, 1267–1272.

Bernstein, R. H. (1990, October 28). The rising hegemony of the politically correct. *The New York Times*.

Bernstein, R. J. (1983). *Beyond objectivism and relativism: Science, hermeneutics, and praxis*. Philadelphia, PA: University of Pennsylvania Press.

Bialystok, L., & Kukar, P. (2018). Authenticity and empathy in education. *Theory and Research in Education, 16*(1), 23–39.

Bibby, R. (2010). *Alberta's emerging millennials: A national survey reading of Alberta teens and other teens*. Lethbridge, AB: Project Canada Books.

Bibby, T. (2011). *Education – An 'impossible profession'? Psychoanalytic explorations of learning and classrooms*. New York, NY: Routledge.

Black, M. J. (2016). Introduction to the 2016 edition. In S. J. Mitchell, & M. J. Black (Eds.), *Freud and beyond: A history of modern psychoanalytic thought* (2nd ed.). New York, NY: Basic Books.

Blake, W. (1908). *Jerusalem*, f. 55, 11. In *The Poetical Works*. Retrieved from www.bartleby.com/235/322.html

Boaler, J. (2016). *Mathematical mindsets: Unleashing students' potential through creative math, inspiring messages and innovative teaching*. San Francisco, CA: Josey-Bass.

Boaler, J., Williams, C., Dieckmann, J., Woodbury, E., Dance, K., Cordero, M., . . . Corkins, S. (n.d.). *YouCubed at Stanford University*. Retrieved from www.youcubed.org

Bollas, C. (1993). An interview with Christopher Bollas. *Psychoanalytic Dialogues, 3*(3), 401–430. doi:10.1080/10481889309538985

Boulenger, V., Shtyrov, Y., & Pulvermüller, F. (2011). When do you grasp the idea? MEG evidence for instantaneous idiom understanding. *NeuroImage, 59*, 3502–3513.

Bradshaw, C. P., Waasdorp, T. E., & Leaf, P. J. (2012). Effects of school-wide positive behavioral interventions and supports on child behavior problems. *Pediatrics, 130*(5), e1136–e1145.

Bransford, J. D., Brown, A. L., & Cocking, R. R. (with Donovan, M. S., Pellegrino, J. W.) (Eds.). (2003). *How people learn: Brain, mind, experience and school*. Washington, DC: National Academy Press.

Brinkmann, S. (2017). *Stand firm: Resisting the self-improvement craze*. Cambridge, UK: Polity Press. (Originally published in Danish, 2014)

Britzman, D. P. (1998). *Lost subjects, contested objects*. New York, NY: SUNY Press.

Britzman, D. P. (2003). *Practice makes practice: A critical study of learning to teach* (2nd ed.). Albany, NY: State University of New York Press.

Britzman, D. P. (2006). *Novel education: Psychoanalytic studies of learning and not learning*. New York, NY: Peter Lang.

References **283**

Britzman, D. P. (2013). What gives with psychoanalysis and education? An essay review: Peter Taubman. Disavowed Knowledge: Psychoanalysis, Education, and Teaching. *Journal of the American Association for the Advancement of Curriculum Studies, 9*, 1–12.

Britzman, D. P. (2016). *Melanie Klein: Early analysis, play, and the question of freedom.* New York, NY: Springer.

Bruner, J. (1990). *Acts of meaning.* Cambridge, MA: Harvard University Press.

Bruner, J. (2004). A short history of psychological theories of learning. *Doedalus,* Winter, 13–20.

Buber, M. (1970). *I and thou* (1996 ed.; W. Kaufman, Trans.). New York, NY: Simon & Schuster. (Original work published 1923)

Burke-Harris, N. (2014). How childhood trauma affects health across a lifetime. *TEDMED2014.* Retrieved from www.ted.com/talks/nadine_burke_harris_how_childhood_trauma_affects_health_across_a_lifetime/transcript?language=en

Burns, M. (1998). *Math: Facing an American phobia.* Sausalito, CA: Math Solutions Publications.

Butler, J. (1990). *Gender trouble* (1st ed.). New York, NY: Routledge.

Butler, J. (1992). Contingent foundations. In J. Butler & J. W. Scott (Eds.), *Feminist theorise the political* (pp. 3–21). New York, NY: Routledge.

Butler, J. (1997). *The psychic life of power: Theories in subjection.* Chicago, IL: Stanford University Press.

Butler, J. (1999). *Gender trouble* (2nd ed.). New York, NY: Routledge.

Butler, J. (2004). *Undoing Gender.* New York, NY: Routledge.

Butler, J. (2005). *Giving an account of oneself.* New York, NY: Fordham University Press.

Cain, S. (2012). *Quiet: The power of introverts in a world that can't stop talking.* New York, NY: Crown Publishers.

Canadian Association of University Teachers. (2011, November 4). *Open letter to the Association of Universities and Colleges of Canada.* Retrieved from www.caut.ca/docs/default-document-library/caut_to_aucc_academic_freedom.pdf?sfvrsn=0

Canadian Federation of Students. (2018). Education Justice. Retrieved from https://cfs-fcee.ca/wp-content/uploads/2018/10/CFS-EducationJustice-Report-ENG-nobleed-1-1.pdf

Carey, B. (2006, January 24). A shocker: Partisan thought is unconscious. *The New York Times.* Retrieved from www.nytimes.com/2006/01/24/science/a-shocker-partisan-thought-is-unconscious.html

Carpendale, J., & Lewis, C. (2004). Constructing an understanding of mind: The development of children's social understanding within social interaction. *Behavioral and Brain Sciences, 27,* 79–151.

Carpendale, J., & Lewis, C. (2006). *How children develop social understanding.* Malden, MA: Blackwell.

Carter, P. D., Skiba, R., Arredondo, M. I., & Pollock, M. (2017). You can't fix what you don't look at: Acknowledging race in addressing racial discipline disparities. *Urban Education, 52*(2), 207–235.

Carver, R. (1989). Late Fragment [poem], in author *A new path to the waterfall.* Atlantic Monthly Press. Retrieved from https://wordsfortheyear.com/2014/07/07/late-fragment-by-raymond-carver/

Case, R. (1987). Neo-Piagetian theory: Retrospect and prospect. *International Journal of Psychology, 22*(5–6), 773–791. doi:10.1080/00207598708246802

Cassidy, J. (2008). The nature of the child's ties. In J. Cassidy & P. R. Shaver (Eds.), *Handbook of attachment: Theory, research, and clinical applications* (2nd ed., pp. 3–22). New York, NY: Guilford Press.

Cavarero, A. (2000). *Relating narratives: Storytelling and selfhood* (P. Kottman, Trans.). New York, NY: Routledge. (Original work published 1997)

284 References

Cederström, C. (2019). *The happiness fantasy.* Cambridge, UK: Polity Press.

Center for Applied Special Technology. (2018). *About universal design for learning.* Retrieved from www.cast.org/our-work/about-udl.html#.Wnj-c2bMyMI

Chau, A. (2011). *Battle hymn of the tiger mother.* New York, NY: Bloomsbury.

Christiansen, I. M. (1997). When negotiation of meaning is also negotiation of task. *Educational Studies in Mathematics, 34*(1), 1–25.

Clement, C. S. (2014). Ronald Fairbairn's theory of object relations and the microanalysis of mother-infant interaction. In B. Beebe & F. M. Lachmann (Eds.), *The origins of attachment: Infant research and adult treatment* (pp. 159–162). New York, NY: Routledge.

Coburn, C. E. (2004). Beyond decoupling: Rethinking the relationship between the institutional environment and the classroom. *Sociology of Education, 77*(3), 211–244.

Collishaw, S., Maughan, B., Natarajan, L., & Pickles, A. (2010). Trends in adolescent emotional problems in England: A comparison of two national cohorts twenty years apart. *Journal of Child Psychology and Psychiatry, 51*(8), 885–894.

Connell, R. (2013). The neoliberal cascade and education: an essay on the market agenda and its consequences. *Critical Studies in Education, 54*(2), 99–112. doi:10.1080/1750848 7.2013.776990

Cooper, A. (2011). 8 amazing kids who make a difference. *Parenting Magazine.* Retrieved from www.parenting.com/gallery/kids-who-make-difference

Council for Inclusive Education. (2017). *BOATS: Behaviour, observation, assessment, teaching, strategies* (3rd ed.). Edmonton, AB: Alberta Teachers' Association.

Cozolino, L. (2010). *The neuroscience of psychotherapy: Healing the social brain* (2nd ed.). New York, NY: W. W. Norton.

Crary, A., & Wilson, W. S. (2013, June 16). The faulty logic of the "math wars." *The New York Times.* Retrieved from https://opinionator.blogs.nytimes.com

Crawford, M. (2015). *The world beyond your head: On becoming an individual in an age of distraction.* New York, NY: Farrar, Straus & Giroux.

Cruikshank, D. R., & Haefele, D. (2001). Good teachers, plural. *Educational Leadership, 58*(5), 26–30.

Csibra, G., & Gergely, G. (2011). Natural pedagogy as evolutionary adaptation. *Philosophical Transactions of the Royal Society B, 366,* 1149–1157. doi:10.1098/rstb.2010.0319

Curtis, A., & Kelsall, L. (Producers), & Curtis, A. (Director). (2002). *The century of the self* [Motion picture documentary series]. UK: BBC Two. Retrieved from www.youtube.com/watch?v=eJ3RzGoQC4s

Damasio, A. (2003). *Looking for Spinoza: Joy, sorrow, and the feeling brain.* Toronto, CA: Harcourt.

Damasio, A. (2010). *Self comes to mind: Constructing the conscious brain.* New York, NY: Random House.

Damasio, A. (2018). *The strange order of things: Life, feeling, and the making of cultures.* Toronto, ON: Random House of Canada.

D'Amour, L. (2010, July). Shifting associations: Mind, mathematics, and culture. In M. F. Pinto & T. F. Kawasaki (Eds.), *Proceedings of the 34th conference of the international group for the psychology of mathematics education, Vol. 2* (pp. 289–296). Belo Horizonte, Brazil: PME.

D'Amour, L. (2011, June). *Toward a phenomenology of trust for teaching and learning.* Presented at the Canadian Society for the Study of Education Conference, Fredericton, NB.

D'Amour, L. (2013). *Addressing anxiety through mathematics: From demanding performances to giving audience.* Doctoral thesis. Retrieved from https://circle.ubc.ca/bitstream/handle/2429/44555/ubc_2013_fall_damour_lissa.pdf?sequence=1

D'Amour, L., & Markides, J. (2017). Identities of exceptionality: The giving and making of selves in the eye of expectation's storm. In E. R. Lyle (Ed.), *At the intersection of selves and subject: Exploring the curricular landscape of identity* (pp. 133–142). Rotterdam, The Netherlands: Sense Publishing.

Dasgupta, P. (2000). Trust as a commodity. In D. Gambetta (Ed.), *Trust: Making and breaking cooperative relations* (pp. 49–72). Retrieved from www.sociology.ox.ac.uk/papers/dasgupta49-72.pdf

Davis, B., & Renert, M. (2014). *The math teachers know: Profound understanding of emergent mathematics.* New York, NY: Routledge.

Davis, B., & Simmt, E. (2003). Understanding learning systems: Mathematics education and complexity science. *Journal for Research in Mathematics Education, 34*(2), 137–167.

Davis, B., & Sumara, D. (2006). *Complexity and education: Inquiries into learning, teaching, and research.* Mahwah, NJ: Lawrence Erlbaum.

Deacon, T. W. (1989). *Holism and associationism in neuropsychology: An anatomical synthesis.* Retrieved from www.researchgate.net/publication/246381903

De Bei, F. & Dazzi, N. (2014). Attachment and relational psychoanalysis: Bowlby according to Mitchell. *Psychoanalytic Dialogues: The International Journal of Relational Perspectives, 24*(5), 562–577.

Debnam, K. J., Pas, E. T., Bottiani, J., Cash, A. H., & Bradshaw, C. P. (2015). An examination of the association between observed and self-reported culturally proficient teaching practices. *Psychology in the Schools, 52*(6), 533–548.

De Freitas, E. & Sinclair, N. (2012). Diagram, gesture, agency: Theorizing embodiment in the mathematics classroom. *Educational Studies in Mathematics, 80*(1–2), 133–152.

Dewey, J. (1997). *Experience and education.* New York, NY: Touchstone. (Original work published 1938)

Dewey, J. (2004). *Democracy and education: An introduction to the philosophy of education.* Mineola, NY: Dover Publications. (Original work published 1916)

DeYoung, P. A. (2000). *Thriving on difficult knowledge: Poststructuralist pedagogy and relational psychoanalysis* (doctoral dissertation). Toronto, ON: University of Toronto.

Dienes, Z. P. (1960). *Building up mathematics.* London, UK: Hutchinson Educational.

Dobbin, F., & Kalev, A. (2016, July/August). Why diversity programs fail. *Harvard Business Review,* 52–60. Retrieved from https://hbr.org/2016/07/why-diversity-programs-fail

Doidge, N. (2007). *The brain that changes itself: Stories of personal triumph from the frontiers of brain science.* New York, NY: Penguin.

Donald, M. (2001). *A mind so rare: The evolution of human consciousness.* New York, NY: Norton.

Dowker, A. (2005). "Maths doesn't like me anymore": The role of attitudes and emotions. In Author (Ed.), *Individual differences in arithmetic: Implications for psychology, neuroscience and education* (pp. 211–228). Hove, UK: Psychology Press.

Dweck, C. S. (2016). *Mindset: The new psychology of success. How we can learn to fulfill our potential.* New York, NY: Random House. (Original work published 2006)

Edelman, E. M. (2006). *Second nature: Brain science and human knowledge.* New Haven, CT: Yale University Press.

Edelson, D. C., & Reiser, B. J. (2006). Making authentic practices accessible to learners. In R. K. Sawyer (Ed.), *The Cambridge handbook of the learning sciences* (pp. 335–354). New York, NY: Cambridge University Press.

Eigen, M. (1999). The area of faith in Winnicott, Lacan and Bion. In S. A. Mitchell & L. Aron (Eds.), *Relational Psychoanalysis: The emergence of a tradition* (pp. 3–36). Hillsdale, NJ: Analytic Press. (Original work published 1981)

Eigen, M. (2018). *Faith.* New York, NY: Routledge. (Original work published 2014)

Einstein, A. (1932, July 30). *The Einstein-Freud correspondence (1931–1932)* [Letter from Freud to Einstein]. Retrieved from www.public.asu.edu/~jmlynch/273/documents/Freud Einstein.pdf

286 References

Ellsworth, E. (1989). Why doesn't this feel empowering? Working through the repressive myths of critical pedagogy. *Harvard Educational Review, 59*(3), 297–325. Retrieved from https://populardigitaleducation.files.wordpress.com/2012/12/why-doesnt-this-feel-empowering.pdf

Ennis, C. D., & McCauley, M. T. (2002). Creating urban classroom communities worthy of trust. *Journal of Curriculum Studies, 34*(2), 149–172.

Ernest, P. (2006). Reflections on theories of learning. *ZDM: Mathematics Education, 38*(1), 3–7.

Erreich, A. (2016). An exchange with Thomas Nagel: The mind-body problem and psychoanalysis. *Journal of the American Psychoanalytic Association, 64*(2), 389–403. doi:10.1177/0003065116647053

Ervin, R. A., Radford, P. M., Bertsch, K., Piper, A. L., Ehrhardt, K. B., & Poling, A. (2001). A descriptive analysis and critique of the empirical literature on school-based functional assessment. *School Psychology Review, 30*(2), 193–222.

Essig, T. (2018, December). *Psychoanalysis, technology and innovation: How "local therapy" is the future.* Presentation by Chicago Center for Psychoanalysis and Psychotherapy.

Essig, T., Turkle, S., & Russell, G. (2018, June 7). Sleepwalking towards artificial intimacy: How psychotherapy is failing the future. *Forbes.* Retrieved from www.forbes.com

Etzioni, A. (2002). A communitarian position on character education. In W. Damon (Ed.), *Bringing in a new era in character education* (pp. 113–128). Stanford, CA: Hoover Institution Press.

Farmer, T., McAuliffe Lines, M., & Hamm, J. (2011). Revealing the invisible hand: The role of teachers in children's peer experiences. In Authors (Eds.), Special issue: Teachers and classroom social dynamics (pp. 247–256). *Journal of Applied Developmental Psychology, 32*(5), 247–312.

Felitti, V. C., Anda, R. F., Nordenberg, D., Williamson, D. F., Spitz, A. M., Edwards, V. . . . Marks, J. S. (1998). The adverse childhood experiences (ACE) study: Relationship of childhood abuse and household dysfunction to many of the leading causes of death in adults. *American Journal of Preventive Medicine, 14*(4), 245–258. Retrieved from www.ajpmonline.org/article/S0749-3797(98)00017-8/pdf

Felman, S. (1982). Psychoanalysis and education: Teaching terminable and interminable. *Yale French Studies, 63,* 21–44. Retrieved from http://links.jstor.org/sici?sici=0044-0078%281982%290%3A63%3C21%3APAETTA%3E2.0.CO%3B2-3

Ferenczi, S. (1988). Confusion of tongues between adults and the child – The language of tenderness and of passion. *Contemporary Psychology, 24,* 196–206. (Original work published 1933)

Fonagy, P., Gergely, G., & Target, M. (2007). The parent–infant dyad and the construction of the subjective self. *Journal of Child Psychology and Psychiatry, 48*(3/4), 288–328. doi:10.1111/j.1469–7610.2007.01727.x

Fonagy, P. & Target, M. (1996). Playing with reality: I. Theory of mind and the normal development of psychic reality. *International Journal of Psychoanalysis, 77*(2), 217–233.

Fonagy, P., & Target, M. (2006). Playing with reality: IV. A theory of external reality rooted in intersubjectivity. *International Journal of Psychoanalysis, 88,* 917–937.

Fonagy, P., & Target, M. (2007). The rooting of the mind in the body: New links between attachment theory and psychoanalytic thought. *Journal of American Psychoanalytic Association, 55*(2), 411–456. doi:10.1111/j.1469-7610.2007.01727.x

Fortun, M., & Bernstein, H. J. (1998). *Muddling through: Pursuing science & truths in the 21st century.* Washington, DC: Counterpoint.

Foucault, M. (1995). *Discipline and punish: The birth of the prison* (2nd ed., A. Sheridan, 1977 Trans.). Toronto: Random House of Canada. (Original work published 1975)

Fox, L., Carta, J., Strain, P. S., Dunlap, G., & Hemmeter, M. L. (2010). Response to intervention and the pyramid model. *Infants & Young Children, 23*(1), 3–13.

Frasier, D., Hill, E., & Kear, J. (2018). Most people are good [Recorded by Luke Bryan]. On *What makes you country*. Nashville: Capitol Records.

Freire, P. (2000). *Pedagogy of the oppressed: 30th anniversary edition*. (1993 ed.; M. Bergman Ramos, Trans.). New York, NY: Continuum International Publishing Group. (Original work published 1970)

French, J. (2016, June 19). As new school curriculum looms, Alberta parents say math woes unresolved. *Edmonton Journal*. Retrieved from http://edmontonjournal.com/news

Freud, S. (1932, September). *The Einstein-Freud correspondence (1931–1932)* [Letter from Freud to Einstein]. Retrieved from www.public.asu.edu/~jmlynch/273/documents/FreudEinstein.pdf

Frie, R. (2009). Introduction: Coherence or fragmentation? Modernism, postmodernism, and the search for continuity. In R. Frie & D. Orange (Eds.), *Beyond postmodernism: New dimensions in clinical theory and practice* (pp. 1–24). New York, NY: Routledge.

Frie, R., & Orange, D. (Eds.). (2009). *Beyond postmodernism: New dimensions in clinical theory and practice*. New York, NY: Routledge.

Frost, R. (1916). The road not taken. In Author (Ed.), *Mountain interval*. New York, NY: Henry Holt & Co. Poem retrieved from www.poetryfoundation.org/poems/44272/the-road-not-taken

Gadamer, H.-G. (2004). *Truth and method* (2nd ed.; J. Weinsheimer & D. G. Marshall, Trans.). New York, NY: Continuum Group. (Original work published 1975)

Gardner, H. (2016). Foreword. In M. H. Immordino-Yang (Ed.), *Emotion, learning, and the brain: Exploring the educational implications of affective neuroscience* (pp. 7–10). New York, NY: Norton.

Gartner, J. E. (2017). Lessons learned treating traumatized teachers. In R. B. Gartner (Ed.), *Trauma and countertrauma, resilience and counterresilience: Insights from psychoanalysts and trauma experts* (pp. 191–214). New York, NY: Routledge.

Gergely, G. (2007). The social construction of the subjective self. In L. Mayes, P. Fonagy, & M. Target (Eds.), *Developmental science and psychoanalysis: Integration and innovation* (pp. 45–82). London, UK: Karnac Books.

Ghent, E. (1990). Masochism, submission, surrender: Masochism as a perversion of surrender. *Contemporary Psychoanalysis, 26*, 108–136.

Ghent, E. (2002). Relations: Introduction to the first IARPP conference. *IARPP eNEWS, 1*(1), 6–9.

Ginot, E. (2015). *The neuropsychology of the unconscious: Integrating brain and mind in psychotherapy*. New York, NY: Norton.

Glasersfeld, E. v. (1989). Cognition, construction of knowledge, and teaching. *Synthese, 80*(1), 121–140.

Glassman, M. (1994). All things being equal: The two roads of Piaget and Vygotsky. *Developmental Review, 14*, 186–214.

Goodman, A., & Mann, J. J. (2018, June 11). The daily show. *Democracy Now*. Retrieved from www.democracynow.org/shows/2018/6/11?autostart=true

Gopnik, A. (2007). Why babies are more conscious than we are. *Behavioral and Brain Sciences, 30*(5/6), 503–504. doi:10.1017/S0140525X07002786

Göransson, K., & Nilholm, C. (2014). Conceptual diversities and empirical shortcomings – A critical analysis of research on inclusive education. *European Journal of Special Needs Education, 29*(3), 265–280. doi:10.1080/08856257.2014.933545

Gorski, P. C. (2009). What we're teaching teachers: An analysis of multicultural teacher education coursework syllabi. *Teaching and Teacher Education, 25*, 309–318.

Gould, S. J. (2003). *The hedgehog, the fox, and the magister's pox: Mending the gap between science and the humanities*. New York, NY: Harmony Books.

Gredler, M. E. (2012). Understanding Vygotsky for the classroom? Is it too late? *Educational Psychology Review, 24*(1), 113–131.

Greenberg, J. R., & Mitchell, S. J. (1983). *Object relations in psychoanalytic theory.* Cambridge, MA: Harvard University Press.

Gregory, J., & Miller, S. (1998). *Science in public: Communication, culture, and credibility.* New York, NY: Plenum Press.

Grumet, M. R. (2006). Psychoanalytic foundations. In W. F. Pinar & M. R. Grumet (Eds.) *Toward a poor curriculum* (pp. 111–146). Troy, NY: Educator's International Press. (Original work published 1976)

Grumet, M. R. (2010). The public expression of the citizen teacher. *Journal of Teacher Education, 61,* 66–76.

Grumet, M. R., & Stone, L. (2000). Feminism and curriculum: Getting our act together. *Journal of Curriculum Studies, 32*(2), 183–197.

Haque, O. S., & Waytz, A. (2012). Dehumanization in medicine: Causes, solutions, and functions. *Perspectives on Psychological Science, 7*(2), 176–186. doi:10.1177/1745691611429706

Hardt, O. (2019, January 4). Why we have to forget to remember [Radio podcast interview]. In *The Sunday Edition.* Toronto, ON: CBC Radio-Canada. Retrieved from www.cbc.ca/radio/thesundayedition/why-we-have-to-forget-to-remember-1.4964849

Hardy, I., & Woodcock, S. (2015). Inclusive education policies: Discourses of difference, diversity and deficit. *International Journal of Inclusive Education, 19*(2), 141–164. doi:10.1080/13603116.2014.908965

Harris, M. (2017). *Kids these days: Human capital and the making of millennials.* New York, NY: Little Brown.

Hattie, J. (2009). *Visible learning: A synthesis of over 800 meta-analyses relating to achievement.* New York, NY: Routledge.

Hayler, M., & Moriarty, J. (Eds.). (2007). *Self-narrative and pedagogy: Stories of experience within teaching and learning.* Boston, MA: Sense Publishers.

Haynal, A. (2002). *Disappearing and reviving: Sandor Ferenczi in the history of psychoanalysis.* London, UK: Karnac Books.

Heyman, D. (1987). Weeping [Recorded by Bright Blue: Dan Heyman, Ian Cohen, Peter Cohen, & Groovesong (Tom Fox)]. On *Yesterday Night – Weeping* [45 rpm single vinyl recording]. Johannesburg, South Africa: No contract. Retrieved from www.weeping.info/index.html

Hilt, L. (2015). Included as excluded and excluded as included: Minority language pupils in Norwegian inclusion policy. *International Journal of Inclusive Education, 19*(2), 145–182. doi:10.1080/13603116.2014.908966

Hirschfeld Davis, J. (2015, December 10). President Obama signs into law a rewrite of No Child Left Behind. *New York Times.* Retrieved October 10, 2018 from www.nytimes.com/2015/12/11/us/politics/president-obama-signs-into-law-a-rewrite-of-no-child-left-behind.html?_r=0

Hood, B., Howard-Jones, P., Laurillard, D., Bishop, D., Coffield, F., Frith, U., ... Foulsham, T. (2017, March 12). No evidence to back idea of learning styles [Letter to the editor]. *The Guardian: International Edition.* Retrieved February 5, 2018 from www.theguardian.com/education/2017/mar/12/no-evidence-to-back-idea-of-learning-styles

Hope, M. A., & Hall, J. J. (2018). "This feels like a whole new thing": A case study of a new LGBTQ-affirming school and its role in developing "inclusions". *International Journal of Inclusive Education, 22*(12), 1230–1332. doi:10.1080/13603116.2018.1427152

Horowitz, M. (2014). *Identity and the new psychoanalytic explorations of self-organization.* New York, NY: Routledge.

Hoy, A. W. Davis, H. A., Anderman, E. M. (2013). Theories of learning and teaching in *TIP*. *Theory into Practice, 52*, 9–21. doi:10.1080/00405841.2013.795437

Hoyt, J. K., & Roberts, K. L. (1922). *Hoyt's new cyclopedia of practical quotations*. Retrieved from www.bartleby.com/78/413.html

Hughes, S. A. (2008). Maggie and me: A black professor and a white urban school teacher connect autoethnography and critical race pedagogy. *Educational Foundations, 22*(3/4), 73–95.

Hutchings, P., & Shulman, L. (1999). The scholarship of teaching: New elaborations, new developments. *Change: The magazine of higher learning, 31*(5), 10–15. doi:10.1080/00091389909604218

International Association for Relational Psychoanalysis and Psychotherapy. (n.d.). *About us*. Retrieved October 27, 2016 from http://iarpp.net

Jacobs, B. (2015, November 24). Donald Trump on waterboarding: "Even if it doesn't work they deserve it". *The Guardian*. Retrieved from www.theguardian.com/us-news/2015/nov/24/donald-trump-on-waterboarding-even-if-it-doesnt-work-they-deserve-it

Journal of the Learning Sciences. (n.d.). *Aims and scope*. Retrieved from www.tandfonline.com/toc/hlns20/current

Juarrero, A. (2002). *Dynamics in action: Intentional behavior as a complex system* (1st paperback ed.). Cambridge, MA: MIT Press. (Original work published 1999)

Kahn-Harris, K. (2018). *Denial: The unspeakable truth*. Cumbria, UK: Notting Hill Editions.

Kandel, E. R. (2005). From metapsychology to molecular biology: Explorations into the nature of anxiety. In Author (Ed.), *Psychiatry, psychoanalysis, and the new biology of mind* (pp. 107–156). Washington, DC: American Psychiatric. (Original work published 1999)

Kavale, K. A., & Mostert, M. P. (2003). River of ideology, islands of evidence. *Exceptionality, 11*(4), 191–208. doi:10.1207/S15327035EX1104_1

Kennedy, M. M. (2005). *Inside teaching: How classroom life undermines reform*. Cambridge, MA: Harvard University Press.

Kernberg, O. F., & Caligor, E. (2005). A psychoanalytic theory of personality disorders. In M. F. Lenzenweger & J. F. Clarkin (Eds.), *Major theories of personality disorder* (2nd ed., pp. 114–157). New York, NY: Guilford Press.

Khazan, O. (2018, April 23). People voted for Trump because they were anxious, not poor. *The Atlantic: Science*. Retrieved from www.theatlantic.com/science/archive/2018/04/existential-anxiety-not-poverty-motivates-trump-support/558674/

Klin, A., & Jones, W. (2007). Embodied psychoanalysis. In L. Mayes, P. Fonagy, & M. Target (Eds.), *Developmental science and psychoanalysis: Integration and innovation* (pp. 5–38). London, UK: Karnac Books.

Koebele, J., & Villines, Z. (n.d.). 10 things to know about the psychology of cults. *Online Psychology Degree Guide*. Retrieved from www.onlinepsychologydegree.info/what-to-know-about-the-psychology-of-cults/

Kohut, H. (2009). *The analysis of the self: A systematic approach to the psychoanalytic treatment of narcissistic personality disorders*. Chicago, IL: University of Chicago Press. (Original work published 1971)

Kounin, J. S. (1970). *Discipline and group management in classrooms*. New York, NY: Holt, Rinehart & Winston.

Kreber, C., Klampfleitner, M., McCune, V., Bayne, S., & Knottenbelt, M. (2007). What do you mean by "authentic"? A comparative review of the literature on conceptions of authenticity in teaching. *Adult Education Quarterly, 58*, 22–43.

Krinzinger, H., Kaufmann, L., & Willmes, K. (2009). Math anxiety and math ability in early primary school years. *Journal of Psychoeducational Assessment, 27*(3), 206–225. doi:10.1177/0734282908330583

290 References

Kuhn, T. S. (1996). *The structure of scientific revolutions* (3rd ed.). Chicago, IL: University of Chicago Press. (Original work published 1962)

Lachmann, F. M. (2008). *Transforming narcissism: Reflections on empathy, humor, and expectations.* New York, NY: Analytic Press, Taylor & Francis Group.

Laible, D. J., & Thompson, R. A. (2000). Attachment and self-organization. In M. D. Lewis & I. Granic (Eds.), *Emotion, development, and self-organization: Dynamic systems approaches to emotional development* (pp. 298–323). New York, NY: Cambridge University Press.

Lakoff, G., & Johnson, M. (1999). *Philosophy in the flesh: The embodied mind and its challenge to western thought.* New York, NY: Basic Books.

Lampert, M. (1990). When the problem is not the question and the solution is not the answer: Mathematical knowing and teaching. *American Educational Research Journal, 27*(1), 29–63.

Lasch, C. (1984). *The minimal self: Psychic survival in troubled times.* New York, NY: Norton.

Laucius, J. (2019, March 22). Ontario is poised to require every high school student take four online courses. What does it mean? *Ottawa Citizen.* Retrieved from https://ottawacitizen. com/news/local-news/ontario-is-poised-to-require-every-high-school-student-take-four-online-courses-what-does-it-mean

Lave, J., & Wenger, E. (1991). *Situated learning: Legitimate peripheral participation.* Cambridge, MA: Cambridge University Press.

Leckman, J. F., Feldman, R., Swain, J. E., & Mayes, L. (2007). Primary parental preoccupation: Revisited. In L. Mayes, P. Fonagy, & M. Target (Eds.), *Developmental science and psychoanalysis: Integration and innovation* (pp. 89–108). London, UK: Karnac Books.

Lee, F. (2018, November 3). When the political is too personal. Personal essay. *CBC Radio, The Sunday Edition.* Retrieved from www.cbc.ca/radio/thesundayedition/when-the-political-is-too-personal-1.4927292

Lerman, S. (1996). Intersubjectivity in mathematics learning: A challenge to the radical constructivist paradigm? *Journal for Research in Mathematics Education, 27*(2), 133–150.

Lewis, M. D., & Granic, I. (Eds.). (2000). *Emotion, development, and self-organization: Dynamic systems approaches to emotional development.* New York, NY: Cambridge University Press.

Lindgren, R., & Johnson-Glenberg, M. (2013). Emboldened by embodiment: Six precepts for research on embodied learning and mixed reality. *Education Researcher, 42*(8), 445–452.

Lindsay, G. (2007). Educational psychology and the effectiveness of inclusive education/mainstreaming. *British Journal of Educational Psychology, 77*, 1–24.

Lipsett, A.-B. (2011). Supporting emotional regulation in elementary school: Brain-based strategies and classroom interventions to promote self-regulation. *Learning Landscapes, 5*(1), 157–175.

Lourenço, O. (2012). Piaget and Vygotsky: Many resemblances, and a crucial difference. *New Ideas in Psychology, 30*, 281–295.

Lourenço, O., & Machado, A. (1996). In defense of Piaget's theory: A reply to 10 common criticisms. *Psychological Review, 103*(1), 143–164.

Low, C. (2001). Have disability rights gone too far? *City Insights Lecture,* 3 April 2001. London: City University. Retrieved from http://unipd-centrodirittiumani.it/public/docs/29743_rights.pdf

Lunau, K. (2012, September). Professional at a steep price: What students will do to finance their degrees. *Macleans, 125*(36), 64, 66–67.

Mackenzie, N. (2008). *Supporting positive behaviour in Alberta schools: A school-wide approach.* Edmonton, AB: Alberta Education.

Mackenzie, S., Wiegel, J. R., Mundt, M., Brown, D., Saewyc, E., Heiligenstein, E. Harahan, B., & Fleming, M. (2011). Depression and suicide ideation among students accessing campus health care. *American Journal of Orthopsychiatry, 81*(1), 101–107.

Maiese, M. (2014). How can emotions be both cognitive and bodily? *Phenomenology and the Cognitive Sciences, 13*, 513–531.

Martin, H. (2016, June 10). Rules and improvisation can sit happily together. *Times Educational Supplement, 5201.*

Martin, J. (2007). The selves of educational psychology: Conceptions, contexts, and critical considerations. *Educational Psychologist, 42*(2), 79–89.

Marton, F. (1981). Phenomenography – Describing conceptions of the world around us. *Instructional Science, 10*, 177–200. Retrieved from www.ped.gu.se/biorn/phgraph/misc/constr/phegraph.html

Marton, F. (1986). Phenomenography: A research approach to investigating different understandings of reality. *Journal of Thought, 21*(3), 28–49.

Marton, F. (1996). Cognosco ergo sum: Reflections on reflections. In G. Dall'Alba & B. Hasselgren (Eds.), *Reflections on phenomenography: Toward a methodology?* (pp. 163–187). Göeborg: Acta Universitatis Gothoburgensis.

Marton, F. (2000). The structure of awareness. In J. A. Bowden & E. Walsh (Eds.), *Phenomenography*. Qualitative research methods series: Vol. 2 (pp. 102–116). Melbourne: RMIT University Press.

Marton, F. (2014). *Necessary conditions of learning*. New York, NY: Routledge.

Marton, F., Wen, Q., & Wong, K. C. (2005). "Read a hundred times and the meaning will appear . . ." Changes in Chinese university students' views of the temporal structure of learning. *Higher Education, 49*, 291–318. doi:10.1007/s10734-004-6667-z

Mascialino, G. (2008). *A critical appraisal of relational approaches to psychoanalysis*. Doctoral dissertation, University of Texas at Austin, TX. Retrieved October 25, 2016 from www.lib.utexas.edu/etd/d/2008/mascialinog81965/mascialinog81965.pdf

Maturana, H. R. (1970). Biology of cognition. In *Autopoiesis and cognition: The realization of the living* (pp. 5–58). Dordecht: D. Reidel, 1980. Retrieved from www.enolagaia.com/M70-80BoC.html

Maturana, H. R. with Verden-Zöller, G. (2008). *The origin of humanness in the biology of love* (P. Bunnell, Ed.). Charlottesville, VA: Imprint Academic.

Maturana, H. R., & Varela, F. J. (1972). *Autopoiesis and cognition: The realization of the living*. Dordrecht, NL: Reidel.

Maturana, H. R., & Varela, F. J. (1980). *Autopoiesis and cognition: The realization of the living*. Boston, MA: Kluwer Boston. (Original work published 1972 as *De Maquinas y Seres Vivos*)

Maturana, H. R., & Varela, F. J. (1998). *The tree of knowledge: The biological roots of human understanding* (3rd ed.; J. Z. Young, Trans.). Boston, MA: Shambhala. (Original work published 1987)

Mayes, L., Fonagy, P., & Target, M. (Eds.). (2007). *Developmental science and psychoanalysis: Integration and innovation* (pp. 5–38). London, UK: Karnac Books.

McAnallen, R. R. (2010). *Examining mathematics anxiety in elementary classroom teachers*. University of Connecticut, CN: ProQuest Dissertations Publishing. Retrieved from https://opencommons.uconn.edu/dissertations/AAI3464333/

McDonald, M. (2013, September 13). Frustrated professors convince elementary schools to step back from "new math" and go "back to basics." *National Post*. Retrieved from https://nationalpost.com/news/canada

McTighe, J., & Wiggins, G. (2012). *Understanding by design® framework*. Alexandria, VA: ASCD.

Mead, G. H. (2015). *Mind, self, & society: The definitive edition* (C. W. Morris, ed. & D. R. Huebner & H. Joas, annotated eds.). Chicago, IL: Chicago University Press. (Original work published 1934)

292 References

Merleau-Ponty, M. (1962). *Phenomenology of perception* (C. Smith, Trans.). New York, NY: Routledge Classics. (Original work published 1945)

Metz, M., Preciado-Babb, P., Sabbaghan, S., Davis, B., & Ashebira, A. (2017). Attending and responding to what matters: A protocol to enhance mathematics pedagogy. In P. Preciado-Babb, L. Yeworiew, & S. Sabbaghan (Eds.). *Selected Proceedings of the IDEAS conference: Leading educational change* (pp. 179–190). Calgary, Canada: Werklund School of Education, University of Calgary.

Metz, M., Preciado-Babb, A., Sabbaghan, S., Davis, B., Pinchbeck, G., & Aljarrah, A. (2016). *Transcending traditional/reform dichotomies in mathematics education* (draft). Retrieved from www.researchgate.net/publication/303480105

Meyer, B., & Pilkonis, P. A. (2005). An attachment model of personality disorders. In M. F. Lenzenweger & J. F. Clarkin (Eds.), *Major theories of personality disorder* (2nd ed., pp. 231–281). New York, NY: Guilford Press.

Michailakis, D., & Reich, W. (2009). Dilemmas of inclusive education. *ALTR, European Journal of Disability Research, 3*, 24–44.

Mills, J. (2005). A critique of relational psychoanalysis. *Psychoanalytic Psychology, 22*(2), 155–188.

Milner, M. (1987). 1945: Some aspects of phantasy in relation to general psychology. In M. Milner (Ed.), *The suppressed madness of sane men: Forty-four years of exploring psychoanalysis* (pp. 39–62). New York, NY: Routledge.

Milner, M. (1987). 1956: The sense in nonsense (Freud and Blake's *Job*). In M. Milner (Ed.), *The suppressed madness of sane men: Forty-four years of exploring psychoanalysis* (Chapter 11, pp. 168–192). New York, NY: Routledge.

Milner, M. (1987). 1957: The ordering of chaos. In M. Milner (Ed.), *The suppressed madness of sane men: Forty-four years of exploring psychoanalysis* (pp. 216–233). New York, NY: Routledge.

Mitchell, S. A. (2002). *Can love last? The fate of romance over time*. New York, NY: W. W. Norton.

Mitchell, S. A., & Aron, L. (Eds.). (1999). *Relational Psychoanalysis: The emergence of a tradition*. Hillsdale, NJ: Analytic Press.

Mitchell, S. A., & Black, M. J. (2016). *Freud and beyond: A history of modern psychoanalytic thought* (2nd ed.). New York, NY: Basic Books. (Original work published 1995)

Mitchell, S. J. (1988). *Relational concepts in psychoanalysis: An integration*. Cambridge, MA: Harvard University Press.

Mithaug, D. E. (1998). The alternative to ideological inclusion. In S. J. Vitello & D. E. Mithaug (Eds.), *Inclusive schooling: National and international perspectives*. Mahwah, NJ: Lawrence Erlbaum Associates.

Molenaar, P. C. M., Lerner, R. M., & Newell, K. M. (Eds.) (2014). *Handbook of developmental systems theory and methodology*. New York, NY: Guilford Press.

Molesworth, M., Nixon, E., & Scullion, R. (2009). Having, being and higher education: The marketisation of the university and the transformation of the student into consumer. *Teaching in Higher Education, 14*(3), 277–287. doi:10.1080/13562510902898841

Möllering, G. (2005). The trust/control duality: An integrative perspective on positive expectations of others. *International Sociology, 20*(3), 283–305.

Möllering, G. (2006). *Trust: Reason, routine, reflexivity*. Oxford, UK: Elsevier.

Nadesan, M. H. (2002). Engineering the entrepreneurial infant: Brain science, infant development toys, and governmentality. *Cultural Studies, 16*(3), 401–432.

Nancy, J.-L. (2000). *Being singular plural* (R. D. Richardson & A. E. O'Bryne, Trans.). Stanford, CA: Stanford University Press. (Original work published 1996)

References 293

Naraian, S. (2011). Seeking transparency: The production of an inclusive classroom community. *International Journal of Inclusive Education, 15*(9), 955–973. doi:10.1080/13603110903477397

National College for School Leadership [NCSLFutures]. (2008, December 16). *Engage me! Robin Hood pupils, Birmingham* [Video file]. Retrieved from www.youtube.com/watch?v=s1YoCx384GQ

National Psychological Association for Psychoanalysis [NPAP]. (2016, September 16). *NPAP's Michael Eigen captures the essence of psychoanalysis in graduation speech: Where are we going?* NPAP Graduation. Retrieved December 20, 2016 from http://npap.org

Nichols, T. (2017). *The death of expertise: The campaign against established knowledge and why it matters.* Oxford, UK: Oxford University Press.

Noddings, N. (2003). *Caring: A feminine approach to ethics and moral education* (2nd ed.). Berkeley, CA: University of California Press.

Noddings, N. (2005). *The challenge to care in schools: An alternative approach to education* (2nd ed.). New York, NY: Teachers College Press.

Novak, E., & Tassell, J. L. (2017). Studying preservice teacher math anxiety and mathematics performance in geometry, word, and non-word problem solving. *Learning and Individual Differences, 54,* 20–29. Retrieved from www.sciencedirect.com/science/article/pii/S1041608017300055?via%3Dihub

One of these things. (2015, October 4). Retrieved from https://sites.psu.edu/aspsy/2015/10/04/www-youtube-comwatchvkzci3eoafk0/

Opfer, V. D., & Pedder, D. (2011). Conceptualizing teacher professional learning. *Review of Educational Research, 81*(3), 376–407. doi:10.3102/0034654311413609

Organization for Economic Cooperation and Development. (1996). *The knowledge-based economy.* Paris, France: OECD Publishing. Retrieved November 25, 2016 from www.oecd.org/sti/sci-tech/1913021.pdf

Organization for Economic Cooperation and Development. (2013). *Supporting investment in knowledge capital, growth and innovation.* OECD Publishing. doi:10.1787/9789264193307-en

Ormrod, J. E., Saklofske, D. H., Schewean, V. L., Andrews, J. W., & Shore, B. M. (2010). *Principles of educational psychology* (2nd Canadian ed.). Toronto, ON: Pearson Education.

Overton, W. F. (2014). Relational developmental systems and developmental science: A focus on methodology. In P. C. M. Molenaar, R. M. Lerner, & K. M. Newell (Eds.), *Handbook of developmental systems theory and methodology* (pp. 19–65). New York, NY: Guilford Press.

Palmer, P. J. (1997). The heart of a teacher identity and integrity in teaching. *Change: The Magazine of Higher Learning, 29*(6), 14–21. doi:10.1080/00091389709602343.

Panksepp, J., & Biven, L. (2012). *The archaeology of mind: Neuroevolutionary origins of human emotion.* New York, NY: Norton.

Park, S., & Auchincloss, E. (2006). Psychoanalysis in textbooks of introductory psychology: A review. *Journal of the American Psychoanalytic Association, 54,* 1361–1380.

Paulston, R. G., & Liebman, M. (1994). An invitation to postmodern social cartography. *Comparative Education Review, 38*(2), 215–232.

Peay, P. (2015, December 10). Psychoanalyst Michael Eigen on violence: An interview. *Psychology Today.* Retrieved May 19, 2018 from www.psychologytoday.com/blog/america-the-couch/201512/psychoanalyst-michael-eigen-violence

Peltokangas, H. (2015). Self-esteem, tenure, and narcissistic leader's performance. *International Journal of Business and Social Research, 5*(12), 26–39.

Peters, D. (2009, June 8). Overprotected children. *Today's Parent.* Retrieved from www.todaysparent.com/family/parenting/overprotected-children/

294 References

Piaget, J. (1971). *Biology and knowledge: An essay on the relations between organic regulations and cognitive processes* (B. Walsh, Trans.). Chicago, IL: University of Chicago Press. (Original work published 1967)

Piaget, J. (2000). Commentary on Vygotsky's criticisms of *Language and thought of the child* and *Judgement and reasoning in the child*. (L. Smith, Trans.). *New Idea in Psychology, 18,* 241–259. (Original work published 1962)

Pinar, W. F. (1975). *The method of "currere".* Retrieved from http://curriculumstudies. pbworks.com/f/Pinar(1975)TheMethodOfCurrere.pdf

Pinar, W. F. (1978). The reconceptualisation of curriculum studies. *Journal of Curriculum Studies, 10*(3), 205–214.

Pinar, W. F. (1994). Autobiography and an architecture of self. In *Autobiography, politics and sexuality: Essays in curriculum theory 1972–1992* (pp. 201–222). New York, NY: Peter Lang. (Original work published 1985)

Pinar, W. F. (2004). *What is curriculum theory?* Mahwah, NJ: Lawrence Erlbaum.

Pinar, W. F. (2009). *The worldliness of a cosmopolitan education: Passionate lives in public service.* New York, NY: Routledge.

Pinar, W. F., & Irwin, R. L. (2015). *Curriculum in a new key: The collected works of Ted T. Aoki.* Mahwah, NJ: Lawrence Erlbaum.

Pinarski, J. (2014, March 28). Confessions of a free-range parent. *Today's Parent.* Retrieved from www.todaysparent.com/family/confessions-of-free-range-parent/

Piontelli, A. (2006). On the onset of human fetal behavior. In M. Mancia (Ed.), *Psychoanalysis and neuroscience* (pp. 391–418). Milan, Italy: Springer-Verlag.

Pitt, A. J. (2003). *The play of the personal: Psychoanalytic narratives of feminist education.* New York, NY: Peter Lang.

Pitt, A. J., & Britzman, D. (2003). Speculations on qualities of difficult knowledge in teaching and learning: an experiment in psychoanalytic research. *International Journal of Qualitative Studies in Education, 6,* 755–776.

Purdon, N., & Palleja, L. (2019, April 27). Once a white supremacist always a white supremacist? *The National, CBC News.* Retrieved from www.cbc.ca/news/thenational/white-supremacist-sikh-friendship-fighting-hate-1.5107715

Qvortrup, A., & Qvortrup, L. (2018). Inclusion: Dimensions of inclusion in education. *International Journal of Inclusive Education, 22*(7), 803–817. doi:10.1080/13603116.2017.1412506

Raposo, J., & Hart, B. [*Sesame Street*]. (1969). One of these things [lyrics]. New York, NY: EMI Music Publishing. Lyrics retrieved from https://mojim.com/usy129026x6x51.htm

Raposo, J., & Moss, J. [*Sesame Street*]. (1970). Three of these things belong together [lyrics]. New York, NY: EMI Music Publishing. Lyrics retrieved from https://mojim.com/usy129026x6x51.htm

Reavis, G. H. (1999). *The animal school.* Peterborough, NH: Crystal Springs Books. Retrieved from https://madalen.files.wordpress.com/2009/09/14037268-the-animal-school.pdf

Redmond, J., & Shulman, M. (2008). Access to psychoanalytic ideas in American undergraduate institutions. *Journal of the American Psychoanalytic Association, 56*(2), 391–408. doi:10.1177/0003065108318639

Reich, K. B. (2014/2015). Psycho lawyer, qu'est-ce que c'est: The high incidence of psychopaths in the legal profession and why they thrive. *Law & Psychology Review, 39,* 287–299.

Reid, L., Bennett, S., Specht, J., White, R., Somma, M., Li, Xiaobin . . . Patel, A. (2018, May 4). *If inclusion means everyone, why not me?* (Public report). Toronto, ON: Ryerson University. Retrieved from www.inclusiveeducationresearch.ca/docs/why-not-me.pdf

Richter S. (2012). Learning tasks. In N. M. Seel (Ed.), *Encyclopedia of the sciences of learning* (pp. 113–211). Boston, MA: Springer. Retrieved from https://link.springer.com/referenceworkentry/10.1007%2F978-1-4419-1428-6_342

Roche, R., Mullally, S. L., McNulty, J. P., Hayden, J., Brennan, P. Doherty, C. P. . . . O'Mara, S. M. (2009). Prolonged rote learning produces delayed memory facilitation and metabolic changes in the hippocampus of the ageing human brain. *BMC Neuroscience, 10*, 136. doi:10.1186/1471-2202-10-136.

Rorty, R. (1989). *Contingency, irony, and solidarity.* Cambridge, UK: Cambridge University Press.

Roth, W.-M. (2011). *Passibility: At the limits of the constructivist metaphor.* New York, NY: Springer.

Ryan, J. (2016, May 26). *Dean James Ryan's prepared remarks at the 2016 HGSE [Harvard Graduate School of Education] Presentation of diplomas and certificates* [Transcript]. Retrieved from www.gse.harvard.edu/news/16/05/good-questions

Safran, J. (2016). *Introduction to relational models and their implications for treatment: NYU postdoctoral program in psychotherapy & psychoanalysis.* Retrieved December 1 from http://postdocpsychoanalytic.as.nyu.edu/object/pd.trk.relational

Salvio, P. M. (2007). *Anne Sexton: Teacher of weird abundance.* Albany, NY: SUNY Press.

Sandler, J. (1995). On attachment to internal objects. Paper presented at the conference *The Clinical Implications of Attachment: The Work of Mary Main.* University College London.

Santrock, J. W., Woloshyn, V. E., Gallagher, T. L., Di Petta, T., & Marini, Z. A. (2004). *Educational psychology: First Canadian edition.* Toronto, ON: McGraw-Hill Ryerson.

Saul, J. (2006). *Writing the roaming subject: The biotext in Canadian literature.* Toronto, ON: University of Toronto Press.

Sawyer, K. (2006a). Introduction: The new science of learning. In Author (Ed.), *The Cambridge handbook of the learning sciences* (pp. 1–16). New York, NY: Cambridge University Press.

Sawyer, K. (2006b). Conclusion: The schools of the future. In Author (Ed.), *The Cambridge handbook of the learning sciences* (pp. 567–580). New York, NY: Cambridge University Press.

Schoenfeld, A. H. (1999). Looking toward the 21st century: Challenges of educational theory and practice. *Educational Researcher, 48*(7), 4–14.

Schoenfeld, A. H. (2004). The math wars. *Educational Policy, 18*(1), 253–286. doi:10.1177/0895904803260042

Schonert-Reichl, K. A., Kitil, M. J., & Hanson-Peterson, J. (2017). *To reach the students, teach the teachers: A national scan of teacher preparation and social & emotional learning.* A report prepared for the Collaborative for Academic, Social, and Emotional Learning (CASEL). Vancouver, BC: University of British Columbia. Retrieved from www.casel.org/wp-content/uploads/2017/02/SEL-TEd-Full-Report-for-CASEL-2017-02-14-R1.pdf

Seligman, S. (2005). Dynamic systems theories as a metaframework for psychoanalysis. *Psychoanalytic Dialogues, 15*(2), 285–319.

Senge, P., Scharmer, C. O., Jaworski, J., & Flowers, B. S. (2004). *Presence: Human purpose and the field of the future.* Cambridge, MA: The Society for Organizational Learning.

Shakespeare, T. (2017). Education for all. In *Disability: The basics* (pp. 106–120). New York, NY: Routledge.

Shaver, P., & Mikulincer, M. (2004). Self-report measures of attachment. In W. Rholes & J. Simpson (Eds.), *Adult attachment: Theory, research, and clinical implications* (pp. 17–54). New York, NY: Guilford Press.

Shedler, J. (2010). The efficacy of psychodynamic psychotherapy. *American Psychologist, 65*(2), 98–109.

Shore, C., & Wright, S. (2000). Coercive accountability: The rise of audit culture in higher education. In M. Strathern (Ed.), *Audit cultures: Anthropological studies in accountability, ethics and the academy* (pp. 57–89). New York, NY: Routledge.

Shulman, L. S. (2005a). To dignify the profession of the teacher. *Change, 37*(5), Business Premium Collection, 22–29.

Shulman, L. S. (2005b). Signature pedagogies in the professions. Daedalus, *134*(3), 52–59. Retrieved from www.mitpressjournals.org/doi/pdf/10.1162/0011526054622015

Sleeter, C. E. (2017). Critical race theory and the whiteness of teacher education. *Urban Education, 52*(2), 155–169.

Slochower, J. (2018). D. W. Winnicott: Holding, playing and moving toward mutuality. In M. Charles (Ed.), *Introduction to contemporary psychoanalysis: Defining terms and building bridges* (pp. 97–117). New York, NY: Routledge.

Smith, H. (2017, June 16). No longer is the teacher the sage on the stage but rather the guide at the side. *Perspectives, 25*. Retrieved from https://perspectives.ctf-fce.ca/en/article/3136/

Smith, T. E. C., Polloway, E., Patton, J., Dowdy, C., & McIntyre, L. (2012). *Teaching students with special needs in inclusive settings* (4th Canadian ed.). Toronto, ON: Pearson Canada.

Snow, C. P. (1959). *The two cultures and the scientific revolution – The Rede lecture.* New York, NY: Cambridge University Press.

Social Sciences and Humanities Research Council of Canada [SSHRC]. (2016). *Guidelines for effective knowledge mobilization.* Ottawa, ON: SSHRC. Retrieved November 22, 2016 from www.sshrc-crsh.gc.ca/funding-financement/policies-politiques/knowledge_mobilisa-tion-mobilisation_des_connaissances-eng.aspx

Souveny, D. (2008). *Supporting positive behaviour in Alberta schools: An intensive individualized approach.* Edmonton, AB: Alberta Education.

Sriraman, B., & English, L. D. (2005). Theories of mathematics education: A global survey of theoretical frameworks/trends in mathematics education research. *ZDM, 37*(6), 450–456.

Stern, D. B. [Donnel]. (2003). *Unformulated experience: From dissociation to imagination in psychoanalysis.* New York, NY: Routledge. (Reprint of original 1997 publication)

Stern, D. B. [Donnel]. (2010). *Partners in thought: Working with unformulated experience, dissociation, and enactment.* New York, NY: Routledge.

Stern, D. B. [Donnel]. (2015). *Relational freedom: Emergent properties of the interpersonal field.* New York, NY: Routledge.

Stern, D. N. [Daniel]. (2000). *The interpersonal world of the infant: A view from psychoanalysis & developmental psychology.* New York, NY: Basic Books. (Original work published 1985)

Stern, D. N. [Daniel]. (2000). Introduction. In Author (Ed.), *The interpersonal world of the infant: A view from psychoanalysis & developmental psychology.* New York, NY: Basic Books.

Stern, D. N. [Daniel]. (2004). *The present moment: In psychotherapy and everyday life.* New York, NY: W. W. Norton.

Stockall, N., & Gartin, B. (2002). The nature of inclusion in a blue ribbon school: A revelatory case. *Exceptionality, 10*(3), 171188. doi:10.1207/S15327035EX1003_2

Stolorow, R. D. (2009). Trauma and human existence: The mutual enrichment of Heidegger's existential analytic and a psychoanalytic understanding of trauma. In R. Frie & D. Orange (Eds.), *Beyond postmodernism: New dimensions in clinical theory and practice* (pp. 143–161). New York, NY: Routledge.

Strathearn, L. (2007). Exploring the neurobiology of attachment. In L. Mayes, P. Fonagy, & M. Target (Eds.), *Developmental science and psychoanalysis: Integration and innovation* (pp. 117–130). London, UK: Karnac Books.

Strathern, M. (Ed.). (2000). *Audit cultures: Anthropological studies in accountability, ethics and the academy.* New York, NY: Routledge.

Target, M., & Fonagy, P. (1996). Playing with reality: II. The development of psychic reality from a theoretical perspective. *International Journal of Psycho-Analysis, 77*, 459–479.

Taubman, P. (2012). *Disavowed knowledge: Psychoanalysis, education, and teaching.* New York, NY: Routledge.

Taussig, M. (1993). *Mimesis and alterity: A particular history of the senses.* New York, NY: Routledge.

Teicholz, J. G. (2009). A strange convergence: Postmodern theory, infant research, and psychoanalysis. In R. Frie & D. Orange (Eds.), *Beyond postmodernism: New dimensions in clinical theory and practice* (pp. 69–91). New York, NY: Routledge.

Thom, J., D'Amour, L., Preciado, P., & Davis, B. (2015). Spatial knowing, being, and doing. In Davis, B. & the Spatial Reasoning Study Group (Eds.), *Spatial reasoning in the early years: Principles, assertions, and speculations* (pp. 63–82). New York, NY: Routledge.

Thomas, G., & Dowker, A. (2000, September). *Mathematics anxiety and related factors in young children.* Paper presented at the British Psychological Society, Developmental Section, Conference, Bristol, UK.

Thompson, E. (2007). *Mind in life: Biology, phenomenology, and the sciences of mind.* Cambridge, MA: Belknap Press of Harvard University Press.

Thompson, E., & Stapleton, E. (2009). Making sense of sense-making: Reflections on enactive and extended mind theories. *Topoi: An International Review of Philosophy, 28,* 23–30. doi:10.1007/s11245-008-9043-2

Thompson, M. (2015). Authenticity in education: From narcissism and freedom to the messy interplay of self-exploration and acceptable tension. *Studies in Philosophy of Education, 34,* 603–618. doi:10.1007/s11217-015-9459-2

Thornton, H. J. (2018). *The it factor: What makes a great teacher?* Leiden, The Netherlands: Koninklijke Brill. doi:10.1163/9789004364486

Todd, S. (2003). *Learning from the other: Levinas, psychoanalysis, and ethical possibilities in education.* Albany, NY: SUNY Press.

Tone, A. (2009). *The age of anxiety: A history of America's turbulent affair with tranquilizers.* New York, NY: Basic Books.

Torre, M. E. (2014). Participatory action research. In T. Teo (Ed.), *Encyclopedia of critical psychology.* New York, NY: Springer. doi:10.1007/978-1-4614-5583-7 (Personal workshop version)

Tremonti, A.-M. (Host). (2018, February 20). The secret to happiness? Ask this Yale professor (and the 1,200 students taking her class) [Radio program]. In *The Current.* Toronto, ON: CBC Radio One.

Trevarthen, C. (2011). What is it like to be a person who knows nothing? Defining the active intersubjective mind of a newborn human being. *Infant and Child Development, 20*(1), 119–135. Retrieved from http://citeseerx.ist.psu.edu/viewdoc/download?doi=10.1.1.4 75.9911&rep=rep1&type=pdf

Tronick, E. (2001). Emotional connection and dyadic consciousness in infant-mother and patient-therapist interaction. *Psychoanalytic Dialogues, 11,* 187–194.

Tronick, E., Als, H., Adamson, L., Wise, S., & Brazelton, T. (1978). The infant's response to entrapment between contradictory messages in face-to-face interaction. *Journal of the Academy of Child and Adolescent Psychiatry, 17*(1), 1–13.

Trueit, D. (2005). *Complexifying the poetic: Toward a* poiesis *of curriculum.* Doctoral dissertation, Louisiana State University and Agricultural and Mechanical College, Louisiana. Retrieved from http://etd.lsu.edu/docs/available/etd-11152005-184410/

Tschannen-Moran, M., & Hoy, W. K. (2000). A multidisciplinary analysis of the nature, meaning, and measurement of trust. *Review of Educational Research, 70*(4), 547–593.

Tuck, E. (2009). Suspending damage: A letter to communities. *Harvard Educational Review, 79*(3), 409–427.

References

Turkle, S. (2015). *Reclaiming conversation: The power of talk in a digital age.* New York, NY: Penguin Press.

Twenge, J. M. (2006). *Generation me: Why today's young Americans are more confident, assertive, entitled – and more miserable than ever before.* New York, NY: Free Press.

Twenge, J. M., & Campbell, W. K. (2009). *The narcissistic epidemic: Living in the age of entitlement.* New York, NY: Free Press.

Uljens, M. (1996). On the philosophical foundation of phenomenography. In G. Dall'Alba & B. Hasselgren (Eds.), *Reflection on phenomenography: Toward a methodology?* (pp. 105–130). Göteborg: Acta Universitatis Gothoburgensis.

United Nations Educational Scientific and Cultural Organization [UNESCO]. 2009. *Policy guidelines on inclusion in education.* Paris, France: Author. (ED-2009/WS/31)

U. S. Department of Education, Office of Elementary and Secondary Education. (2002). *No child left behind: A desktop reference.* Washington, DC.

Varela, F. G. (1999). *Ethical know-how: Action, wisdom, and cognition.* (Leland Stanford Junior University, Trans.). Stanford, CA: Stanford University Press. (Original work published 1991)

Varela, F. G., Maturana, H. R., & Uribe, R. (1974). Autopoiesis: The organization of living systems, its characterization and a model. *Biosystems, 5,* 187–196.

Varela, F. G., Thompson, E., & Rosch, E. (1991). *The embodied mind: Cognitive science and human experience.* Cambridge, MA: MIT Press.

Vygotsky, L. (1986). *Thought and language* (A. Kozulin, Trans.). Cambridge, MA: MIT Press. (Original work published 1934)

Wallin, D. J. (2007). *Attachment in psychotherapy.* New York, NY: Guilford Press.

Walsh, G. (2017, October 1). Character education and social justice [Blog post]. In *Curriculum for equity: Exploring the relationship between education, equity and social justice.* Retrieved from https://curriculumforequity.org/2017/10/01/character-education-and-social-justice/

Watson, A., & Mason, J. (2006). Seeing an exercise as a single mathematical object: Using variation to structure sense-making. *Mathematical Thinking and Learning, 8*(2), 91–111. doi:10.1207/s15327833mtl0802_1

Waverman, E. (2015, January 14). Snowplow parenting: The latest controversial technique. *Today's Parent.* Retrieved from www.todaysparent.com/blogs/snowplow-parenting-the-latest-controversial-technique/

Werklund School of Education. (n.d.). *Signature pedagogies.* Retrieved March 2, 2018 from https://werklund.ucalgary.ca/tandl/resources

Westen, D. (1998). The scientific legacy of Sigmund Freud: Toward a psychodynamically informed psychological science. *Psychological Bulleting, 124*(3), 333–371.

Wilson, E. O. (1998). *Consilience: The unity of knowledge.* New York, NY: Vintage Books.

Winnicott, D. W. (2005). *Playing and reality* (2nd ed.). New York, NY: Routledge. (Original work published 1971)

INDEX

affect attunement 97–99
affective contours 85, 93–94
agency: in childhood development 89,
103–105, 200, 230, 252–254; compromised
68, 146, 153, 251; enhancement of 68,
87, 81–82, 98, 195, 209, 266; intellectual
freedom and teacher agency 29–30, 33,
124, 140; and labels as performative acts
235–236; and responsibility 20, 24, 187;
will and power 21, 43, 65, 138, 174–175,
235; *see also* integrity
anxiety: and early affect-regulation 99;
and performance 151; prevalence in
schooling 33, 37, 45, 67, 68, 252; in
regulated and enforced success 37, 44–45,
150, 157–158 (*see also* entitlement);
see also dissociation
Aron, L. 249, 264, 265
attachment theory 90–91
autopoietic systems: boundary maintenance
132, 136, 144–145, 149; coupling to
niche; dynamic flux 132, 136, 148;
embeddedness in milieu 135, 138; nested
137; principle of sufficiency 136, 147;
recursively self-producing 132; structure-
determined 135, 147

Benjamin, J. 63–64, 104–105, 169, 200,
214–215, 255, 264, 265–266
best teaching practices 124, 177, 183;
collaboration 37–38, 126–127,
177–178, 186, 193, 196; differentiated
instruction 65–66, 121, 187–188, 190,
212; learner-centred 66, 203–204, 255,
259; rich problems and engaging tasks
177–178, 194–196; signature pedagogies
46; STEM technologies 177–178, 218–219
Bibby, T. 17, 18–19
boundaries: in autopoietic (learning/
life) systems 132, 135–136, 144, 147;
negotiation under threat 137, 144–145,
149, 160–161 (*see also* dissociation); and
psychic survival 88, 104–105, 160–161
Britzman, D. 16, 18–19
Buber, M. 214, 250, 252, 265
business of knowledge as capital:
governments, sponsors, and stakeholders
32, 211, 228; information as knowledge
and knowledge as commodity
(promoting ignorance) 27–29, 30–31, 33
Butler, J. 114, 235–236

Cartesianism 11–13
complex systems *see* autopoietic systems
conscious knowing *see* thinking
continuity 63, 87, 94, 148, 244, 270; *see also*
integrity
critical theory *see* curriculum studies
Csibra, G. 102, 237
curriculum studies 1, 32, 46–47, 185,
266–267; critical theory and social
justice 42–43, 188; reconceptualisation of
34, 41, 46–47

Damasio, A. 68, 79
Dewey, J. 65, 123, 126, 194–196

300 Index

Deweyan revisionism 193–197
difficult knowledge 18–19, 24
discernment: associative reasoning 224–225; phenomenography and variation theory 225–226; student proclivities and capacities 227–228; teaching for 223; *see also* neurobiology
dissociation 60, 153–161, 172, 223, 262; and folk psychology 145, 213–214; impasses 257, 271–274; me/not-me 146–147, 153, 155, 160, 191, 199, 253 (*see also* boundaries); objectivity as defence 238–240; *vs.* recognition 169, 247, 265–266; *vs.* repression 20; and systemic pathology 44–45, 153, 158–159, 166, 193, 251; *see also* anxiety
drives *see* object relations
Dweck, C. 120

educational fields 4, 41–43
educational leadership 41–42
educational psychology 31, 41–42, 117–118, 119–121, 129, 183–185
educational research 26–27, 46, 129–130, 228, 251, 277
educational theory to practice 122, 176, 183
education wars 64–65, 219; a politics of given and made 64–72, 143, 218–219
Eigen, M. 22–24
empowerment 42–43; everyone can 43, 177; growth-mindedness 70; positive psychology and self-empowerment 157–158, 177, 200–201
engagement 36–37, 38, 106, 173, 195, 251; for disengagement (*see* dissociation); and meaning 173–174; *see also* entitlement
entitlement: and appropriate responsibility 67–68, 204–206; labels and identities 192–193; *see also* empowerment

Fonagy, P. 98–99, 103, 128, 156
formulation 74; articulation 76–77, 222 (*see also* thinking); and illusion 25, 63–64, 74, 221–222; realisation 74–75 (*see also* creativity); *see also* theory of learning
Foucault, M. 41, 44–45
Freud, S. 7–9, 12–13, 18–19, 141, 274

Gergely, G. 102, 237; *see also* Fonagy, P.
good enough mother 99

holding environments 208–209; and one fathomable small theatre 278–279

illusion/disillusionment: and language's bifurcating effects 108–111; in learning

25, 63–64, 67–68, 71, 89, 203–204, 208–209, 264–265 (*see also* transitional phenomena); in modernity and postmodernity 277; *see also* recognition theory
inclusion: classrooms as holding environments 213–217; connecting to meaning 173–175; an elusive ideal 180–182; essence of 276–277; imagining what could be 278–279; mitigating trust 168–173; supporting capacity 167 (*see also* discernment); what it would take 187–191
inclusion's questionable practices: atonement 197–199; capitulating responsibilities 203–206; celebrating experience and forcing community 193–197; clinical approaches 182–185; labels 192–193; lessons in being good 199–200; positive psychology and self-regulation practices 201–202; withholding feedback 202
integrity (as self-coherence, continuity, and agency) 63–64, 87, 138; development of 85–87, 94, 150, 252–253, 276
interpersonal complementarity: in care-relationships 265; and dissociation 153, 155, 157, 169; doer/done-to relations 55, 253–255, 266; relevance to teaching 191, 194; vignettes from the classroom 257–260, 270–274
intersubjective mutuality: in asymmetry of responsibility 264–265; relations of being/being-with 25, 89, 214–216, 256; rupture and repair 88, 256, 257–258, 265, 277; surrender and thirdness 56, 61, 105, 259, 265–266; *see also* recognition theory; witnessing

Juarrero, A. 141, 143, 215

Klein, M. 9, 11, 17–18, 23–24
knowing: as embodied 12, 128, 132–133, 134, 136; given yet made 68–69, 71–72; interpretive 55–56, 61, 71, 141; and vitality affects in development 80, 93, 100, 102, 109; *see also* thinking
knowledge: as commodity 27–30, 38, 219; folk psychology 115, 117–119, 145; spontaneous and nonspontaneous 106, 115–116, 125–126, 133, 230, 231

language: development of 106–112, 116; and thought (*see also* categories)
learning: amplifying one's known 195; defined 125; disassembling one's known

152–153, 227; as interpretive 138, 141; as structure-determined 134–135, 136; as structure-determining 77; toward viability and vitality 113, 132, 137–139, 147; *see also* theory of learning
learning sciences 39–41, 42–44; and STEM education 218–219; and technological rationality 31, 34–36

Marton, F. 220, 244
Maturana, H. 130–132, 134–135, 137, 138–139, 149
Mead, G. H. 107–108
meaning 173–174; affective salience 75–77, 85, 144, 229–232; and objectivity 40, 54, 60, 76, 106–108, 231; relationally shaped from gestures to words and thought 106–109, 128; transitionally given and made 76–77, 89, 100–101, 107–111; and the unconscious 21, 29, 35, 48, 59; *see also* engagement
Milner, M. 17, 191, 273
mimesis/poiesis: in learning 241–244; *see also* education wars
Mitchell, S. 8–11

Nancy, J.–L. 114, 137, 193–194, 198
natural human pedagogy 102
neurobiology: of discernment 229–230; drives as responsive subcortical systems 19–20; emotions *vs.* feelings 79; neural proclivities to assemblage 84–85; principles of salience 75; sensation types 79
new managerialism 35, 44–46, 251; the production of teachers 175–176; schools as factories 34, 36–39
Noddings, N. 46, 265
non-linear dynamic systems (NLDS) *see* autopoietic systems

object relations 8–10, 11; external objects and triadic relations 101–102; internal objects in dyadic relations 79–80; object- and subject-others 103–105; *see also* illusion/disillusionment; recognition theory
objects, ambiguous meanings 47–49; *see also* object relations

paradoxes of the living 61, 138; individuation-through-belonging and belonging-through-individuation 105, 255; knowing as given and made 53, 64, 80, 143, 218–219; learning as structure-determined 135; singular-plural being 105, 114, 131, 138, 143, 206; thirdness,

mutuality, and the co-recognition of intersubjectivity 89, 99, 214–216, 219, 252; yet self-organising (structure-determining) 24
phenomenography *see* discernment
Pinar, W. 1, 26, 27, 32, 33, 34, 41, 266–267
playing 53–54, 70–72, 168, 214, 221, 237, 278–279; and creativity 23–24, 76, 110–111, 143–147, 240–242; and curiosity 86, 203–204, 256; at reality (out-there *vs.* in-mind) 103–104, 110–112, 145, 156; *see also* transitional phenomena
primary consciousness 85
primary intersubjectivity 91–93
psychoanalysis in education 11–12, 16–19
psychoanalytic thought: historical trajectory 8–11, 17–18; on schooling as civilising 18–20, 22; *see also* educational fields; relational psychoanalysis

recognition theory 88–89, 96, 105, 154, 155, 168, 169, 199–200, 206, 216, 250, 252–253, 255–257; holding and object mothers 208, 277; rapprochement 80–81, 102–105, 208–209
relational psychoanalysis: an accessible field 15–17, 260–262; historical roots 4, 7–11, 16–17, 18; philosophical orientations 11–17; and sciences of brain development and function 19, 21, 28, 73, 91, 128, 256; in teaching and learning 55–56; on trauma and joy 17–20, 22–25

Sawyer, K. 35, 39
schooling marketable products: facts, gizmos, and credentials 32–33; students as entitled consumers and quality controlled products 33–34, 36, 37, 192–193
secondary intersubjectivity 96–97
sense-making *see* learning
Stern, Daniel 59, 77–78, 80, 85, 90, 92, 93–99, 109–110
Stern, Donnel 20, 146–147, 155–156, 172, 223, 228, 247–248, 250, 255, 259, 270–271
subjects, ambiguous meanings 47–49; *see also* object relations

Target, M. 98–99, 103, 128, 156
teacher development, some possibilities 170–172, 175, 256, 263, 269–270
teacher experiences: and anxiety 256–257, 262–263; benevolent collusion 186; rupture and repair 257–259;

302 Index

service rationing 211; transference–
countertransference 270–274; in the
trenches 2–3; untenable expectations
251–252; with unwieldy guidelines and
protocols 119–121

theories of learning: compendial
collections 117–121; enactivism
129–134 (*see also* autopoietic systems);
first generation cognitivism 127–128;
historicised narratives 121–129; personal
constructivism 124–125; second
generation cognitivism 128–129; social
constructivism 125–127

theory of learning, a dialectic model *62,
142*, 61, 63–64, 143–145; applicable
across all autopoietic systems 134–140;
applicable from birth 74–75, 77–80,
86–87; centrifugal moment 67–68,
171, 220, 242; centripetal moment 74
(*see also* formulation); dialectic recursion
61, 63–64, 72, 78, 138–139, 144, 224;
mimesis and poiesis 241–244; violations
of expectation 80, 82, 151, 241

thinking: and language 106–112, 116, 133,
230–233; relationship to unconscious
and nonconscious knowing 57–61,

74–76, 228–230; words, categories, and
labels 232–238; *see also* formulation

transitional phenomena 72, 103–104, 109,
228, 231; criticality of the teacher 111,
153, 214–215, 219; and education wars
143; given and made in learning 53–56,
63, 89, 166; *see also* paradoxes of the living

trust: and attachment 80–82, 83, 87, 96, 102,
104–105, 171–172 (*see also* integrity);
and inclusion 187, 190–191, 214–215;
in learning 166–169, 175, 201–203,
209–210; for mis/distrust (*see* anxiety); and
responsibility 66–69, 109–110, 203–206,
253; and witnessing 253, 255–256, 266

Turkle, S. 36, 66

Varela, F. 130–132, 133, 135, 138
variation theory *see* discernment
vitality affects 82–84

ways-of-being-with 89–90, 94–96
Winnicott, D. 18, 23–24, 53–54, 81, 105,
111, 205, 208
witnessing 169, 250, 254, 255–256,
265–266; teacher role in 35–36, 105, 111;
see also affect attunement